The American Record

The American Record

Images of the Nation's Past
Volume II: Since 1865

FOURTH EDITION

EDITED BY

William Graebner
*State University of New York
College at Fredonia*

Leonard Richards
*University of Massachusetts,
Amherst*

Boston   Burr Ridge, IL   Dubuque, IA   Madison, WI
New York   San Francisco   St. Louis
Bangkok   Bogotá   Caracas   Lisbon   London   Madrid   Mexico City
Milan   New Delhi   Seoul   Singapore   Sydney   Taipei   Toronto

McGraw-Hill Higher Education

A Division of The **McGraw-Hill** Companies

THE AMERICAN RECORD: IMAGES OF THE NATION'S PAST
VOLUME II: SINCE 1865, FOURTH EDITION

Published by McGraw-Hill, an imprint of The McGraw-Hill Companies, Inc., 1221 Avenue of the Americas, New York, NY 10020. Copyright © 2001, 1995, 1988, 1982 by The McGraw-Hill Companies, Inc. All rights reserved. No part of this publication may be reproduced or distributed in any form or by any means, or stored in a database or retrieval system, without the prior written consent of The McGraw-Hill Companies, Inc., including, but not limited to, in any network or other electronic storage or transmission, or broadcast for distance learning.

Some ancillaries, including electronic and print components, may not be available to customers outside the United States.

This book is printed on acid-free paper.

1 2 3 4 5 6 7 8 9 0 DOC/DOC 0 9 8 7 6 5 4 3 2 1 0

ISBN 0–07–231737–X

Vice president and editor-in-chief: *Thalia Dorwick*
Editorial director: *Jane E. Vaicunas*
Senior sponsoring editor: *Lyn Uhl*
Developmental editor: *Kristen Mellitt*
Marketing manager: *Janise A. Fry*
Project manager: *Mary E. Powers*
Production supervisor: *Laura Fuller*
Cover/interior designer: *Gino Cieslik*
Cover photo: *Jacob Lawerence, "The Migration of the Negro People no.1," 1940–1941, The Phillips Collection, Washington, DC.*
Senior photo research coordinator: *Carrie K. Burger*
Photo research: *PhotoSearch, Inc.*
Supplement coordinator: *Brenda A. Ernzen*
Compositor: *ElectraGraphics, Inc.*
Typeface: *10/12 Palatino*
Printer: *R. R. Donnelley & Sons Company/Crawfordsville, IN*

Library of Congress Cataloging-in-Publication Data

The American record : images of the nation's past / [edited by] William Graebner, Leonard Richards. — 4th ed.
    p. cm.
  Includes bibliographical references.
  Contents: v. I. To 1877 – v. II. Since 1865.
  ISBN 0–07–231737–X
  1. United States—History. 2. United States—History—Sources. I. Graebner, William.
II. Richards, Leonard L.

E178.6 .A4145 2001
973—dc21   00-056087
                                                                    CIP

www.mhhe.com

About the Editors

WILLIAM GRAEBNER is Professor of History at the State University of New York at Fredonia. He received the Frederick Jackson Turner Award from the Organization of American Historians for *Coal-Mining Safety in the Progressive Period: The Political Economy of Reform*. Another book, *A History of Retirement: The Meaning and Function of an American Institution, 1885–1978*, was published in 1980. He is also the author of *The Engineering of Consent: Democracy and Authority in Twentieth-Century America* (1987); *Coming of Age in Buffalo: Youth and Authority in the Postwar Era* (1990); *The Age of Doubt: American Thought and Culture in the 1940s* (1991), and the editor of *True Stories from the American Past* (1993, 1997). In 1993, he was Fulbright Professor of American Studies at the University of Rome. He currently serves as Associate Editor of *American Studies*.

LEONARD RICHARDS is Professor of History at the University of Massachusetts at Amherst. He was awarded the 1970 Beveridge Prize by the American Historical Association for his book *"Gentlemen of Property and Standing": Anti-Abolition Mobs in Jacksonian America*. Professor Richards is also the author of *The Advent of American Democracy, The Life and Times of Congressman John Quincy Adams*, which was a finalist for the Pulitzer Prize, and *The Slave Power: The Free North and Southern Domination, 1780–1860*. He has just finished a study of the thousand families who fought in "Shays's Rebellion." He hopes to publish their story in the near future.

Contents

Preface

During the past three or four decades, the study of history in the United States has become in many ways more sophisticated and more interesting. Until the mid-1960s the dominant tradition among American historians was to regard the historian's domain as one centered on politics, economics, diplomacy, and war. Now, at the dawn of the twenty-first century, historians are eager to address new kinds of subjects and to include whole sections of the population that were neglected in the traditional preoccupation with presidential administrations, legislation, and treaties. Women and children, the poor and economically marginal, African Americans and native Americans, have moved nearer the center of the historians' stage. We have become almost as eager to know how our ancestors dressed, ate, reared their children, made love, and buried their dead as we are to know how they voted in a particular presidential election. In addition, ordinary Americans now appear on the stage of history as active players who possess the power to shape their lives, rather than as passive victims of forces beyond their control. The result is a collective version of our national past that is more inclusive, more complex, and less settled.

About the New Edition

The fourth edition of *The American Record* continues the effort begun in previous editions. We have attempted to bridge the gap between the old history and the new, to graft the excitement and variety of modern approaches to the past on an existing chronological and topical framework with which most of us feel comfortable. Most of the familiar topics are here; we have included essays on the early colonial settlements, the Revolutionary War, the Constitution, progressivism, the Great Depression, World War II, and the consensual society of the 1950s. But by joining these essays to primary sources, we have tried to make it possible for teachers and students to see links between the Puritan social order and the lessons children learned from their primers; between the Revolutionary

War and the colonial class structure; between the Constitution and the physical layout of the nation's capital; between progressivism and the turn-of-the-century cult of masculinity; between the Great Depression and the murals that were painted on post office walls across the nation in the mid-1930s; between the Second World War and emerging conflicts over the status of women; and between the idea of consensus and the integration of Little Rock, Arkansas's public schools. The fourth edition also takes up themes and materials that are not so universally familiar, but which are beginning to reshape our understanding of the American past—among them, the rise of a consumer society, the history of popular music, the impact of the mass media, the late-twentieth-century conflict over "culture," and the issue of "family values." This book teaches the skill of making sense out of one's whole world.

Throughout, we have attempted to incorporate materials with *texture:* documents that are not only striking but can be given more than one interpretation; photographs that invite real examination and discussion; tables and maps that have something new and interesting to contribute; and essays, such as James H. Merrell's account of the "New World" as it appeared to the Catawba Indians, Kenneth Cmiel's treatment of the "politics of civility" in the turbulent 1960s, and Susan J. Douglas's playful essay on growing up female with the mass media in the 1970s, that are at once superb examples of recent historical scholarship and accessible to undergraduates. To foreground the agency of ordinary people, we have added sections called **"Voices,"** which feature firsthand commentaries such as Sarah Winnemucca's account of the California migrations and the testimony of John Morrison, a New York machinist, before the U.S. Senate in 1883. Another new section, labeled **"Debates,"** juxtaposes differing perspectives on selected issues, including the adoption of the Constitution, the nature of American aristocracy in the early republic, imperialism, the role of women in the 1940s, and Vietnam.

Learning Aids for Students

From the beginning, we realized that our approach to American history would require some adjustment for many students and teachers. It was one thing to call on students to place an address by Albert J. Beveridge in the context of turn-of-the-century imperialism, yet quite another to ask them to do the same with a young woman's account of the African exhibit at the 1901 Pan-American Exposition in Buffalo, New York. For this reason, we have offered a good deal of guidance. **Introductions** to primary and secondary materials are designed not just to provide basic background information, but to suggest productive avenues of interpretation. Interpretive essays and questions are intended to create a kind of mental chemistry that provides students with enough information to experience the excitement of putting things together, and yet not so much guidance that conclusions become obvious. For this edition, we have added to each chapter a brief section called **"The Big Picture,"** where some of the broader questions are posed.

Instructor's Manual

An instructor's manual is available in conjunction with *The American Record*. It includes resources for every chapter, including suggestions for using the book in the classroom and for stimulating student discussion.

Acknowledgments

We remain indebted to R. Jackson Wilson, who inspired the first edition of this book. We also wish to thank our editors at Alfred A. Knopf and McGraw-Hill—first David Follmer and Chris Rogers, later Niels Aaboe and Peter Labella, now Kristen Mellitt and Lyn Uhl—for their patient supervision of a difficult project. And we are grateful to the teachers and students who used the first, second, and third editions of *The American Record* and showed us how to make the book better. In particular, we would like to thank the following reviewers of the third edition for their many helpful suggestions: Michael Cassella-Blackburn, Green River Community College; Priscilla Ferguson Clement, Penn State University–Delaware County; Robert Greenblatt, Massachusetts Bay Community College; Lisa M. Lane, Mira Costa College; Margaret M. Mulrooney, Marymount University; Heather R. Parker, Hofstra University; Mario A. Perez, Crafton Hills College; R. B. Rosenburg, University of North Alabama; Susan A. Strauss, Santa Fe Community College; Cam Walker, College of William and Mary; and Robert S. Wolff, Central Connecticut State University.

William Graebner
State University of New York
at Fredonia

Leonard Richards
University of Massachusetts
at Amherst

February, 2000

chapter one

RECONSTRUCTION

When it was first coined in the crisis months between the election of Lincoln and the beginnings of the Civil War, the term "Reconstruction" meant simply the reunification of the nation. By the time the war ended in 1865, the idea of Reconstruction was more complicated: it now meant more than simple political reestablishment of the Union; it meant reconstructing the South, refashioning its social and economic life to some degree or other. For the freedmen—many only days removed from slavery—Reconstruction would soon come to represent freedom itself. Even in 1865, most southern blacks realized that without thoroughgoing Reconstruction, in which freedmen obtained land as well as the right to vote, freedom would mean only a new kind of economic oppression.

Twelve years later, in 1877, many people, north and south, realized that Reconstruction had ended. But by then the term had taken on intense moral meanings. To most white southerners, it was a term of resentment, the name of a bleak period during which vindictive Yankee politicians had tried to force "black rule" on a "prostrate South." The North tried and finally failed, for the South had in the end been "redeemed" by its own leaders. Slavery had ended, but white supremacy had been firmly reestablished. To perhaps a majority of whites in the North, Reconstruction had over the years become a nuisance, and they were glad to let go of it, to reaffirm the value of the Union, and to let the bitter past die. There were other northerners, however, who looked back from

1877 to twelve years of moral failure, of lost opportunities to force freedom and equality on an unrepentant South.

There were hundreds of thousands of freedmen who experienced this "moral failure" in very real ways. Instead of farming their own land, they farmed the lands of whites as tenants and sharecroppers. Far from benefiting from meaningful voting rights, most blacks were denied the franchise, and those who continued to exercise it did so in a climate of hostility hardly conducive to political freedom. Nonetheless, it was possible for blacks to look back positively at the Reconstruction experience. The 1866 Civil Rights Act granted blacks both citizenship and all the civil rights possessed by whites. When the constitutionality of that statute seemed in doubt, Congress made ratification of the Fourteenth Amendment (accomplished in 1868) a precondition for southern restoration to the Union. In theory, that amendment made the federal government the protector of rights that might be invaded by the states. Under "Radical" Reconstruction, carried out by Congress after 1867, hundreds of thousands of southern blacks voted, and many held high elective office. And in 1875, when whites had reestablished their authority throughout most of the region, a new civil rights act "guaranteed" blacks equal rights in theaters, inns, and other public places. If in the end it proved impossible to maintain these gains, Reconstruction still remained the bright spot in the lives of many former slaves.

interpretive essay

Elizabeth Rauh Bethel

PROMISED LAND

Most accounts of the Reconstruction period have been written largely from the perspective of powerful white men such as presidents, northern congressmen, or southern "Redeemers." As a result, students often get the impression that all decisions were made by whites, and blacks were idly sitting on their hands, just the beneficiaries or victims of white actions. That was not the case. Throughout the South black men and women, just months after the end of slavery, actively shaped their own futures and challenged the power and prejudices of their white neighbors. Most wanted to own land and become family farmers. The odds against them were immense, and many struggled valiantly only to see their hopes dashed by their lack of money, or by political decisions made in distant Washington, or by white terrorists such as the Ku Klux Klan. But some, as Elizabeth Rauh Bethel documents in the following selection, overcame great obstacles and established tightly knit communities. What do you think accounts for the courage and determination of the families Bethel describes? Do you think the course of American history would have been changed if most black families during Reconstruction had obtained a forty-acre farm? In what respect?

The opportunity to acquire land was a potent attraction for a people just emerging from bondage, and one commonly pursued by freedmen throughout the south. Cooperative agrarian communities, instigated in some cases by the invading Union Army and in other cases by the freedmen themselves, were scattered across the plantation lands of the south as early as 1863. Collective land purchases and cooperative farming ventures developed in the Tidewater area of Virginia, the Sea Islands of South Carolina and Georgia, and along the Mississippi River as refugees at the earliest contraband camps struggled to establish economic and social stability.

These initial land tenure arrangements, always temporary, stimulated high levels of industrious labor among both those fortunate enough to obtain land and those whose expectations were raised by their neighbors' good fortunes.

From Elizabeth Rauh Bethel, *Promiseland: A Century of Life in a Negro Community,* Temple University Press, Philadelphia, 1981, pp. 5–8, 17–21, 23, 25–33, 39–40. © 1981 by Temple University. Reprinted by permission of Temple University Press.

Although for most freedmen the initial promise of landownership was never realized, heightened expectations resulted in "entire families laboring together, improving their material conditions, laying aside money that might hopefully be used to purchase a farm or a few acres for a homestead of their own" during the final years of the war.

The desire for a plot of land dominated public expressions among the freedmen as well as their day-to-day activities and behaviors. In 1864 Secretary of War Stanton met with Negro leaders in Savannah to discuss the problems of resettlement. During that meeting sixty-seven-year-old freedman Garrison Frazier responded to an inquiry regarding living arrangements by telling Stanton that "we would prefer to 'live by ourselves' rather than 'scattered among the whites.' " These arrangements, he added, should include self-sufficiency established on Negro-owned lands. The sentiments Frazier expressed were not unusual. They were repeated by other freedmen across the south. Tunis Campbell, also recently emancipated, testified before the congressional committee investigating the Ku Klux Klan that "the great cry of our people is to have land." A delegate to the Tennessee Colored Citizens' Convention of 1866 stated that "what is needed for the colored people is land which they own." A recently emancipated Negro representative to the 1868 South Carolina Constitutional Convention, speaking in support of that state's land redistribution program, which eventually gave birth to the Promised Land community, said of the relationship between landownership and the state's Negro population: "Night and day they dream" of owning their own land. "It is their all in all."

At Davis Bend, Mississippi, and Port Royal, South Carolina, as well as similar settlements in Louisiana, North Carolina, and Virginia, this dream was in fact realized for a time. Freedmen worked "with commendable zeal . . . out in the morning before it is light and at work 'til darkness drives them to their homes" whenever they farmed land that was their own. John Eaton, who supervised the Davis Bend project, observed that the most successful land experiments among the freedmen were those in which plantations were subdivided into individually owned and farmed tracts. These small farms, rather than the larger cooperative ventures, "appeared to hold the greatest chance for success." The contraband camps and federally directed farm projects afforded newly emancipated freedmen an opportunity to "rediscover and redefine themselves, and to establish communities." Within the various settlements a stability and social order developed that combined economic self-sufficiency with locally directed and controlled schools, churches, and mutual aid societies. In the years before the Freedmen's Bureau or the northern missionary societies penetrated the interior of the south, the freedmen, through their own resourcefulness, erected and supported such community institutions at every opportunity. In obscure settlements with names like Slabtown and Acreville, Hampton, Alexandria, Saxtonville, and Mitchelville, "status, experience, history, and ideology were potent forces operating toward cohesiveness and community." . . .

. . . In South Carolina, perhaps more intensely than any of the other southern states, the thirst for land was acute. It was a possibility sparked first by

General William T. Sherman's military actions along the Sea Islands, then dashed as quickly as it was born in the distant arena of Washington politics. Still, the desire for land remained a goal not readily abandoned by the state's freedpeople, and they implemented a plan to achieve that goal at the first opportunity. Their chance came at the 1868 South Carolina Constitutional Convention.

South Carolina was among the southern states that refused to ratify the Fourteenth Amendment to the Constitution, the amendment that established the citizenship of the freedmen. Like her recalcitrant neighbors, the state was then placed under military government, as outlined by the Military Reconstruction Act of 1867. Among the mandates of that federal legislation was a requirement that each of the states in question draft a new state constitution incorporating the principles of the Fourteenth Amendment. Only after such new constitutions were completed and implemented were the separate states of the defeated Confederacy eligible for readmission to the Union.

The representatives to these constitutional conventions were selected by a revolutionary electorate, one that included all adult male Negroes. Registration for the elections was handled by the army with some informal assistance by "that God-forsaken institution, the Freedman's Bureau." Only South Carolina among the ten states of the former Confederacy elected a Negro majority to its convention. The instrument those representatives drafted called for four major social and political reforms in state government: a statewide system of free common schools; universal manhood suffrage; a jury law that included the Negro electorate in county pools of qualified jurors; and a land redistribution system designed to benefit the state's landless population, primarily the freedmen.

White response to the new constitution and the social reforms that it outlined was predictably vitriolic. It was condemned by one white newspaper as "the work of sixty-odd Negroes, many of them ignorant and depraved." The authors were publicly ridiculed as representing "the maddest, most unscrupulous, and infamous revolution in history." Despite this and similar vilification, the constitution was ratified in the 1868 referendum, an election boycotted by many white voters and dominated by South Carolina's 81,000 newly enfranchised Negroes, who cast their votes overwhelmingly with the Republicans and for the new constitution.

That same election selected representatives to the state legislature charged with implementing the constitutional reforms. That body, like the constitutional convention, was constituted with a Negro majority; and it moved immediately to establish a common school system and land redistribution program. The freedmen were already registered, and the new jury pools remained the prerogative of the individual counties. The 1868 election also was notable for the numerous attacks and "outrages" that occurred against the more politically active freedmen. Among those Negroes assaulted, beaten, shot, and lynched during the pre-election campaign months were four men who subsequently bought small farms from the Land Commission and settled at Promised Land. Like other freedmen in South Carolina, their open involvement in the state's Republican political machinery led to personal violence.

Wilson Nash was the first of the future Promised Land residents to encounter white brutality and retaliation for his political activities. Nash was nominated by the Republicans as their candidate for Abbeville County's seat in the state legislature at the August 1868 county convention. In October of that year, less than two weeks before the general election, Nash was attacked and shot in the leg by two unidentified white assailants. The "outrage" took place in the barn on his rented farm, not far from Dr. Marshall's farm on Curltail Creek. Wilson Nash was thirty-three years old in 1868, married, and the father of three small children. He had moved from "up around Cokesbury" within Abbeville County, shortly after emancipation to the rented land further west. Within months after the Nash family was settled on their farm, Wilson Nash joined the many Negroes who affiliated with the Republicans, an alliance probably instigated and encouraged by Republican promises of land to the freedmen. The extent of Nash's involvement with local politics was apparent in his nomination for public office; and this same nomination brought him to the forefront of county Negro leadership and to the attention of local whites.

After the attack Nash sent his wife and young children to a neighbor's home, where he probably believed they would be safe. He then mounted his mule and fled his farm, leaving behind thirty bushels of recently harvested corn. Whether Nash also left behind a cotton crop is unknown. It was the unprotected corn crop that worried him as much as his concern for his own safety. He rode his mule into Abbeville and there sought refuge at the local Freedman's Bureau office where he reported the attack to the local bureau agent and requested military protection for his family and his corn crop. Captain W. F. DeKnight was sympathetic to Nash's plight but was powerless to assist or protect him. DeKnight had no authority in civil matters such as this, and the men who held that power generally ignored such assaults on Negroes. The Nash incident was typical and followed a familiar pattern. The assailants remained unidentified, unapprehended, and unpunished. The attack achieved the desired end, however, for Nash withdrew his name from the slate of legislative candidates. For him there were other considerations that took priority over politics.

Violence against the freedmen of Abbeville County, as elsewhere in the state, continued that fall and escalated as the 1868 election day neared. The victims had in common an involvement with the Republicans, and there was little distinction made between direct and indirect partisan activity. Politically visible Negroes were open targets. Shortly after the Nash shooting young Willis Smith was assaulted, yet another victim of Reconstruction violence. Smith was still a teenager and too young to vote in the elections, but his age afforded him no immunity. He was a known member of the Union League, the most radical and secret of the political organizations that attracted freedmen. While attending a dance one evening, Smith and four other League members were dragged outside the dance hall and brutally beaten by four white men whose identities were hidden by hoods. This attack, too, was an act of political vengeance. Like other crimes committed against politically active Negroes, this one remained unsolved.

On election day freedmen Washington Green and Allen Goode were precinct managers at the White Hall polling place, near the southern edge of the Marshall land. Their position was a political appointment of some prestige, their reward for affiliation with and loyalty to the Republican cause. The appointment brought them, like Wilson Nash and Willis Smith, to the attention of local whites. On election day the voting proceeded without incident until midday, when two white men attempted to block Negroes from entering the polling site. A scuffle ensued as Green and Goode, acting in their capacity as voting officials, tried to bring the matter to a halt and were shot by the white men. One freedman was killed, two others injured, in the incident that also went unsolved. In none of the attacks were the assailants ever apprehended. Within twenty-four months all four men—Wilson Nash, Willis Smith, Washington Green, and Allen Goode—bought farms at Promised Land.

Despite the violence surrounding the 1868 elections, the Republicans carried the whole of the state. White Democrats refused to support an election they deemed illegal, and they intimidated the newly enfranchised Negro electorate at every opportunity. The freedmen, nevertheless, flocked to the polls in an unprecedented exercise of their new franchise and sent a body of legislative representatives to the state capitol of Columbia who were wholly committed to the mandates and reforms of the new constitution. Among the first legislative acts was one that formalized the land redistribution program through the creation of the South Carolina Land Commission.

The Land Commission program, as designed by the legislature, was financed through the public sale of state bonds. The capital generated from the bond sales was used to purchase privately owned plantation tracts that were then subdivided and resold to freedmen through long-term (ten years), low-interest (7 percent per annum) loans. The bulk of the commission's transactions occurred along the coastal areas of the state where land was readily available. The labor and financial problems of the rice planters of the low-country were generally more acute than those of the up-country cotton planters. As a result, they were more eager to dispose of a portion of the landholdings at a reasonable price, and their motives for their dealings with the Land Commission were primarily pecuniary.

Piedmont planters were not so motivated. Many were able to salvage their production by negotiating sharecropping and tenant arrangements. Most operated on a smaller scale than the low-country planters and were less dependent on gang labor arrangements. As a consequence, few were as financially pressed as their low-country counterparts, and land was less available for purchase by the Land Commission in the Piedmont region. With only 9 percent of the commission purchases lying in the up-country, the Marshall lands were the exception rather than the rule.

The Marshall sons first advertised the land for sale in 1865. These lands, like others at the eastern edge of the Cotton Belt, were exhausted from generations of cultivation and attendant soil erosion; and for such worn-out land the price was greatly inflated. Additionally, two successive years of crop failures, low cotton prices, and a general lack of capital discouraged serious planters from purchasing the lands. The sons then advertised the tract for rent, but the land stood idle. The family wanted to dispose of the land in a single transaction rather than subdivide it, and Dr. Marshall's farm was no competition for the less expensive and more fertile land to the west that was opened for settlement after the war. In 1869 the two sons once again advertised the land for sale, but conditions in Abbeville County were not improved for farmers, and no private buyer came forth.

Having exhausted the possibilities for negotiating a private sale, the family considered alternative prospects for the disposition of a farm that was of little use to them. James L. Orr, a moderate Democrat, former governor (1865 to 1868), and family son-in-law, served as negotiator when the tract was offered to the Land Commission at the grossly inflated price of ten dollars an acre. Equivalent land in Abbeville County was selling for as little as two dollars an acre, and the commission rejected the offer. Political promises took precedence over financial considerations when the commission's regional agent wrote the Land Commission's Advisory Board that "if the land is not bought the (Republican) party is lost in this district." Upon receipt of his advice the commission immediately met the Marshall family's ten dollar an acre price. By January 1870 the land had been subdivided into fifty small farms, averaging slightly less than fifty acres each, which were publicly offered for sale to Negro as well as white buyers.

The Marshall Tract was located in the central sector of old Abbeville County and was easily accessible to most of the freedmen who were to make the lands their home. . . .

The farms on the Marshall Tract were no bargain for the Negroes who bought them. The land was only partially cleared and ready for cultivation, and that which was free of pine trees and underbrush was badly eroded. There was little to recommend the land to cotton farming. Crop failures in 1868 and 1869 severely limited the local economy, which further reduced the possibilities for small farmers working on badly depleted soil. There was little credit available to Abbeville farmers, white or black; and farming lacked not only an unqualified promise of financial gain but even the possibility of breaking even at harvest. Still, it was not the fertility of the soil or the possibility of economic profit that attracted the freedmen to those farms. The single opportunity for landownership, a status that for most Negroes in 1870 symbolized the essence of their freedom, was the prime attraction for the freedmen who bought farms from the subdivided Marshall Tract.

Most of the Negroes who settled the farms knew the area and local conditions well. Many were native to Abbeville County. In addition to Wilson Nash, the Moragne family and their in-laws, the Turners, the Pinckneys, the Letmans, and the Williamses were also natives of Abbeville, from "down over by Bordeaux" in the southwestern rim of the county that borders Georgia. Others came to their new farms from "Dark Corner, over by McCormick," and another nearby Negro settlement, Pettigrew Station—both in Abbeville County. The Redd family lived in Newberry, South Carolina before they bought their farm;

and James and Hannah Fields came to Promised Land from the state capital, Columbia, eighty miles to the east.

Many of the settlers from Abbeville County shared their names with prominent white families—Moragne, Burt, Marshall, Pressley, Frazier, and Pinckney. Their claims to heritage were diverse. One recalled "my grandaddy was a white man from England," and others remembered slavery times to their children in terms of white fathers who "didn't allow nobody to mess with the colored boys of his." Others dismissed the past and told their grandchildren that "some things is best forget." A few were so fair skinned that "they could have passed for white if they wanted to," while others who bought farms from the Land Commission "was so black there wasn't no doubt about who their daddy was."

After emancipation many of these former bondsmen stayed in their old neighborhoods, farming in much the same way as they had during slavery times. Some "worked for the marsters at daytime and for theyselves at night" in an early Piedmont version of sharecropping. Old Samuel Marshall was one former slaveowner who retained many of his bondsmen as laborers by assuring them that they would receive some land of their own—promising them that "if you clean two acres you get two acres; if you clean ten acres you get ten acres" of farmland. It was this promise that kept some freedmen on the Marshall land until it was sold to the Land Commission. They cut and cleared part of the tract of the native pines and readied it for planting in anticipation of ownership. But the promise proved empty, and Marshall's death and the subsequent sale of his lands to the state deprived many of those who labored day and night on the land of the free farms they hoped would be theirs. "After they had cleaned it up they still had to pay for it." Other freedmen in the county "moved off after slavery ended but couldn't get no place" of their own to farm. Unable to negotiate labor or lease arrangements, they faced a time of homelessness with few resources and limited options until the farms became available to them. A few entered into labor contracts supervised by the Freedman's Bureau or settled on rented farms in the county for a time.

The details of the various postemancipation economic arrangements made by the freedmen who settled on the small tracts at Dr. Marshall's farm, whatever the form they assumed, were dominated by three conscious choices all had in common. The first was their decision to stay in Abbeville County following emancipation. For most of the people who eventually settled in Promised Land, Abbeville was their home as well as the site of their enslavement. There they were surrounded by friends, family, and a familiar environment. The second choice this group of freedmen shared was occupational. They had been Piedmont farmers throughout their enslavement, and they chose to remain farmers in their freedom.

Local Negroes made a third conscious decision that for many had long-range importance in their lives and those of their descendants. Through the influence of the Union League, the Freedman's Bureau, the African Methodist Church, and each other, many of the Negroes in Abbeville aligned politically with the Republicans between 1865 and 1870. In Abbeville as elsewhere in the state, the alliance was established enthusiastically. The Republicans promised land as well as suffrage to those who supported them. If their political activities became public knowledge, the freedmen "were safe nowhere"; and men like Wilson Nash, Willis Smith, Washington Green, and Allen Goode who were highly visible Negro politicians took great risks in this exercise of freedom. Those risks were not without justification. It was probably not a coincidence that loyalty to the Republican cause was followed by a chance to own land.

. . . The Land Commission first advertised the farms on the Marshall Tract in January and February 1870. Eleven freedmen and their families established conditional ownership of their farms before spring planting that year. They were among a vanguard of some 14,000 Negro families who acquired small farms in South Carolina through the Land Commission program between 1868 and 1879. With a ten-dollar down payment they acquired the right to settle on and till the thin soil. They were also obliged to place at least half their land under cultivation within three years and to pay all taxes due annually in order to retain their ownership rights.

Among the earliest settlers to the newly created farms was Allen Goode, the precinct manager at White Hall, who bought land in January 1870, almost immediately after it was put on the market. Two brothers-in-law, J. H. Turner and Primus Letman, also bought farms in the early spring that year. Turner was married to LeAnna Moragne and Letman to LeAnna's sister Francis. Elias Harris, a widower with six young children to raise, also came to his lands that spring, as did George Hearst, his son Robert, and their families. Another father-son partnership, Carson and Will Donnelly, settled on adjacent tracts. Willis Smith's father, Daniel, also bought a farm in 1870.

Allen Goode was the wealthiest of these early settlers. He owned a horse, two oxen, four milk cows, and six hogs. For the other families, both material resources and farm production were modest. Few of the homesteaders produced more than a single bale of cotton on their new farms that first year; but all, like Wilson Nash two years earlier, had respectable corn harvests, a crop essential to "both us and the animals." Most households also had sizable pea, bean, and sweet potato crops and produced their own butter. All but the cotton crops were destined for household consumption, as these earliest settlers established a pattern of subsistence farming that would prevail as a community economic strategy in the coming decades.

This decision by the Promised Land farmers to intensify food production and minimize cotton cultivation, whether intentional or the result of other conditions, was an important initial step toward their attainment of economic self-sufficiency. Small-scale cotton farmers in the Black Belt were rarely free agents. Most were quickly trapped in a web of chronic indebtedness and marketing restrictions. Diversification of cash crops was inhibited during the 1870s and 1880s not only by custom and these economic entanglements but also by an absence of local markets, adequate roads, and methods of transportation to move crops other than cotton to larger markets. The Promised Land farmers, generally unwilling to incur debts with the local lien men if they could avoid it, turned to a modified form of subsistence farming as their only realistic land-use option. Through this strategy many of them avoided the "economic nightmare" that fixed the status of other small-scale cotton growers at a level of permanent peonage well into the twentieth century.

The following year, 1871, twenty-five more families scratched up their ten-dollar down payment; and upon presenting it to Hollinshead obtained conditional titles to farms on the Marshall Tract. The Williams family, Amanda and her four adult sons—William, Henry, James, and Moses—purchased farms together that year, probably withdrawing their money from their accounts at the Freedmen's Savings and Trust Company Augusta Branch for their separate down payments. Three of the Moragne brothers—Eli, Calvin, and Moses—joined the Turners and the Letmans, their sisters and brothers-in-law, making five households in that corner of the tract soon designated "Moragne Town." John Valentine, whose family was involved in A.M.E. organizational work in Abbeville County, also obtained a conditional title to a farm, although he did not settle there permanently. Henry Redd, like the Williamses, withdrew his savings from the Freedman's Bank and moved to his farm from Newberry, a small town about thirty miles to the east. Moses Wideman, Wells Gray, Frank Hutchison, Samuel Bulow, and Samuel Burt also settled on their farms before spring planting.

As the cluster of Negro-owned farms grew more densely populated, it gradually assumed a unique identity; and this identity, in turn, gave rise to a name, Promised Land. Some remember their grandparents telling them that "the Governor in Columbia [South Carolina] named this place when he sold it to the Negroes." Others contend that the governor had no part in the naming. They argue that these earliest settlers derived the name Promised Land from the conditions of their purchase. "They only promised to pay for it, but they never did!" Indeed, there is some truth in that statement. For although the initial buyers agreed to pay between nine and ten dollars per acre for their land in the original promissory notes, few fulfilled the conditions of those contracts. Final purchase prices were greatly reduced, from ten dollars to $3.25 per acre, a price more in line with prevailing land prices in the Piedmont.

By the end of 1873 forty-four of the fifty farms on the Marshall Tract had been sold. The remaining land, less than seven hundred acres, was the poorest in the tract, badly eroded and at the perimeter of the community. Some of those farms remained unsold until the early 1880s, but even so the land did not go unused. Families too poor to consider buying the farms lived on the state-owned property throughout the 1870s. They were squatters, living there illegally and rent-free, perhaps working a small cotton patch, always a garden. Their condition contrasted sharply with that of the landowners who, like other Negroes who purchased farmland during the 1870s, were considered the most prosperous of the rural freedmen. The freeholders in the community were among the pioneers in a movement to acquire land, a movement that stretched across geographical and temporal limits. Even in the absence of state or federal assistance in other regions, and despite the difficulties Negroes faced in negotiating land purchases directly from white landowners during Reconstruction, by 1875 Negroes across the south owned five million acres of farmland. The promises of emancipation were fulfilled for a few, among them the families at Promised Land.

Settlement of the community coincided with the establishment of a public school, another of the revolutionary social reforms mandated by the 1868 constitution. It was the first of several public facilities to serve community residents and was built on land still described officially as "Dr. Marshall's farm." J. H. Turner, Larkin Reynolds, Iverson Reynolds, and Hutson Lomax, all Negroes, were the first school trustees. The families established on their new farms sent more than ninety children to the one-room school. Everyone who could be spared from the fields was in the classroom for the short 1870 school term. Although few of the children in the landless families attended school regularly, the landowning families early established a tradition of school attendance for their children consonant with their new status. With limited resources the school began the task of educating local children.

The violence and terror experienced by some of the men of Promised Land during 1868 recurred three years later when Eli and Wade Moragne were attacked and viciously beaten with a wagon whip by a band of Klansmen. Wade was twenty-three that year, Eli two years older. Both were married and had small children. It was rumored that the Moragne brothers were among the most prominent and influential of the Negro Republicans in Abbeville County. Their political activity, compounded by an unusual degree of self-assurance, pride, and dignity, infuriated local whites. Like Wilson Nash, Willis Smith, Washington Green, and Allen Goode, the Moragne brothers were victims of insidious political reprisals. Involvement in Reconstruction politics for Negroes was a dangerous enterprise and one that addressed the past as well as the future. It was an activity suited to young men and those who faced the future bravely. It was not for the timid.

The Republican influence on the freedmen at Promised Land was unmistakable, and there was no evidence that the "outrages" and terrorizations against them slowed their participation in local partisan activities. In addition to the risks, there were benefits to be accrued from their alliance with the Republicans. They enjoyed appointments as precinct managers and school trustees. As candidates for various public offices, they experienced a degree of prestige and public recognition that offset the element of danger they faced. These men, born slaves, rose to positions of prominence as landowners, as political figures, and as makers of a community. Few probably had dared to dream of such possibilities a decade earlier.

During the violent years of Reconstruction there was at least one official attempt to end the anarchy in Abbeville County. The representative to the state legislature, J. Hollinshead—the former regional agent for the Land Commission—stated publicly what many local Negroes already knew privately, that "numerous outrages occur in the county and the laws cannot be enforced by civil authorities." From the floor of the General Assembly of South Carolina Hollinshead called for martial law in Abbeville, a request that did not pass unnoticed locally. The editor of the *Press* commented on Hollinshead's request for martial law by declaring that such outrages against the freedmen "exist only in the imagination of the legislator." His response was probably typical of the cavalier attitude of southern whites toward the problems of their former bondsmen. Indeed, there were no further reports of violence and attacks against freedmen carried by the *Press,* which failed to note the murder of County Commissioner Henry Nash in February 1871. Like other victims of white terrorists, Nash was a Negro.

While settlement of Dr. Marshall's farm by the freedmen proceeded, three community residents were arrested for the theft of "some oxen from Dr. H. Drennan who lives near the 'Promiseland.'" Authorities found the heads, tails, and feet of the slaughtered animals near the homes of Ezekiel and Moses Williams and Colbert Jordan. The circumstantial evidence against them seemed convincing; and the three were arrested and then released without bond, pending trial. Colonel Cothran, a former Confederate officer and respected barrister in Abbeville, represented the trio at their trial. Although freedmen in Abbeville courts were generally convicted of whatever crime they were charged with, the Williamses and Jordan were acquitted. Justice for Negroes was always a tenuous affair; but it was especially so before black, as well as white, qualified electors were included in the jury pool. The trial of the Williams brothers and Jordan signaled a temporary truce in the racial war, a truce that at least applied to those Negroes settling the farms at Promised Land.

In 1872, the third year of settlement, Promised Land gained nine more households as families moved to land that they "bought for a dollar an acre." There they "plow old oxen, build log cabin houses" as they settled the land they bought "from the Governor in Columbia." Colbert Jordan and Ezekiel Williams, cleared of the oxen stealing charges, both purchased farms that year. Family and kinship ties drew some of the new migrants to the community. Joshuway Wilson, married to Moses Wideman's sister Delphia, bought a farm near his brother-in-law. Two more Moragne brothers, William and Wade, settled near the other family members in "Moragne Town." Whitfield Hutchison, a jack-leg preacher, bought the farm adjacent to his brother Frank. "Old Whit Hutchison could sing about let's go down to the water and be baptized. He didn't have no education, and he didn't know exactly how to put his words, but when he got to singing he could make your hair rise up. He was a number one preacher." Hutchison was not the only preacher among those first settlers. Isaac Y. Moragne, who moved to Promised Land the following year, and several men in the Turner family all combined preaching and farming.

Not all the settlers came to their new farms as members of such extensive kinship networks as the Moragnes, who counted nine brothers, four sisters, and an assortment of spouses and children among the first Promised Land residents. Even those who joined the community in relative isolation, however, were seldom long in establishing kinship alliances with their neighbors. One such couple was James and Hannah Fields, who lived in Columbia before emancipation. While still a slave, James Fields owned property in the state capital, which was held in trust for him by his master. After emancipation Fields worked for a time as a porter on the Columbia and Greenville Railroad and heard about the up-country land for sale to Negroes as he carried carpet bags and listened to political gossip on the train. Fields went to Abbeville County to inspect the land before he purchased a farm there. While he was visiting, he "run up on Mr. Nathan Redd," old Henry Redd's son. The Fields's grand-daughter Emily and Nathan were about the same age, and Fields proposed a match to young Redd. "You marry my granddaughter, and I'll will all this land to you and her." The marriage was arranged before the farm was purchased, and eventually the land was transferred to the young couple.

By the conclusion of 1872 forty-eight families were settled on farms in Promised Land. Most of the land was under cultivation, as required by law; but the farmers were also busy with other activities. In addition to the houses and barns that had to be raised as each new family arrived with their few posses-sions, the men continued their political activities. Iverson Reynolds, J. H. Turner, John and Elias Tolbert, Judson Reynolds, Oscar Pressley, and Washington Green, all community residents, were delegates to the county Republican convention in August 1872. Three of the group were landowners. Their political activities were still not received with much enthusiasm by local whites, but reaction to Negro involvement in politics was lessening in hostility. The *Press* mildly observed that the fall cotton crop was being gathered with good speed and "the farmers have generally been making good use of their time." Cotton picking and politics were both seasonal, and the newspaper chided local Negroes for their priorities. "The blacks have been indulging a lit-tle too much in politics but are getting right again." Iverson Reynolds and Washington Green, always among the community's Republican leadership during the 1870s, served as local election managers again for the 1872 fall elec-tions. The men from Promised Land voted without incident that year.

Civic participation among the Promised Land residents extended beyond partisan politics when the county implemented the new jury law in 1872. There had been no Negro jurors for the trial of the Williams brothers and Colbert Jordan the previous year. Although the inclusion of Negroes in the jury pools was a reform mandated in 1868, four years passed before Abbeville authorities drew up new jury lists from the revised voter registration rolls. The jury law was as repugnant to the whites as Negro suffrage, termed "a wretched attempt at legislation, which surpasses anything which has yet been achieved by the Salons in Columbia." When the new lists were finally completed in 1872 the *Press*, ever the reflection of local white public opinion, predicted that "many of [the freedmen] probably have moved away; and the chances are that not many of them will be forthcoming" in the call to jury duty. Neither the initial con-demnation of the law nor the optimistic undertones of the *Press* prediction stopped Pope Moragne and Iverson Reynolds from responding to their notices from the Abbeville Courthouse. Both landowners rode their mules up Five Notch Road from Promised Land to Abbeville and served on the county's first integrated jury in the fall of 1872. Moragne and Reynolds were soon followed by others from the community—Allen Goode, Robert Wideman, William Moragne, James Richie, and Luther (Shack) Moragne. By 1874, less than five years after settlement of Dr. Marshall's farm by the new Negro landowners began, the residents of Promised Land remained actively involved in Abbeville County politics. They were undaunted by the *Press* warning that "just so soon as the colored people lose the confidence and support of the North their doom is fixed. The fate of the red man will be theirs." They were voters, jurors, taxpayers, and trustees of the school their children attended. Their collective identity as an exclusively Negro community was well established. . . .

The representatives to the 1868 South Carolina Constitutional Convention who formulated the state's land redistribution hoped to establish an economically independent Negro yeomanry in South Carolina. The Land Commission intended the purchase and resale of Dr. Marshall's farm to solidify the interests of radical Republicanism in Abbeville County, at least for a time. Both of these designs were realized. A third and unintended consequence also resulted. The land fostered a socially autonomous, identifiable community. Drawing on resources and social structures well established within an extant Negro culture, the men and women who settled Promised Land established churches and schools and a viable economic system based on landownership. They maintained that economic autonomy by subsistence farming and supported many of their routine needs by patronizing the locally owned and operated grist mills and general store. The men were actively involved in Reconstruction politics as well as other aspects of civil life, serving regularly on county juries and paying their taxes. Attracted by the security and prestige Promised Land afforded and the possible hope of eventual landownership, fifty additional landless households moved into the community during the 1870s, expanding the 1880 population to almost twice its original size. Together the eighty-nine households laid claim to slightly more than four square miles of land, and within that small territory they "carved out their own little piece of the world."

THE MEANING OF FREEDOM

What did it mean to be free? As Bethel's account of the settlers of Promised Land indicates, there were many obstacles in the path of every freedman and only a few succeeded in becoming independent small farmers. Some twentieth-century writers have argued that the gains for most blacks were miniscule, that being a poor tenant farmer or sharecropper was often even worse than being a slave. But these writers, of course, never experienced the change from slavery to freedom. Here is a man who did.

Dayton, Ohio, August 7, 1865

To My Old Master, Colonel P. H. Anderson, Big Spring, Tennessee

Sir: I got your letter and was glad to find you had not forgotten Jourdon, and that you wanted me to come back and live with you again, promising to do better for me than anybody else can. I have often felt uneasy about you. I thought the Yankees would have hung you long before this for harboring Rebs they found at your house. I suppose they never heard about your going to Col. Martin's to kill the Union soldier that was left by his company in their stable. Although you shot at me twice before I left you, I did not want to hear of your being hurt, and am glad you are still living. It would do me good to go back to the dear old home and see Miss Mary and Miss Martha and Allen, Esther, Green, and Lee. Give my love to them all, and tell them I hope we will meet in the better world, if not in this. I would have gone back to see you all when I was working in the Nashville hospital, but one of the neighbors told me Henry intended to shoot me if he ever got a chance.

I want to know particularly what the good chance is you propose to give me. I am doing tolerably well here; I get $25 a month, with victuals and clothing; have

From Lydia Maria Child, ed., *The Freedmen's Book,* Boston, 1865, pp. 265–267.

a comfortable home for Mandy (the folks here call her Mrs. Anderson), and the children, Milly, Jane and Grundy, go to school and are learning well; the teacher says Grundy has a head for a preacher. They go to Sunday-School, and Mandy and me attend church regularly. We are kindly treated; sometimes we overhear others saying, "Them colored people were slaves" down in Tennessee. The children feel hurt when they hear such remarks, but I tell them it was no disgrace in Tennessee to belong to Col. Anderson. Many darkies would have been proud, as I used to was, to call you master. Now, if you will write and say what wages you will give me, I will be better able to decide whether it would be to my advantage to move back again.

As to my freedom, which you say I can have, there is nothing to be gained on that score, as I got my free-papers in 1864 from the Provist-Marshal-General of the Department at Nashville. Mandy says she would be afraid to go back without some proof that you are sincerely disposed to treat us justly and kindly—and we have concluded to test your sincerity by asking you to send us our wages for the time we served you. This will make us forget and forgive old scores, and rely on your justice and friendship in the future. I served you faithfully for thirty-two years and Mandy twenty years. At $25 a month for me, and $2 a week for Mandy, our earnings would amount to $11,680. Add to this the interest for the time our wages has been kept back and deduct what you paid for our clothing and three doctor's visits to me, and pulling a tooth for Mandy, and the balance will show what we are in justice entitled to. Please send the money by Adams Express, in care of V. Winters, esq., Dayton, Ohio. If you fail to pay us for faithful labors in the past we can have little faith in your promises in the future. We trust the good Maker has opened your eyes to the wrongs which you and your fathers have done to me and my fathers, in making us toil for you for generations without recompense. Here I draw my wages every Saturday night, but in Tennessee there was never any pay day for the negroes any more than for the horses and cows. Surely there will be a day of reckoning for those who defraud the laborer of his hire.

In answering this letter please state if there would be any safety for my Milly and Jane, who are now grown up and both good-looking girls. You know how it was with poor Matilda and Catherine. I would rather stay here and starve and die if it comes to that than have my girls brought to shame by the violence and wickedness of their young masters. You will also please state if there has been any schools opened for the colored children in your neighborhood, the great desire of my life now is to give my children an education, and have them form virtuous habits.

P.S.—Say howdy to George Carter, and thank him for taking the pistol from you when you were shooting at me.

> From your old servant,
> Jourdon Anderson

THE CARTOONIST'S VIEW OF RECONSTRUCTION

Thomas Nast was America's foremost political cartoonist. He also was a Radical Republican who had no love for the white South or the Democratic Party. The touchstone cause of Radical Republicans was black civil rights—particularly the right to vote—and conflict with the Democrats and the white South often focused on this issue. Nast's drawings in Harper's Weekly, *as you will notice, illustrated vividly this ongoing battle. The high point for Nast came when Hiram Revels, a black, occupied the Senate seat from Mississippi once held by Jefferson Davis. The low point came shortly afterward. What effect do you think each cartoon had on the electorate? Were any more compelling than the others?*

Columbia—"Shall I Trust These Men, . . .

And Not This Man?"
Thomas Nast, Harper's Weekly, *August 5, 1865.*

"This Is a White Man's Government."
"We regard the Reconstruction Acts (so called) of Congress as usurpations, and unconstitutional, revolutionary, and void."—Democratic platform.
Thomas Nast, Harper's Weekly, *September 5, 1868, Courtesy of The Research Libraries, The New York Public Library, Astor, Lenox and Tilden Foundations.*

"Time Works Wonders Government." Thomas Nast, Harper's Weekly, *April 9, 1870.*

The Commandments in South Carolina.
"We've pretty well smashed that; but I suppose, Massa Moses, you can get another one."
Thomas Nast, Harper's Weekly, *September 26, 1874.*

"To Thine Own Self Be True."
Thomas Nast, Harper's Weekly, *October 24, 1874.*

The Target.
"* * * They (Messrs. Phleps & Potter) seem to regard the White League as innocent as a Target Company."—Special dispatch to the N.Y. *Times,* from Washington, Jan. 17, 1875. *Thomas Nast,* Harper's Weekly, *February 6, 1875.*

"These Few Precepts in Thy Memory"
Beware of entrance to a quarrel; but, being in,
Bear it that the opposer may beware of thee.
Give every man thine ear, but few thy voice:
Take each man's censure, but reserve thy judgment.
Costly thy habit as thy purse can but,
But not express'd in fancy; rich, not gaudy:
For the apparel oft proclaims the man.

This above all,—To thine own self be true;
And it must follow, as the night the day,
Thou canst not then be false to any man.

—Shakespeare

Thomas Nast, Harper's Weekly, *April 24, 1875.*

The "Civil Rights" Scare Is Nearly Over.
The game of (Colored) fox and (White) goose.
Thomas Nast, Harper's Weekly, *May 22, 1875.*

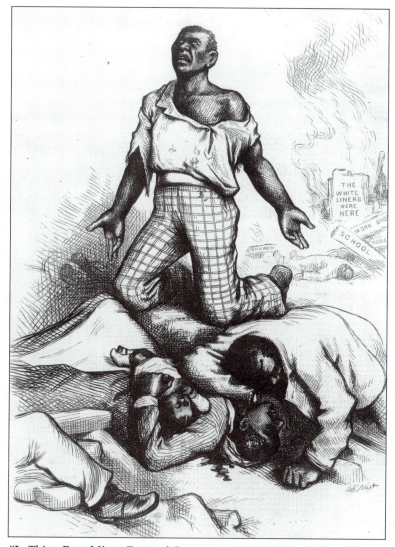

"Is *This* a Republican Form of Government? Is *This* Protecting Life, Liberty, or Property? Is *This* the Equal Protection of the Laws?"
Mr. Lamar (Democrat, Mississippi): "In the words of the inspired poet, 'Thy gentleness has made thee great.'" [Did Mr. Lamar mean the colored race?]
Thomas Nast, Harper's Weekly, *September 2, 1876. The Newberry Library*

THE SOUTH REDEEMED

As Nast's cartoons indicate, the crusade for black voting rights and other civil rights ran into stiff opposition and eventually failed. By 1877, white supremacy was firmly reestablished throughout the South, and black political voices were almost completely stilled. The South, according to many white southerners, had been "redeemed" by its white leaders. But the white South did not get back everything it wanted. Black men had refused to work as gang laborers, and black families had refused to let women and children work long hours in the field. Grudgingly, white landowners had let blacks work the land in family plots, usually as either tenant farmers or sharecroppers. Thus, despite "redemption," the southern landscape would look startlingly different from Reconstruction. Here are maps of the same Georgia plantation in 1860 and in 1880. What, in your judgment, were the important features in the new and the old landscape? Do the changes match up with the kinds of attitudes discussed in Bethel's essay? How many of the 1880 families, would you guess, once lived in the old slave quarters?

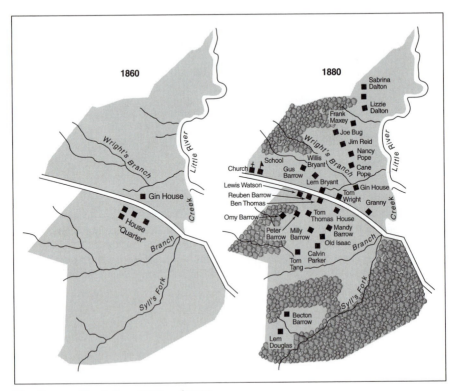

The Barrow Plantation, 1860 and 1880.
Adapted from Scribner's Monthly, *vol. 21, April 1881, 832–833.*

the big picture

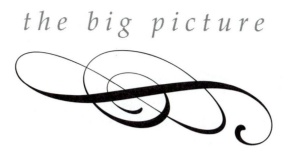

The problem of reconstruction was to bring eleven states back into the Union, rebuild the war-torn nation, and achieve racial justice. The latter did not happen. Why didn't it happen? What, in your opinion, would have been an appropriate and effective method for achieving racial justice in 1865?

chapter two

THE GILDED AGE

Nineteenth-century Americans were obsessed with change, progress, development, and growth. And this obsession reached a new peak during the decades after the Civil War. An American who had matured in the 1850s or 1860s could look backward from 1890 or 1900 and remember a lifetime filled with what seemed to be the most astonishing kinds of transformations.

The facts were there to support such memories of change. The population more than doubled between 1870 and 1900. The telegraph, the telephone, the electric light, and the Linotype were only four of the dozens of inventions that made life—and work—remarkably different. In 1850, most workers were artisans, plying their crafts in small shops under employers working beside them on similar tasks. By 1900, larger industrial enterprises were employing thousands of workers; employers seldom had any personal knowledge of their employees; and much of the skill had been removed from the work process. There were new cities, too—six in 1900 with populations of more than 500,000. The United States leapfrogged over England, France, and Germany to become the leading industrial nation of the world. Steel production increased 2,000 percent between the Civil War and the end of the century. Many firms for the first time supplied national and urban markets rather than local and rural ones. This meant new opportunities, more intense competition, and, finally, the emergence of the big corporations that have become the hallmark of the American economy. Change was a whirling, accelerating affair that altered the horizons of experience in every decade.

Above the whirl, a kind of official opinion developed, an orthodox opinion that change was "progress." Presidents and senators, newspaper editors and magazine writers, preachers and book publishers—all the molders of what was coming to be thought of as "public opinion"—voiced a belief that industrialization was creating a better life for the republic. Within this view, industrial growth meant opportunity. Competition meant success. All the inventions created leisure and material comfort. The great new factories meant a sort of democracy of well-being for the workers in them. And, in national terms, industrial growth meant the potential triumph in the world of American principles of freedom and equality.

But the awareness of change also generated problems and anxieties. For the wealthy and the sophisticated, there was the possibility that industrialization might lead to a world of materialism, greed, and speculation, a world with only a thin and false veneer of culture and moral values. This fear was a theme of the book that gave a name to the period, Mark Twain and Charles Dudley Warner's *Gilded Age,* published in 1873.

What became known as the "labor question" or the "labor problem" was really a collection of doubts and anxieties. Could the United States absorb the huge pool of immigrants who were attracted to the industrializing cities and towns? Would the new industrial work force tolerate long hours, factory conditions, and gross disparities of wealth, or would they form labor unions and even take to the streets to protest and redress their grievances? Would ordinary Americans continue to believe in the possibilities of success and self-improvement, and so resign themselves to a place in the new order of things? Or would radical ideologies—socialism, communism, anarchism—thrive in the new industrial environment and bring American capitalism crashing down?

interpretive essay

David R. Roediger

AMERICA'S FIRST GENERAL STRIKE: THE ST. LOUIS "COMMUNE"* OF 1877

In the midst of the great economic changes of the latter half of the nineteenth century, most Americans believed that their country could somehow avoid the deep social conflicts and sharp ideological struggles associated with industrialization in Europe. There were, to be sure, disquieting signs. American workers had come together in unions as early as the 1790s, formed workingmen's political parties in the 1820s and 1830s, and, like Philadelphia textile workers in 1844, gone out on strike against their employers. In the decade after the Civil War, national unions, bringing together workers in similar occupations, had grown dramatically in number and influence, led by the iron molders and the railroad "brotherhoods." Yet even as Americans suffered through the depression of the 1870s, it was easy to believe that race and sectionalism, not class and economics, were the nation's most critical problems.

With the fourth year of the depression came the rude awakening known as the 1877 railroad strike. Although less familiar to most students of American history than the Pullman strike or the Homestead strike of the 1890s, the railroad conflict was probably more significant. It began on a Monday in mid-July, 1877, in Martinsburg, West Virginia, where workers employed by the Baltimore and Ohio Railroad refused to move the trains until the company rescinded a previously announced wage cut of 10 percent. There, and elsewhere, the use of state militia and federal troops to move the trains and bring order angered railroad workers and those in other industries. By the end of the week, the strike had spread to other lines and to other communities in the East, Midwest, and South, including Baltimore, Buffalo, Pittsburgh, Columbus, Chicago, Louisville, and Galveston. In many communities, railroad workers

---

*The word "commune" refers to an alternative municipal government (commune) organized by Parisians of various political persuasions in 1871, in the wake of a humiliating peace with Prussia. The Paris Commune was defeated with military force and more than 17,000 were executed for their participation.—Ed.

were joined by workers in other industries in citywide "general" strikes, in which most of the city's industries were shut down. The St. Louis general strike, described and interpreted by David Roediger, was the most important of these confrontations.

Events of this sort would seem highly improbable today. What conditions— political, economic, social, or technological—made the St. Louis general strike possible? How did workers understand their situation? What did they want out of the strike, and were their demands reasonable? What role did ethnicity, class, and race play in the strike? What was the role of government?

Eads' magnificent bridge opened 106 years ago to link the bustling trading city of St. Louis with the busy rail town of East St. Louis. For a torrid July week in 1877, the bridge came to carry neither shoppers nor railroad cars but a highly contagious strike wave which swept over both sides of the river. From its modest beginning as a walkout in the East Side rail yards the strike movement spread across the bridge to all major industries in the area. St. Louis, then America's third-ranking manufacturing city, witnessed the nation's first general strike in an industrial city. To the wealthy it seemed clear that a St. Louis "Commune" was taking shape.

Political passions blazed in 1877. A new president, Rutherford B. Hayes, took office after having defeated Samuel Tilden by one hotly contested electoral vote. To secure his victory, Hayes pledged to remove federal troops protecting the civil rights of black Southerners. In the Northwest, Indian wars raged in the afterglow of Custer's 1876 defeat. Most seriously, the entire nation plunged into the worst depression in U.S. history. Farm organizations (especially the Grange) and the urban poor alike blamed reckless, high-living rail speculators for the economic disaster that left 5 million jobless.

When rail corporations tried to push through a series of wage cuts for those still employed, the railwaymen of Baltimore and Pittsburgh reacted. Unwilling to accept Henry Ward Beecher's admonition that "the man who cannot live on bread and water is not fit to live," they stopped rail traffic with spontaneous strikes. The strike movement fanned out from east to west, following rail and telegraph lines and taking them over as it proceeded. By Sunday, July 22, it had reached East St. Louis. That evening representatives of the many rail lines which traversed that town filed into Traubel's Hall, elected an Executive Committee and issued an order to halt all freight traffic. Within hours a mass meeting convened and made the Relay Depot and telegraph offices the property of the strikers. Mayor John Bowman, an emigrant from Germany's 1848 revolution, had neither the police nor, perhaps, the inclination to challenge the strikers. Rather he deputized the workmen themselves, entrusting them to protect East St. Louis property.

However impressive, the east-side events would be but a footnote in the history of 1877 had they not sparked so much further strike activity.

From David R. Roediger, "America's First General Strike: The St. Louis 'Commune' of 1877," *The Midwest Quarterly,* 21 (Winter 1980): 196-206.

The Sixth Maryland Regiment, Fighting Its Way Through Baltimore During the Great Strike of 1877.
From a photograph by D. Bendann. Library of Congress.

Predictably, the strike spilled over into the meatpacking industries of East St. Louis, virtually closing industry in that town of 9000. And the contagion came also to St. Louis' Union Depot, which became a new rail strike center. All this still hardly compared with the tense demonstrations and bloody pitched battles that characterized the strikes in Pittsburgh, Chicago, Reading, San Francisco and New York. Only through the actions of the small but potent political party did the strike overspread St. Louis' 300,000 inhabitants and did the Mound City catapult into the national news.

Before July, the Workingmen's Party scarcely looked capable of leading so momentous a strike. A spinoff of the dying Marxist First International Workingmen's Association, the St. Louis group had perhaps 1,000 members. Language divided even this small core. A German-speaking federation loomed larger than the French, English and Bohemian contingents. The party's meager work consisted primarily of sporadic leafletting and of vigorously refusing to march in the city's Fourth of July parades.

As soon as the railroad strike erupted, however, the unlikely Workingmen's Party seized the moment. On the Sunday night that East St. Louis railroad workers voted to strike, the party sent a delegation of several hundred across Eads' well-travelled bridge to address the strikers. At least one party member, railroad machinist Harry Eastman, won a place on the railroaders' five-man strike committee. By Monday, the Workingmen's Party undertook even more fruitful activities west of the river. That evening in Carondolet, an industrial enclave which had just been annexed to St. Louis, Iron Mountain Railroad workers joined forces with the employees of the mammoth Vulcan Iron Works in a massive strike meeting. Party leader Martin Becker quickly assumed leadership of the Carondolet strikers.

A second Monday night mass meeting grew to huge proportions. The demonstration, called by the Workingmen's Party, brought throngs to old Lucas Market (Twelfth Street from Olive to Chestnut). The best estimates, those of strike historian David T. Burbank, point to a tumultuous crowd which included some 8,000 to 10,000 people. After cheering several speakers, the meeting elected a five-man Executive Committee of party members to request that St. Louis' mayor *not* ask for federal troops in St. Louis. The nighttime rally's effect, summed up by a *Chicago Tribune* reporter, was "to set the lower classes on fire."

On Tuesday, the Workingmen's Party kindled that fire by sending out committees to various plants to call for extension of the strike. Coopers quickly struck, as did some newsboys, gas workers, wire workers, and longshoremen. Tuesday evening saw a parade of 1,500, mostly iron moulders and mechanics, headed by a fife, a drum, and a lone torch. The Lucas Market demonstration that evening could only be measured, said the *St. Louis Times*, "by acres." The crowd was at least 10,000 when the Executive Committee members unveiled specific demands: an eight-hour day and an end to child labor. The party's proclamation called for a general strike in all industries to enforce the demands:

PROCLAMATION

St. Louis, Mo., July 25th, 1877.

FELLOW-CITIZENS: The daily press of the city—both English and German—persisting in misrepresentation of our movement in the present great struggle of our fellow-workingmen against the overbearing oppression of capitalists and monopolists,—we are compelled to issue the following in order to clear ourselves of the charges and abuses, which the daily press of St. Louis sees fit to throw upon us. Liberal thinking men may then judge, who is right and who is wrong.

As you all well know, work is very scarce now in all branches, and the compensation for work done is so little, to make it almost impossible for any man to make his bare living, and it is utterly impossible for married men to support their families. Where shall this end? If now, during the summer season, such is the case, what shall we do next winter? Has our government done anything for us workingmen? We say No! emphatically No! Therefore, fellow-workingmen, me (sic) MUST act ourselves, unless we want starvation to stare to our faces the coming winter. There is only one way—Help yourself!

To this purpose a meeting was held last night at the Lucas Market, where the following resolutions were passed!

Resolved, that we, the authorized executive committee of the Workingmen's party of the United States, do not hold ourselves responsible for any act of violence which may be perpetrated during the present excitement; but that we will do all that lies in our power to aid the authorities in keeping order and preventing acts of violence, and will do our utmost to detect and bring to punishment all guilty parties. We make an issue for our constitutional rights as American citizens—that is, the right of life, liberty, and the pursuit of happiness. Our motto is, "Death to thieves, incendiaries and murderers."

Resolved, that, as every man willing to perform a use to society is entitled to a living, therefore, if our present system of production and distribution fails to provide for our wants, it then becomes the duty of the government to enact such laws as will insure equal justice to all the people of the nation.

Resolved, that, as the condition of an immense number of people now is forced idleness, and the great suffering for the necessaries of life caused by the monopoly in the hands of capitalists, appeals strongly to all industrial classes for prompt action, therefore, to avoid bloodshed or violence, we recommend a general strike of all branches of industry for eight hours as a days work, and we call on the legislature for the immediate enactment of an eight hour law, and the enforcement of a severe penalty for its violation, and that the employment of all children under fourteen years of age be prohibited.

Resolved, that it is our purpose never to give up the strike till these propositions are enforced.

The Executive Committee.

By Wednesday the battle lines emerged clearly. On one side the Workingmen's Party placed itself at the head of a burgeoning movement of pop-ular discontent. The leadership of the strike reflected St. Louis' cosmopolitan na-ture. Peter Lofgreen, leader of the party's American section, but a native Dane, graduated from the University of Copenhagen and qualified as a lawyer in Chicago before coming to St. Louis and finding a job as a clerk for the *Globe-*

Democrat. (Lofgreen would later, under the name Laurence Gronlund, produce works on "ethical socialism" which influenced both Eugene Debs and Edward Bellamy). Albert Currlin, head of the German contingent, fled to the U.S. in 1874 to avoid Germany's draft and worked as a baker before becoming a full-time political organizer. Henry Allen, the top-ranking American native in the group, was a self-taught doctor and a visionary heavily influenced by the mystical religion of Emmanuel Swedenborg. A fourth major leader, a black American identified only as Wilson, was not a member of the apparently all-white Workingmen's Party but was among the most popular speakers at strike meetings.

James Dacus, a *Globe-Democrat* writer unsympathetic to the strike, reported that "circumstances had conspired to create a general feeling of uneasiness among the 'propertied classes.'" Those classes, perhaps more than uneasy, led the forces arrayed against the strikers and the Workingmen's Party. Mayor Henry Overstolz had few police at his disposal and could not move quickly against the strike. The largely American-born upper classes chafed at the boldness of the mostly foreign strikers and were quick to deride the German mayor as pusillanimous if not traitorous. Rail magnate James H. Wilson tried to remedy the situation by writing federal officials to request troops.

Others of the rich formed a "citizens' militia" to repress the strike. Fearing a reincarnation of the notorious Paris Commune of 1871, the militiamen took a page from the book of the French middle class and christened themselves the Committee of Public Safety. Headquartered in the Four Courts building and very strong in the exclusive Lafayette Park area, the "citizens' militia" suffered on Wednesday from an excess of inexperienced leaders. Only as the week wore on and federal troops arrived would the militia's superior firepower prove decisive.

Wednesday belonged to the strikers. In the morning the Workingmen's Party Executive Committee sent delegations to various workplaces, especially the levees, to spread the strike. The response was overwhelming, and by 2:00 P.M. a crowd of 5,000 had gathered at Lucas Market to overspread the city and shut down industries. A brass band led the procession along with a flagstaff on which was stuck a loaf of bread—the symbol of the strike. The march was an astonishing success—flour mills, smelting plants, foundries—virtually all major industries shut down. Carondolet's heavy industries ground to a similar halt, and East St. Louis women marched in support of the strike. That night the Lucas Market crowd rose to well in excess of 10,000. Even the bars and brothels closed.

Ironically, the very successes of Wednesday may have paralyzed the Workingmen's Party. Leadership of the Wednesday afternoon demonstrations fell, according to the *Republican,* to a band of several hundred black rivermen. Party leader Albert Currlin told an interviewer after the strike that "We did all we could to get the crowd to disperse and to dissuade any white men from going with the niggers." Currlin probably exaggerated his group's pacifism to save himself at his coming trial, but he hardly exaggerated the racism which infected some white workers. Linked to the fear of black activity, was the Workingmen's Party's fear that violence might upset its strategy. Party leaders vainly hoped that their ability to keep order during the strike might cause Mayor Overstolz to deputize and arm their members. When marchers looted small amounts of bread and soap on Wednesday, party leaders hesitated to call further demonstrations.

The main work of the party hierarchy on Thursday was to issue a circular asking that Mayor Overstolz and the employers feed the strikers to forestall rioting. The city did have two soup kitchens to aid the destitute, but the philanthropists were not about to take over the feeding of an entire city of strikers. Fighting, not feeding, was on the minds of the upper class. The morale of the "citizen's militias" improved dramatically when Missouri Governor John Phelps sent 1,500 rifles to quell the strike. The arms entered on a passenger train under U.S. infantry guard. In one wire works, the heartened police succeeded in facing down strike committee members and keeping the plant open.

Thursday saw some gains for the strikers—the closing of several more plants and the winning of wage increases in some industries—but the momentum was shifting. The leaders of the increasingly immobilized Workingmen's Party failed to appear on the platform at Lucas Market that evening. Others, perhaps angry at the party's apparent abdication, bandied about improbable schemes for a military siege of the city by the strikers. In one of the oddest mo-

Robert M. Ammon, the Leader of the Pittsburgh and Fort Wayne Railroad Strike, at His Post, Directing the Movements of the Strikers.
From a sketch by John Donaghy. Library of Congress.

ments of the strike, party leaders apparently begged police to arrest an especially incendiary orator.

By Friday, the militia, poised to take advantage of disarray in the ranks of
the strikers, drilled determinedly at the Four Courts. Civic leader Leigh Knapp
doubling as an "Adjutant General" headed the militia (or "posse" as he called
them) into the streets. Reinforced by troops from Fort Leavenworth, the militiamen cut into the effectiveness of the strike, especially on the levee. The
Executive Committee of the strikers met frantically at Schuler's Hall (having
been evicted from the Turners' Hall) and presided over the eroding strike. The
debates at Schuler's Hall were doubtless heated enough, but the police agents
who relayed news of the proceedings to Four Courts were superfluous. Strike
leaders had banked on the mayor deputizing them as police; when all the arms
and authority went to the "citizens' militia," strikers could only await the
inevitable.

The inevitable came quickly. Late Friday morning, Mayor Overstolz issued
orders to capture "Fort Schuler." Perhaps stung by criticism of his earlier vacil-
lation, Overstolz ordered that all who resisted at Schuler's Hall be shot. As 700
police and militiamen slogged through the rain from Four Courts to the strike
headquarters, the crowd in Schuler's Hall thinned from 500 to 100. Police, city
fathers, cavalry and artillery all massed before the hall by 3:00 P.M. A throng of
bystanders drew the wrath of the cavalry's horsewhips as a police board official sat beneath an umbrella chanting "Ride 'em down." Except for a small
group which jumped to freedom from the higher stories of Schuler's Hall, the
strikers submitted to arrest without resistance. Of the 73 seized, 49 were incar-
cerated at Four Courts and the rest released.

Strike leaders apparently slipped away before police arrived, but shortly
after the arrests Currlin and another spokesperson voluntarily visited
Overstolz's office still hoping to arrive at some compromise. Both were arrested, and others of the Executive Committee soon joined them in jail. Few
workers gathered in Lucas Market that evening as the forces of order demolished the empty speaker's platform. The Carondolet strike lasted several more
hours, but by Saturday, the west side of the river was returning to work. Just as
the strike had spread from the east, the defeat of the strike flowed from the
west. At the insistence of edgy St. Louis businessmen, federal troops crossed
the river to end the rail strike at bayonet point.

On August 10, the Workingmen's Party had its day in court. Currlin,
Lofgreen, Allen and others in the leadership faced penitentiary sentences on the
felony charge of "riot." Rank-and-file party members had already received
terms in the workhouse. All the leaders went free after a very brief trial in
which the defendants stressed their disdain for violence and disorder. The
party suffered decimation in the wake of the strike's defeat, but individual
leaders, especially Currlin, continued as important figures in St. Louis politics.

The St. Louis press, so terrified during late July, slowly recovered from the
shock. Editors even began to show a certain strange pride that St. Louis had
spawned America's only *genuine* Commune." After a time, few cared to remember the strike, however. Among the upper classes, neither the terrifying

early days of the week nor the lopsided, almost farcical, "battle of Fort Schuler" proved popular memories. The strike leaders, free but chastened, had little reason to recall those hot July days when promises of an 8-hour day and an end to child labor melted in a Friday afternoon rain. Supporters of a beefed-up police force did make frequent (and successful) references to the 1877 events in appealing for municipal funds, but even they soon dwelled on more contemporary threats to order and property. Schuler's Hall was razed in 1956 to make way for the Mark Twain Expressway. Few mourned the passing of a St. Louis landmark or remembered the 1877 week when the whole city struck.

The strike was forgotten long before its centennial. Did the 1877 exertions of thousands of St. Louisians prove ephemeral? Perhaps not. Even as police rounded up the last Workingmen's Party leaders on that eventful Friday night cigar makers, inspired by the strike, met to form a durable union. That union and its leader, David Kreyerling, helped sustain the Missouri Federation of Labor in its early years and well into the 1930's. Other unions, especially in shoe manufacturing, also drew strength and leadership from the 1877 strike. In 1879, reacting to mild electoral successes by St. Louis socialists (and surely recalling the strike), Governor Phelps established the State Bureau of Labor Statistics. Even the 1880 plans to build public baths in St. Louis are thought to have resulted in part from pressure brought to bear by Currlin and ex-supporters of the strike.

These were small beginnings. Even such basic reforms as the 8-hour day and an end to child labor were years in coming. But the flexed muscles of St. Louis labor during America's first general strike may have hastened their arrival. If so the July days of the St. Louis "Commune" are still worthy of our attention even after more than a century has passed.

E. L. Godkin

THE WORKING CLASS

In the aftermath of the great labor upheaval of 1877, journalists and social analysts across the country pondered the meaning of the conflict. Among them was E. L. Godkin, the influential editor of The Nation. *In politics, Godkin was a thoughtful, independent liberal; he supported civil service reform and attacked political corruption and the high protective tariffs favored by business. As the following selection reveals, he was also an opponent of organized labor and deeply concerned about the strikes and violence in the summer of 1877. How did Godkin interpret those events? What, according to Godkin, was at stake? What aspects of his analysis do you find most objectionable?*

A WIDESPREAD RISING . . .

It is impossible to deny that the events of the last fortnight constitute a great national disgrace, and have created a profound sensation throughout the civilized world. They are likely to impress the foreign imagination far more than the outbreak of the Civil War, because the probability that the slavery controversy would end in civil war or the disruption of the Union had been long present to people's minds both at home and abroad. . . . There has for fifty years been throughout Christendom a growing faith that outside the area of slave-soil the United States had—of course with the help of great natural resources—solved the problem of enabling labor and capital to live together in political harmony, and that this was the one country in which there was no proletariat and no dangerous class, and in which the manners as well as legislation effectually prevented the formation of one. That the occurrences of the last fortnight will do, and have done, much to shake or destroy this faith, and that whatever weakens it weakens also the fondly cherished hopes of many millions about the future of the race, there is unhappily little question. We have had what appears a

"A Widespread Rising . . . Against Society Itself," *The Nation*, XXV (August 2, 1877), pp. 68–69.

widespread rising, not against political oppression or unpopular government, but against society itself. What is most curious about it is that it has probably taken people here nearly as much by surprise as people in Europe. The optimism in which most Americans are carefully trained, and which the experience of life justifies to the industrious, energetic, and provident, combined with the long-settled political habit of considering riotous poor as the products of a monarchy and aristocracy, and impossible in the absence of "down-trodden masses," has concealed from most of the well-to-do and intelligent classes of the population the profound changes which have during the last thirty years been wrought in the composition and character of the population, especially in the great cities. Vast additions have been made to it within that period, to whom American political and social ideals appeal but faintly, if at all, and who carry in their very blood traditions which give universal suffrage an air of menace to many of the things which civilized men hold dear. So complete has the illusion been that up to the day of the outbreak at Martinsburg thousands, even of the most reflective class, were gradually ridding themselves of the belief that force would be much longer necessary, or, indeed, was now necessary in the work of government. . . .

The kindest thing which can be done for the great multitudes of untaught men who have been received on these shores, and are daily arriving, and who are torn perhaps even more here than in Europe by wild desires and wilder dreams, is to show them promptly that society as here organized, on individual freedom of thought and action, is impregnable, and can be no more shaken than the order of nature. The most cruel thing is to let them suppose, even for one week, that if they had only chosen their time better, or had been better led or better armed, they would have succeeded in forcing it to capitulate. In what way better provision, in the shape of public force, should be made for its defense we have no space left to discuss, but that it will not do to be caught again as the rising at Martinsburg caught us; that it would be fatal to private and public credit and security to allow a state of things to subsist in which 8,000 or 9,000 day laborers of the lowest class can suspend, even for a whole day, the traffic and industry of a great nation, merely as a means of extorting ten or twenty cents a day more wages from their employers, we presume everybody now sees. Means of prompt and effectual prevention—so plainly effectual that it will never need to be resorted to—must be provided, either by an increase of the standing army or some change in the organization of the militia which will improve its discipline and increase its mobility. There are, of course, other means of protection against labor risings than physical ones, which ought not to be neglected, though we doubt if they can be made to produce much effect on the present generation. The exercise of greater watchfulness over their tongues by philanthropists, in devising schemes of social improvement, and in affecting to treat all things as open to discussion, and every question as having two sides, for purposes of legislation as well as for purposes of speculation, is one of them. Some of the talk about the laborer and his rights that we have listened to on the platform and in literature during the last fifteen years, and of the capacity even of the most grossly ignorant, such as the South Carolina fieldhand, to reason upon and even manage the interests of a great community, has been enough, considering the sort of ears on which it now falls, to reduce our great manu-facturing districts to the condition of the Pennsylvania mining regions, and put our very civilization in peril. Persons of humane tendencies ought to remember that we live in a world of stern realities, and that the blessings we enjoy have not been showered upon us like the rain from heaven. Our superiority to the Ashantees or the Kurds is not due to right thinking or right feeling only, but to the determined fight which the more enlightened part of the community has waged from generation to generation against the ignorance and brutality, now of one class and now of another. In trying to carry on the race to better things nobody is wholly right or wise. In all controversies there are wrongs on both sides, but most certainly the presumptions in the labor controversy have al-ways been in favor of the sober, orderly, industrious, and prudent, who work and accumulate and bequeath. It is they who brought mankind out of the woods and caves, and keep them out; and all discussion which places them in a position of either moral or mental inferiority to those who contrive not only to own nothing, but to separate themselves from property holders in feeling or interest, is mischievous as well as foolish, for it strikes a blow at the features of human character which raise man above the beasts.

ALMOST PART OF THE MACHINERY

The depression of the 1870s finally ended, but conflict between capital and la-bor did not; every year brought hundreds of strikes, boycotts, and lockouts. In 1883, deeply concerned about the deteriorating climate of labor relations, the U.S. Senate held extensive hearings. One of those who testified was John Morrison, a New York City machinist. With variations, his story is the story of the American industrial working class in the closing decades of the late nineteenth century. In reading Morrison's testimony, imagine that you are E. L. Godkin (see his editorial on page 41), seated in the hearing room, taking notes for an upcoming feature in The Nation. *What is your reaction? Should something be done to help Morrison, or to deal with the problems he reveals? What, if anything, could government do?*

 **VOICES**

BY MR. GEORGE:

Q. State your age, residence, and occupation.
A. I am about twenty-three years old; I live in this city; I am a machinist, and have been in that business about nine years.
Q. Do you work in a shop?
A. Yes, sir; I work in different shops.

*   *   *

Testimony of John Morrison, August 28, 1883, U.S. Congress, Senate, *Report of the Committee of the Senate upon the Relations between Labor and Capital* (Washington, D.C.: GPO, 1885) I, 755–759.)

Q. Is there any difference between the conditions under which machinery is made now and those which existed ten years ago?

A. A great deal of difference.

Q. State the differences as well as you can.

A. Well, the trade has been subdivided and those subdivisions have been again subdivided, so that a man never learns the machinist's trade now. Ten years ago he learned, not the whole of the trade, but a fair portion of it. Also, there is more machinery used in the business, which again makes machinery. In the case of making the sewing machine, for instance, you find that the trade is so subdivided that a man is not considered a machinist at all. Hence, it is merely laborers' work and it is laborers that work at that branch of our trade. The different branches of the trade are divided and subdivided so that one man may make just a particular part of a machine and may not know anything whatever about another part of the same machine. In that way machinery is produced a great deal cheaper than it used to be formerly, and in fact, through this system of work, 100 men are able to do now what it took 300 or 400 men to do fifteen years ago. By the use of machinery and the subdivision of the trade they so simplify the work that it is made a great deal easier and put together a great deal faster. There is no system of apprenticeship, I may say, in the business. You simply go in and learn whatever branch you are put at, and you stay at that unless you are changed to another.

Q. Does a man learn his branch very rapidly?

A. Yes, sir; he can learn his portion of the business very rapidly. Of course he becomes very expert at it, doing that all the time and nothing else, and therefore he is able to do a great deal more work in that particular branch than if he were a general hand and expected to do everything in the business as it came along. . . .

Q. Have you noticed the effect upon the intellect of this plan of keeping a man at one particular branch?

A. Yes. It has a very demoralizing effect upon the mind throughout. The man thinks of nothing else but that particular branch; he knows that he cannot leave that particular branch and go to any other; he has got no chance whatever to learn anything else because he is kept steadily and constantly at that particular thing, and of course his intellect must be narrowed by it.

Q. And does he not finally acquire so much skill in the manipulation of his particular part of the business that he does it without any mental effort?

A. Almost. In fact he becomes almost a part of the machinery.

BY THE CHAIRMAN:

Q. Then if he gets so skilled that he has not to think about his work, why cannot he compose poetry, or give range to his imagination, or occupy his mind in some other way while he is at work?

A. As a rule a man of that kind has more to think of about his family and his belly than he has about poetry.

THE CHAIRMAN: That is right.

BY MR. GEORGE:

Q. Has there been in the last ten or fifteen years any great revolution in the making of machinery so far as regards the capital that is required to start the business?

A. Well, I understand that at this present day you could not start in the machinist's business to compete successfully with any of these large firms with a capital of less than $20,000 or $30,000. That is my own judgment. There have been cases known where men started ten or fifteen years ago on what they had earned themselves, and they have grown up gradually into a good business. One of these firms is Floyd & Sons, on Twentieth Street. That man started out of his own earnings; he saved enough to start a pretty fair-sized shop, and he is occupying it today; but since that time it appears the larger ones are squeezing out the smaller, and forcing more of them into the ranks of labor, thus causing more competition among the workers.

Q. What is the prospect for a man now working in one of these machine shops, a man who is temperate and economical and thrifty to become a boss or a manufacturer of machinery himself from his own savings? Could a man do it without getting aid from some relative who might die and leave him a fortune, or without drawing a lottery prize, or something of that sort?

A. Well, speaking generally, there is no chance. They have lost all desire to become bosses now.

Q. Why have they lost that desire?

A. Why, because the trade has become demoralized. First they earn so small wages; and, next, it takes so much capital to become a boss now that they cannot think of it, because it takes all they can earn to live.

Q. Then it is the hopelessness of the effort that produces the loss of the desire on their part; is that it?

A. That is the idea. . . .

Q. What is the social condition of the machinists in New York and the surrounding towns and cities?

A. It is rather low compared to what their social condition was ten or fifteen years ago.

Q. Do you remember when it was better?

A. When I first went to learn the trade a machinist considered himself more than the average workingman; in fact he did not like to be called a workingman. He liked to be called a mechanic. Today he recognizes the fact that he is simply a laborer the same as the others. Ten years ago even he considered himself a little above the average workingman; he thought himself a mechanic, and felt he belonged in the middle class; but today he recognizes the fact that he is simply the same as any other ordinary laborer, no more and no less.

Q. What sort of houses or lodgings do the machinists occupy as a general rule?

A. As a general rule they live in tenement houses, often on the top floor.

Q. How is it as to the size of the apartments that they occupy, the conveniences and comforts they afford, their healthfulness, the character of the neighborhood and the general surroundings?

A.   That depends a great deal upon the size of the families. In most cases they are compelled to send their families to work, and of course they have to have rooms in proportion to the size of their families, and of course it often robs them of their earnings to pay rent; but as a rule the machinists live in the lowest quarters of the city, between Eighth and Eleventh Avenues, on the west side, and on the east side between Third Avenue and the river. You will find the machinists stuck in those quarters on both sides of the city.

• • •

One great trouble with our trade is that there is such a surplus of machinists in the market now that every day sees seven or eight at the door of every shop looking for a job. In fact they are denied the right to labor, and that is what we kick about. About two months ago, I believe there was about one-fifth of our trade in this city entirely out of work.

Q.   Do you know from reading the papers or from your general knowledge of the business whether there are places in other cities or other parts of the country that those men could have gone and got work?

A.   I know from general reports of the condition of our trade that the same condition existed throughout the country generally.

Q.   Then those men could not have bettered themselves by going to any other place, you think?

A.   Not in a body.

Q.   I am requested to ask you this question: Dividing the public, as is commonly done, into the upper, middle, and lower classes, to which class would you assign the average workingman of your trade at the time when you entered it, and to which class would you assign him now?

A.   I now assign them to the lower class. At the time I entered the trade I should assign them as merely hanging on to the middle class, ready to drop out at any time.

Q.   What is the character of the social intercourse of those workingmen? Answer first with reference to their intercourse with other people outside of their own trade—merchants, employers, and others.

A.   Are you asking what sort of social intercourse exists between the machinists and the merchants? If you are, there is none whatever, or very little if any.

Q.   What sort of social intercourse exists among the machinists themselves and their families, as to visiting, entertaining one another, and having little parties and other forms of sociability, those little things that go to make up the social pleasures of life?

A.   In fact with the married folks that has died out—such things as birthday parties, picnics, and so on. The machinists today are on such small pay, and the cost of living is so high, that they have very little, if anything, to spend for recreation, and the machinist has to content himself with enjoying himself at home, either fighting with his wife or licking his children.

Q.   I hope that is not a common amusement in the trade. Was it so ten years ago?

A.   It was not; from the fact that they then sought enjoyment in other places, and had a little more money to spend. But since they have had no organization worth speaking of, of course their pay has gone down. At that time they had a form of organization in some way or other which seemed to keep up the wages, and there was more life left in the machinist then; he had more ambition, he felt more like seeking enjoyment outside, and in reading and such things, but now it is changed to the opposite; the machinist has no such desires.

Q. What is the social air about the ordinary machinist's house? Are there evidences of happiness, and joy, and hilarity, or is the general atmosphere solemn, and somber, and gloomy?

A. To explain that fully, I would state first of all, that machinists have got to work ten hours a day in New York, and that they are compelled to work very hard. In fact the machinists of America are compelled to do about one-third more work than the machinists do in England in a day. Therefore, when they come home they are naturally played out from shoving the file, or using the hammer or the chisel, or whatever it may be, such long hours. They are pretty well played out when they come home, and the first thing they think of is having something to eat and sitting down, and resting, and then of striking a bed. Of course when a man is dragged out in that way he is naturally cranky, and he makes all around him cranky; so, instead of a pleasant house it is every day expecting to lose his job by competition from his fellow workman, there being so many out of employment, and no places for them, and his wages being pulled down through their competition, looking at all times to be thrown out of work in that way, and staring starvation in the face makes him feel sad, and the head of the house being sad, of course the whole family are the same, so the house looks like a dull prison instead of a home.

Q. Do you mean to say that that this is the general condition of the machinists in New York and in this vicinity?

A. That is their general condition, with, of course, a good many exceptions. That is the general condition to the best of my knowledge.

VICTORIAN AMERICA

Although the term Victorian *derives from the reign of Queen Victoria of England (1837–1901), when American historians use the term they are referring to the values, beliefs, and assumptions shared by middle-class and upper-class Americans in the late nineteenth century. A contrasting term,* modernism, *refers to a different set of values and beliefs that had made inroads within the same social classes by the turn of the century. The materials assembled in this section—a selection from a book on etiquette published in 1885 and some illustrations and photographs that depict the home life and leisure activities of Victorian Americans—are designed to suggest and reveal certain aspects of Victorian thought.*

At first, this inquiry into Victorian America may seem far removed from the 1877 railroad strike or the other documents in this chapter. But there are connections. E. L. Godkin was a classic Victorian gentleman. So were his readers—mostly middle-class and upper-middle-class people—and so, too, were the St. Louis elites who opposed the general strike in that community. Their anxieties about labor, class, and the social order were reflected in Victorian customs and values. Victorian manners helped them feel as if they were in control of their world, even as it was changing around them. "Good manners"— the kind one found in etiquette books—were also a sign that one deserved one's privileged position in the social and economic order. Like the federal troops that came to St. Louis to help defeat the strikers, manners were a tool in the struggle between classes.

By carefully examining the following materials, you may be able to locate evidence to demonstrate these claims, or perhaps to think of other ways that manners, and the advice in etiquette books, might be useful to particular social and economic groups. Think, too, about Victorian institutions and values: What did Victorian Americans think about the home? About the roles of men and women? How did they furnish their homes, and what might these furnishings tell us about the people who lived in and used these rooms?

Frontispiece to John H. Young, *Our Deportment,* **1885.**

John H. Young

MANNERS, CONDUCT, AND DRESS

Introductory

Knowledge of etiquette has been defined to be a knowledge of the rules of society at its best. These rules have been the outgrowth of centuries of civilization, had their foundation in friendship and love of man for his fellow man—the vital principles of Christianity—and are most powerful agents for promoting peace, harmony, and good will among all people who are enjoying the blessings of more advanced civilized government. In all civilized countries the influence of the best society is of great importance to the welfare and prosperity of the nation, but in no country is the good influence of the most refined society more powerfully felt than in our own, "the land of the future, where mankind may plant, assay, and resolve all social problems." These rules make social intercourse more agreeable, and facilitate hospitalities, when all members of society hold them as binding rules and faithfully regard their observance. They are to society what our laws are to the people as a political body, and to disregard them will give rise to constant misunderstandings, engender ill-will, and beget bad morals and bad manners. . . .

Originally a gentleman was defined to be one who, without any title of nobility, wore a coat of arms. And the descendants of many of the early colonists preserve with much pride and care the old armorial bearings which their ancestors brought with them from their homes in the mother country. Although despising titles and ignoring the rights of kings, they still clung to the "grand old name of gentleman." But race is no longer the only requisite for a gentleman, nor will race united with learning and wealth make a man a gentleman, unless there are present the kind and gentle qualities of the heart, which find expression in the principles of the Golden Rule. Nor will race, education, and wealth combined make a woman a true lady if she shows a want of refinement and consideration of the feelings of others.

Good manners are only acquired by education and observation, followed up by habitual practice at home and in society, and good manners reveal to us the lady and the gentleman. He who does not possess them, though he bear the highest title of nobility, cannot expect to be called a gentleman; nor can a woman, without good manners, aspire to be considered a lady by ladies. Manners and morals are indissolubly allied, and no society can be good where they are bad. It is the duty of American women to exercise their influence to form so high a standard of morals and manners that the tendency of society will be continually upward, seeking to make it the best society of any nation. . . .

In a society where the majority are rude from the thoughtfulness of ignorance, or remiss from the insolence of bad breeding, the iron rule, "Do unto others, as

John H. Young, *Our Deportment: Or the Manners, Conduct, and Dress of the Most Refined Society*, F. B. Dickerson & Co., Detroit, 1885.

they do unto you," is more often put into practice than the golden one. The savages know nothing of the virtues of forgiveness, and regard those who are not revengeful as wanting in spirit; so the ill-bred do not understand undeserved civilities extended to promote the general interests of society, and to carry out the injunction of the Scriptures to strive after the things that make for peace.

Society is divided into sets, according to their breeding. One set may be said to have no breeding at all, another to have a little, another more, and another enough; and between the first and last of these, there are more shades than in the rainbow. Good manners are the same in essence everywhere—at courts, in fashionable society, in literary circles, in domestic life—they never change, but social observances, customs and points of etiquette, vary with the age and with the people. . . .

Our Manners

No one quality of the mind and heart is more important as an element conducive to worldly success than civility—that feeling of kindness and love for our fellow-beings which is expressed in pleasing manners. Yet how many of our young men, with an affected contempt for the forms and conventionalities of life, assume to despise those delicate attentions, that exquisite tenderness of thought and manner, that mark the true gentleman.

Manners As An Element of Success   History repeats, over and over again, examples showing that it is the bearing of a man toward his fellow men which, more than any other one quality of his nature, promotes or retards his advancement in life. The success or failure of one's plans have often turned upon the address and manner of the man. Though there are a few people who can look beyond the rough husk or shell of a fellow-being to the finer qualities hidden within, yet the vast majority, not so keen-visaged nor tolerant, judge a person by his appearance and demeanor, more than by his substantial character. Experience of every day life teaches us, if we would but learn, that civility is not only one of the essentials of high success, but that it is almost a fortune of itself, and that he who has this quality in perfection, though a blockhead, is almost sure to succeed where, without it, even men of good ability fail.

A good manner is the best letter of recommendation among strangers. Civility, refinement, and gentleness are passports to hearts and homes, while awkwardness, coarseness, and gruffness are met with locked doors and closed hearts. Emerson says: "Give a boy address and accomplishments, and you give him the mastery of palaces and fortunes wherever he goes; he has not the trouble of earning or owning them; they solicit him to enter and possess." . . .

Manner An Index of Character   A rude person, though well meaning, is avoided by all. Manners, in fact, are minor morals; and a rude person is often assumed to be a bad person. The manner in which a person says or does a thing furnishes a better index of his character than what he does or says, for it is by the incidental expression given to his thoughts and feelings, by his looks, tones, and gestures, rather than by his words and deeds, that we prefer to judge him, for the reason that the former are involuntary. The manner in which a favor is granted or a kindness done often affects us more than the deed itself. The deed may have been prompted by vanity, pride, or some selfish motive or interest; the warmth or coldness with which the person who has done it speaks to you, or grasps your hand, is less likely to deceive. The manner of doing any thing, it has been truly said, is that which stamps its life and character on any action. A favor may be performed so grudgingly as to prevent any feeling of obligation, or it may be refused so courteously as to awaken more kindly feelings than if it had been ungraciously granted. . . .

The True Gentleman   Politeness is benevolence in small things. A true gentleman must regard the rights and feelings of others, even in matters the most trivial. He respects the individuality of others, just as he wishes others to respect his own. In society he is quiet, easy, unobtrusive, putting on no airs, nor hinting by word or manner that he deems himself better, or wiser, or richer than any one about him. He never boasts of his achievements, or fishes for compliments by affecting to underrate what he has done. He is distinguished, above all things, by his deep insight and sympathy, his quick perception of, and prompt attention to, those small and apparently insignificant things that may cause pleasure or pain to others. In giving his opinions he does not dogmatize; he listens patiently and respectfully to other men, and, if compelled to dissent from their opinions, acknowledges his fallibility and asserts his own views in such a manner as to command the respect of all who hear him. Frankness and cordiality mark all his intercourse with his fellows, and, however high his station, the humblest man feels instantly at ease in his presence.

The True Lady   Calvert says: "Ladyhood is an emanation from the heart subtilized by culture"; giving as two requisites for the highest breeding transmitted qualities and the culture of good training. He continues:

> Of the higher type of ladyhood may always be said what Steele said of Lady Elizabeth Hastings, "that unaffected freedom and conscious innocence gave her the attendance of the graces in all her actions." At its highest, ladyhood implies a spirituality made manifest in poetic grace. From the lady there exhales a subtle magnetism. Unconsciously she encircles herself with an atmosphere of unruffled strength, which, to those who come into it, gives confidence and repose. Within her influence the diffident grow self-possessed, the impudent are checked, the inconsiderate are admonished; even the rude are constrained to be mannerly, and the refined are perfected; all spelled, unawares, by the flexible dignity, the commanding gentleness, the thorough womanliness of her look, speech and demeanor. A sway is this, purely spiritual. Every sway, every legitimate, every enduring sway is spiritual; a regnancy of light over obscurity, of right over brutality. The only real gains ever made are spiritual gains—a further subjection of the gross to the incorporeal, of body to soul, of the animal to the human. The finest and most characteristic acts of a lady involve a spiritual ascension, a growing out of herself. In her being and bearing, patience, generosity, benignity are the graces that give shape to the virtues of truthfulness.

Here is the test of true ladyhood. Whenever the young find themselves in the company of those who do not make them feel at ease, they should know that they are not in the society of true ladies and true gentlemen, but of pretenders; that well-bred men and women can only feel at home in the society of the well-bred.

VICTORIAN PHOTOGRAPHS

The following photographs portray the experience of well-to-do Victorian families. "Bedroom in the Finch House" requires that we ask the meaning of possessions for these late-nineteenth-century elites and that we try to come up with some reason why the feeling, or tone, of this room is so different from what we would expect to find in its late-twentieth-century equivalent.

"Family Gathering Around a Portrait of Its Patriarch" also tells us something about Victorian family life and especially, of course, about patriarchy (a form of community in which the father is the supreme authority in the family). Was the notion of patriarchy still relevant to the society of the Gilded Age?

Bedroom in the Finch House, 1884.
Minnesota Historical Society. Photo by T. W. Ingersoll.

Family Gathering Around a Portrait of Its Patriarch, c. 1890.
Photograph by Charles Currier. Library of Congress.

the big picture

Is there evidence of class conflict in late-nineteenth-century America? How was class conflict managed, or contained?

chapter three

THE WEST

The terms *America* and the *West* had seemed synonymous, from the time of the earliest penetration of the Atlantic coastline down into the nineteenth century. But during the years after the Civil War, a new kind of frontier waited to be conquered by white settlers and surrendered in bitter defeat by the Indians. Beyond the Mississippi lay a vast expanse of plains, known officially as "the Great American Desert." Farther west were the seemingly impenetrable mountains and the real deserts of the Southwest. To most Americans, even as late as the 1850s, this half of the continent appeared to be good for little but a permanent reservation for native American tribes.

Amazingly, in little over a generation, the trans-Mississippi West was settled. The first transcontinental railroad was opened shortly after the Civil War. It was followed by others and by a network of rail lines spreading out into Iowa, Missouri, Texas, and the Dakotas. California became a state on the eve of the Civil War, and by the end of the century the process of state making had filled in almost all the continental map. The last effective native American resistance was broken in the 1870s and 1880s, when the old policy of war and extermination was replaced with a new form of aggression, called "assimilation." Mining towns sprang from nothing in Nevada, Colorado, and Montana. Texas and Oklahoma became primary cotton-producing states. Cowboys drove Texas longhorns into the new cow towns of Kansas and Nebraska, where the animals could be loaded onto trains headed for eastern slaughterhouses. New techniques of dry farming created one of the world's most productive wheat belts in the western half of the Great Plains. In 1890, just twenty-five years after Grant had accepted Lee's surrender, the United States Bureau of the Census officially declared that the frontier had ended forever.

The story was not a simple one of geographical expansion. The settlers of the new West were armed with a new technology that helped explain the remarkable rapidity of their success. The repeating rifle and the Gatling gun subdued the native American. The railroad took the wheat and cattle east at heretofore incredible speeds. Miners used steam power and dynamite to pry gold and silver from the mountains. Farmers—the big ones, at least—had the new mechanical reaper to bring in wheat at a rate that manual labor could not have approached. Californians were tied to the rest of the Union by the railroad and the new telegraph.

On the surface, then, the experience was one of triumph—at least for the white society. But there was a dark side to things, too. Even dry farming could not overcome periodic droughts, and the droughts came. There was competition from Russian and Australian wheat, so prices were very unstable. Some railroads gouged the farmers. Worst of all, the new technology proved not to be a blessing at all. The new agriculture was just *too* efficient. By 1890, one farmer could produce and get to market what it had taken eight farmers to produce fifty years before. Together, they produced more food than could be sold. So prices fell and stayed down, and farmers often could not recoup the cost of their seed, much less earn the money to pay interest on their mortgages and on the loans they had made to buy their reapers and plows. Agricultural depression was so severe and frequent that the whole second half of the nineteenth century—except for the war years—was really one long and chronic economic crisis for farmers, not only in the new West, but everywhere.

Agriculture in the South labored under a different set of burdens. The Civil War created a long-term capital shortage and, of course, severed the bond that had held slave labor to the plantation. Southerners responded with two systems. The first, designed to establish a link between free black farm workers and the plantation, was sharecropping. Under this system, blacks (and poor whites) agreed to farm the land in return for a share of the crop—usually one-third. Under the second system, the crop-lien, sharecroppers and tenant farmers borrowed money and received credit for supplies and food from merchants and landowners, while pledging in return a percentage of their crop. Together, sharecropping and the crop-lien fostered throughout the South a system of peonage, in which poor whites and blacks were legally bound by debt to work the lands of others.

Farmers sought to redress their grievances through a variety of protest movements, each linked to a particular organization. In the 1860s, midwestern farmers established the Patrons of Husbandry, better known as the Grange. Its purposes were partly social and partly economic—to lower the costs of shipment and storage of grain. By the 1890s, farmers in the South, the Great Plains, and the Far West had turned to state and national politics. Through the People's Party, or Populists, they sought the aid of the national government in inflating a depressed currency and in regulating the railroads and other trusts. Populist influence peaked in 1896, when William Jennings Bryan was the presidential nominee of both the Democrats and the Populists, but declined after Bryan was defeated for the presidency by Republican William McKinley.

There were other, less political, ways of coming to grips with the market revolution, the heritage of slavery, and the dislocation caused by being transplanted, body and soul, onto a remote prairie. Plains farmers brought with them a weapon that helped them overcome the initial reluctance to move onto the hard, unyielding sod of Nebraska and the Dakotas. The weapon was *myth*: the myth that the West was the source of unprecedented opportunity; the myth that climate would respond to the migration of people; the myth that the yeoman farmer—half frontiersman, half man-of-the-soil—could handle anything; the myth that all whites were superior to all native Americans.

If the West was all this to the people who lived there, to the majority of Americans—who lived in cities or just "back east"—it was a mirror of what Americans were and wanted to be. Frederick Jackson Turner triggered an ongoing debate on the meaning of the West in 1893, when he read an essay, "The Significance of the Frontier in American History," to an audience of fellow historians assembled in Chicago. Turner read American history as the story of the frontier, a continually receding area of free land that had placed generations of Americans on the cutting edge between civilization and savagery. This experience had shaped the national character. It had made Americans intensely individualistic, nationalistic, and democratic. When he linked his frontier thesis to the announcement in the 1890 federal census that the frontier had ceased to exist, Turner implied that these values were in danger—his way, perhaps, of sharing his sadness that an era had come to an end.

interpretive essay

Richard White

THE FEDERAL GOVERNMENT AND THE INDIANS

During the course of the nineteenth century, the policy of the American government toward the Indian tribes within its boundaries went through several very different configurations. As the century opened, Indian tribes were treated as "sovereign" nations—as nations within a nation—an understanding that meant that only the federal government, as the sole practitioner of foreign relations, could purchase Indian lands. When this notion of Indian sovereignty was challenged by President Andrew Jackson and the state of Georgia in the 1830s, the U.S. Supreme Court upheld it, but with a subtle change. In the language of the Court, the Indians were "domestic dependent nations," at once sovereign and dependent, essentially wards of the federal government. When Jackson removed thousands of Cherokee Indians to the West, the idea of dependency came into play; Indian removal was justified on the grounds that the removed Indians would be protected by their new western location. But that was not what happened. Instead, migrating whites who wanted Indian lands fought with Indians and forced them to make one cession of their territory after another.

Faced with these pressures, the federal government tried to "reserve" lands for Indians under a system of direct and elaborate supervision—the reservation system that emerged in about 1850. The reservation system failed, too; the federal government could not control the desire of its citizens for Indian lands, and the Indians could not make a reasonable living on the reserved lands made available to them. The result was a series of Indian wars, culminating in the 1870s and 1880s, that effectively destroyed the power of the Sioux, the Comanches, the Kiowas, the Apaches, the Cheyenne, and the Nez Perces. At the same time, Protestant reformers in the East, shocked at the

Richard White, *"It's Your Misfortune and None of My Own": A History of the American West* (Norman, Oklahoma: University of Oklahoma Press, 1991) pp. 108–9, 111–17. © 1991 by the University of Oklahoma Press, Norman, Publishing Division of the University. All rights reserved.

bloodshed and convinced that a stronger federal government could help rescue the Indians from imminent extinction, came to favor a policy of "peace" and "reform." As the fighting ended, the reformers had their way. Historian Richard White describes the results. While reading White's account, think about the policy of assimilation. Why did this goal appeal to reformers? That is, what sorts of values or assumptions were behind it? Was it a reasonable policy? If not, what would have been a reasonable alternative? In what specific ways was the policy of assimilation carried out? What is the significance of the role of the federal government in carrying out that policy?

FROM SOVEREIGNTY TO WARDSHIP

Whether they were allies of the Americans, whether they remained neutral, or whether they opposed the American advance, all Indian peoples in the years after the Civil War saw their sovereignty erode. The national wardship implied in Chief Justice Marshall's formulation of "domestic dependent nations" became instead an individual wardship. The United States would administer the affairs of its Indian wards as if they were incompetent children.

Reformers regarded Indian nations as legal fictions which the federal government should no longer recognize. As bitterly as advocates of civilian control over Indian affairs quarreled with proponents of military control, their disagreements masked a deeper consensus. Both groups disdained Indian sovereignty; both agreed that the treaty system was dead. Each camp regarded Indians as powerless savages and the treaties as a farce, as Indians had no means of compelling the United States to honor them. As early as 1868, the Indian Peace Commission had asserted that the time had come to cease regarding the Indians as domestic dependent nations; Indians instead should be "individually subject to the laws of the United States." It would be better, reformers said, to treat the Indians as wards, to stop negotiating treaties, and to find a "just" way to abrogate those that existed.

In 1871 the United States did abandon the treaty system, but it did so for reasons that had little to do with the reformers' objectives. The House of Representatives had long wanted a voice in agreements with Indians, since the terms of Indian treaties often affected their constituents' access to land. The constitution, however, gave only the president and the Senate a role in treaty making. Denied an equal voice, the House moved to abolish the treaty system altogether. The Senate agreed as long as existing treaties, which governed potentially lucrative transfers of land to individuals and corporations, remained in force.

The end of treaty making, however, neither ended negotiations with Indian nations nor abrogated Indian sovereignty. Congress continued to negotiate "agreements" to obtain land cessions from Indians. These differed from treaties largely in that both houses of Congress and not just the Senate had to ratify them. With the old treaties in force and with sovereignty ignored instead of being legally terminated, the United States proceeded to reform Indian policy by

deepening its contradictions. Reformers pushed the federal government toward direct supervision of the lives of individual Indians whom the law now
defined as wards of the state. A partial and reduced sovereignty and a new doctrine of wardship stood uncomfortably side by side.

PROGRAMS OF ASSIMILATION

During the 1870s, the churches lost control of administering the agencies, but
Protestant reformers nonetheless continued to steer American Indian policy.
The friends of the Indians exerted tremendous influence on Indian policy
through the Indian Rights Association, the Womens National Indian
Association, and the annual conferences that brought government officials and
reformers together at Lake Mohonk, New York. Effective publicists with strong
connections in the eastern Protestant churches, Indian reformers capitalized on
the outrage best-sellers such as Helen Hunt Jackson's *Century of Dishonor* provoked among the public at large when these books exposed past and present
American duplicity and corruption in dealings with the Indians.

Well into the twentieth century, reformers continued to see themselves as a
heroic and dedicated minority working for the good of the Indians. Given the
context in which they worked, this was not an unreasonable view. Reformers
challenged prevailing racist assumptions by proclaiming Indian capabilities
and their equality with whites. Reformers demanded efficient and honest administration at a time when Indian land and property was the focus of considerable white greed. Reformers struggled to preserve Indian peoples in a society
in which many Americans were convinced that Indians must disappear and
were not sorry to see them go. That Indians themselves resisted the reformers'
efforts seemed to the reformers only more evidence of the ignorant and be-
nighted state from which the Indians had to be rescued.

The reform policy had three basic components. The first was the suppression of Indian norms of family life, community organization, and religion.
Reformers sought to accomplish this suppression by persuasion when possible
and by force when necessary. Simultaneously, reformers tried to educate Indian
children in order to instill mainstream American Protestant values in place of
tribal values. Finally, reformers sought a policy of land allotment that would
break up communal landholding patterns and create private ownership. In the
end, Indians would be Christian farmers living in nuclear families on their own
land. The remaining lands could then be opened to white farmers. In the end,
all supposedly would be reconciled.

In imposing these policies on the Indians, the reformers operated at a con-
siderable advantage. Not only had the military made effective resistance by
Indians impossible, but conquest itself also had proceeded to destroy existing
Indian subsistence systems. With the exception of some tribes in the Southwest
and the Pacific Northwest and the Five Civilized Tribes of Oklahoma, most
Indian peoples could no longer feed or clothe themselves without federal aid.
Most reservation Indians depended for survival on payments due them from

the government for their lands and on rations issued by the government. This condition of dependency gave government officials significant control over the social and cultural life of Indian peoples. Agents could use annuities to reward friends and punish enemies; they could use the distribution of supplies to alter the usual political arrangements of a community.

The strength of Indian communities during this period declined while the power of the federal bureaucracy that supervised them increased. The Bureau of Indian Affairs had made its first moves toward centralization before the Civil War, when the government began removing the supervision of Indian affairs from the duties of the territorial governors and transferring them to special officers, the superintendents. The failure of the churches to supervise Indian affairs adequately—and subsequent scandals under Columbus Delano, President Grant's particularly corrupt secretary of the interior—increased pressure for a strengthened bureaucracy. The need to assimilate Indians and protect federal wards thus spurred the growth of the Bureau of Indian Affairs from a corrupt patronage system into a not as corrupt group of professional bureaucrats. Between 1881 and 1897 the bureau nearly doubled in size, and although its 4,000 employees would be a small staff by twentieth-century standards, it was a significant one by those of the nineteenth century.

The struggle to turn the Bureau of Indian Affairs into a centralized organization with standardized procedures was a long one. Perhaps the secretary of the interior most responsible for eventual bureaucratic centralization success was Carl Schurz, an exiled German revolutionary who helped organize the Republican party in Wisconsin. General, ambassador, senator, newspaperman and editor, historian, and later renegade from Grant's Republican party, his tenure as secretary of the interior under President Rutherford B. Hayes from 1877 to 1881 was but one stop in a tumultuous career. A fervent supporter of civil service reform, Schurz took the office of Indian inspector and made it a tool for centralizing the bureau. He appointed former superintendents and agents to the post, used the inspectors to investigate irregularities in the agencies, and had those men report directly to him. They were officials whose loyalties were to Washington and not to the agents or locally controlled Indian rings—that is, coalitions of government officials and businessmen designed to divert Indian funds into white hands. As reform proceeded, the bureau increasingly controlled its employees by an elaborate set of rules and procedures. Complete bureaucratization occurred in the early twentieth century when all important field employees of the Indian Bureau came under the Civil Service System. Now administrators rose within the Bureau of Indian Affairs, were familiar with its procedures, and had more loyalty to the organization. Political appointees finally lost out to professional bureaucrats.

Weakened tribes, an increasingly assertive and professional bureaucracy, and a conviction among reformers that change must come quickly allowed the Bureau of Indian Affairs to launch what amounted to a wholesale assault on Indian culture and community organization in the 1880s. In 1883 the Indian Bureau banned "medicine making," polygamy, and bride payments and set up a system of courts of Indian offenses—staffed by Indians—to enforce their directives. When a few whites protested such actions, claiming that these were the natural conditions of an Indian's life, the commissioner of Indian affairs replied that "So are superstition and sin but that is no reason against trying to improve his condition."

By withholding rations, imprisoning recalcitrants, forcibly cutting adult men's hair, seizing children for schools, physically breaking up religious ceremonies, and seizing religious objects, the Indian Bureau mounted direct assaults on Indian cultural and religious practices that would continue well into the twentieth century. The government successfully banned the Sun Dance among the Lakotas for the first time in 1884. That tribe thus lost not only its central religious ceremony but also associated social and religious rituals. The Sun Dance had been a time of courting and fun, and other rituals had flourished in the shadow of the sacred tree of the Sun Dance. In the encampments visionaries had acted out their experiences, healers had demonstrated their power, and babies' ears had been pierced in a ceremony as central to identification as a Lakota as circumcision was to the identity of a Jewish man.

In 1888 the government enforced a further prohibition by banning bundles. When a person died among the Lakotas, the family had cut a lock of his or her hair and saved it in a ritual bundle for a year, thus causing that person's spirit to remain with the people. At the end of the year the spirit was released, and goods amassed over the course of the year were given away in honor of the deceased. The government, it seemed, would not even let the dead escape its power. As Short Bull, a Lakota religious leader, saw it: "The white people made war on the Lakotas to keep them from practicing their religion. . . . The white people wish to make us cause the spirits of our dead to be ashamed."

Most reformers backed repression in prohibiting cultural and religious practices among adults, but they had real hopes of getting Indian children to change their ways voluntarily once they were properly educated. Indian schools would both refute those who believed that the Indians were racially inferior, and thus ineducable, and would also break the resistance of those Indians who tried to preserve old ways. With proper education, reformers contended, Indian religions and practices would disappear within a generation.

The most famous of the Indian educators was Richard Henry Pratt, an army officer who was in charge of those Kiowa and Comanche prisoners sent to Florida after the Red River War. Pratt's success in working with those prisoners convinced him that education was the key to the "Indian problem," and in 1879 he convinced the government to help fund the Carlisle Indian School in Pennsylvania. At Carlisle, Pratt adopted a policy of isolating children from their tribe, forcing them to speak English, and compelling them to follow Anglo American customs. With its mixture of academic training and manual labor, Carlisle resembled Booker T. Washington's Tuskegee Institute for blacks. It set the pattern for the Indian boarding schools that followed it.

Reformers like Pratt were quite determined to destroy existing Indian cultures. Reformers believed that until they eliminated existing Indian beliefs and social forms, they could not assimilate Indians into American life. And if Indians were not assimilated into American life, then they would disappear. As

Pratt put it, the goal was to "kill the Indian and save the man." The deculturization Pratt demanded was virtually total: "the sooner all tribal relations are broken up; the sooner the Indian loses all his Indian ways, even his language, the better it will be for him and for the government and the greater will be the economy for both."

The reformers were unwilling to brook any opposition to their goals from Indian parents. Commissioner of Indian Affairs Thomas Morgan told parents that they did not "have any right to forcibly keep their children out of school to grow up like themselves, a race of barbarians and semi-savages." Yet many Indian parents did resist. Not only was the avowed goal of these schools to make the children strangers to their own people, but they were also often cruel, dangerous, and sickly places where disease claimed the lives of many students. Indian reform policies placed Indian parents in a difficult position. Their children obviously needed new skills, but the price exacted for those skills was cultural destruction and loss of identity. And for many children the culmination of schooling was not graduation but death on a sickbed hundreds of miles from their home.

In the end, however, the resistance of Indian peoples was probably less important in halting the expansion of boarding schools than the cost of the schools themselves and their failure to achieve the results they had promised. Some students returned to the reservations without skills. Others came with skills that had no application in the stunted reservation economy. Often, too, these returned students found themselves out of place in communities whose values they no longer fully understood or shared. The attempt to eradicate tribal values and practices through education would continue into the twentieth century, but increasingly the main educational tool would be local schools, not boarding schools.

If the suppression of Indian cultural practices and education were two supports of the reform program, land allotment formed the third. The middle-class reformers who controlled Indian policy believed that private property and individual autonomy formed the heart of civilization. As long as Indians held their land in common, that heart could not beat, and the entire "civilizing" process could not take place. Reformers were determined to divide tribal lands among tribal members. Because with dwindling populations many tribes held what the reformers regarded as too much land for the members to use efficiently, reformers proposed selling the excess to white settlers. Proposals to allot land in severalty, as this division was called, were not new. They had already been written into some of the first treaties establishing reservations in the years before the Civil War, and Congress had passed several partial measures following the war.

The main severalty measure, however, came in 1887 when Senator Henry Dawes of Massachusetts sponsored the Dawes Act. The law provided varying amounts of land for all tribal members with the maximum amount, 160 acres, being allotted to a head of a family. This land was to be held in trust by the government—it could neither be sold nor taxed—for twenty-five years. The decision to allot a reservation was not up to the Indians. It rested with the president. If he decided that a reservation should be allotted, there was nothing Indians could do to stop him.

The law pleased both eastern reformers, who saw it as vital to the civilization program, and western settlers and developers, who were less interested in assimilating Indians than in gaining access to Indian lands. With the passage of the Dawes Act, reformers believed that the end to the "Indian problem" was in sight. Reservations, the commissioner of Indian affairs wrote in 1889, belonged to the vanishing order of things. He declared that "tribal relations should be broken up, socialism destroyed and the family and autonomy of the individual substituted. The allotment of land in severalty, the establishment of local courts and police, the development of a personal sense of independence and the universal adoption of the English language are means to this end."

As with education, the reformers failed to achieve their goals, but they once more exacted a heavy price from those they wished to help. In the late nineteenth and early twentieth centuries, the Bureau of Indian Affairs applied the Dawes Act with a speed and a lack of safeguards that appalled even its sponsor. In 1881, Indians held 155,632,312 acres of land. By 1890 this figure had dwindled to 104,314,349, and by 1900 it had declined to 77,865,373 acres. Most Indians did not become independent farmers, and the federal government did not fulfill its trust responsibilities. Particularly during the early twentieth century, fraud and relaxation of trust provisions allowed allotted lands to pass to whites. Between 1887 and 1934, Indians lost 60 percent of their remaining land and 66 percent of their allotted lands.

As the sovereignty of native western tribes buckled before the reformers' zeal, the Five Civilized Tribes of Oklahoma initially held out as a bastion of the older order of domestic dependent nations. They managed to obtain exemption from the Dawes Act, but the sovereignty they had been promised in the West was about to be undermined once more. The same combination of reformist zeal and white desire for Indian land that had contributed to the Dawes Act strengthened the desire of corporations for access to Indian resources and created pressure for the dissolution of the governments of the old Indian Territory. With reformers ideologically committed to severalty, even the success of Indian governments became an argument for disbanding them. As one reformer explained after interviewing a chief of one of the Five Civilized Tribes, there was not a family in the nation without a home of its own. Nor was there a pauper in the nation. Nor did the nation owe a dollar. It had built its own capitol, schools, and hospitals. Yet he argued that their system was defective: "They have got as far as they can go, because they own their land in common. . . . There is no enterprise to make your home any better than that of your neighbors. There is no selfishness, which is at the bottom of civilization. . . . Till this people will consent to give up their lands, and divide them among their citizens so that each can own the land he cultivates, they will not make much more progress."

Indians had no recourse against this kind of stubborn ideology that used even the Indians' success against them. The reformers rarely made their case for individualization so revealingly; at bottom, they believed, civilization was based on selfishness. Progress came only through the uninhabited pursuit of self-interest. Indians were not innately inferior. They simply lived in a society whose communal values inhibited the greed and selfishness necessary for progress. The reformer's program, in essence, was to give selfishness its head.

Such ideology, powerfully buttressed by federal power and by the self-interest of railroad companies that would by law get large grants of land if Indian Territory was dissolved, created an unstoppable momentum for dissolving the governments of the Five Civilized Tribes. What the federal government had failed to get at once, however, it worked at obtaining piecemeal. From the 1870s onward there was intense pressure from surrounding whites to organize Indian Territory as a federally governed western territory, to allot lands to the Indians, and to open up the remainder for white settlement. While representatives of the Five Civilized Tribes fought off proposals to make the Indian Territory a federally governed western territory, they lost other battles. As corporations built the railroads and opened coal mines, the federal government limited the ability of the Indian nations to regulate these corporations or their workers. In 1889 government extended the federal judicial system into the region, establishing a court at Muskogee for whites living in Indian Territory.

The assault on the sovereignty of the Five Civilized Tribes culminated in the efforts of the Dawes Commission of 1893. Assigned the task of negotiating with the Five Civilized Tribes for an end to national or tribal title to their lands, the Dawes Commission finally brought allotment of lands in severalty to the Indian Territory. With allotment secured, Congress then demanded the end to the tribal governments themselves. When some of the Five Civilized Tribes resisted, the Curtis Act of 1898 unilaterally terminated the governments of those tribes that had not already agreed to disband "voluntarily."

TRAJECTORIES OF POWER

By the early twentieth century all available choices seemed bad for American Indian peoples. They had reached their population nadir, and in many respects their cultural and social nadir as well. The reformers and federal policy makers, whose own programs had accelerated this descent, began to lose faith in their own solutions. The reformers did not admit their own fault. Instead, they blamed Indian capacities. Indians, they said, might not be the equal of whites after all. The reformers did not abandon their goal of assimilation, but relying on the resurgent racism of the early twentieth century, they slowed their timetable. Accepting Indian abilities as limited, they no longer thought assimilation would be rapid. This did not, however, stop the alienation of Indian land and resources at a rate even faster than that of the late nineteenth century.

Together the decline of the tribes and the rise of the Bureau of Indian Affairs traced the trajectories of power in the nineteenth-century West. Americans had fought and conquered Indians, but this was only part of the change, for the Indians who never fought the United States as well as those who had allied themselves with the Americans declined in power. American officials gradually perverted the promises of one sovereign nation to protect other far weaker, but still sovereign, nations into a mandate for bureaucrats appointed by one government to oversee the personal lives of individual members of those weaker nations.

Federal officials succeeded in imposing this altered definition of wardship on Indians for several reasons. First, Indian power had declined to a point at which Indians themselves could not prevent the government from acting unilaterally. Second, government officials following the Civil War recognized a real need to protect at least some of the remaining Indian property against rapacious whites. Finally, as the courts accepted assimilation as the ultimate goal of Indian policy and wardship, they granted the government extraordinary coercive powers in order to force assimilation on the Indians. In 1903 the Supreme Court ruled in *Lone Wolf* v. *Hitchcock* that Congress had a plenary (or absolute) power to regulate Indian affairs even when congressional actions violated existing treaty provisions. "It is to be presumed," the Court said, "that in this matter the United States would be governed by such considerations of justice as would control a Christian people in their treatment of an ignorant and dependent race." Such plenary power mocked Indian sovereignty as fully as the reasoning mocked actual history.

In reducing the Indians to wardship, the federal government had enhanced its own power. Congress could, according to the courts, dictate the fates of hundreds of thousands of people in the American West and control tens of millions of acres of Indian land. In gaining such powers, the federal government had also built up the means to exercise them. The military had subdued the Indians, and a modern bureaucracy, the Bureau of Indian Affairs, had arisen to administer the reservations and steer the government's wards toward citizenship.

It is true that reformers believed both the reservations and the bureaucracy would be temporary, that they would disappear as the Indians assimilated and joined with the larger populations. Indians and bureaucrats would supposedly vanish together. But it would not turn out to be that way. The significance of Indians in the West did not end when they were herded onto reservations. The plenary power that the courts granted Congress would in practice only limit instead of destroy Indian sovereignty. The history of nineteenth-century Indian policy clearly marks the decline of sovereignty and the rise of wardship, but the process was never complete. Indian sovereignty would have its own resurgence. Both bureaucrats and Indians would turn out to have a much larger role to play in the West than nineteenth-century reformers imagined.

Zitkala-Sǎ

GROWING UP INDIAN, IN A WHITE MAN'S WORLD

In the following account, Zitkala-Sǎ recalls her Indian childhood. Born Gertrude Simmons in 1876 on a Sioux reservation in South Dakota, she was the daughter of an Indian woman and a white man. Zitkala-Sǎ, as she later christened herself, left the reservation at the age of eight for White's Manual Institute in Wabash, Indiana, a school operated by Quakers that followed the assimilationist policies of the Bureau of Indian Affairs, described by Richard White in the previous essay. Written without the assistance of an interpreter or editor, the stories first appeared in 1900 and 1901 in Harper's *and the* Atlantic Monthly, *where they were meant to inform and entertain the elite, liberal readers of those magazines.*

Why did Zitkala-Sǎ want to leave the reservation, and why did her mother agree to allow her to do so? How did Zitkala-Sǎ experience the Institute? More generally, how should one evaluate her reaction to the white man's school? Is it appropriate to see what happened to Zitkala-Sǎ as a kind of tragedy? Or should one view her experience as an understandable and necessary aspect of her transition from one culture to another?

𝒱 VOICES The Big Red Apples.

The first turning away from the easy, natural flow of my life occurred in an early spring. It was in my eighth year; in the month of March, I afterward learned. At this age I knew but one language, and that was my mother's native tongue.

From some of my playmates I heard that two paleface missionaries were in our village. They were from that class of white men who wore big hats and carried large hearts, they said. Running direct to my mother, I began to question

67

her why these two strangers were among us. She told me, after I had teased much, that they had come to take away Indian boys and girls to the East. My mother did not seem to want me to talk about them. But in a day or two, I gleaned many wonderful stories from my playfellows concerning the strangers.

"Mother, my friend Judéwin is going home with the missionaries. She is going to a more beautiful country than ours; the palefaces told her so!" I said wistfully, wishing in my heart that I too might go.

Mother sat in a chair, and I was hanging on her knee. Within the last two seasons my big brother Dawée had returned from a three years' education in the East, and his coming back influenced my mother to take a farther step from her native way of living. First it was a change from the buffalo skin to the white man's canvas that covered our wigwam. Now she had given up her wigwam of slender poles, to live, a foreigner, in a home of clumsy logs.

"Yes, my child, several others besides Judéwin are going away with the palefaces. Your brother said the missionaries had inquired about his little sister," she said, watching my face very closely.

My heart thumped so hard against my breast, I wondered if she could hear it.

"Did he tell them to take me, mother?" I asked, fearing lest Dawée had forbidden the palefaces to see me, and that my hope of going to the Wonderland would be entirely blighted.

With a sad, slow smile, she answered: "There! I knew you were wishing to go, because Judéwin has filled your ears with the white man's lies. Don't believe a word they say! Their words are sweet, but, my child, their deeds are bitter. You will cry for me, but they will not even soothe you. Stay with me, my little one! Your brother Dawée says that going East, away from your mother, is too hard an experience for his baby sister."

Thus my mother discouraged my curiosity about the lands beyond our eastern horizon; for it was not yet an ambition for Letters that was stirring me. But on the following day the missionaries did come to our very house. I spied them coming up the footpath leading to our cottage. A third man was with them, but he was not my brother Dawée. It was another, a young interpreter, a paleface who had a smattering of the Indian language. I was ready to run out to meet them, but I did not dare to displease my mother. With great glee, I jumped up and down on our ground floor. I begged my mother to open the door, that they would be sure to come to us. Alas! They came, they saw, and they conquered!

Judéwin had told me of the great tree where grew red, red apples; and how we could reach out our hands and pick all the red apples we could eat. I had never seen apple trees. I had never tasted more than a dozen red apples in my life; and when I heard of the orchards of the East, I was eager to roam among them. The missionaries smiled into my eyes and patted my head. I wondered how mother could say such hard words against him.

"Mother, ask them if little girls may have all the red apples they want, when they go East," I whispered aloud, in my excitement.

The interpreter heard me, and answered: "Yes, little girl, the nice red apples are for those who pick them; and you will have a ride on the iron horse if you go with these good people."

I had never seen a train, and he knew it.

"Mother, I am going East! I like big red apples, and I want to ride on the iron horse! Mother, say yes!" I pleaded.

My mother said nothing. The missionaries waited in silence; and my eyes began to blur with tears, though I struggled to choke them back. The corners of my mouth twitched, and my mother saw me.

"I am not ready to give you any word," she said to them. "Tomorrow I shall send you my answer by my son."

With this they left us. Alone with my mother, I yielded to my tears, and cried aloud, shaking my head so as not to hear what she was saying to me. This was the first time I had ever been so unwilling to give up my own desire that I refused to hearken to my mother's voice.

There was a solemn silence in our home that night. Before I went to bed I begged the Great Spirit to make my mother willing I should go with the missionaries.

The next morning came, and my mother called me to her side. "My daughter, do you still persist in wishing to leave your mother?" she asked.

"Oh, mother, it is not that I wish to leave you, but I want to see the wonderful Eastern land," I answered.

My dear old aunt came to our house that morning, and I heard her say, "Let her try it."

I hoped that, as usual, my aunt was pleading on my side. My brother Dawée came for mother's decision. I dropped my play, and crept close to my aunt.

"Yes, Dawée, my daughter, though she does not understand what it all means, is anxious to go. She will need an education when she is grown, for then there will be fewer real Dakotas, and many more palefaces. This tearing her away, so young, from her mother is necessary, if I would have her an educated woman. The palefaces, who owe us a large debt for stolen lands, have begun to pay a tardy justice in offering some education to our children. But I know my daughter must suffer keenly in this experiment. For her sake, I dread to tell you my reply to the missionaries. Go, tell them that they may take my little daughter, and that the Great Spirit shall not fail to reward them according to their hearts."

Wrapped in my heavy blanket, I walked with my mother to the carriage that was soon to take us to the iron horse. I was happy. I met my playmates, who were also wearing their best thick blankets. We showed one another our new beaded moccasins, and the width of the belts that girdled our new dresses. Soon we were being drawn rapidly away by the white man's horses. When I saw the lonely figure of my mother vanish in the distance, a sense of regret settled heavily upon me. I felt suddenly weak, as if I might fall limp to the ground. I was in the hands of strangers whom my mother did not fully trust. I no longer felt free to be myself, or to voice my own feelings. The tears trickled down my cheeks, and I buried my face in the folds of my blanket. Now the first step, parting me from my mother, was taken, and all my belated tears availed nothing.

Having driven thirty miles to the ferryboat, we crossed the Missouri in the evening. Then riding again a few miles eastward, we stopped before a massive brick building. I looked at it in amazement, and with a vague misgiving, for in our village I had never seen so large a house. Trembling with fear and distrust of the palefaces, my teeth chattering from the chilly ride, I crept noiselessly in my soft moccasins along the narrow hall, keeping very close to the bare wall. I was as frightened and bewildered as the captured young of a wild creature. . . .

The Cutting of My Long Hair.

The first day in the land of apples was a bitter-cold one; for the snow still covered the ground, and the trees were bare. A large bell rang for breakfast, its loud metallic voice crashing through the belfry overhead and into our sensitive ears. The annoying clatter of shoes on bare floors gave us no peace. The constant clash of harsh noises, with an undercurrent of many voices murmuring an unknown tongue, made a bedlam within which I was securely tied. And though my spirit tore itself in struggling for its lost freedom, all was useless.

A paleface woman, with white hair, came up after us. We were placed in a line of girls who were marching into the dining room. These were Indian girls, in stiff shoes and closely clinging dresses. The small girls wore sleeved aprons and shingled hair. As I walked noiselessly in my soft moccasins, I felt like sinking to the floor, for my blanket had been stripped from my shoulders. I looked hard at the Indian girls, who seemed not to care that they were even more immodestly dressed than I, in their tightly fitting clothes. While we marched in, the boys entered at an opposite door. I watched for the three young braves who came in our party. I spied them in the rear ranks, looking as uncomfortable as I felt.

A small bell was tapped, and each of the pupils drew a chair from under the table. Supposing this act meant they were to be seated, I pulled out mine and at once slipped into it from one side. But when I turned my head, I saw that I was the only one seated, and all the rest at our table remained standing. Just as I began to rise, looking shyly around to see how chairs were to be used, a second bell was sounded. All were seated at last, and I had to crawl back into my chair again. I heard a man's voice at one end of the hall, and I looked around to see him. But all the others hung their heads over their plates. As I glanced at the long chain of tables, I caught the eyes of a paleface woman upon me. Immediately I dropped my eyes, wondering why I was so keenly watched by the strange woman. The man ceased his mutterings, and then a third bell was tapped. Every one picked up his knife and fork and began eating. I began crying instead, for by this time I was afraid to venture anything more.

But this eating by formula was not the hardest trial in that first day. Late in the morning, my friend Judéwin gave me a terrible warning. Judéwin knew a few words of English; and she had overheard the paleface woman talk about cutting our long, heavy hair. Our mothers had taught us that only unskilled warriors who were captured had their hair shingled by the enemy. Among our people, short hair was worn by mourners, and shingled hair by cowards!

We discussed our fate some moments, and when Judéwin said, "We have to submit, because they are strong," I rebelled.

"No, I will not submit! I will struggle first!" I answered.

I watched my chance, and when no one noticed I disappeared. I crept up the stairs as quietly as I could in my squeaking shoes,—my moccasins had been exchanged for shoes. Along the hall I passed, without knowing whither I was going. Turning aside to an open door, I found a large room with three white beds in it. The windows were covered with dark green curtains, which made the room very dim. Thankful that no one was there, I directed my steps toward the corner farthest from the door. On my hands and knees I crawled under the bed, and cuddled myself in the dark corner.

From my hiding place I peered out, shuddering with fear whenever I heard footsteps near by. Though in the hall loud voices were calling my name, and I knew that even Judéwin was searching for me, I did not open my mouth to answer. Then the steps were quickened and the voices became excited. The sounds came nearer and nearer. Women and girls entered the room. I held my breath and watched them open closet doors and peep behind large trunks. Some one threw up the curtains, and the room was filled with sudden light. What caused them to stoop and look under the bed I do not know. I remember being dragged out, though I resisted by kicking and scratching wildly. In spite of myself, I was carried downstairs and tied fast in a chair.

I cried aloud, shaking my head all the while until I felt the cold blades of the scissors against my neck, and heard them gnaw off one of my thick braids. Then I lost my spirit. Since the day I was taken from my mother I had suffered extreme indignities. People had stared at me. I had been tossed about in the air like a wooden puppet. And now my long hair was shingled like a coward's! In my anguish I moaned for my mother, but no one came to comfort me. Not a soul reasoned quietly with me, as my own mother used to do; for now I was only one of many little animals driven by a herder. . . .

The School Days of an Indian Girl The Devil.   Among the legends the old warriors used to tell me were many stories of evil spirits. But I was taught to fear them no more than those who stalked about in material guise. I never knew there was an insolent chieftain among the bad spirits, who dared to array his forces against the Great Spirit, until I heard this white man's legend from a paleface woman.

Out of a large book she showed me a picture of the white man's devil. I looked in horror upon the strong claws that grew out of his fur-covered fingers. His feet were like his hands. Trailing at his heels was a scaly tail tipped with a serpent's open jaws. His face was a patchwork: he had bearded cheeks, like some I had seen palefaces wear; his nose was an eagle's bill, and his sharp-pointed ears were pricked up like those of a sly fox. Above them a pair of cow's horns curved upward. I trembled with awe, and my heart throbbed in my throat, as I looked at the king of evil spirits. Then I heard the paleface woman say that this terrible creature roamed loose in the world, and that little girls who disobeyed school regulations were to be tortured by him.

That night I dreamt about this evil divinity. Once again I seemed to be in my mother's cottage. An Indian woman had come to visit my mother. On opposite sides of the kitchen stove, which stood in the center of the small house, my mother and her guest were seated in straight-backed chairs. I played with a train of empty spools hitched together on a string. It was night, and the wick burned feebly. Suddenly I heard some one turn our door-knob from without.

My mother and the woman hushed their talk, and both looked toward the door. It opened gradually. I waited behind the stove. The hinges squeaked as the door was slowly, very slowly pushed inward.

Then in rushed the devil! He was tall! He looked exactly like the picture I had seen of him in the white man's papers. He did not speak to my mother, because he did not know the Indian language, but his glittering yellow eyes were fastened upon me. He took long strides around the stove, passing behind the woman's chair. I threw down my spools, and ran to my mother. He did not fear her, but followed closely after me. Then I ran round and round the stove, crying aloud for help. But my mother and the woman seemed not to know my danger. They sat still, looking quietly upon the devil's chase after me. At last I grew dizzy. My head revolved as on a hidden pivot. My knees became numb, and doubled under my weight like a pair of knife blades without a spring. Beside my mother's chair I fell in a heap. Just as the devil stooped over me with outstretched claws my mother awoke from her quiet indifference, and lifted me on her lap. Whereupon the devil vanished, and I was awake.

On the following morning I took my revenge upon the devil. Stealing into the room where a wall of shelves was filled with books, I drew forth The Stories of the Bible. With a broken slate pencil I carried in my apron pocket, I began by scratching out his wicked eyes. A few moments later, when I was ready to leave the room, there was a ragged hole in the page where the picture of the devil had once been.

Iron Routine.

A loud-clamoring bell awakened us at half-past six in the cold winter mornings. From happy dreams of Western rolling lands and unlassoed freedom we tumbled out upon chilly bare floors back again into a paleface day. We had short time to jump into our shoes and clothes, and wet our eyes with icy water, before a small hand bell was vigorously rung for roll call.

There were too many drowsy children and too numerous orders for the day to waste a moment in any apology to nature for giving her children such a shock in the early morning. We rushed downstairs, bounding over two high steps at a time, to land in the assembly room.

A paleface woman, with a yellow-covered roll book open on her arm and a gnawed pencil in her hand, appeared at the door. Her small, tired face was coldly lighted with a pair of large gray eyes.

She stood still in a halo of authority, while over the rim of her spectacles her eyes pried nervously about the room. Having glanced at her long list of names and called out the first one, she tossed up her chin and peered through the crystals of her spectacles to make sure of the answer "Here."

Relentlessly her pencil black-marked our daily records if we were not present to respond to our names, and no chum of ours had done it successfully for us. No matter if a dull headache or the painful cough of slow consumption had delayed the absentee, there was only time enough to mark the tardiness. It was next to impossible to leave the iron routine after the civilizing machine had once begun its day's buzzing; and as it was inbred in me to suffer in silence rather than to appeal to the ears of one whose open eyes could not see my pain. I have many times trudged in the day's harness heavy-footed, like a dumb sick brute.

Once I lost a dear classmate. I remember well how she used to mope along at my side, until one morning she could not raise her head from her pillow. At her deathbed I stood weeping, as the paleface woman sat near her moistening the dry lips. Among the folds of the bedclothes I saw the open pages of the white man's Bible. The dying Indian girl talked disconnectedly of Jesus the Christ and the paleface who was cooling her swollen hands and feet.

I grew bitter, and censured the woman for cruel neglect of our physical ills. I despised the pencils that moved automatically, and the one teaspoon which dealt out, from a large bottle, healing to a row of variously ailing Indian children. I blamed the hard-working, well-meaning, ignorant woman who was inculcating in our hearts her superstitious ideas. Though I was sullen in all my little troubles, as soon as I felt better I was ready again to smile upon the cruel woman. Within a week I was again actively testing the chains which tightly bound my individuality like a mummy for burial.

The melancholy of those black days has left so long a shadow that it darkens the path of years that have since gone by. These sad memories rise above those of smoothly grinding school days. Perhaps my Indian nature is the moaning wind which stirs them now for their present record. But, however tempestuous this is within me, it comes out as the low voice of a curiously colored seashell, which is only for those ears that are bent with compassion to hear it.

THE WORLDS OF QUANAH PARKER: A PHOTO ESSAY

Comanche chief Quanah Parker (c. 1852–1911) was the son of a Comanche chief, Peta Nocone, and Cynthia Ann Parker, a white woman taken captive during an 1836 raid on Parker's Fort, Texas. Between 1867 and 1875, Parker led raids on frontier settlements. After his defeat and surrender, he lived another kind of life, one illustrated in the photographs on these pages. What adjectives would you use to describe the Quanah Parker revealed in these photographs?

Quanah Parker, Seated Next to a Portrait of His Mother.
Photo by H. P. Robinson, Fort Sill, Oklahoma Territory. Courtesy Oklahoma Historical Society.

Comanche Chief Quanah Parker on Horseback Near His Home, Cache, Oklahoma Territory, c. 1901.
Photo by N. Losey. Courtesy Oklahoma Historical Society.

Quanah Parker, on the Porch of His Home, c. 1895.
Photo by Irwin and Mankins. Courtesy Oklahoma Historical Society.

Quanah Parker, with One of His Seven Wives.
Courtesy Oklahoma Historical Society.

Quanah Parker's Home, 1912.
Photo by Bates, Lawton Oklahoma. Courtesy Oklahoma Historical Society.

THE POPULIST CHALLENGE

THE ELECTION OF 1892

Farmers were among the victors in the struggle with the Indians over control of the Great Plains and its resources. But victory in that contest did not ensure prosperity, nor even contentment, as the introduction to this chapter explains. In the 1890s, farmers in the Midwest, the South, and on the Great Plains turned to politics to register their frustrations and remedy their grievances. They formed a new political party. In November 1892, the People's (or Populist) Party elected governors in Kansas, North Dakota, and Colorado, as well as an estimated 1,500 county officials and state legislators. James Weaver, the party's presidential candidate, received more than 1 million votes.

From the following items—the text of most of the 1892 Populist party platform and a map that shows the voting pattern in the presidential election of 1892—evaluate the challenge that the Populists leveled at the Republicans and Democrats. Geographically, where did the Populists succeed, and where did they fail? Does it appear that the People's Party was successful in reaching debt-ridden sharecroppers in the cotton belt? Industrial workers in the urban North? Do you think that the platform strengthened or weakened the party's appeal to either of these groups or to the general public? According to the platform, what issues did the Populists emphasize? Several of the measures suggested in the platform, including the provisions dealing with currency and coinage, were designed to produce some measure of inflation (prices fell during most of the late nineteenth century). Assuming that most farmers were debtors, how would they have benefited from an inflationary economy? In general, was the Populist response to the market revolution (see the introduction to this chapter) a reasonable one?

THE PEOPLE'S PARTY PLATFORM, 1892

Preamble

The conditions which surround us best justify our co-operation; we meet in the midst of a nation brought to the verge of moral, political, and material ruin. Corruption dominates the ballot-box, the Legislatures, the Congress, and touches even the ermine of the bench. The people are demoralized; most of the States have been compelled to isolate the voters at the polling places to prevent universal intimidation and bribery. The newspapers are largely subsidized or muzzled, public opinion silenced, business prostrated, homes covered with mortgages, labor impoverished, and the land concentrated in the hands of capitalists. The

Donald Bruce Johnson, ed., *National Party Platforms*, vol. I: *1840–1956*, rev. ed., University of Illinois Press, Urbana, 1978.

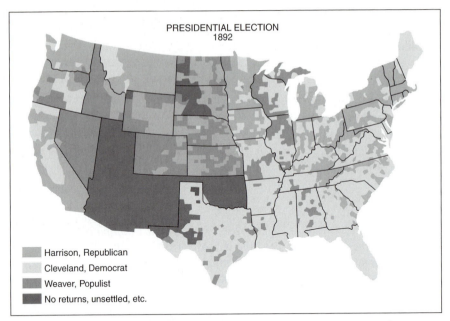

Presidential Election, 1892.
From Atlas of the Historical Geography of the United States, *ed. Charles O. Paullin*
(New York: Carnegie Institution of Washington and the American Geographical Society of
New York, 1932), copyright Carnegie Institution of Washington.

urban workmen are denied the right to organize for self-protection; imported pauperized labor beats down their wages, a hireling standing army, unrecognized by our laws, is established to shoot them down, and they are rapidly degenerating into European conditions. The fruits of the toil of millions are boldly stolen to build up colossal fortunes for a few, unprecedented in the history of mankind; and the possessors of these, in turn despise the Republic and endanger liberty. From the same prolific womb of governmental injustice we breed the two great classes—tramps and millionaires.

The national power to create money is appropriated to enrich bond-holders; a vast public debt payable in legal tender currency has been funded into gold-bearing bonds, thereby adding millions to the burdens of the people.

Silver, which has been accepted as coin since the dawn of history, has been demonetized to add to the purchasing power of gold by decreasing the value of all forms of property as well as human labor, and the supply of currency is purposely abridged to fatten usurers, bankrupt enterprise, and enslave industry. A vast conspiracy against mankind has been organized on two continents, and it is rapidly taking possession of the world. If not met and overthrown at once, it forebodes terrible social convulsions, the destruction of civilization, or the establishment of an absolute despotism.

We have witnessed for more than a quarter of a century the struggles of the two great political parties for power and plunder, while grievous wrongs have been inflicted upon the suffering people. We charge that the controlling influence dominating both these parties have permitted the existing dreadful conditions to develop without serious effort to prevent or restrain them. Neither do they now promise us any substantial reform. They have agreed together to ignore, in the coming campaign, every issue but one. They propose to drown the outcries of a plundered people with the uproar of a sham battle over the tariff, so that capitalists, corporations, national banks, rings, trusts, watered stock, the demonetization of silver, and the oppressions of the usurers may all be lost sight of. They propose to sacrifice our homes, lives, and children on the altar of mammon; to destroy the multitude in order to secure corruption funds from the millionaires.

Assembled on the anniversary of the birthday of the nation, and filled with the spirit of the grand general and chief who established our independence, we seek to restore the government of the Republic to the hands of "the plain people," with which class it originated. . . .

We declare that this Republic can only endure as a free government while built upon the love of the whole people for each other and for the nation; that it cannot be pinned together by bayonets; that the civil war is over and that every passion and resentment which grew out of it must die with it, and that we must be in fact, as we are in name, one united brotherhood of freemen.

Our country finds itself confronted by conditions for which there is no precedent in the history of the world; our annual agricultural productions amount to billions of dollars in value, which must, within a few weeks or months be exchanged for billions of dollars' worth of commodities consumed in their production; the existing currency supply is wholly inadequate to make this exchange; the results are falling prices, the formation of combines and rings, the impoverishment of the producing class. We pledge ourselves that, if given power, we will labor to correct these evils by wise and reasonable legislation, in accordance with the terms of our platform.

We believe that the power of government—in other words, of the people—should be expanded (as in the case of the postal service) as rapidly and as far as the good sense of an intelligent people and the teachings of experience shall justify, to the end that oppression, injustice and poverty, shall eventually cease in the land. . . .

Platform

We declare, therefore,

> *First*—That the union of the labor forces of the United States this day consummated shall be permanent and perpetual; may its spirit enter into all hearts for the salvation of the Republic and the uplifting of mankind.

> *Second*—Wealth belongs to him who creates it, and every dollar taken from industry without an equivalent is robbery. "If any will not work, neither shall he eat." The interests of rural and civic labor are the same; their enemies are identical.

Third—We believe that the time has come when the railroad corporations will either own the people or the people must own the railroads, and should the government enter upon the work of owning and managing all railroads, we should favor an amendment to the Constitution by which all persons engaged in the government service shall be placed under a civil service regulation of the most rigid character, so as to prevent the increase of the power of the national administration by the use of such additional government employees.

Finance—We demand a national currency, safe, sound, and flexible, issued by the general government only, a full legal tender for all debts, public and private, and that without the use of banking corporations, a just, equitable and efficient means of distribution direct to the people, at a tax not to exceed 2 percent per annum, to be provided as set forth by the sub-treasury plan of the Farmers' Alliance, or a better system; also by payments in discharge of its obligations for public improvements.

1. We demand free and unlimited coinage of silver and gold at the present legal ratio of 16 to 1.
2. We demand that the amount of circulating medium be speedily increased to not less than $50 per capita.
3. We demand a graduated income tax.
4. We believe that the money of the country should be kept as much as possible in the hands of the people, and hence we demand that all State and national revenues shall be limited to the necessary expenses of the government, economically and honestly administered.
5. We demand that postal savings banks be established by the government for the safe deposit of the earnings of the people and to facilitate exchange.

Transportation—Transportation being a means of exchange and a public necessity, the government should own and operate the railroads in the interest of the people. The telegraph and telephone, like the post office system, being a necessity for the transmission of news, should be owned and operated by the government in the interest of the people.

Land—The land, including all the natural sources of wealth, is the heritage of the people, and should not be monopolized for speculative purposes, and alien ownership of land should be prohibited. All land now held by railroads and other corporations in excess of their actual needs, and all lands now owned by aliens, should be reclaimed by the government and held for actual settlers only.

THE WONDERFUL WIZARD OF OZ

The following illustrations are intended to stimulate discussion of one of the most popular and influential children's books of the age: The Wizard of Oz, *published by L. Frank Baum in 1900, a few years after the nation's farmers created the Populist party. Indeed, some historians believe that Baum constructed the story as a parable of the Populist effort, with each character and object symbolic of some aspect of the era's politics: the Tin Woodman represents the injured industrial worker; the Scarecrow symbolizes the befuddled farmer; the Lion caricatures Populist presidential candidate William Jennings Bryan; the silver slippers (they became ruby in the 1939 film version) embody Populist dreams of a silver currency that would free farmers from the gold standard—what Bryan referred to in a famous address as a "cross of gold."*

However, Baum's background suggests that other interpretations might have greater validity. Born in 1856 in upstate New York, Baum wrote plays, worked as a traveling salesman, opened a retail store in South Dakota, and, just before he wrote The Wizard of Oz, *worked in Chicago advising retailers on the new art of displaying merchandise in store windows. In short, he seems to have been a student and an admirer of consumer capitalism.*

Use your memory of the film version of The Wizard of Oz *to explore the meaning of the text. What case can be made for the parable-of-Populism interpretation? What impression does the story offer of farm life in the 1890s? Does the story have any of the anticapitalist perspectives that lurk in the People's Party platform? What does the Wizard stand for, and how is the reader (or viewer) supposed to feel about him? What does the Emerald City signify? What is the spirit of the book? Finally, examine the book/film for how it might have spoken to Americans in 1939, after a decade of depression.*

L. Frank Baum, The Wizard of Oz *(1900), illustrations by W. W. Denslow.*

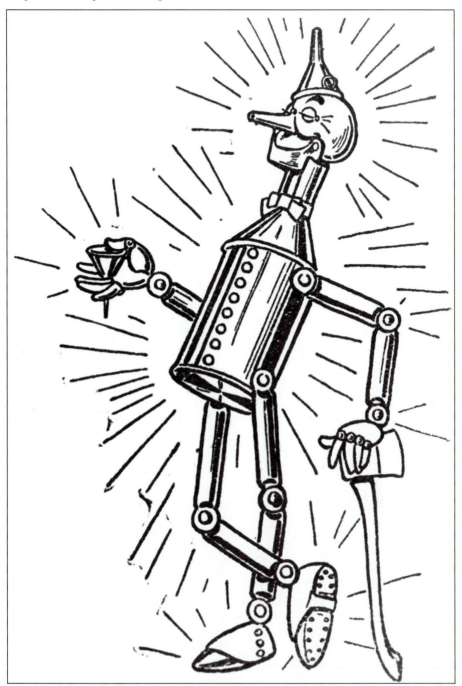

L. Frank Baum, The Wizard of Oz *(1900), illustrations by W. W. Denslow.*

the big picture

What was the role of the federal government in the trans-Mississippi West of the late nineteenth century? Did it act responsibly in that region, or irresponsibly? Should Zitkala-Šǎ and Quanah Parker be considered victims? Why or why not?

chapter four

CITIES AND IMMIGRANTS, CITIES AND MIGRANTS

*I*n 1860 there were only sixteen cities in the United States with populations over 50,000, and only three cities of more than 250,000. By 1900 the corresponding figures were seventy-eight and fifteen. In the half-century after 1850, the population of Chicago grew from less than 30,000 to more than 1 million. For older, eastern cities, growth meant change in function and structure. Boston—in 1850 a concentrated merchant city of some 200,000 persons, dependent on oceangoing commerce—was by 1900 a sprawling industrial city with a population of more than 1 million.

Entirely new cities arose to meet particular demands of time and place. For George Pullman, of sleeping-car fame, big cities were sordid and disorderly places that spawned crime and violence. He planned and built an entirely new community isolated from disruptive influences where (so he believed) his workers would always be happy (he was mistaken). Western cities also expanded rapidly, usually by virtue of some nearby exploitable resource. Wichita was one of several Kansas towns founded on the cattle trade. Seattle was a timber city. Denver had its origins in the 1857 gold rush, but it remained to service the Great Plains, much as Chicago did the Midwest.

The new urban residents were often either immigrants from abroad or migrants from the nation's small towns and rural areas. In 1910 perhaps one-third of the total urban population were native Americans of rural origin; another one-quarter were foreign-born. Although the nonurban population increased absolutely in each decade before 1950, it diminished relatively. During and after the Civil War, the widespread adoption of a variety of labor-saving devices, including cultivators, reapers, mowers, threshers, and corn planters, allowed fewer and fewer farmers to feed the urban populace. Certain areas, such as rural New England, showed marked reductions in population. "We cannot all live in cities," wrote Horace Greeley in the 1860s, "yet nearly all seem determined to do so."

The emigration to the United States from abroad was, simply put, a major folk migration. There were 4.1 million foreign-born in the United States in 1860, 13.5 million foreign-born in 1910. And to these numbers must be added the children of the foreign-born—15.6 million in 1900, 18.9 million (more than one out of every five Americans) by 1910.

Some cities attracted a disproportionate share of the foreign-born. By 1910, New York City and two older Massachusetts cities, Fall River and Lowell, had more than 40 percent foreign-born residents. Twelve major cities, including Boston, Chicago, Milwaukee, Detroit, and San Francisco, had between 30 and 40 percent foreign-born residents. Seventeen other cities, including Seattle, Portland, Omaha, and Oakland, had over 20 percent foreign-born residents. (Most southern cities had less than 10 percent.)

After 1880, another change of importance occurred. The national origin of the nation's foreign-born population shifted from the northern and western European mix characteristic of previous decades to the southern and eastern European, Jewish and Catholic, mix dominant in 1900. In contrast to the earlier immigrants, a larger proportion of the later immigrants concentrated in the ghettos of northeastern industrial cities. On New York City's Lower East Side, more than 30,000 people were squeezed into half a dozen city blocks.

Ethnic clustering was nothing new, but the unfamiliar languages, customs, and religious practices of the Italians, Russians, Poles, and Slavs seemed to many observers to be associated with slums, unemployment, delinquency, and disease. The later immigrants were also held responsible for the growth of "alien" ideologies—anarchism and socialism—in large American cities in the last quarter of the century. And there was enough truth in this charge to give it some credence. "Red" Emma Goldman, one of the nation's most active anarchists, was Russian-born. Her friend Alexander Berkman, who was born in Poland, made an unsuccessful attempt to kill steel magnate Henry Clay Frick during the 1892 Homestead strike. In Chicago, a center of working-class politics, radical political ideas were especially well represented, and radical leaders were more often than not German-born. Germany, after all, had produced Karl Marx, and Russia, the anarchist Mikhail Bakunin. Europe simply had a more well-developed radical tradition than the United States. Many new immigrants brought with them some portion of this tradition when they set foot on American shores.

After 1880, but especially after 1910, the social character of American cities was altered by another migration, this one inside the country. This internal migration—one of the most important events in all of twentieth-century

American history—brought hundreds of thousands, and eventually millions, of African Americans from the rural and urban South to industrial cities of the North and Midwest, and, to a lesser extent, the Far West. Many came with great expectations for a better life, chalking their dreams on the sides of the boxcars that carried them north: "Farewell—We're Good and Gone," "Bound to the Land of Hope," and "Bound for the Promised Land." Aboard a northbound train headed for Chicago from Jackson, Mississippi, in 1925, future novelist Richard Wright wondered what his new circumstances would bring. "If I could meet enough of a different life," he thought, "then, perhaps, gradually and slowly I might learn who I was, what I might be."

White or black, from Europe or the American South, many of the migrants found their new communities to be wellsprings of freedom and economic opportunity. But these gifts were not distributed evenly. Most of the immigrants—Italians, Poles, Russian Jews, Irish, Germans, and others—had within a generation or two of their arrival been largely integrated into the American economic and social order. Most of the migrants—African Americans, in particular—found themselves increasingly separated from the rest of society, their political, social, and economic opportunities limited and restricted in ways that could hardly have been foreseen.

The American city of the late nineteenth and early twentieth centuries was the most complex social space one can imagine: rich and poor, blacks and whites, migrants and immigrants, those who spoke English and those who did not—all seeking some modicum of success, some version of a good life. This chapter explores just a few of the problems raised by the American urban experience. Why did some groups fare better than others? Did the city restrict opportunity, or enhance it? How did rich and poor, white and black, get along? What did Americans imagine their cities were like or could become? How did white, "native" Americans deal with their fears of the "new" immigrants and African Americans?

interpretive essay

Douglas S. Massey and Nancy A. Denton
THE CONSTRUCTION OF THE GHETTO

Inevitably, scholars and students of the American past seek to compare, and to contrast, the experiences of white ethnics—say, Irish, Italians, or Poles—with those of African Americans. Often, what they want to know is why one of the former groups seems to have done rather well, while the latter has not. After all (so the argument goes) both groups were once outsiders. Having begun the race at the same point, why did the white ethnics succeed, while blacks failed? One answer, made famous in a 1965 document called The Moynihan Report, *emphasizes the unique African-American experience with slavery, especially its degrading impact on the African-American family and on African-American men. According to this argument, African Americans began the quest for success with a significant handicap, which even today has not been overcome. Another answer, a favorite with conservatives of the Reagan-Bush era, is that African Americans have been damaged more recently by "welfare" payments and other government programs.*

In the selection that follows, sociologists Douglas S. Massey and Nancy A. Denton offer a very different view, one that foregrounds the African-American experience with racial segregation, rather than slavery, and one in which the urban experience plays a central role. According to Massey and Denton, when was the African-American ghetto constructed, and why? Was the formation of the ghetto inadvertent—and perhaps inevitable? Or was it, as the word "constructed" seems to imply, the result of conscious decisions?

Surveying the harsh black-and-white landscape of contemporary urban America, it is hard to imagine a time when people of European and African origin were not highly segregated from one another. In an era when Watts, Harlem, and Roxbury are synonymous with black geographic and social isolation, it is easy to assume that U.S. cities have always been organized to achieve a physical separation of the races. The residential segregation of blacks and whites has been with us so long that it seems a natural part of the social order, a normal and unremarkable feature of America's urban landscape.

Yet it wasn't always so. There was a time, before 1900, when blacks and whites lived side by side in American cities. In the north, a small native black population was scattered widely throughout white neighborhoods. Even Chicago, Detroit, Cleveland, and Philadelphia—cities now well known for their large black ghettos—were not segregated then. In southern cities such as Charleston, New Orleans, and Savannah, black servants and laborers lived on alleys and side streets near the mansions of their white employers. In this lost urban world, blacks were more likely to share a neighborhood with whites than with other blacks.

In most cities, to be sure, certain neighborhoods could be identified as places where blacks lived; but before 1900 these areas were not predominantly black, and most blacks didn't live in them. No matter what other disadvantages urban blacks suffered in the aftermath of the Civil War, they were not residentially segregated from whites. The two racial groups moved in a common social world, spoke a common language, shared a common culture, and interacted personally on a regular basis. In the north, especially, leading African American citizens often enjoyed relations of considerable trust, respect, and friendship with whites of similar social standing.

Of course, most blacks did not live in northern cities, and didn't experience these benign conditions. In 1870, 80% of black Americans still lived in the rural south, where they were exploited by a sharecropping system that was created by white landowners to replace slavery; they were terrorized by physical violence and mired in an institutionalized cycle of ignorance and poverty. Over the next century, however, blacks in the rural south increasingly sought refuge and betterment in burgeoning cities of the south and north. By 1970, 80% of black Americans lived in urban areas, and nearly half were located outside the south.

The shift of blacks from south to north and from farm to city radically transformed the form, nature, and substance of African American life in the United States. As we shall see, the way in which blacks from the rural south were incorporated into the geographic structure of American cities in the years after 1900 proved to be decisive in determining the path of black social and economic development later in the twentieth century.

Southern blacks were not the only rural people migrating to American cities at the turn of the century. Between 1880 and 1920 millions of eastern and southern Europeans arrived as well, and after 1920 their place was taken by a growing number of Mexicans. For these groups, however, U.S. cities served as vehicles for integration, economic advancement, and, ultimately, assimilation into American life. For rural blacks, in contrast, cities became a trap—yet another mechanism of oppression and alienation. The urban ghetto, constructed during the first half of the twentieth century and successively reinforced thereafter, represents the key institutional arrangement ensuring the continued subordination of blacks in the United States.

The term "ghetto" means different things to different people. To some observers it simply means a black residential area; to others it connotes an area that is not only black but very poor and plagued by a host of social and economic problems. In order to distinguish clearly between race and class in discussing black residential patterns, our use of the term "ghetto" refers only to the racial make-up of a neighborhood; it is not intended to describe anything about a black neighborhood's class composition. For our purposes, a ghetto is a set of neighborhoods that are exclusively inhabited by members of one group, within which virtually all members of that group live. By this definition, no ethnic or racial group in the history of the United States, except one, has ever experienced ghettoization, even briefly. For urban blacks, the ghetto has been the paradigmatic residential configuration for at least eighty years.

The emergence of the black ghetto did not happen as a chance by-product of other socioeconomic processes. Rather, white Americans made a series of deliberate decisions to deny blacks access to urban housing markets and to reinforce their spatial segregation. Through its actions and inactions, white America built and maintained the residential structure of the ghetto. Sometimes the decisions were individual, at other times they were collective, and at still other times the powers and prerogatives of government were harnessed to maintain the residential color line; but at critical points between the end of the Civil War in 1865 and the passage of the Fair Housing Act in 1968, white America chose to strengthen the walls of the ghetto.

BEFORE THE GHETTO

At the close of the Civil War, American cities were just beginning to throw off the trappings of their pre-industrial past. Patterns of urban social and spatial organization still reflected the needs of commerce, trade, and small-scale manufacturing. Public transportation systems were crude or nonexistent, and production was largely organized and carried out by extended households or in small shops. People got around by walking, so there was little geographic differentiation between places of work and residence. Land use was not highly specialized, real estate prices were low, and socially distinctive residential areas had not yet emerged. In the absence of structural steel, electricity, and efficient mechanical systems, building densities were low and urban populations were distributed uniformly.

Such an urban spatial structure is not conducive to high levels of segregation by class, race, or ethnicity, and the small African American population that inhabited northern cities before 1900 occupied a niche in the urban geography little different from that of other groups. Before 1900, blacks were not particularly segregated from whites, and although they were overrepresented in the poorest housing and the meanest streets, their residential status did not differ markedly from that of others in the same economic circumstances.

If the disadvantaged residential condition of blacks in the nineteenth century can be attributed to racial prejudice and discrimination, it is to prejudice and discrimination in employment rather than in housing. Because blacks were systematically excluded from most skilled trades and nonmanual employment, they were consigned to a low economic status that translated directly into poor housing. Those few blacks who were able to overcome these obstacles and achieve success in some profession or trade were generally able to improve their housing conditions and acquire a residence befitting their status. Studies of black residential life in northern cities around the time of the Civil War reveal little systematic exclusion from white neighborhoods on the basis of skin color.

Indeed, before 1900 African Americans could be found in most neighborhoods of northern cities. Although blacks at times clustered on certain streets or blocks, they rarely comprised more than 30% of the residents of the immediate area; and these clusters typically were not spatially contiguous. Maps from the period reveal a widely dispersed spatial pattern, with black households being unevenly but widely scattered around the urban landscape. In no city of the nineteenth century is there anything resembling a black ghetto. . . .

Such modest levels of segregation, combined with small black populations, led to substantial contact between blacks and whites in northern cities. This conclusion accords with historical studies of black communities in nineteenth-century northern cities. In places such as Cleveland, Chicago, Detroit, and Milwaukee, the small black communities were dominated by an elite of educated professionals, business owners, and successful tradespeople, most of whom were northern-born or migrants from border states. Within the upper stratum, interracial contacts were frequent, cordial, and often intimate. Members of this elite were frequently of mixed racial origin and tended to be light-skinned. Although the black lower classes usually did not maintain such amicable interracial ties, they too interacted frequently with whites in their places of work and on the streets.

Typical of the northern black elite of the nineteenth century was John Jones, a mulatto who was the "undisputed leader of Chicago's Negro community until his death in 1879." After his arrival in the city in 1845, he established a tailoring shop and built a successful business making clothes for wealthy whites. Before the Civil War, he was prominent in the abolitionist movement, where he had extensive contact with liberal whites, and after the war he ran for the Cook County Board of Commissioners and was elected with widespread white support.

Other members of Chicago's nineteenth-century African American elite included physicians, dentists, journalists, attorneys, and clergymen, all of whom relied substantially on the white community for economic and political support; and all maintained close social and professional relationships with individual whites. Like Jones, they supported the ideal of integration and opposed the formation of separate black community institutions. Above all they stressed the importance of economic self-improvement for racial progress. . . .

A high degree of interracial contact in northern cities is confirmed by an analysis of the racial composition of the neighborhoods inhabited by nineteenth century blacks. Given racial breakdowns for ward populations, the percentage of blacks in the ward of the average black citizen can be computed. This average, known as the isolation index, measures the extent to which blacks live within neighborhoods that are predominantly black. A value of 100% indicates complete ghettoization and means that all black people live in totally black areas; a value under 50% means that blacks are more likely to have whites than blacks as neighbors.

Stanley Lieberson made this calculation for black Americans in seventeen northern cities between 1890 and 1930, and his results are reproduced in Table [1]. We see from the first column that blacks in the north tended to live in predominantly white neighborhoods during the nineteenth century. The most "ghettoized" city in 1890 was Indianapolis, where the average black person lived in a neighborhood that was 13% black; in three-quarters of the cities, the percentage was under 10%. In other words, the typical black resident of a nineteenth-century northern city lived in a neighborhood that was close to 90% white. Even in cities that later developed large black ghettos, such as Chicago, Cleveland, Detroit, Los Angeles, Newark, and New York, blacks were more likely to come into contact with whites than with other blacks.

There is also little evidence of ghettoization among southern blacks prior to 1900. Indeed, segregation levels in the south tend to be lower than those in the north. Prior to the Emancipation Proclamation, urban slaves were intentionally dispersed by whites in order to prevent the formation of a cohesive African American society. Although this policy broke down in the years leading up to the Civil War—when free blacks and slaves who were "living out" gravitated

TABLE [1]   Indices of Black Isolation Within Wards of Selected Northern Cities, 1890–1930

	Isolation Indices by Year				
	1890	1900	1910	1920	1930
Boston	8.5	6.4	11.3	15.2	19.2
Buffalo	1.0	4.4	5.7	10.2	24.2
Chicago	8.1	10.4	15.1	38.1	70.4
Cincinnati	9.4	10.1	13.2	26.9	44.6
Cleveland	4.7	7.5	7.9	23.9	51.0
Detroit	5.6	6.4	6.8	14.7	31.2
Indianapolis	12.9	15.1	18.5	23.4	26.1
Kansas City	12.7	13.2	21.7	23.7	31.6
Los Angeles	3.3	3.2	3.8	7.8	25.6
Milwaukee	1.4	2.4	1.9	4.1	16.4
Minneapolis	1.6	1.6	1.7	2.1	1.7
Newark	4.1	5.5	5.4	7.0	22.8
New York	3.6	5.0	6.7	20.5	41.8
Philadelphia	11.7	16.4	15.7	20.8	27.3
Pittsburgh	8.1	12.0	12.0	16.5	26.8
St. Louis	10.9	12.6	17.2	29.5	46.6
San Francisco	1.4	1.1	0.7	1.0	1.7
Average	6.7	7.8	9.7	16.8	29.9

Source: Stanley Lieberson, *A Piece of the Pie: Blacks and White Immigrants Since 1880* (Berkeley: University of California Press, 1980), pp. 266, 288. Isolation is measured by ward.

toward black settlements on the urban periphery to escape white supervision—historical studies are consistent in reporting a great deal of racial integration in housing prior to 1900. . . .

In contrast to the situation in the north, however, residential integration in the postbellum south was not accompanied by a relatively open set of race relations among elites. As the Reconstruction Era drew to a close, black-white relations came to be governed by the increasingly harsh realities of the Jim Crow system, a set of laws and informal expectations that subordinated blacks to whites in all areas of social and economic life. The implementation of Jim Crow did not increase segregation, however, or reduce the frequency of black-white contact; it governed the terms under which integration occurred and strictly regulated the nature of interracial social contacts.

Neighborhoods in many southern cities evolved a residential structure characterized by broad avenues interspersed with small streets and alleys. Large homes on the avenues contained white families, who employed black servants and laborers who lived on the smaller streets. The relationship of master and slave was supplanted by one of master and servant, or a paternalistic relationship between boss and worker. Despite their economic and social subjugation, however, blacks in southern cities continued to have direct personal contacts with whites, albeit on very unequal terms. As in the north, the social worlds of the races overlapped.

CREATING THE GHETTO, 1900–1940

The era of integrated living and widespread interracial contact was rapidly effaced in American cities after 1900 because of two developments: the industrialization of America and the concomitant movement of blacks from farms to cities. The pace of change was most rapid in the north, not only because industrialization was quicker and more complete there, but also because the south's Jim Crow system provided an effective alternative to the ghetto in bringing about the subjugation of blacks. Moreover, the interspersed pattern of black and white settlement in southern cities carried with it a physical inertia that retarded the construction of the ghetto.

Industrialization in the north unleashed a set of social, economic, and technological changes that dramatically altered the urban environment in ways that promoted segregation between social groups. Before industrialization, production occurred primarily in the home or small shop, but by the turn of the century manufacturing had shifted decisively to large factories that employed hundreds of laborers. Individual plants clustered in extensive manufacturing districts together demanded thousands of workers. Dense clusters of tenements and row houses were constructed near these districts to house the burgeoning work force.

The new demand for labor could not be met by native white urbanites alone, so employers turned to migrants of diverse origins. Before World War I, the demand for unskilled labor was met primarily by rural immigrants from southern and eastern Europe. Their migration was guided and structured by social networks that connected them to relatives and friends who had arrived earlier. Drawing upon the ties of kinship and common community origin, the new migrants obtained jobs and housing in U.S. cities, and in this way members of specific ethnic groups were channeled to particular neighborhoods and factories.

At the same time, the need to oversee industrial production—and to administer the wealth it created—brought about a new managerial class composed primarily of native white Americans. As their affluence increased, the retail sector also expanded dramatically. Both administration and retail sales depended on face-to-face interaction, which put a premium on spatial proximity and high population densities. The invention of structural steel and mechanical elevators allowed cities to expand upward in skyscrapers, which were grouped into central business districts that brought thousands of people into regular daily contact. The development of efficient urban rail systems permitted the city to expand outward, creating new residential districts in suburban areas to house the newly affluent class of middle-class managers and service workers.

These developments brought about an unprecedented increase in urban social segregation. Not only was class segregation heightened, but the "new" immigrant groups—Jews, Poles, Italians, Czechs—experienced far more segregation from native whites than did the "old" immigrant groups of Irish and Germans. . . .

Southern blacks also formed part of the stream of migrants to American cities, but until 1890 the flow was relatively small; only 70,000 blacks left the south during the 1870s and 80,000 departed during the 1880s. In contrast, the number of European immigrants ran into the millions in both decades. Immigration, however, was cyclical and strongly affected by economic conditions abroad. When the demand for labor in European cities was strong, migration to the United States fell, and when European demand flagged, immigration to the United States rose.

This periodic ebb and flow of European immigration created serious structural problems for American employers, particularly when boom periods in Europe and America coincided. When this occurred, European migrants moved to their own industrial cities and U.S. factories had difficulty attracting new workers. Periodic labor shortages caused northern employers to turn to domestic sources of labor, especially migrants from American rural areas and particularly those in the south. Thus black migration to northern cities oscillated inversely with the ebb and flow of European immigration.

But northern employers also found another reason to employ southern blacks, for by the turn of the century, they had discovered their utility as strikebreakers. Blacks were repeatedly employed in this capacity in northern labor disputes between 1890 and 1930: black strikebreakers were used seven times in New York between 1895 and 1916, and were employed in Cleveland in 1896, in Detroit in 1919, in Milwaukee in 1922, and in Chicago in 1904 and 1905. Poor rural blacks with little understanding of industrial conditions and no experience with unions were recruited in the south and transported directly to northern factories, often on special trains arranged by factory owners.

The association of blacks with strikebreaking was bound to earn them the enmity of white workers, but discrimination against blacks by labor unions cannot be attributed to this animosity alone. European groups had also been used as strikebreakers, but labor leaders overcame these attempts at union-busting by incorporating each new wave of immigrants into the labor movement. Unions never employed this strategy with southern blacks, however. From the start, African Americans suffered unusually severe discrimination from white unions simply because they were black.

Most of the skilled crafts unions within the American Federation of Labor, for example, excluded blacks until the 1930s; and the Congress of Industrial Organizations* accepted blacks only grudgingly, typically within segregated Jim Crow locals that received poorer contracts and lower priorities in job assignments. Being denied access to the benefits of white unions, blacks had little to lose from crossing picket lines, thereby setting off a cycle of ongoing mutual hostility and distrust between black and white workers.

Black out-migration from the south grew steadily from the end of the nineteenth century into the first decades of the new century. During the 1890s, some 174,000 blacks left the south, and this number rose to 197,000 between 1900 and 1910. The event that transformed the stream into a flood, however, was the outbreak of World War I in 1914. The war both increased the demand for U.S. industrial production and cut off the flow of European immigrants, northern factories' traditional source of labor. In response, employers began a spirited recruitment of blacks from the rural south.

The arrival of the recruiters in the south coincided with that of the Mexican boll weevil, which had devastated Louisiana's cotton crops in 1906 before moving on to Mississippi in 1913 and Alabama in 1916. The collapse of southern agriculture was aggravated by a series of disastrous floods in 1915 and 1916 and low cotton prices up to 1914. In response, southern planters shifted production from cotton to food crops and livestock, both of which required fewer workers. Thus the demand for black tenant farmers and day laborers fell just when the need for unskilled workers in northern cities skyrocketed.

This coincidence of push and pull factors increased the level of black out-migration to new heights and greatly augmented the black populations of Chicago, Detroit, Cleveland, Philadelphia, and New York. Between 1910 and 1920, some 525,000 African Americans left their traditional homes in the south and took up life in the north, and during the 1920s the outflow reached 877,000. This migration gradually acquired a dynamic of its own, as established migrants found jobs and housing for their friends and relatives back home. At the same time, northern black newspapers such as the *Chicago Defender*, which were

---

*Founded in 1886, the AFL represented mainly skilled workers in a variety of skilled trades. The CIO, founded in 1935, represented skilled and unskilled workers in basic industries.—Ed.

widely read in the south, exhorted southern blacks to escape their oppression and move northward. As a result of this dynamic, black out-migration from the south continued at a substantial rate even during the Great Depression.

Northern whites viewed this rising tide of black migration with increasing hostility and considerable alarm. Middle-class whites were repelled by what they saw as the uncouth manners, unclean habits, slothful appearance, and illicit behavior of poorly educated, poverty-stricken migrants who had only recently been sharecroppers, and a resurgence of white racist ideology during the 1920s provided a theoretical, "scientific" justification for these feelings. Working-class whites, for their part, feared economic competition from the newcomers; and being first- or second-generation immigrants who were themselves scorned by native whites, they reaffirmed their own "whiteness" by oppressing a people that was even lower in the racial hierarchy. Blacks in the early twentieth century frequently said that the first English word an immigrant learned was "nigger."

As the size of the urban black population rose steadily after 1900, white racial views hardened and the relatively fluid and open period of race relations in the north drew to a close. Northern newspapers increasingly used terms such as "nigger" and "darkey" in print and carried unflattering stories about black crimes and vice. After decades of relatively integrated education, white parents increasingly refused to enroll their children in schools that included blacks. Doors that had permitted extensive interracial contact among the elite suddenly slammed shut as black professionals lost white clients, associates, and friends.

The most dramatic harbinger of the new regime in race relations was the upsurge in racial violence. In city after northern city, a series of communal riots broke out between 1900 and 1920 in the wake of massive black migration. Race riots struck New York City in 1900; Evansville, Indiana, in 1903; Springfield, Illinois, in 1908; East St. Louis, Illinois, in 1917; and Chicago in 1919.* In each case, individual blacks were attacked because of the color of their skin. Those living away from recognized "black" neighborhoods had their houses ransacked or burned. Those unlucky or unwise enough to be caught trespassing in "white" neighborhoods were beaten, shot, or lynched. Blacks on their way to work were pulled from trolleys and pummelled. Rampaging bands of whites roamed the streets for days, attacking blacks at will. Although most of the rioters were white, most of the arrests, and nearly all of the victims, were black.

As the tide of violence rose in northern cities, blacks were increasingly divided from whites by a hardening color line in employment, education, and especially housing. Whites became increasingly intolerant of black neighbors and fear of racial turnover and black "invasion" spread. Those blacks living away from recognized Negro areas were forced to move into expanding "black belts," "darkytowns," "Bronzevilles," or "Niggertowns." Well-educated,

---

*For more on the Chicago riot, see Chapter 7.—Ed.

middle-class blacks of the old elite found themselves increasingly lumped together with poorly educated, impoverished migrants from the rural south; and well-to-do African Americans were progressively less able to find housing commensurate with their social status. In white eyes, black people belonged in black neighborhoods no matter what their social or economic standing; the color line grew increasingly impermeable.

Thus levels of residential segregation between blacks and whites began a steady rise at the turn of the century that would last for sixty years. . . . By World War II the foundations of the modern ghetto had been laid in virtually every northern city. . . .

With a rapidly growing black population being accommodated by an ever-smaller number of neighborhoods and an increasingly uneven residential configuration, the only possible outcome was an increase in the spatial isolation of blacks. As can be seen in Table [1], levels of racial isolation in northern cities began to move sharply upward after 1900, and especially after 1910. By 1930, African Americans were well on their way to experiencing a uniquely high degree of spatial isolation in American cities. Chicago led the way: its isolation index increased from only 10% in 1900 to 70% thirty years later. As of 1930 the typical black Chicagoan lived in a neighborhood that was over two-thirds black. That the level of black racial isolation also rose in other cities indicated the growth of more incipient ghettos: from 8% to 51% in Cleveland, from 5% to 42% in New York, and from 13% to 47% in St. Louis. . . . As the new century wore on, areas of acceptable black residence became more and more narrowly circumscribed: the era of the ghetto had begun.

Migration and industrial development also segregated the "new" European immigrant groups, of course, but recent studies have made it clear that immigrant enclaves in the early twentieth century were in no way comparable to the black ghetto that formed in most northern cities by 1940. To be sure, certain neighborhoods could be identified as "Italian," "Polish," or "Jewish"; but these ethnic enclaves differed from black ghettos in three fundamental ways.

First, unlike black ghettos, immigrant enclaves were never homogeneous and always contained a wide variety of nationalities, even if they were publicly associated with a particular national origin group. In Chicago's "Magyar district" of 1901, for example, twenty-two different ethnic groups were present and only 37% of all family heads were Magyar (26% were Polish). Similarly, an 1893 color-coded block map of Chicago's West Side prepared by the U.S. Department of Labor showed the location of European ethnic groups using eighteen separate colors. The result was a huge rainbow in which no block contained a single color. The average number of colors per block was eight, and four out of five *lots* within blocks were mixed. In none of the "Little Italys" identified on the map was there an all-Italian block. . . .

A second crucial distinction is that most European ethnics did not live in immigrant "ghettos," as ethnically diluted as they were. . . .

Thus even at the height of their segregation early in this century, European ethnic groups did not experience a particularly high degree of isolation from

American society, even in 1910 at the end of the peak decade of European immigration. . . .

The last difference between immigrant enclaves and black ghettos is that whereas ghettos became a permanent feature of black residential life, ethnic enclaves proved to be a fleeting, transitory stage in the process of immigrant assimilation. The degree of segregation and spatial isolation among European ethnic groups fell steadily after 1910, as native-born children of immigrants experienced less segregation than their parents and as spatial isolation decreased progressively with socioeconomic advancement. For European immigrants, enclaves were places of absorption, adaptation, and adjustment to American society. They served as springboards for broader mobility in society, whereas blacks were trapped behind an increasingly impermeable color line.

The emergence of severe racial segregation in the north was not primarily a reflection of black housing preferences or a natural outcome of migration processes. On the contrary, as the ghetto walls grew thicker and higher, well-to-do class blacks complained bitterly and loudly about their increasing confinement within crowded, dilapidated neighborhoods inhabited by people well below their social and economic status. Although they fought the construction of the ghetto as best they could, the forces arrayed against them proved to be overwhelming.

Foremost among the tools that whites used to construct the ghetto was violence. The initial impetus for ghetto formation came from a wave of racial violence, already noted, that swept over northern cities in the period between 1900 and 1920. These disturbances were communal in nature, and victims were singled out strictly on the basis of skin color. As history has repeatedly shown, during periods of communal strife, the only safety is in numbers. Blacks living in integrated or predominantly white areas—or even simply traveling through white areas to their own homes—proved to be extremely vulnerable. . . .

As the black ghetto became more dense and spatially concentrated, a struggle for power, influence, and ideological control emerged within the black community between the old elite and the "New Negroes" of the 1920s and 1930s. The latter were politicians and, to a lesser extent, business owners who benefited from the spatial concentration of black demand within a racially segmented market. In ideological terms, the struggle was symbolized by the debate between the adherents of W. E. B. Du Bois and the followers of Booker T. Washington. The former argued that blacks should fight white injustice and demand their rightful share of the fruits of American society; the latter advocated accommodating white racism while building an independent black economic base.

The rise of the ghetto, more than anything else, brought about the eclipse of the old elite of integrationist blacks who dominated African American affairs in northern cities before 1910. These professionals and tradespeople who catered to white clients and aspired to full membership in American society were supplanted by a class of politicians and entrepreneurs whose source of power and wealth lay in the black community itself. Rather than being caterers, barbers, doctors, and lawyers who served a white or racially mixed clientele, the new elite were politicians and business owners with a self-interested stake in the ghetto. With their ascendancy, the ideal of an integrated society and the fight against racial segregation went into a long remission.

s o u r c e s

SINGING THE BLUES

The blues had its origins in the cotton fields of Mississippi and Alabama, some-time in the late nineteenth century, and it became the musical expression of the great black migration and of the black experience in the urban North. Because Chicago was so easily accessible by rail from the Mississippi delta, that city be-came a center for playing and recording the blues. Between 1920, when the first blues was recorded, and 1926, when country blues played by men began to at-tract interest, women dominated the commercial blues scene. By far the biggest stars of the era were Gertrude "Ma" Rainey and Bessie Smith, who recorded over 250 songs, many in the mid-1920s. Their lyrics, and those of other com-posers whose songs they sang and recorded, are printed on the following pages.

Read the lyrics from a broad perspective. What ideas and themes can you find? What do the songs tell us about the great migration, especially as it was experienced by black women? About gender relations? About the role of sexu-ality? Do you think Rainey and Smith should be viewed as feminists—that is, as "sisters" of the middle-class white women who had recently fought for the right to vote—or as kin to the "New Women" of the 1920s, depicted in Chapter 7? In the hands of these composers, was the blues a music of despair, of triumph, or of survival?

 **VOICES**   **Gone Daddy Blues** *(Gertrude Rainey)*

[Knocking]

[Spoken]

UNKNOWN MAN: Who's that knockin' on that door?
RAINEY: It's me, baby.
MAN: Me who?
RAINEY: Don't you know I'm your wife?
MAN: What?! Wife?!
RAINEY: Yeah!
MAN: Ain't that awful? I don't let no woman quit me but one time.
RAINEY: But I just quit one li'l old time, just one time!

MAN: You left here with that other man, why didn't you stay?
RAINEY: Well, I'll tell you why I didn't stay, baby. I got home and I had to come
    on back home to you!
MAN: Well, I'm leavin' here today, what have you got to say?
RAINEY: Well, all right, I'll tell it, baby.
MAN: Talk fast, then.

[Sung]
    I'm going away, I'm going to stay
    I'll find the man I love some day
    I've got my ticket, clothes in my hand
    Trying to find that South bound land

    I'm gonna ride 'til I find that South bound land
    I'm gonna ride 'til I find that South bound land
    Gon' keep on ridin' 'til I shake hands with my man

    I'm going away, I'm going to stay
    I'll come back for my daddy someday
    But, dad, you'll never know how much I've missed you 'til I'm gone

    I'm going away, I'm going to stay
    I'll long for my daddy some day
    But, dad, you'll never know how much I've missed you 'til I'm gone.

Yes, Indeed He Do *(Porter Grainger)*

    I don't know what makes it rain, can't tell what makes it snow
    Well, I don't claim to know it all, but there's some things I do know

    There's one thing in particular that I never have to guess
    I ask myself this question, and I have to tell me yes

    Oh, do my sweet, sweet daddy love me? Yes, indeed he do
    Is he true as stars above me? What kind of fool is you?

    He don't stay from home all night more than six times a week
    No, I know that I'm his Sheba, and I know that he's my sheik

    And when I ask him where he's been, he grabs a rocking chair
    Then he knocks me down and says, "It's just a little love lick, dear."

    But if some woman looks at him, I'll tear her half in two
    Oh, do my sweet, sweet daddy love me? Yes, indeed he do

    Of course my sweet daddy loves me, yes, indeed he do
    If he beats me or mistreats me, what is that to you?

    I don't have to do no work except to wash his clothes
    And darn his socks and press his pants and scrub the kitchen floor

    I wouldn't take a million for my sweet, sweet daddy Jim
    And I wouldn't give a quarter for another man like him

Gee, ain't it great to have a man that's crazy over you?
Oh, do my sweet, sweet daddy love me? Yes, indeed he do.

Traveling Blues *(Composer unknown)*

Train's at the station, I heard the whistle blow
The train's at the station, I heard the whistle blow
I done bought my ticket and I don't know where I'll go

I went to the depot, looked up and down the board
I went to the depot, looked up and down the board
I asked the ticket agent, "Is my town on this road?"

The ticket agent said, "Woman, don't sit and cry."
The ticket agent said, "Woman, don't you sit and cry
The train blows at this station, but she keeps on passing by."

I hear my daddy calling some other woman's name
I hear my daddy calling some other woman's name
I know he don't need me, but I'm gonna answer just the same

I'm dangerous and blue, can't stay here no more
I'm dangerous and blue, can't stay here no more
Here come my train, folks, and I've got to go.

Lost Wandering Blues *(Gertrude Rainey)*

I'm leavin' this mornin' with my clothes in my hand
Lord, I'm leavin' this mornin' with my clothes in my hand
I won't stop movin' 'til I find my man

I'm standin' here wonderin' will a matchbox hold my clothes
Lord, I'm standin' here wonderin' will a matchbox hold my clothes
I got a trunk too big to be botherin' with on the road

I went up on the mountain, turned my face to the sky
Lord, I went up on the mountain, turned my face to the sky
I heard a whisper, said, "Mama, please don't die."

I turned around to give him my right han'
Lord, I turned around to give him my right han'
When I looked in his face, I was talkin' to my man

Lord, look-a yonder, people, my love has been refused
I said, look-a yonder, people, my love has been refused
That's the reason why mama's got the lost wandering blues.

Poor Man's Blues *(Bessie Smith)*

Mister rich man, rich man, open up your heart and mind
Mister rich man, rich man, open up your heart and mind
Give the poor man a chance, help stop these hard, hard times

While you're livin' in your mansion, you don't know what hard times means
While you're livin' in your mansion, you don't know what hard times means
Poor working man's wife is starvin', your wife's livin' like a queen

Portrait of Bessie Smith, by Carl Van Vechten, 1936.
Library of Congress.

Get a workin' man when you marry, and let all these sweet men be
Child, it takes money to run a business, and with me I know you girls will agree

There's one thing about this married life that these young girls have got to know
If a sweet man enter your front gate, turn out your lights and lock your door

Yes, get a working man when you marry, let all these pinchbacks be
Child, it takes money to run a business, and with me I know you girls will agree

And if this panic stay on much longer, I'll hear all these young girls say
That it's a long way to Oklahoma, but these little pinchbacks, take 'em away.

Blame It on the Blues *(Thomas Dorsey)*

I'm so sad and worried, got no time to spread the news
I'm so sad and worried, got no time to spread the news
Won't blame it on my trouble, can't blame it on the blues

Lord, Lord, Lord, Lordy Lord
Lord, Lord, Lordy Lordy Lord
Lord, Lord, Lord, Lord, Lord, Lord

[Spoken] Lord, who'm I gonna blame it on, then?

I can't blame my daddy, he treats me nice and kind
I can't blame my daddy, he treats me nice and kind
Shall I blame it on my nephew, blame it on that trouble of mine?

This house is like a graveyard, when I'm left here by myself
This house is like a graveyard, when I'm left here by myself
Shall I blame it on my lover, blame it on somebody else?

Can't blame my mother, can't blame my dad
Can't blame my brother for the trouble I've had
Can't blame my lover that held my hand
Can't blame my husband, can't blame my man
Can't blame nobody, guess I'll have to blame it on the blues.

Interior Space: The Dumbbell Tenement

By the 1880s, immigrants to New York and other big cities often found themselves living in "dumbbell" tenements, so called because of their shape. Because it was designed as an improvement on existing structures, the dumbbell was, ironically, labeled a "reform." Perhaps it was, but it also had serious deficiencies. Placed side by side, as was the intention, two dumbbells created an airshaft less than five feet wide between the buildings.

The dumbbell generally housed four families to a floor, with two families living in the four room apartments (to the left in the diagram) and two in the

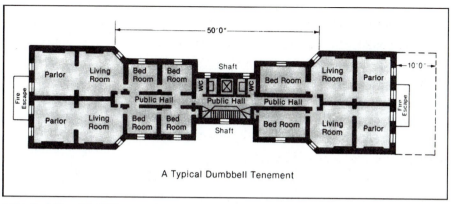

A Typical Dumbbell Tenement

A Typical Dumbbell Tenement.
Reprinted by permission of the publisher from The Promised City *by Moses Rischin,*
Cambridge, Mass.: Harvard University Press, Copyright © 1962 by the President and Fellows
of Harvard College.

three room apartments (to the right). Many families also took in boarders or
used the premises to produce goods. The most spacious room, the front parlor,
was only 10½ feet × 11 feet; bedrooms were 8½ feet × 7 feet. The cooking ap-
parently was done in what is labeled the "living room." Everyone on the floor
shared the bathrooms, marked here with "w.c." (water closet).

From the floor plan reproduced below, imagine what it would have been
like to live in a dumbbell tenement. What kinds of experiences would life in
such a building promote? And what activities would it inhibit? Speculate on
why the building was designed so that the bedrooms in the apartments on the
left could be entered from both the living room and the public hallway.

URBAN IMAGES

By virtue of their size and the new relationships they imposed on their inhab-
itants, American cities of the late nineteenth century required their residents
to live and to communicate in ways unknown just a few decades before. Many
of the adjustments that people made—and the institutions they created to fa-
cilitate those adjustments—involved attempts to reduce racial, ethnic, or class
contact where it was felt to be excessive or inappropriate. Which of the follow-
ing photographs illustrates this kind of effort? This group of illustrations also
includes several that might best be understood as mythic images—images that
tell us more about what the photographer or illustrator desired or believed than
about any existing "reality." Which ones fall in this category, and what does
each tell us about how nineteenth-century Americans understood the city?

Central Park, the Drive, Currier & Ives, 1862.
Library of Congress.

World's Columbian Exposition, Chicago, 1893.
Library of Congress.

Frederick C. Robie House, Chicago, Designed by Frank Lloyd Wright.
Library of Congress.

Delmonico's, New York City, 1903.
Library of Congress.

Bandit's Roost, 39½ Mulberry Street, New York City, c. 1888.
Photography by Jacob A. Riis. The Jacob A. Riis Collection; Museum of the City of New York.

the big picture

The American city of the late nineteenth and early twentieth centuries was a complex social space. What were some of its functions? How was the city experienced, and imagined, by the different groups that lived within it?

chapter five

EMPIRE

*I*n the final years of the nineteenth century, Americans suddenly awoke from their preoccupations with domestic life to find themselves with an empire on their hands. In 1895, while very few Americans paid any attention, inhabitants of Cuba, which was still a Spanish colony, staged an unsuccessful revolution—one more in a series of New World revolutions against European rule that had begun in 1776. But this one failed. The Spanish began a ruthless repression of guerrilla resistance, even herding men, women, and children into concentration camps. The American press took up the Cuban cause in shrill editorials and exaggerated reporting. Before anyone—even those in President McKinley's administration—quite knew what was happening, the American battleship *Maine,* calling at Havana, had been mysteriously sunk, perhaps sabotaged. McKinley asked Congress for a resolution permitting "forcible intervention" in Cuba. An American fleet that Secretary of the Navy Theodore Roosevelt had waiting in the Pacific steamed for Manila Bay in the Philippines to attack Spanish warships there. War was on.

The war lasted for only a few weeks, and when it was over, the United States "possessed" the Philippines, Cuba, and Puerto Rico, and was faced with the task of governing its new colonies for a time under military occupation. The British boasted that the sun never set on their empire. Americans could not yet make the same boast, but they could see from a quick look at the map that the sun never set for *long* on American possessions.

This simple story—of bring drawn innocently into "a splendid little war," as John Hay called it, and waking up blinkingly to an unanticipated empire— probably is a fairly accurate summary of the way most Americans experienced the events of 1898 and 1899. But the story misses a lot.

It overlooks, to begin with, the fact that the history of the United States could be written as a history of expansion and conquest. Through exploration, purchase, treaty, and war, the United States had become, in the course of the nineteenth century, a vast nation. And all along there had been plans and dreams to expand even further, down into Mexico and the Caribbean. In this way, the Spanish-American War was a logical outcome to a long history.

The Cuban and Philippine occupations should also be seen as early examples of many similar interventions over the next two decades that together helped define the distinctly American version of empire. Carried out with the support of presidents known as reformers and progressives, these ventures added up to a major extension of American influence around the globe. Roosevelt's aid to Panamanian rebels in 1903 made possible American domination of the Canal Zone. Under William Taft, the United States asserted its right to intervene and to supervise the collection of customs receipts in Nicaragua, another nation with a potential canal route. Woodrow Wilson sent American forces into Haiti and the Dominican Republic, and in 1914, seeking to topple the Mexican government, he landed American troops and occupied the coastal city of Veracruz.

But this new expansion occurred in a new atmosphere. The 1890s was a decade of deep economic and social crisis. The depression of 1893 to 1897 was the worst in the nation's history and gave rise to the specter of collapse, as bands of tramps wandered the countryside in numbers large enough to be called "armies." Two of the most violent strikes in American history—one at Homestead, Pennsylvania, in 1892; the second at Pullman, Illinois, in 1894— intensified the sense that the country was at a desperate crossroads. For many, particularly for people like Theodore Roosevelt, the Spanish-American War and the chance to be an imperial power were a welcome relief from the brooding sense of decline and collapse that the decade had engendered.

In addition, whatever its origins, the new empire appeared to many Americans to be an opportunity, both for commercial and military development and for reform. The connection may seem odd in retrospect, but many Americans looked on the chance to govern Cuba or the Philippines as a chance to recover a sense of mission, to bring to "backward" nations government that was honest, efficient, enlightened, and democratic. In the process, such people hoped, the nation might begin to set its own house in order. Indeed, the experience of empire may have contributed as much as populism did to the emergence of the atmosphere of reform that was to give the first decades of the new century their characteristic flavor.

interpretive essay

Willard B. Gatewood, Jr.

BLACK SOLDIERS AND THE WHITE MAN'S BURDEN

The quick and decisive defeat of the Spanish in the Philippines did not end conflict on the islands. Led by Emilio Aguinaldo, Filipino nationalists for several years resisted American domination using guerrilla tactics not unlike those employed against another American army by Vietnamese nationalists in the 1960s.

The following selection, by Willard B. Gatewood, Jr., touches on the character of this guerrilla war and the problems it posed for American soldiers. But Gatewood's primary interest is in the Philippines as a site of racial contact and interaction. He chronicles the experiences and feelings of black American combat units, led by white officers, engaging native populations of color and, ironically, taking up the "white man's burden"—and all of this at a time when, back home, whites were legalizing racial segregation and lynching about a hundred blacks each year.

What can be learned about race relations from the experience of these black soldiers in the Philippines? How did the racial contacts brought about by the conflict shape the beliefs of whites, blacks, and Filipinos? What stance did the black troops take toward their role in the imperial process, and how do you explain their outlook?

Black regulars were among the American troops whose service in the Philippines spanned the shift in insurgent strategy from conventional to guerrilla warfare. Arriving in Manila in July and August 1899, Negro soldiers of the Twenty-fourth and Twenty-fifth Infantry immediately took stations around the city from Calacoon to Balic Balic road. By mid-1900 the number of black regulars in the Philippines had increased to 2100 men. In January and February 1900, the Forty-eighth and Forty-ninth Infantry, the two Negro volunteer regiments recruited specifically for service in the islands, disembarked at Manila

Willard B. Gatewood, Jr., *Black Americans and the White Man's Burden, 1898–1903,* University of Illinois Press, Urbana, 1975, chapter 10. Used with permission of Willard B. Gatewood, Jr.

111

and remained in the field in Luzon until their enlistment terms expired a year and a half later. Eight troops of the Ninth Cavalry, originally destined for China to help put down the Boxer Rebellion, arrived in mid-September 1900. The Ninth first saw action in southern Luzon in the vicinity of Nueva Caceres and Legaspi, and later participated in operations in Samar and Panay. By December 1900, when the total strength of American forces stood at 70,000 men and officers, there were over 6000 black regulars and volunteers stationed at dozens of small outposts scattered from northern Luzon to Samar.

During their first weeks in the Philippines the black soldiers became intimately acquainted both with the hazards of a tropical climate and with the deadly tactics of the insurgents. On August 21, 1899, eleven men of the Twenty-fourth Infantry who had started on a reconnaissance mission toward San Mateo drowned when their boat capsized in the Mariquina River, a swift stream swollen by several days of heavy rain. Early in September a party of the Twenty-fourth, on a scouting expedition in the mountains north of Manila, discovered in a valley "a body of Filipinos, drilling on extended order, such as used only in fighting." But upon descending to the site, the soldiers found only "peaceful citizens planting rice"—an occurrence that was to be repeated many times . . . as they pursued their elusive enemy.

Among the numerous engagements in which black regulars participated during the northern offensive, few attracted as much attention as the battle at O'Donnell. The Twenty-fifth, with headquarters at Bamban, learned that a large force of insurgents was encamped fifteen miles away at O'Donnell. Led by a Filipino guide, a detachment of four-hundred black soldiers under the command of Captain H. A. Leonhauser left Bamban on the night of November 17, 1899, headed for O'Donnell on a roundabout route through the foothills of the Zambales Mountains. Arriving at their destination just before sunrise, the troops staged a surprise attack on the insurgent stronghold. Once inside O'Donnell, the colored soldiers "showed a grim and great earnestness in their work of gathering in prisoners, rifles and bolos." One eyewitness reported: "Strong black arms caught fleeing insurgents upon the streets and hauled them from under beds and beneath houses. Native women screamed in alarm and on their knees offered money and food to the American troops." But the soldiers apparently refrained from acts of unnecessary brutality. In fact, a young white officer was deeply impressed by the "humanity and forebearance of the colored men of the 25th Infantry" in their taking of O'Donnell. "There might have been a hundred of these pitiful Filipino warriors killed," he wrote, "but the men apparently couldn't bring themselves to shoot them." Instead, the soldiers were satisfied to capture over one-hundred insurgents and a large supply of weapons, food, and ammunition . . .

. . . By early 1900 resistance to American rule was almost wholly in the form of guerrilla warfare. Few engagements thereafter deserved to be called battles. But the hit-and-run tactics of Aguinaldo's widely dispersed forces and the marauding bands of robbers (ladrones) proved to be no less deadly to American troops who were constantly on patrol and scouting duty. Black volunteers of the Forty-eighth and Forty-ninth Infantry arrived in the Philippines early in

1900 anxious to confront the insurgents in conventional warfare; they were disappointed to discover that most of their efforts were devoted to "looking for rebel forces which are no where to be found." A Negro lieutenant probably expressed the sentiments of his comrades when on January 31, 1900, he wrote home: "While there is no enemy in sight, yet we are always on the lookout and we have slept in our shoes ever since we landed. The war may be over or it may have just commenced. No one can tell what these devils will do next." . . .

McKinley's victory in November was the signal for General MacArthur* to inaugurate a new policy designed to ensure the establishment of permanent control over the islands. This policy represented a shift from "benevolent pacification" to a more stringent approach, promising punishment for natives who continued to resist American authority and stressing the importance of isolating insurgents from their bases of supply in the villages. It also emphasized the need to protect villagers from intimidation and terror at the hands of insurgents. For the black soldiers, including the Tenth Cavalry, which arrived in May 1901, the new military policy meant not only garrison duty in towns and villages scattered over hundreds of miles across the archipelago, but also an endless succession of expeditions through rice paddies and dense forests and over treacherous mountains and swollen streams. . . .

From early 1901 until their departure from the Philippines more than a year later, the black troops who garrisoned numerous outposts on the islands did more than perform the usual scouting, patrol, and guard duties, and other activities involved in keeping the peace. They also assisted in laying "the foundations of civil government" and generally functioned as agents of the Americanization process. Their civil duties included the supervision of elections, the organization of educational and legal systems, and the maintenance of public health facilities. Lieutenant David J. Gilmer of the Forty-ninth Infantry, a former member of the Third North Carolina Volunteers, not only was popular with enlisted men but also won the affection of the people of Linao as commander of the post there. Gilmer later secured a commission in the Philippine Scouts, an army of natives organized and officered by Americans. Captain Frank R. Steward, also of the Forty-ninth, who was a graduate of the Harvard Law School, served as provost judge in San Pablo; there he organized and presided over the first American-type court. His father, Chaplain Theophilus Steward of the Twenty-fifth Infantry, supervised a series of schools taught by soldiers in the towns and villages north of Manila under the protection of his regiment. According to one observer, the chaplain's command of the Spanish language and capacity for hard work enabled him to achieve excellent results and to instill in Filipinos an appreciation for American values. Black soldiers often displayed considerable pride in their nonmilitary activities, which they described as significant contributions to the improvement of life among the natives. An enlisted man in the Twenty-fifth Infantry boasted in 1902 that "the colored American soldier has taught the Filipino thrift, economy and above all the customs of polite society." . . .

*General Arthur MacArthur, military commander in the Philippines.

. . . No less than whites, blacks suffered from the boredom endemic to existence in remote outposts. Their diversions sometimes included activities considerably less wholesome than fishing, swimming, playing baseball, or participating in choral groups. Gambling and overindulgence in various alcoholic concoctions constituted the chief diversions of some soldiers, and drinking gamblers had a tendency to spawn fights. Black soldiers on leave in Manila sometimes became involved in disturbances in the tenderloin districts, especially in houses of prostitution that attempted to establish a color line.

For many soldiers, black and white, female companionship offered the best respite from a monotonous existence. It was common practice for a Negro soldier to acquire a "squaw." Richard Johnson of the Forty-eighth Infantry claimed that the "first to acquire a querida' or lover (kept woman) was our captain and this set the pattern for all the men." Perhaps, as Archibald Cary Coolidge later wrote, "their pursuits of the native women provoked much anger among the [Filipino] men." But whether such activity gave "rise to fresh insurrection in districts which had been called pacified," as Coolidge claimed, is open to question. Some black soldiers, especially those who planned to remain permanently in the Philippines at the termination of their military service, married Filipino women and settled in various parts of Luzon. For most soldiers, however, these relationships ended when they sailed for the United States in 1902. An enlisted man of the Twenty-fifth observed that in view of the number of deluded women who crowded the pier as soldiers shipped out for home, it was altogether appropriate for the band to play "The Girl I Left Behind."

Whatever the consequences of their relations with native women, black soldiers generally appear to have treated Filipinos with respect and compassion. Throughout the war, and especially after the army adopted a harsher policy toward insurgents, reports of atrocities circulated widely in the United States. Few prompted as much indignation as those regarding the use of the so-called water cure as "a persuader . . . to induce bad hombres to talk." Some Americans maintained that troops in the Philippines engaged in brutalities that surpassed anything committed by "Butcher" Weyler in Cuba. In May 1900, black newspapers in the United States published a letter from a Negro soldier who expressed horror at the looting, stealing, desecration of churches, and daily indignities against Filipinos committed by his white comrades. Even some high-ranking military officers protested against the severity of the war. The charges of unwarranted brutality achieved even greater credence late in 1901 when General Jacob Smith, in retaliation against the insurgents for their massacre of a contingent of American troops in Samar, ordered his army to turn the island into "a howling wilderness" and to kill every human being over the age of ten.

Although one writer asserted in 1904 that "the brutal conduct" of black soldiers "in the interior seriously jeopardized the hope of a peaceful solution" to the Philippine insurrection, the weight of testimony in regard to their treatment of natives contradicts this observation. Oswald Garrison Villard* maintained

---

*The liberal, pacifist editor of the *New York Evening Post*.

that "neither the officers nor the men of any colored regiment" figured in "the charges and counter-charges arising out of the use of the water torture, except one man who at the time of his offense was not with his regiment." There were, of course, other exceptions of which Villard was undoubtedly ignorant. For example, Lieutenant Samuel Lyons of the Twenty-fifth confided in a letter to his wife that he and his men had on occasion administered the water cure to recalcitrant insurgents. Nevertheless, it does appear that the black regiments used this particular form of torture far less frequently than some of the white outfits.

The Ninth Cavalry developed its own method for extracting information from captured insurgents. In describing it one authority wrote: "A native . . . was taken into a semi-dark room and securely bound. Then a huge black, dressed only in a loin cloth and carrying a cavalry sabre, entered and danced around the victim making threatening gesticulations with the sabre. To an ignorant Filipino he undoubtedly looked like a devil incarnate." The method proved amazingly successful as a persuader; whatever its psychological consequences, it was obviously preferable to the physical torture inflicted by the water cure.

By the time the black troops departed from the Philippines, it was generally agreed that their relationships with natives were more cordial than those of white soldiers. When the Negro soldiers first arrived in the islands, Filipinos viewed them with awe and fear as an "American species of bête noir." A typical reaction was: "These are not Americans; they are Negritoes." But their fear quickly turned into friendliness and their awe into admiration. Filipinos came to accept black Americans as "very much like ourselves only larger" and gave them the affectionate appellation, "Negritos Americanos." Negro soldiers generally reciprocated the good will of peaceful natives and treated them with consideration and respect. In letters home they often referred to the contempt that white soldiers displayed toward all Filipinos and insisted that such an attitude underlay much of the natives' hostility to American rule. Military authorities, quick to recognize the rapport between black soldiers and natives, generally agreed that in towns and districts "garrisoned by colored troops the natives seem to harbor little or no enmity toward the soldiers and the soldiers themselves seem contented with their lot and are not perpetually pining for home." In 1902 Colonel [Andrew S.] Burt could "not recall of the many places where the 25th Infantry has been stationed on these Islands that the inhabitants were not genuinely sorry when they have been ordered to leave their towns." General Robert P. Hughes fully agreed, noting that black soldiers "mixed with the natives at once" and "whenever they came together, they became great friends." Hughes recalled that when he withdrew "a darkey company" from Santa Rita, the residents wept and begged him to allow the black soldiers to remain.

Not all white Americans in the Philippines were so favorably disposed toward black soldiers and their friendly relations with Filipinos. "While the white soldiers, unfortunately, got on badly with the natives," the correspondent Stephen Bonsal reported, "the black soldiers got on much too well." Some white officers came to suspect that Negro troops had more sympathy for the Filipinos' aspirations for independence than for American policy regarding the islands. Others complained that the racial identity that black soldiers established with the natives had resulted in a color line that discriminated against whites. Governor Taft* apparently shared some of these concerns. He felt that black troops "got along fairly well with the natives . . . too well with the native women"; the result was "a good deal of demoralization in the towns where they have been stationed." Taft was credited with engineering the withdrawal of Negro troops from the islands in 1902 "out of their regular turn."

Whatever the reaction of white soldiers to the rapport between their black comrades and the Filipinos, their overt expressions of racial prejudice toward both only strengthened that relationship. Writing about American forces in the Philippines early in 1900, Frederick Palmer maintained that color was a crucial factor and that if a man was nonwhite, "we include him in a general class called 'nigger,' a class beneath our notice, to which, so far as our white soldier is concerned, all Filipinos belonged." Another correspondent, Albert Gardiner Robinson, reported from Manila that "the spirit of our men is far too much one of contempt for the dark-skinned people of the tropics." White soldiers "almost without exception" referred to the natives as "niggers," and, as Major Cornelius Gardner of the Thirtieth Infantry observed, "the natives are beginning to understand what the word 'nigger' means." In 1899 both the *Manila Times* and the *Army and Navy Journal* became so concerned about the mischief done by the widespread use of the term in referring to black soldiers and Filipinos that they called upon Americans to banish it from their vocabulary. For quite a different reason white southerners in the islands also objected to calling Filipinos "niggers"—a term that they reserved for Negro Americans, soldiers as well as civilians. James H. Blount of Georgia, an officer in the Twenty-ninth Infantry who remained in the Philippines as a civil judge, claimed that southerners "instinctively resented any suggestion comparing Filipinos and negroes," because such comparison implied that their social intercourse with natives was "equivalent to eating, drinking, dancing and chumming with negroes"—things that no self-respecting white man would do.

Black soldiers were keenly aware of the racial attitudes of their white comrades toward all colored people, themselves as well as Filipinos. The men of the Twenty-fifth Infantry had scarcely landed in the islands in 1899 when, as they marched into Manila, a white spectator yelled: "What are you coons doing here?" The sentiment implicit in the question found expression in the establishment of "white only" restaurants, hotels, barber shops, and even brothels, and in tunes such as "I Don't Like a Nigger Nohow" sung by white soldiers. In mid-1900 a Negro regular observed that "already there is nowhere in Manila you can hardly [*sic*] get accommodated and you are welcomed nowhere." The color line being drawn against the black soldier in the Philippines was, in his opinion, "enough to make a colored man hate the flag of the United States." Patrick Mason of the Twenty-fourth Infantry wrote home not long before he was killed in combat: "The first thing in the morning is the 'Nigger' and the last thing at night is the 'Nigger.'" Such talk, according to Mason, was prompted by

*Governor of the Philippines and future president, William Taft.

the assumption of white soldiers that no one except Caucasians had "any rights or privileges." Late in 1899 a black infantryman on duty near San Isidro wrote: "The whites have begun to establish their diabolical race hatred in all its home rancor . . . even endeavoring to propagate the phobia among the Spaniards and Filipinos so as to be sure of the foundation of their supremacy when the civil rule . . . is established." White officers often expressed admiration for the light-hearted, cheerful mood with which black soldiers undertook even the most difficult assignments, but few indicated an awareness of their deep resentment of the insults and discrimination to which they were regularly subjected.

A major source of black soldiers' grievances was the racial prejudice displayed by some of their white officers. While in the Philippines, the officer personnel of the four Negro regiments of the regular army changed frequently; according to black enlisted men and noncommissioned officers, the replacements too often included whites who, protected by their rank, gave full vent to their animosities against people of color. Though always generous in their praise of white officers whom they considered fair-minded, black soldiers complained bitterly about their treatment at the hands of those with a prejudice against Negroes. Specifically, they charged such officers with cursing and abusing enlisted men and with subjecting them to inhuman treatment for even minor infractions of military regulations. In a few instances the grievances found their way to the War Department; but as a member of the Twenty-fifth who filed a complaint correctly predicted, "an abnegation will confront this statement as has been the case heretofore."

The color prejudice manifested by white Americans in the Philippines substantially affected the black soldiers' view of the Filipino. The soldiers early classified the natives as colored people and looked upon themselves as part of an experiment pitting "Greek against Greek." Although some white Americans claimed that Filipinos deeply resented the presence of black troops because they regarded themselves "as belonging to a race superior to the African," such a view was contradicted by the testimony of black soldiers who almost without exception noted how the affinity of complexion between themselves and the natives provided the basis for mutual respect and good will. After a series of interviews with well-educated Filipinos, a black infantryman reported that although natives had been told of the "brutal natures" of black Americans and had at first feared for the safety of their senoritas, personal experience had demonstrated that Negro soldiers were "much more kindly and manly in dealing with us" than [were] whites.

Black soldiers might refer to Filipino insurgents as "gugus," a term used by white Americans usually to identify hostile natives, but they obviously did not join white soldiers in applying the more general term "nigger" to all Filipinos. Nor did they "kick and cuff" natives at will. According to one Filipino, the black soldier differed from his white comrade in one principal respect: he did not "connect race hatred with duty." Eugene R. Whitted of the Twenty-fifth Infantry agreed that the Negro soldier's lack of racial animosity toward colored people gave him an advantage over whites in dealing with the Filipinos. "Our men met treatment with like treatment," he declared, "and when they were in the field they were soldiers and when in town gentlemen." Despite breaches in the gentleman's code, Negro troops appear, as one Negro regular put it, to have gotten "along well with everybody but American [white] people."

Although color was important in determining the attitude of black soldiers toward Filipinos, it was not the only consideration. Some soldiers early detected a similarity between the predicament of the black man in the United States and the brown man in the Philippines: both were subjects of oppression. For such soldiers the struggle of colored Filipinos against their white oppressors had obvious ideological as well as racial implications. In view of the plight of colored citizens in the United States, it was not surprising that some black soldiers expressed doubts as to whether Filipinos under American rule would "be justly dealt by." Private William R. Fulbright of the Twenty-fifth described the war against the Filipinos as "a gigantic scheme of robbery and oppression." Writing from a military station on Luzon on Christmas Eve, 1900, a Tuskegee alumnus confided to Booker T. Washington that "these people are right and *we* are wrong and terribly wrong." The black soldier assured Washington that he would not re-enlist because no man "who has any humanity about him at all" would desire "to fight against such a cause as this." Another Negro infantryman who believed that the Filipinos had "a just grievance" maintained that the insurrection would never "have occurred if the army of occupation . . . [had] treated them as people." But the occupation forces, he declared, attempted to apply to the Filipinos the "home treatment for colored people," which they would not tolerate.

Few black soldiers were so forthright in expressing doubts about the wisdom and correctness of the American position in the Philippines. More typical was a statement by Sergeant M. W. Saddler: "Whether it is right to reduce these people to submission is not a question for the soldier to decide." Like others, Saddler preferred to emphasize the resolve with which Negro troops in the Philippines performed their duty in order to "add another star to the already brilliant crown of the Afro-American soldier." Captain W. H. Jackson of the Forty-ninth acknowledged that the soldiers of his regiment identified racially with the natives, but he insisted that, as members of the American army, black men took the position that "all enemies of the U.S. government look alike to us, hence we go along with the killing."

Despite such explanations, the correspondence of Negro soldiers revealed that they were continually plagued by misgivings about their role in the Philippines. For black regular William Simms of Muncie, Indiana, such misgivings were forcefully driven home by a Filipino boy who asked him: "Why does the American Negro come from America to fight us when we are much a friend to him and have not done anything to him [?] He is all the same as me and me all the same as you. Why don't you fight those people in America who burn Negroes, that make a beast of you . . . ?" For introspective and thoughtful soldiers like Simms, their racial and ideological sympathy for a colored people struggling to achieve freedom seemed always to be at war with their notions of duty as American citizens and their hope that the fulfillment of that duty would somehow ameliorate the plight of their people at home. As Sergeant John W.

Galloway indicated, "the black men here are so much between the 'Devil and the deep sea' on the Philippine Question." But even those without such qualms who believed that the soldier's oath knew "neither race, color, nor nation" were troubled by the increasing hostility of black Americans at home toward the war in the Philippines. Negro soldiers, according to one infantryman, were "rather discouraged over the fact that the sacrifice of life and health has to be made for a cause so unpopular among our people."

Anti-imperialists in the United States were quick to detect the irony involved in the use of black troops to suppress the Filipino insurrection. A succession of poets, novelists, humorists, and journalists attacked the racist notions implicit in the doctrine of the white man's burden and pointed up the disparities between the rhetoric and realities of "benevolent assimilation." George Ade and Finley Peter Dunne called attention to the incongruities in the nation's use of black troops to shoulder the "white man's burden" in the Philippines where they, as representatives of an unassimilated segment of the American population, were supposed to bring about the "benevolent assimilation" of the Filipino. According to Dunne's Mr. Dooley, the government's policy in the Philippines was to "Take up th' white man's burden an' hand it to th' coons." Having succeeded to the presidency in September 1901, upon McKinley's assassination, Theodore Roosevelt admitted that Dunne's "delicious phrase about 'take up the white man's burden and put it on the coons' exactly hit off the weak spot" in his expansionist theory. But Roosevelt assured Dunne that he was not willing "to give up the theory yet."

No less aware of the "weak spot" were the Filipino insurgents, who were also thoroughly familiar with the plight of Negroes in the United States and with the widespread anti-imperialist sentiment within the black community. Cognizant of the ambivalent attitude of the black troops who found themselves combatting an independence movement by another people of color, insurgent propagandists directed special appeals "To the Colored American Soldier." Here is one such proclamation signed by Aguinaldo and addressed to the Twenty-fourth Infantry during its operations in 1899 in the vicinity of Mabalacat:

> It is without honor that you are spilling your costly blood. Your masters have thrown you into the most iniquitous fight with double purpose—to make you the instrument of their ambition and also your hard work will soon make the extinction of your race. Your friends, the Filipinos, give you this good warning. You must consider your situation and your history, and take charge that the blood . . . of Sam Hose proclaims vengeance.

Such appeals were sources of embarrassment for the vast majority of black soldiers, who protested that they were "just as loyal to the old flag as white Americans." Nevertheless, the insurgents' propaganda was not altogether barren of results, and a few black soldiers actually joined the rebel ranks. . . .

Despite the publicity that a dozen or so Negro deserters attracted, the overwhelming majority of black soldiers in the Philippines ignored the blandishments of the insurgents and hoped that their service would result in rewards commensurate with their record. The Negro regular still believed that he was entitled to "a commission from the ranks." During the congressional consideration of the Army Reorganization Bill, which passed in February, 1901, the black press in the United States pleaded not only for an increase in the number of Negro regiments in the regular army, but also for the appointment of black officers. Their efforts were unsuccessful in both respects. . . .

Despite such discrimination, black soldiers throughout their service in the islands reported favorably on opportunities for enterprising black Americans. They described the soil and climate as conducive to productive agriculture and particularly emphasized the openings awaiting the Negro in business. F. H. Crumbley of the Forty-ninth Infantry urged black Americans "of Christian education" who desired to labor "among an appreciative people" to migrate to the Philippines at once. "They should not wait till the field is covered by others," he advised, "but should come in the front ranks and assist in developing these people." Sharing Crumbley's enthusiasm, a black enlisted man of the Twenty-fourth wrote home: "I shall say to all industrious and energetic colored Americans . . . that they cannot do anything more beneficial to themselves than to come over here while the country is still in its infancy and help . . . reap the harvest which we shall soon begin to gather in. In this country will be many fortunes made." The soldiers believed that the friendly relations that they had established with the Filipinos would operate to the advantage of Negro Americans who sought their fortunes in the islands.

On July 2, 1902, President Roosevelt issued a proclamation that, in effect, announced the end of the Filipino Insurrection. Even before his announcement American troops had begun to depart from the Philippines; beginning in May, the first black troops had shipped out of Manila for San Francisco. By mid-autumn all Negro soldiers, except those who chose to be mustered out in the Philippines, had taken stations in the United States. Most of those taking up residence in the islands secured jobs in hotels and restaurants in Manila or appointments as clerks in the civil government. In addition, there were "several school teachers, one lawyer and one doctor of medicine." One black American to remain in Manila when his regiment left in 1902 was T. N. McKinney of Texas, who first served on the city's police force and later as a minor civil servant. Ultimately McKinney acquired considerable wealth as the proprietor of the Manila Commission House Company; he became the recognized leader of the "colored colony in the capital city." Late in 1902 a black veteran of the Philippine campaign stationed at Fort Assiniboine, Montana, made public his views on the emigration of Negro Americans to the islands. Despite the fact that racial prejudice had "kept close in the wake of the flag" and was "keenly felt in that far-off land of eternal sunshine and roses," he was nonetheless convinced that the islands offered "our people the best opportunities of the century."

William Connor

COMBAT: AN OFFICER'S ACCOUNT

In the spring of 1899, Lt. William Connor wrote the following letter to Lt. Frederick Sladen, describing his experiences in a series of engagements that took place in and around Pasig, Malolos, and other locations within fifty miles of Manila on the island of Luzon. What attitude does Connor take toward the Filipino enemy? Toward combat? What can the account tell us about why Americans went to war in the Philippines and, more broadly, about why the nation became an imperial power?

𝒱 VOICES   [April 1, 1899]

. . . On Thursday reconnaissances were made in all directions to locate the enemy who had fled precipitately on Wednesday. This developed quite an engagement at Cainta when a Batallion of the 20th routed nearly 1000 natives behind entrenchments with a swamp in front. They then retired to Pasig, the natives burning the town before retiring. Every one who could walk had left Pasig during the bombardment and from the looks of several buildings I fancy they did so wisely. On one bell in the church belfry I counted fourteen bullet marks and four of them had passed through the metal. . . .

On Saturday night some of the Insurgents crept up and attacked a Company of the Washingtons and the outposts of the 22nd Infantry. We lost pretty heavily for a small engagement and the General was mad all through. We chased the Indians that night until 9, bivouacking for the night and all the next day followed them down the shore as far as San Pedro Tuason. (I hope you have a map of the country.) It was a running fight all the way, the Indian loss was heavy and they were going too rapidly to carry off their dead or wounded.

At the end of the week I simply had to come back to Manila and catch up in [*sic*] the office work (which needed it) so left the brigade and the last part of its operations.

Lt. William Connor to Lt. Frederick Sladen, April 1, 1899, Personal Correspondence, Sladen Family Papers (Box 5), Archives, U.S. Military History Institute, Carlisle Barracks, Pennsylvania.

I had burned my face to a blister and that, with a scrubby beard I looked more like a highway ruffian than a U.S. Officer.

I was in town just a week when I received a telegram from Gen. Wheaton asking if I could accompany him as A.D.C. [aide de camp] on the campaign to be made against Malolos. . . .

Oregon was meantime advancing toward Polo on the left and we could hear the rest of the Division firing on our right. As soon as line[s] could be formed the Indians opened fire and I took orders to General Egbert, 22nd Inft. to advance and take the trenches at the top of the hill. Those were the last orders the little General ever got. I saw him 15 minutes later shot through and through. He died before he got to the dressing station. He recovered from a wound received in the Wilderness in the Civil war, was shot through the lungs in Cuba and recovered and then was caught by a bullet of one of the worthless niggers. The 22nd went right up and over one hill and up the next and the Indian was hunting other quarters at a splendid gait. . . .

The morning of the first advance was beautiful and to see those thousands of men (about 9000) leave the trenches just as day was breaking, to hear how the rifles commenced to crack and a distant boom of Hall's cannon, to see those lines march straight ahead all with their flags flying, to hear the shrill officers whistles and the trumpet calls and the faint [. . .] calls in the insurgent lines, then to see the dust fly up with more and more frequency when bullets struck, to get the Ping: Ping of the Mauser and the Ugh of the Remington and then to see men commence to drop and be carried off to the rear, were all things that now seem more and more like stories told by some one else than actual experience. . . .

There were lots of brave things done that day, many doubtless that will never be known to the world at large, but not done for the world at large, but for duty's sake.

It takes a few weeks of work like this to make one proud that he is an American. The average man here in the Army (Volunteer and Regular) is a type that the country can be proud of, daring fearless and generous. A Mighty poor "peace soldier" but a more than mighty good "war soldier."

William Connor

DEBATING EMPIRE

Cuba and Puerto Rico, the Philippines and Guam—these were the spoils of the short and bloody war with Spain in the spring of 1898. But what to do with them? Fortunately, the decision on Cuba and Puerto Rico had already been made; the Teller Amendment, passed by Congress before it would agree to a declaration of war, prohibited outright annexation. Besides, most Americans felt reasonably comfortable with a mini-empire in the Caribbean, traditionally seen as an American lake.

> *The Pacific acquisitions were another matter. They were not covered by the Teller Amendment, and their annexation had the look of a European-style empire—of purposeful imperialism. A national discussion began—one of the great debates in all of American history. The debate took place wherever people gathered: in barber shops and women's clubs, in schools and churches, in debating societies and general stores, and on the floor of the United States Senate, where, finally, a tie-breaking vote by the vice president announced that the Philippines would be annexed.*
>
> *Among the voices that made a difference in that debate were those of Albert J. Beveridge, Republican Senator from Indiana and a spokesman for the pro-empire position; and William Jennings Bryan, the Democratic candidate for president in 1896, and a representative of the anti-imperialist position. The Beveridge and Bryan positions presented here are each taken from two speeches. One of the central issues was whether an overseas empire was consistent with the American historical experience. How did each man deal with that issue? What other issues were involved?*

Albert J. Beveridge

MARCH OF THE FLAG

It is a noble land that God has given us; a land that can feed and clothe the world; a land whose coastlines would inclose half the countries of Europe; a land set like a sentinel between the two imperial oceans of the globe, a greater England with a nobler destiny.

It is a mighty people that He has planted on this soil; a people sprung from the most masterful blood of history; a people perpetually revitalized by the virile, man-producing working-folk of all the earth; a people imperial by virtue of their power, by right of their institutions, by authority of their Heaven-directed purposes—the propagandists and not the misers of liberty.

It is a glorious history our God has bestowed upon His chosen people; a history heroic with faith in our mission and our future; a history of statesmen who flung the boundaries of the Republic out into unexplored lands and savage wilderness; a history of soldiers who carried the flag across blazing deserts and through the ranks of hostile mountains, even to the gates of sunset; a history of a multiplying people who overran a continent in half a century; a history of prophets who saw the consequences of evils inherited from the past and of martyrs who died to save us from them; a history divinely logical, in the process of whose tremendous reasoning we find ourselves to-day.

Therefore, in this campaign, the question is larger than a party question. It is an American question. It is a world question. Shall the American people continue their march toward the commercial supremacy of the world? Shall free

Excerpts from "March of the Flag" (1898) and "Our Philippine Policy" (1900), in Albert J. Beveridge, *The Meaning of the Times and Other Speeches* (Freeport, New York: Bobbs-Merrill, 1908).

institutions broaden their blessed reign as the children of liberty wax in strength, until the empire of our principles is established over the hearts of all mankind?

Have we no mission to perform, no duty to discharge to our fellow-man? Has God endowed us with gifts beyond our deserts and marked us as the people of His peculiar favor, merely to rot in our own selfishness, as men and nations must, who take cowardice for their companion and self for their deity—as China has, as India has, as Egypt has?

Shall we be as the man who had one talent and hid it, or as he who had ten talents and used them until they grew to riches? And shall we reap the reward that waits on our discharge of our high duty; shall we occupy new markets for what our farmers raise, our factories make, our merchants sell—aye, and, please God, new markets for what our ships shall carry?

Hawaii is ours; Porto Rico is to be ours; at the prayer of her people Cuba finally will be ours; in the islands of the East, even to the gates of Asia, coaling stations are to be ours at the very least; the flag of a liberal government is to float over the Philippines, and may it be the banner that Taylor unfurled in Texas and Fremont carried to the coast.

The Opposition tells us that we ought not to govern a people without their consent. I answer, The rule of liberty that all just government derives its authority from the consent of the governed, applies only to those who are capable of self-government. We govern the Indians without their consent, we govern our territories without their consent, we govern our children without their consent. How do they know that our government would be without their consent? Would not the people of the Philippines prefer the just, humane, civilizing government of this Republic to the savage, bloody rule of pillage and extortion from which we have rescued them?

And, regardless of this formula of words made only for enlightened, self-governing people, do we owe no duty to the world? Shall we turn these peoples back to the reeking hands from which we have taken them? Shall we abandon them, with Germany, England, Japan, hungering for them? Shall we save them from those nations, to give them a self-rule of tragedy?

They ask us how we shall govern these new possessions. I answer: Out of local conditions and the necessities of the case methods of government will grow. If England can govern foreign lands, so can America. If Germany can govern foreign lands, so can America. If they can supervise protectorates, so can America. Why is it more difficult to administer Hawaii than New Mexico or California? Both had a savage and an alien population; both were more remote from the seat of government when they came under our dominion than the Philippines are to-day.

Will you say by your vote that American ability to govern has decayed; that a century's experience in self-rule has failed of a result? Will you affirm by your vote that you are an infidel to American power and practical sense? Or will you say that ours is the blood of government; ours the heart of dominion; ours the brain and genius of administration? Will you remember that we do but what our fathers did—we but pitch the tents of liberty farther westward, farther southward—we only continue the march of the flag?

The march of the flag! In 1789 the flag of the Republic waved over 4,000,000 souls in thirteen states, and their savage territory which stretched to the Mississippi, to Canada, to the Floridas. The timid minds of that day said that no new territory was needed, and, for the hour, they were right. But Jefferson, through whose intellect the centuries marched; Jefferson, who dreamed of Cuba as an American state; Jefferson, the first Imperialist of the Republic—Jefferson acquired that imperial territory which swept from the Mississippi to the mountains, from Texas to the British possessions, and the march of the flag began! . . .

And, now, obeying the same voice that Jefferson heard and obeyed, that Jackson heard and obeyed, that Monroe heard and obeyed, that Seward heard and obeyed, that Grant heard and obeyed, that Harrison heard and obeyed, our President to-day plants the flag over the islands of the seas, outposts of commerce, citadels of national security, and the march of the flag goes on! . . .

The ocean does not separate us from lands of our duty and desire—the oceans join us, rivers never to be dredged, canals never to be repaired. Steam joins us; electricity joins us—the very elements are in league with our destiny. Cuba not contiguous! Porto Rico not contiguous! Hawaii and the Philippines not contiguous! The oceans make them contiguous. And our navy will make them contiguous.

OUR PHILIPPINE POLICY

. . . the times call for candor. The Philippines are ours, "territory belonging to the United States," as the Constitution calls them. And just beyond the Philippines are China's illimitable markets. We will not retreat from either. We will not repudiate our duty in the archipelago. We will not abandon our opportunity in the Orient. We will not renounce our part in the mission of our race. And we will move forward to our work, not howling out regrets, like slaves whipped to their burdens, but with gratitude for a task worthy of our strength, and thanksgiving to Almighty God that He has deemed us worthy of His work.

This island empire is the last land left in all the oceans. If it should prove a mistake to abandon it, the blunder, once made, would be irretrievable. If it proves a mistake to hold it, the error can be corrected when we will. Every other progressive nation stands ready to relieve us.

But to hold it will be no mistake. Our increasing trade henceforth must be with Asia. More and more Europe will manufacture what it needs, secure from its colonies what it consumes. Where shall we turn for consumers of our surplus? Geography answers the question. China is our natural customer. She is nearer to us than to England, Germany or Russia, the commercial powers of the present and the future. They have moved nearer to China by securing permanent bases on her borders. The Philippines give us a base at the door of all the East. . . .

And the Pacific is the ocean of the commerce of the future. Most future wars will be conflicts for commerce. The power that rules the Pacific, therefore, is the power that rules the world. And, with the Philippines, that power will be the American Republic. . . .

It will be hard for Americans who have not studied them to understand the people. They are a barbarous race, modified by three centuries of contact with a decadent race. The Filipino is the South Sea Malay, put through a process of three hundred years of dishonesty in dealing, disorder in habits of industry, and cruelty, caprice, and corruption in government. It is barely possible that 1,000 men in all the archipelago are now capable of self-government in the Anglo-Saxon sense. . . .

. . . *it would be better to abandon the Philippines, and count our blood and treasure already spent a profitable loss, than to apply any academic arrangement of self-government to these children.* They are not yet capable of self-government. How could they be? They are not a self-governing race; they are Orientals, Malays, instructed by Spaniards in the latter's worst estate.

They know nothing of practical government, except as they have witnessed the weak, corrupt, cruel, and capricious rule of Spain. What magic will any one employ to dissolve in their minds and characters those impressions of governors and governed which three centuries of misrule has created? What alchemy will change the oriental quality of their blood, in a year, and set the self-governing currents of the American pouring through their Malay veins? How shall they, in a decade, be exalted to the heights of self-governing peoples which required a thousand years for *us* to reach?

William Jennings Bryan

AMERICA'S MISSION

When the advocates of imperialism find it impossible to reconcile a colonial policy with the principles of our government or with the canons of morality; when they are unable to defend it upon the ground of religious duty or pecuniary profit, they fall back in helpless despair upon the assertion that it is destiny. "Suppose it does violate the Constitution," they say; "suppose it does break all the commandments; suppose it does entail upon the nation an incalculable expenditure of blood and money; it is destiny and we must submit."

The people have not voted for imperialism; no national convention has declared for it; no Congress has passed upon it. To whom, then, has the future been revealed? Whence this voice of authority? We can all prophesy, but our prophecies are merely guesses, colored by our hopes and our surroundings. Man's opinion of what is to be is half wish and half environment. Avarice paints destiny with a dollar mark before it; militarism equips it with a sword. . . .

We have reached another crisis. The ancient doctrine of imperialism, banished from our land more than a century ago, has recrossed the Atlantic and challenged democracy to mortal combat upon American soil.

Excerpts from "America's Mission" (1899) and "Imperialism" (1900), in *Speeches of William Jennings Bryan*, ed. William Jennings Bryan (New York: Funk & Wagnalls, 1909), 2 vols., volume II.

Whether the Spanish war shall be known in history as a war for liberty or as a war of conquest; whether the principles of self-government shall be strengthened or abandoned; whether this nation shall remain a homogeneous republic or become a heterogeneous empire—these questions must be answered by the American people—when they speak, and not until then, will destiny be revealed.

Destiny is not a matter of chance; it is a matter of choice; it is not a thing to be waited for, it is a thing to be achieved.

So with our nation. If we embark upon a career of conquest no one can tell how many islands we may be able to seize or how many races we may be able to subjugate; neither can any one estimate the cost, immediate and remote, to the Nation's purse and to the Nation's character, but whether we shall enter upon such a career is a question which the people have a right to decide for themselves. Unexpected events may retard or advance the Nation's growth, but the Nation's purpose determines its destiny.

What is the Nation's purpose?

The main purpose of the founders of our Government was to secure for themselves and for posterity the blessings of liberty, and that purpose has been faithfully followed up to this time. Our statesmen have opposed each other upon economic questions, but they have agreed in defending self-government as the controlling national idea. They have quarreled among themselves over tariff and finance, but they have been united in their opposition to an entangling alliance with any European power. . . .

This sentiment was well-nigh universal until a year ago. It was to this sentiment that the Cuban insurgents appealed; it was this sentiment that impelled our people to enter into the war with Spain. Have the people so changed within a few short months that they are now willing to apologize for the War of the Revolution and force upon the Filipinos the same system of government against which the colonists protested with fire and sword? . . .

The forcible annexation of the Philippine Islands is not necessary to make the United States a world-power. For over ten decades our Nation has been a world-power. During its brief existence it has exerted upon the human race an influence more potent for good than all the other nations of the earth combined, and it has exerted that influence without the use of sword or Gatling gun. Mexico and the republics of Central and South America testify to the benign influence of our institutions, while Europe and Asia give evidence of the working of the leaven of self-government. In the growth of democracy we observe the triumphant march of an idea—an idea that would be weighted down rather than aided by the armor and weapons proffered by imperialism.

Much has been said of late about Anglo-Saxon civilization. Far be it from me to detract from the service rendered to the world by the sturdy race whose language we speak. . . .

Anglo-Saxon civilization has, by force of arms, applied the art of government to other races for the benefit of Anglo-Saxons; American civilization will, by the influence of example, excite in other races a desire for self-government and a determination to secure it.

Anglo-Saxon civilization has carried its flag to every clime and defended it with forts and garrisons. American civilization will imprint its flag upon the hearts of all who long for freedom.

"To American civilization, all hail!
"Time's noblest offspring is the last!"

IMPERIALISM

Even now we are beginning to see the paralyzing influence of imperialism. Heretofore this Nation has been prompt to express its sympathy with those who were fighting for civil liberty. While our sphere of activity has been limited to the Western Hemisphere, our sympathies have not been bounded by the seas. We have felt it due to ourselves and to the world, as well as to those who were struggling for the right to govern themselves, to proclaim the interest which our people have, from the date of their own independence, felt in every contest between human rights and arbitrary power.

Three-quarters of a century ago, when our nation was small, the struggles of Greece aroused our people, and Webster and Clay gave eloquent expression to the universal desire for Grecian independence. In 1898 all parties manifested a lively interest in the success of the Cubans, but now when a war is in progress in South Africa, which must result in the extension of the monarchical idea, or in the triumph of a republic, the advocates of imperialism in this country dare not say a word in behalf of the Boers. . . .

The forcible annexation of territory to be governed by arbitrary power differs as much from the acquisition of territory to be built up into States as a monarchy differs from a democracy. The Democratic party does not oppose expansion when expansion enlarges the area of the Republic and incorporates land which can be settled by American citizens, or adds to our population people who are willing to become citizens and are capable of discharging their duties as such.

The acquisition of the Louisiana territory, Florida, Texas and other tracts which have been secured from time to time enlarged the Republic and the Constitution followed the flag into the new territory. It is now proposed to seize upon distant territory already more densely populated than our own country and to force upon the people a government for which there is no warrant in our Constitution or our laws.

Even the argument that this earth belongs to those who desire to cultivate it and who have the physical power to acquire it cannot be invoked to justify the appropriation of the Philippine Islands by the United States. If the islands were uninhabited American citizens would not be willing to go there and till the soil. The white race will not live so near the equator. Other nations have tried to colonize in the same latitude. The Netherlands have controlled Java for three hundred years and yet today there are less than sixty thousand people of European birth scattered among the twenty-five million natives. . . .

The Republican platform assumes that the Philippine Islands will be retained under American sovereignty, and we have a right to demand of the Republican leaders a discussion of the future status of the Filipino. Is he to be a citizen or a subject? Are we to bring into the body politic eight or ten million Asiatics, so different from us in race and history that amalgamation is impossible? Are they to share with us in making the laws and shaping the destiny of this nation? No Republican of prominence has been bold enough to advocate such a proposition. . . .

Let us consider briefly the reasons which have been given in support of an imperialistic policy. . . .

It is argued by some that the Filipinos are incapable of self-government and that, therefore, we owe it to the world to take control of them. Admiral Dewey, in an official report to the Navy Department, declared the Flipinos more capable of self-government than the Cubans and said that he based his opinion upon a knowledge of both races. But I will not rest the case upon the relative advancement of the Filipinos. Henry Clay, in defending the right of the people of South America to self-government, said:

> "It is the doctrine of thrones that man is too ignorant to govern himself. Their partizans assert his incapacity in reference to all nations; if they cannot command universal assent to the proposition, it is then demanded to particular nations; and our pride and our presumption too often make converts of us. I contend that it is to arraign the disposition of Providence himself to suppose that he has created beings incapable of governing themselves, and to be trampled on by kings. Self-government is the natural government of man."

Clay was right. There are degrees of proficiency in the art of self-government, but it is a reflection upon the Creator to say that he denied to any people the capacity for self-government. Once admit that some people are capable of self-government and that others are not and that the capable people have a right to seize upon and govern the incapable, and you make force—brute force—the only foundation of government and invite the reign of a despot. I am not willing to believe that an all-wise and an all-loving God created the Filipinos and then left them thousands of years helpless until the islands attracted the attention of European nations. . . .

Some argue that American rule in the Philippine Islands will result in the better education of the Filipinos. Be not deceived. If we expect to maintain a colonial policy, we shall not find it to our advantage to educate the people. The educated Filipinos are now in revolt against us, and the most ignorant ones have made the least resistance to our domination. If we are to govern them without their consent and give them no voice in determining the taxes which they must pay, we dare not educate them, lest they learn to read the Declaration of Independence and Constitution of the United States and mock us for our inconsistency.

The principal arguments, however, advanced by those who enter upon a defense of imperialism are:

First—That we must improve the present opportunity to become a world power and enter into international politics.

Second—That our commercial interests in the Philippine Islands and in the Orient make it necessary for us to hold the islands permanently.

Third—That the spread of the Christian religion will be facilitated by a colonial policy.

Fourth—That there is no honorable retreat from the position which the nation has taken. . . .

It is sufficient answer to the first argument to say that for more than a century this nation has been a world power. For ten decades it has been the most potent influence in the world. Not only has it been a world power, but it has done more to shape the politics of the human race than all the other nations of the world combined. . . .

. . . the commercial argument . . . is based upon the theory that war can be rightly waged for pecuniary advantage, and that it is profitable to purchase trade by force and violence. . . .

But a war of conquest is as unwise as it is unrighteous. A harbor and coaling station in the Philippines would answer every trade and military necessity and such a concession could have been secured at any time without difficulty.

It is not necessary to own people in order to trade with them. We carry on trade today with every part of the world, and our commerce has expanded more rapidly than the commerce of any European empire. We do not own Japan or China, but we trade with their people. We have not absorbed the republics of Central and South America, but we trade with them. It has not been necessary to have any political connection with Canada or the nations of Europe in order to trade with them. Trade cannot be permanently profitable unless it is voluntary.

IMAGINING THE AFRICAN "OTHER"

Mabel E. Barnes

TOURING "DARKEST AFRICA"

America's flirtation with empire created a new and deep curiosity about "exotic" peoples and nations. The World's Fairs at Buffalo (1901) and St. Louis (1904) both had elaborate Filipino "villages," designed to show visitors what life was really like in that remote archipelago. The Filipino compound in Buffalo included houses with thatched roofs, natives making rope on a rope walk, a primitive cart drawn by water buffalo, and a reproduction of a Catholic church, where the imported Filipinos attended Sunday services.

Mabel E. Barnes, "Peeps at the Pan-American," vol. III, August 29, 1901, Nineteenth Visit, pp. 70–72, 81–88. The Barnes diary is in the collections of the Buffalo and Erie County Historical Society.

Although not an object of the nation's imperial ambition, Africa was a compelling subject of the American imagination. In that imagination, Africa was what the United States was not: primitive, sensual, black, and (always) "dark." In the following account of a visit to the African exhibit at Buffalo's Pan-American Exposition, Mabel Barnes offers us a glimpse of how Americans understood peoples who were remote and different from themselves. According to Barnes's account, what aspects of African society and culture did the exhibit highlight? What aspects of that culture touched Barnes most deeply, and why? What assumptions did Barnes make that proved not to be true? How might one relate Barnes's experience to the "Victorian" values described in Chapter 2?

𝒱 V O I C E S   Then we went on an exploring tour into "Darkest Africa." In the ballyhoo, a real pygmy, with a sheep's skin about his head, a piece of cotton cloth about his loins and glistening flesh visible everywhere else, with a quiver full of supposedly poisoned arrows hanging from his neck, executed a few steps of a barbaric dance to attract the attention of passersby.

Within there is a presentation of real African life in a real African village. The exhibit was made possible only by the cooperation of England, France, Germany, and Italy with the Buffalo Society of National Science, which accepted the sponsorship of the expedition into Africa to gather materials under the leadership of Xavier Pené, a French geographer and explorer. The original purpose of the expedition contemplated chiefly an ethological and anthropological exhibit to specially include rare types of African natives. But it was realized that an added interest would be given if the natives could be shown in their natural surroundings—and living in the native way. To this end, these natives cut and brought with them the bamboos with which to build and the reeds with which to thatch the huts they live in. They brought, also, their primitive household utensils, implements of labor, and weapons of war and of the chase, and to make the exhibit complete, there were added to the cannibals, pygmies, and semi-barbarous natives, representative native craftsmen, cloth weavers, workers in gold, and carvers of ivory. The occasional chatter of monkeys and the constant screaming of the flock of African parrots give a final touch of local color to the scene.

There are said to be ninety-eight men, women, and children. This number includes, besides the specimens of pygmies and cannibals, representatives of eleven different tribes. The latter are, for the most part, semi-civilized, as they are from the mission stations along the Congo River. This is the first time, however, that they have been outside of Africa and they are to be returned there when the exposition is over. Within their bark stockade, beyond which they are not allowed to go, they live their own lives, with some necessary concessions to the white man's ideas in the matter of clothes, etc. They may be seen at work and at play, carving ivory, weaving nets, working gold, engaging in their dances of war and peace, or indulging in the simple sports and pastimes of village life.

"Tickets Here for Darkest Africa."
Buffalo and Erie County Historical Society.

The headman, Chief Ogolaurie is a fine speciman [*sic*] of the semi-barbarous African. He has in all fifty-six wives, fifty-three of these having been left behind. The three who are with him treat him with the deference paid by oriental women to their lords. They speak only when spoken to, but stand ready to obey his every behest. The chief's son, Ogandaga is the active head of the native life and decked out in barbarous finery conducts the fetish dances.

In one of the buildings constructed by the native workmen is a construction of musical instruments, weapons, idols, and curios. . . . Here is a queer shaped native drum, almost as high as the roof, that has sounded the call to cannibal orgies. . . . These spears have been bathed in the blood of battle, those lances have stood the lion's charge, and that quiver is filled with arrows so deadly that a prick from their poisoned tips means quick death. Here are the gods of fetishism, every one of which has a tale of human sacrifice to its credit, and in that corner is a tusk carved with a long procession of women winding round and round from base to top, a sort of family tree, the carver of which added a new figure every time he took a new wife. . . .

But the finest exhibits are the natives themselves. Their bodies are slender, strong, and clean; their eyes large, clear, and full of life; their teeth milk white, firm and well-shaped. They are great bathers, these barbarians; they demand a bath every night, and they rub themselves daily with palm oil. The result is a skin so smooth, so fine in texture that it resembles brown satin. To the unpracticed eye there is little to distinguish a native of one tribe from another, but to an expert, each tribe differs in dress, decoration, or mutilation. Some have their teeth filed in a distinctive manner; others are curiously tattooed, the tattooing being not a mere pattern printed on the skin, but markings raised by some painful process to stand out in relief against the flat surface of the body. We saw two women who were decorated in this way from the throat down with a design in arabesque. The women seem more addicted to this sort of decoration than the men. One of the latter, in whom we became especially interested, had a skin so free from blemish, so clean and smooth that it almost tempted one to lay hands upon it. Miss Hale and I were making some comment upon it, not realizing that the owner of the skin, who, moreover, was of rather an intelligent appearance, could understand English, when a knowing and amused expression on his face led me to ask hastily, "Do you understand?," and his reply was, "a little." So we had a few words of conversation as we watched him weave a net of intricate pattern which he explained was for fishing, and then he had to leave us to join in one of the native dances given in an open pavilion.

Each dance has its own significance, and this was described for the instruction of the spectators. . . . [for example], in a time of plague, a dance is begun while the obiman, or witch-doctor, moves along the line to "smell out" the witch who has laid a spell upon the people and their cattle. Imagine the terror of the natives who shrink from the man whose touch means death. Some victory must be had, and if any unfortunate has incurred the ill will of the obiman, he knows that the hour of vengeance has come. It is in such settings as these that the spectator must frame the picture on the stage and remember that the performers have gone through the same ceremonials in darkest Africa to avert threatened famine or present plague and that their hearts have throbbed to the rhythm and the drums which called for a sacrifice to the blood-thirsty deity.

The two extremes of the native religions are illustrated in the village,—Mohammedanism and Fetishism. The representative of the one—the mullah—calls the faithful to prayer with the same call that rises from the lips of the muezzin on oriental minarets. The chief priest of the other leads the barbaric fetish dance about the grotesque image of stone that he worships.

At the farther end of the enclosure are clustered the little huts in which the native craftsmen ply their arts. Here a goldworker with a few primitive tools forges and decorates a ring of yellow African gold; there a carver in ivory reproduces a Midway type with excellent fidelity, for simple as they are, these natives are also quick at observing the customs of the world outside their bark enclosure, a world of which they catch glimpses only from the watchtowers on the stockade. One ivory group shows a woman, an American, with an [sic] parasol in a jinrickisha, another depicts the parade of the Mexican vaqueros next door.

We spent two interesting hours in the African village, and when it began to grow dark, we left the grounds for home.

THE SEARCH FOR THE PRIMITIVE: TARZAN OF THE APES

The Cover of the September 10, 1912, Issue of *The All-Story*
Magazine, in Which Edgar Rice Burroughs's *Tarzan of the Apes*
First Appeared. The epic tale was very much about empire and
race. The story concerns an Englishman, Lord Greystoke
(Tarzan), raised from infancy entirely by apes and mothered by
the ape Kala, whose death—at the hands of a black man—
Tarzan avenges. Does the cover image resonate with Mabel
Barnes's experience at Buffalo's African exhibit?

the big picture

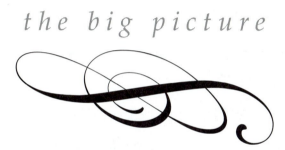

Why did the American people take on an empire—even a small one—at the turn of the century? Do you think Mabel Barnes would have sided with Albert J. Beveridge or with William Jennings Bryan?

c h a p t e r   s i x

PROGRESSIVISM: THE AGE OF REFORM

H istorian Richard Hofstadter gave us the theme for this chapter in 1955 when he published his conclusions about populism and progressivism in a book titled *The Age of Reform*. A half century later, it is not at all clear what this phenomenon called "progressivism" was, or whether its agents, the "progressives," were really very progressive. Hofstadter in fact argued that at the heart of progressivism was a vision of the past, an attempt to restore economic individualism and political democracy, values that had been buried under giant corporations, burgeoning unions, and corrupt political bosses. With the exception of Theodore Roosevelt, who believed that most big business could not and should not be eliminated, progressives, according to Hofstadter, generally tried to disassemble existing institutions. The progressive movement, he wrote, was "the complaint of the unorganized against the consequences of organization."

Others have argued that progressivism was not nostalgic but aggressively future-oriented. According to this view, progressivism cannot be separated from the "organizational revolution" taking place at the turn of the century. Products of that revolution include trade associations, new government agencies, the organized professions, and an increased willingness to use federal rather than state and local agencies to achieve economic and social goals. But there are real problems even in placing specific movements within this organizational context. Did new government regulations represent the past or the future? Were they designed to bring change or to preserve the status quo?

The most recent effort to understand progressivism emphasizes the prominence of women in setting the progressive agenda and in the legislative process. This view foregrounds the creation of the U.S. Children's Bureau in 1912 (the first government agency run by women), the passage of mothers' pension laws in most states, and the Sheppard-Towner Act of 1921 (money for health-care clinics and to reduce infant mortality). At bottom, this women's perspective holds that the foundations of the American welfare state were poured not by male-dominated political parties but by women—most of them still without the right to vote—organized in a variety of voluntary associations.

The title of Hofstadter's study implies the ability to recognize a reform when we see one, and much of the history of the progressive period has been written from this assumption. But here, too, there are difficulties. When Theodore Roosevelt broke with the Republican Party in 1912 and campaigned for the presidency under the banner of the Progressive Party (not to be confused with the more general term "progressivism"), his Bull Moose platform was a classic summary of social reforms long identified with progressivism— minimum wages for women, prohibition of child labor, the eight-hour workday, and workmen's compensation. For years, however, Roosevelt had been involved with birth-control advocate Margaret Sanger and with Stanford University president David Starr Jordan and other luminaries in another "reform" effort, the eugenics movement, which many progressives found unappealing. In a letter written in 1914, Roosevelt described and explained his interest in eugenics:

> I wish very much that the wrong people could be prevented entirely from breeding; and when the evil nature of these people is sufficiently flagrant, this should be done. Criminals should be sterilized and feeble-minded persons forbidden to leave offspring behind them. But as yet there is no way possible to devise a system which could prevent all undesirable persons from breeding.

For Roosevelt, eugenics deserved the label "reform" every bit as much as the movement to abolish child labor. Others, including historians, have disagreed, and therein lies a central problem with the word *reform.*

Nor is the difficulty resolved simply by focusing on what seem to be clearly benign reforms. One of the most popular progressive-period programs was state workmen's compensation legislation, under which injured workers were compensated according to predetermined schedules, rather than by virtue of what they could recover through legal action. By what standards is workmen's compensation "reform"? Is it an example of progressivism? Feminists of the 1970s and 1980s would raise similar, and worthwhile, questions about the many progressive-era laws that regulated hours and conditions for working women. In 1910 those laws seemed to be important measures of protection; today they seem to be obstacles to equality of the sexes. Where those laws, even in 1910, a clear example of social progress?

Still, certain features of progressivism stand out. One need only mention the major regulatory measures of the period to grasp the importance of regulation (a word, it should be emphasized, with no more real content than *reform*).

Out of a financial panic in 1907 came the Federal Reserve System, created in 1913 to provide a more flexible currency. Several pieces of railroad legislation, including the Elkins Act (1903) and the Hepburn Act (1906), were designed to limit rebates (unfair price cutting by the carriers) and to give the Interstate Commerce Commission, then two decades old, the authority to fix maximum rates. Congress also provided for federal inspection of meat packers that shipped in interstate commerce and created the Federal Trade Commission (1914) to supervise the competitive relations of interstate businesses. State and local governments were also active in the regulatory movement and were the major agencies of change in such social-justice areas as hours of labor, child labor, mothers' pensions, and tenement-house reform. The progressive period is also well known for a series of measures designed to change the terms of access to the political system. For example, a 1913 amendment to the Constitution provided that U.S. senators would be elected directly by the people of their states, rather than by the state legislatures. And some western states enacted reforms known as initiative (by which the electorate could make laws directly, while voting), referendum (by which voters expressed opinions on issues), and recall (allowing voters to remove public officials from office). The impact of these political reforms was mixed. They did, indeed, increase the role of ordinary citizens in public affairs. But often they were co-opted and used by big business or political machines.

Aside from the dramatic rise in the use of government as a social tool, the qualities that gave unity to progressivism were attitudinal and ideological. Progressives believed in data. They believed in the possibilities of "scientific" social welfare, supported by research; of market research in selling; and of measuring the abilities of employees through psychological testing. This faith in science was often accompanied by a fear of national moral collapse. It was this kind of thinking that led to the founding of the Boy Scouts of America in 1910 and to Roosevelt's enchantment with eugenics.

Finally, progressivism was not, at least on the surface, a matter of class interests, of one group seeking hegemony over another. For progressives, the political system was not a device by which conflicting interests compromised (or failed to compromise) their essential differences; it was a means through which the essential harmony of all interests might be expressed. Perhaps because of this emphasis on harmony, the declaration of war in April 1917 ushered in a brief period in which the progressive spirit of reform was reincarnated as a struggle against German autocracy. Led by Woodrow Wilson, Americans came to understand the war as a holy crusade, a great struggle, as Wilson put it, to "make the world safe for democracy."

interpretive essay

Robyn Muncy

BUSTING THE TRUSTS,
FOR MANHOOD'S SAKE

It is common knowledge that the progressives "busted the trusts"—that is, broke up big business. The term "trust" had once meant a specific kind of business corporation, created when stockholders transferred their stock to "trustees." The Standard Oil Company, created in 1882, was the first trust of this sort, and it was followed by dozens of others, including the Amalgamated Copper Company (1889, 35 plants or properties controlled); American Tobacco (1904, about 200 plants controlled); and U.S. Steel Corporation (1901, nearly 800 plants controlled). By 1902, when President Theodore Roosevelt moved to break up the Northern Securities Corporation, a giant railroad conglomerate, "trust" had become a generic word, connoting a business so big and powerful that it was dangerous to the public interest.

Had some big businesses become too big, too powerful? If so, what should be done about them? Should they be regulated and controlled, or broken up? For more than a decade, Americans discussed and debated these programs. Or did they? Robyn Muncy's essay returns us to these familiar issues, only to cut the ground from under the easy and familiar assumption that the trusts were of concern to everyone. Viewing the issue from the perspective of multiculturalism— that is, using race, class, and gender as categories of analysis—she finds that some people took up the issue while others did not, and that those who took it up may have had something other than the economy in mind when they did so.

Muncy's analysis raises a variety of questions. First, if something as basic as busting the trusts can be reduced to an issue of gender, could not the same be said for any issue, in any period? If so, are not all issues—political, economic, social—to be understood primarily as questions of gender? Can you think of issues—historical or current—that would not reflect gender differences?

Robyn Muncy, "Trustbusting and White Manhood in America, 1898–1914," *American Studies,* 38 (fall 1997): 21–37. Reprinted from *American Studies* by permission. © Mid-American American Studies Association.

A second question has to do with what it takes, or means, to be a "man" or
a "woman" in different eras (that is, Muncy's essay assumes that gender roles
are socially and historically determined). If, as Muncy seems to suggest, it was
increasingly hard to be manly at the turn of the twentieth century, is it even
more difficult at the turn of the twenty-first? Similarly, do black men face more
obstacles to masculinity today than they did a century ago, or fewer? Finally,
what difference, if any, has a century made in how men achieve masculinity?

"I care more for the independence and manliness of the American citizen than for all the gold or silver in the world," declared the Progressive governor of Michigan in 1899. Hazen Pingree thus concluded a speech denouncing the trusts, those huge corporations that seemed to be swallowing up individual enterprises at the turn-of-the-century. Indeed, Governor Pingree believed that those corporations were undermining the foundation of American manhood, and, in order to restore manliness, he was willing to sacrifice the greater wealth that giant enterprises might create. This essay returns to the Progressive-era debate over trusts and argues that, as Pingree's speech suggested, that debate was in part an argument over the shape that white manhood should take in the twentieth-century United States.

Historians often set responses to corporations at the heart of Progressivism, that early twentieth-century hodgepodge of "shifting coalitions" which ultimately produced such a range of reforms as Prohibition and women's suffrage, a graduated income tax and mothers' pensions, workmen's compensation and the direct election of senators. Richard Hofstadter, for instance, insisted that "big business was the ultimate enemy of the Progressive." In most analyses, this turn-of-the-century concern has been construed as an anxiety about how to preserve local autonomy, a competitive economic system with a fairly equal distribution of wealth, and ultimately a representative political system. Large corporations, according to many Progressives and their historians, swallowed up smaller enterprises, robbing men of the economic independence on which democracy itself depended. Other commentators both then and later also showed that organized capital corrupted the political process by buying off legislators and in that way, too, threatened representative government. "The life of the Trusts or the life of the republic—which?" This was America's stark choice according to muckraking journalist Charles Edward Russell.

Although perhaps no issue in United States history would seem mustier than Progressive-era trustbusting, I have revisited many of the speeches, editorials, books, and essays produced by the furor over big business and discovered two new and related aspects of it. The first is the degree to which the trust question was, in the early twentieth-century, a race and gender specific issue. My research suggests that the debate occurred almost exclusively within the community of white men. Black Progressives—men and women—and white women activists, volubly discussing other problems of the day, largely ignored this issue. Second, for at least some of the white men who participated in the struggle over the proper response to large corporations, the debate embodied a contest over the meaning of white manhood. This is not to argue that many other issues were not also at stake in the debate over corporations. Rather, this essay seeks simply to illuminate a previously undetected dimension of the controversy: for some, this debate was partly a battle over gender identities. For many of these men, of course, gender—or the particular shape that manhood would take—was integral to the fate of democracy. As Governor Pingree insisted: "A democratic republic cannot survive the disappearance of a democratic population," by which he meant "our independent and intelligent business men and artisans. . . ."

Pingree's belief that particular forms of manhood were integral to particular forms of government coincides with the current claim that gender has always been a constitutive element of institutions. Building on that insight, recent historians of the Progressive era have gone a long way toward understanding how gender (modified by race and class) structured political cultures and legislative agendas. We have come to see, for instance, that women and men reformers often had different public values and employed different strategies for effecting change and that only by understanding the interplay of these gendered political cultures can we fully comprehend Progressive reform. We have also begun to understand the ways that notions about proper manhood and womanhood shaped policies like mothers' pensions and workmen's compensation. This essay carries the same project into a more unlikely area of Progressive agitation: the debate over the shape of economic institutions. It shows that gender structured even the debate over "trusts."

At the turn of the century, Americans staked out a variety of positions with regard to the emergence of huge corporate enterprises, often lumped together under the name "trusts." While conservatives believed that businesses should be left alone to grow as big as markets allowed them to, progressive reformers believed that the federal government should intervene. But reformers did not agree on the goal of intervention. Some believed that the federal government should break up corporate combinations. "I favor complete and prompt annihilation of the trust," Pingree baldly put it. Others insisted that the trusts were here to stay and that the federal obligation was to regulate them in the interest of workers and consumers. Representing this position, progressive mayor of Toledo, Samuel Jones, insisted: "our problem is not how to destroy them, but how to use them for the good of all." Others, like Theodore Roosevelt during his presidency (1901–1909), supported both trustbusting and regulation as they came to believe that some trusts were good and others bad. Bad trusts had to be busted; good trusts had to be regulated to make sure that they honestly served the public.

TRUSTBUSTERS

Trustbusters, those who advocated breaking up big businesses, believed that large corporations threatened free enterprise and representative government; they also sometimes argued explicitly that enormous corporations were destroying American manhood. According to those like Hazen Pingree, this destruction occurred because corporate combinations snatched away the possibility of economic independence, which these commentators construed as the most significant foundation of American manhood.

This perception was laid out in some detail, for instance, in a 1902 editorial in the weekly news magazine, the *Independent.* Because of trusts like Standard Oil and U.S. Steel, the editor argued, "there are left to-day few opportunities for the man who would prefer economic independence to a life of service as a salaried employee." During the nineteenth century, he insisted, young men sought the economic independence offered by ownership of their own businesses, but, in the present day, corporate capitalism was reducing such aspiring businessmen to "industrial dependents, receiving fixed salaries and liable to dismissal without warning. . . ." The editor argued that if businesses continued to combine in ever larger corporate entities, then

> Every man who is not a multimillionaire will be a *millionaire's man,* dependent upon the good will of a superior for his daily bread. Could there be a more melancholy outcome of our great American attempt to build up a civilization in which every man might be independent and self-respecting?

Within corporations, in other words, all employees were analogous to servants; they could not achieve the independence of mind and action that this writer believed had previously characterized white American men. "As the number of economic dependents increases," the author worried, *"Where will independent manhood be?"*

Although such commentators exaggerated the degree to which their nineteenth-century predecessors actually achieved and maintained economic independence, their ideas about the past embodied cultural meanings well established in the nineteenth century. A generation of historians have gathered evidence showing that Americans who wielded cultural and political power in the mid-nineteenth century associated "dependence" with women and black men, and "independence" with white men only. In fact, recent studies suggest that dependence became more exclusively associated with women in the nineteenth-century United States than it had been ever before. In early modern Europe, independence was ascribed only to the few men who owned property. "Dependence" had marked not only women but also the majority of men, who were peasants or retainers laboring on someone else's land or in someone else's household. Only in the late eighteenth-century United States, with its relatively widespread landownership and a political commitment to "independence" for all white men, did property ownership (usually ownership of a farm or business) become accepted as the norm for white men and thus a basis of white manhood itself.

The emergence of industrial capitalism complicated this construction of white manhood. It began to create a working class in which few men could, even in the nineteenth century, hope to own a farm or business, the quintessential foundation of manly independence. As the pre-industrial organization of labor gave way to industrial production, journeymen in transformed industries lost hope of ever owning their own shop. They became permanent wage-earners in someone else's business. Even so, because independence had become so crucial to white manhood itself, these workers refused to see themselves outside the realm of "independent" men. In order to satisfy the cultural imperative that real men be "independent," these workers, according to analysts Linda Gordon and Nancy Fraser, began to insist that "independence" rested less on property ownership than on earning a family wage, that is, on supporting a dependent wife and children.

Thus, by the time of the trustbusting debate, "independence" was culturally connected with manhood for both working- and middle-class white men. For middle-class white men, this manly independence rested especially on ownership of a farm or business. For working-class white men, it rested especially on earning a family wage.

In addition to these cultural ideals, trustbusters were responding to material circumstances that dominated American life at the beginning of the twentieth century. Economic changes did indeed seem to be luring increasing numbers of men away from the kind of economic independence that early twentieth-century commentators believed American men had enjoyed earlier in the nineteenth century. According to historian Naomi Lamoreaux, for instance, "more than 1800 firms disappeared into consolidations" between 1895 and 1904. Nell Irvin Painter put it another way: between 1897 and 1904 "one-third of all companies disappeared through mergers." Furthermore, farm owners accounted for a smaller and smaller proportion of gainfully employed Americans between 1900 and 1930. In contrast, positions for salaried professionals, managers and clerks multiplied rapidly. This "new middle-class" of salaried employees constituted the fastest growing sector of the labor market at the turn of the century, and, by 1910, the people in this new middle class actually outnumbered independent businessmen and professionals by 5,609,000 to 3,261,000.

These numbers did not, of course, signal the disappearance of small business or demonstrate that men in large corporations did not enjoy any independence. Statistics show the contrary: that the absolute number of small firms actually increased in the 1890s and during the two subsequent decades as well. Especially in sectors of the economy not dominated by capital-intensive mass production, smaller enterprises continued to rule the day. Moreover, historian Olivier Zunz has shown that the first generation of salaried corporate managers exercised considerable autonomy in creating a new, rationalized work culture and bureaucratic organizations. Indeed, Zunz argues that, for some middle managers at least, the early years of building corporations offered wider ranging responsibilities and possibilities than ownership of a smaller business would have.

Nevertheless, Zunz agrees with turn-of-the-century critics that such managers did indeed "relinquish individualism." Furthermore, the implication of his argument is that managerial autonomy diminished with the passing of the first generation of managers, and the much larger and ever growing group of white-collar clerks never exercised such autonomy. Finally, no one has denied that self-employment accounted for a continually decreasing proportion of the work force at the turn of the century.

Thus, despite the persistence of small business and the relative autonomy enjoyed by the first generation of managers, antitrust agitators had material foundations for their claims. They had reason to believe that "bigness" was the inevitable trend if businesses were allowed to go their own way without government intervention. They were right to think that increasing numbers of American men would find employment only as the employees of someone else and that most such men would have less freedom of action than they would have had in their own enterprises.

Trustbusters continually lamented the demotion from independence to dependence that they believed was increasingly the fate of these men. As one commentator put it: "The middle class is becoming a salaried class and rapidly losing the economic and moral independence of former days." In his condemnation of what he called the Tobacco Trust, the muckraker Charles Edward Russell wrote: "On a certain stretch of Broadway where ten years ago were thirty-six independent cigar stores are now but six; and the former proprietors of the other thirty are either salesmen for the Trust, servitors, dependent for their bread upon whim, fancy, and caprice . . . or they have sought other work; or they have died."

That this loss of independence constituted a loss of manliness in the eyes of many turn-of-the-century commentators is further supported by the classic antitrust work, *The History of the Standard Oil Company.* In this analysis, Ida Tarbell narrated the struggles of Midwestern oil refiners and producers to remain independent in the face of unfair business practices by John Rockefeller during the late nineteenth century. So, as long as those valiant businessmen fought against Rockefeller's attempts to reduce them to "industrial dependents," they in her words "struggled manfully."

Tarbell's contemporary, Samuel Gompers, had much to say about manful struggle as well, but while Tarbell saw such struggle among small businessmen, Gompers located it in workingmen's determination to unionize in the face of corporate hostility. For example, in response to U.S. Steel's attempt to crush workers' organizations in 1910, Gompers reported that the men "did resist and are resisting manfully, grandly, heroically."

Although Gompers and his American Federation of Labor urged the breakup of U.S. Steel, they were not wholesale trustbusters. They rather accepted large corporations as a permanent part of the American economy, advocating demolition only of corporations bent on destroying workers' collective efforts to affect working conditions and compensation. Given the expectation of wage-earning among these men, one might expect that they viewed themselves as "industrial dependents" and rested their manhood on some other foundation. This was not so. Workingmen in the AFL defined "independence" in a different way from middle-class men, and they continued to see this form of independence as crucial to their manly identities.

For organized labor in the early twentieth century, "independence" referred to a worker's ability to unite with other workers to gain some control over their working lives. One labor journalist wrote: "The methods of the trade unionists of America . . . free labor from a *slavish dependence* either upon the unstable philanthropy or the contemptuous labor trafficking which are features of today's multi-millionaires." Another insisted that the goal of unionization was "to improve the standard of life, to uproot ignorance and foster education, to instill character, manhood, and independent spirit among our people. . . ." "If the workers are to be deprived of their opportunities for self-improvement and independence," this last writer continued, "if they are to be held at the will of the employer . . . the industrial condition of our country would sink lower than that of slavery."

Anti-union trusts, then, threatened workingmen's independence as well as that of middle-class men, and working-class men connected their manly identities with this independence. Gompers, for instance, argued that corporate attempts to break unions constituted an "effort to curb and crush American manhood and its spirit of sovereignty and independence." Speaking of U.S. Steel, the AFL leader said, "The gigantic trust . . . has used and is using its great wealth and power in an effort to rob the toilers, not only of their livelihood, but of their rights of American manhood. . . ." He believed that the only hope for limiting the trusts' influence over American life lay in the "virile power" of organized labor. Finally, workers striking U.S. Steel needed support from fellow workers "to maintain themselves, their wives, and little ones . . . so that their independence, character, and American conception of manhood may be sustained. . . ."

In the 1912 presidential election, Gompers supported Woodrow Wilson, who agreed that trusts undermined American manhood. During the campaign, Wilson exaggerated the earlier analogy between a salaried man and a servant, invoking instead the metaphor of master and slave. Wilson represented his most powerful opponent's plan to regulate a big business as a consummation of the partnership between monopolies and the federal government, which would create, in Wilson's words, "a master." "I don't care how benevolent the master is going to be," Wilson warned, "I will not live under a master. That is not what America was created for. . . . *Benevolence never developed a man* or a nation."

Wilson's words and those of other trustbusters embodied the belief that economic independence—defined differently by middle- and working-class men—had been the foundation of American manhood. Acceptance of large corporations and government regulation, they thought, threatened that independence. Indeed, some Americans—perhaps the majority in 1912—could not imagine manliness without independence.

NONCOMBATANTS

As Wilson's analogy between a salaried man and a slave suggests, the manhood at issue in battles between trustbusters and their opponents was specifically *white* manhood. This was evidenced further by the fact that black

Progressives rarely participated in the debate. For instance, the *Crisis*, journalistic organ of the National Association for the Advancement of Colored People and voice of many black progressives, did not devote one single article or editorial to government policy toward big business from 1911–1913, years when policy toward corporations was hotly debated in the white-dominated press. Indeed, only one column mentioned trusts at all, and it was a brief article on a black community in Alabama that was built on land somehow ceded by the state legislature to an interstate power company. The community was going to court to protest.

Other sources, too, reveal the unimportance of the trust issue among black men. When the National Baptist Convention endorsed William Howard Taft for president in 1912, the body published its reasons for supporting the incumbent in a presidential contest especially focused on trusts and tariffs: the Convention did not mention economic policy at all. Articles in the black-run newspaper, *The Bee*, even when they took up the high cost of living—usually a prelude to lambasting the trusts in white-dominated publications—never mentioned the conglomerates as a probable culprit.

Moreover, in one of his editorials several months after Woodrow Wilson took office in 1913, W.E.B. Du Bois, the country's leading black male progressive, explicitly stated the relative unimportance to black people of the issues that had dominated the campaign of 1912, among them the issues connected with big business. "Of course, the real trouble is," he insisted, "that President Wilson . . . may continue to think that the Tariff and Corporate control and China are the only pressing questions in National politics." Du Bois wanted to set the record straight: "The *Crisis* is here to emphasize the fact that Lynching, Disfranchisement, Peonage and Discrimination in Civil Rights are just as large and in many respects larger questions. . . ."

Indeed, it was precisely in these abrogations of civil and political rights that black men saw assaults on their manhood. In Mississippi, for instance, black leaders called disfranchisement a "policy of crushing out the manhood of the Negro citizen." In an early issue of the *Crisis*, Du Bois resolved "to be satisfied with no treatment which ignores my manhood," which required him "to be ready at all times and in all places to bear witness with pen, voice, money and deed against the . . . wrong of disfranchisement. . . ." Reverend I. N. Ross, pastor of the Metropolitan A.M.E. Church in Washington, D.C., insisted "The man who asks me or my people to vote the Democratic ticket [in 1912] . . . places a low estimate upon the manhood of a people who have been sold in bondage by the sponsors of Democracy. . . ." "As long as the jim-crow car, disfranchisement, lynching, and segregation remain as the ruling principle of the Democratic party," Ross wrote, "it is absolutely impossible for any self-respecting Negro to vote for its candidates."

Historian Neil McMillan has shown that the modifications that Southern whites forced on race relations in the 1890s also required a return to rigid rituals of social deference from black people toward whites. This, too, black men experienced as an attack on their manhood. Du Bois insisted that "playing the man" included a resolve "to stand straight, look the world squarely in the eye, and walk to my work with no shuffle or slouch . . . to refuse to cringe in body or in soul, to resent deliberate insult, and assert my just rights in the face of wanton aggression." Richard Wright would later call the requirement of deference the denial of "manly self-assertion on the part of the Negro." A Mississippi mother discouraged her Northern-educated son from returning to his home state, arguing that the deference required of him "would make him much less than the man we would have him be."

Black men, then, at the turn-of-the-century, did not see huge corporations as the threat to their manliness that some white men did. This was not only because of fiercer assaults from elsewhere (as outlined above) but also because black men were not swept up in the corporate mergers of the late nineteenth and early twentieth centuries to the degree that white men were. The overwhelming number of black men continued to live in rural communities in the South, and many continued to strive for the kind of independence that a family farm might provide. Racial discrimination prevented black men from finding employment among the ranks of managers in ever-growing, white-dominated corporations, and especially before World War I, African-American men even had trouble getting employment as waged workers in many industries.

The popularity of the economic self-help movement among African Americans opens another window on issues of black manhood. It suggests first of all just how unaffected by corporate mergers African Americans were: Booker T. Washington and his colleagues were not preaching a return to or preservation of individual proprietorships but the *initial* development of small business enterprises serving local African American communities. Second, the goal of the National Negro Business League and similar organizations was the achievement of the same economic independence cherished by white trustbusters, and some black commentators explicitly connected this independence to black manhood. R.L. Smith, for instance, founder of the Farmers' Improvement Society of Texas, believed his organization would "bring about a self-reliant manhood. . . ."

But, finally, for African American men, building a small business or buying a farm was not made difficult by competition from larger businesses. It was made difficult by racist financial institutions and lending practices; by wages so low and sharecropping so unlucrative that saving for the creation of a business was nearly impossible; by racist white consumers who often refused to purchase goods or services from black businessmen; and by the poverty of black communities, which could not support many entrepreneurs. Thus, although Washington's gospel of self-help promoted an understanding of manhood similar to that advocated by white trustbusters, the very different relations of black and white men to corporate combinations meant that this shared notion of manhood did not bring black and white men together in the movement against the trusts.

Just as black men showed little concern over the trusts so American women, black and white, mostly ignored this "problem." While the debate between busters and regulators raged in such periodicals as the *Independent, Nation, Outlook,* and *Harper's Weekly* as well as in academic social science journals, women's magazines virtually ignored the issue. Among the 246 articles that the *Readers' Guide to Periodical Literature* listed under the topic of trusts between 1910 and 1914, only 2 appeared in women's magazines, both published in *The Ladies Home Journal,* and both of them condescending to women and written by men. In fact, of the 72 articles written by authors whose gender is known, all were written by men. This includes the many articles that appeared in social science periodicals where women were debating other issues of the day but remained silent on the issue of the trusts. Even the *Woman's Journal,* a more politically engaged women's periodical than those indexed in the *Readers' Guide,* did not in the years between 1905–1908 or 1911–13 take up the issue of corporate control. Indeed, the only woman who wrote substantially about the trusts was Ida Tarbell, whose exposes on Standard Oil early in the century made her a name as a muckraking journalist.

The problem of trusts also did not show up on the agenda of organized women. One place where progressive black women gathered regularly was in the national conventions of the National Association of Colored Women. Organized in 1896 and growing throughout the Progressive era, the NACW studied and took action on lynching, jim crow, women's suffrage, juvenile justice, and many other issues of the day. But again, while the white-dominated press was vigorously debating government policy toward corporations, the issue never appeared on a national program of the NACW from 1896 through 1918. Neither did the issue of corporate combinations appear on a program of the General Federation of Women's Clubs in this period despite the participation of those clubs in numerous other progressive causes.

In fact, progressive women routinely discussed many other economic/industrial issues, including some that were raised by the emergence of giant corporations. In civic organizations, white women wrestled with municipal ownership of utilities, urban transportation systems, homework, and factory inspection. Moreover, although women's magazines almost never touched the *general* issue of government policy toward big business, they did report on and educate their readers as to the effects of specific governmental regulations on women's lives as consumers and domestic managers. These articles and discussions made the lack of interest in trusts all the more meaningful.

Occasionally, women campaigning for the Progressive party in 1912 mentioned the problem of large corporations. In a meeting of progressives in October 1912, for instance, Jane Addams insisted "we must have concentration in our industries just as we have concentration in our cities. We need control of business, however, and that is what the Progressive Party is seeking." Another activist, Kate Robinson from Tennessee, listed ten reasons that she was a Progressive party member and included "the Progressives are the only body of men and women who understand what to do with 'the trust.'"

Such references to big business were the very rare exception, however, even among female activists in this political party devoted to regulating big business. Its position on the trusts was the tenth out of ten reasons that Kate Robinson was a Progressive, and Jane Addams in her speech acknowledged that the issue of trusts was "not generally regarded as a woman's subject."

When women organized state level progressive groups that in every other way mirrored the organization of the national party, they nevertheless omitted committees on trusts.

This lack of interest makes sense insofar as the growth of huge corporations did not rob women of some previous foundation for womanhood. The kind of economic independence offered to American men in the nineteenth century had never been generally available to women, and, if anything, the growth of corporations opened new opportunities for some white women to achieve greater economic independence than before. Employment as secretaries and clerks, sometimes accountants and bookkeepers, within corporate enterprises made possible a degree of independence from individual male relatives previously rare for women, but, because women hardly ever moved into managerial positions or sat on boards of directors, they for the most part remained subordinate to men within corporate structures themselves. Within the context of corporations, then, the accepted gender hierarchy remained intact. Moreover, the new job possibilities held out for middle-class women by corporate growth did not block them from earlier gender identities as seemed to be the case for men; it merely created new options for those who wanted them.

This debate, then, sometimes represented as the vital center of Progressivism, was very race- and gender-specific.

PROPONENTS OF BIG BUSINESS

In opposition to trustbusters, a range of white men believed that big businesses were best for America: laissez-faire Republicans, socialists, and those progressive reformers who supported governmental regulation of business. All of these advocates had to respond to accusations that huge corporate combinations destroyed American manhood. I read these responses as evidence that the trustbusting debate was indeed in part about the meaning of white manhood and offer some examples of those responses here.

Some advocates of big business simply asserted that competition remained so important within corporate life that independent thought and action—supposedly elements of nineteenth-century manhood—continued to be fostered there. One writer for *Harper's Weekly* noted that "the great indictment" against the corporations "has been that in the development of so huge a machine the value of the individual has been lost, his personal qualifications as well as his *identity merged in the mass*, opportunity for distinction and field for personal accomplishment abolished." In response to that indictment, *Harper's* surveyed the largest American industries and not surprisingly found that corporate executives insisted: "Individuality counts for more to-day than ever before." The same claim was made by James Dill, a corporate lawyer, who, at the commencement ceremonies of Williams College in 1900, responded to fears that college men would not enjoy the same opportunities as their fathers: "Individualism is not dead."

But in both cases, speakers for corporate enterprise were on the defensive, trying to convince their audiences that the manly qualities admired in the nineteenth century would continue to be rewarded in an entirely new economic context. Nevertheless, everything that these apologists described about life in a large corporation suggested that only a very few men could be rewarded by advancement to creative levels of authority and that the primary goal of all men in a corporation was to learn the system already in place and dutifully follow the routines established for efficient operation of their departments. Nothing that these advocates described confirmed their conclusion that individualism or independence were qualities generally nurtured by large corporate concerns.

Less defensive were those who named alternative sources for American manhood. For example, Rev. Henry A. Stimson argued in 1901 that "there has been no more important agency for the production of character than the responsibility of managing an individual business." Consequently, it was frightening that "individual business is disappearing." He went on to say that corporations could not, however, hope to survive "with men in whom manhood in its finer forms is not both stimulated and rewarded." The only institution left, Stimson argued, that could create "that type of manhood" was the church. Unlike those who simply asserted without evidence that an earlier form of manhood would continue to be created by the new corporations, Stimson believed that they could not. But, rather than taking this to mean that the corporations must be destroyed, he identified the church as an alternative source of traditional manly qualities.

A completely different kind of case for big business—under government regulation and possibly government ownership—was made by the socialist and naturalist Jack London. London turned on its head the assumption that individual enterprise allowed men to be free while salaried employees were forced to be yes-men to their superiors. London argued that the "nineteenth century business man . . . is the *slave* of his desk, the genie of the dollar." Because every man has, in a competitive economic system, to worry about nothing else except making a living, "individuality is repressed, forced to manifest itself in acquisitiveness and selfishness." London argued that there "should be no one type of man." But, a competitive economy created only one sort of man—"from the factory hand to the millionaire there will be the one stamp of material acquisitiveness." Only after Americans achieved the wealth and security promised by big business operating under government regulation could varieties of men, that is, true individuality, flourish.

London not only shrewdly re-envisioned competition among individual enterprises as the creator of slaves but he also articulated the belief that manhood was created not inborn. In one section of his essay, he argued, for instance, that Renaissance Spain "had lost the greater part of the variety which was hers in former times." This was, he insisted, not "due to an innate degeneracy of her people, but to her social, political and religious structures." His closing line was: "government should make men by giving them the freedom to make themselves."

London was not the only regulator who believed it possible deliberately to build a new kind of manhood. Another supporter of governmental regulation explicitly stated the same belief in the plasticity of identity: "We cannot change human nature? Oh, yes, we can." He argued that the institutions that could change men's nature were legislatures, churches, homes, and schools, all of which could "give to ambition and to acquisitiveness a new meaning and a new direction." Interestingly, this social critic argued that some big businesses were good and that the distinguishing feature of good businesses was that they "received their fortunes in return for the service which they have rendered to the community." He was trying to define good businessmen as servants of the community: "The ambition for service is the merchant's ambition." Bad businessmen were rather "gamblers" filled only with the "ambition for gain." Legislation, he suggested, could send to jail those whose only goal was private gain and could reward those whose goal was service to the community. In contrast to Woodrow Wilson or the *Independent,* this writer construed servanthood as a worthy position for American men. But his form of servanthood was voluntary and rendered to a community of peers rather than involuntary and rendered to superiors within a corporate hierarchy.

The most popular proponent of big business under governmental regulation was eventually Theodore Roosevelt. By 1912, when he was the presidential candidate of the Progressive party, Roosevelt became the spokesperson for federal regulation of big business rather than trustbusting, which he left to his major opponent, Woodrow Wilson. I believe that Roosevelt could with political impunity accept enormous corporations precisely because he offered clear alternative bases for American manhood to the basis of economic self-sufficiency. Indeed, when Woodrow Wilson compared the relationship between a monopoly-regulating government and American men to the master/slave relationship, he was on to something important in Roosevelt's scheme: Roosevelt's new foundations for American manhood in many ways recalled those of white antebellum Southern manhood. White manhood in the antebellum South had rested more on violence, honor, and control of other people than had the manhood of the North.

In Roosevelt's scheme, well-known through recent historical analyses, a new white manhood would rest especially on three pillars: violence—played out on football fields, battlefields, and in boxing rings; on honor, about which he railed incessantly in his discussions of foreign policy; and on ruling races he considered inferior, a stand that had won the day in America's decision to rule the Philippines rather than to grant it independence.

Every student of American history is familiar with Roosevelt's rambunctiousness, safaris, and love of the West. We know that the twenty-sixth president cheered for college football, boxed, rode, roped, camped, hunted and cherished the company of men who met those challenges more gracefully than he. Rough sports, in fact, Roosevelt offered as one of the foundations of American manhood.

We also know Roosevelt as a proponent of a new American militarism and imperialism. In Roosevelt's mind, these initiatives provided further foundations for American manhood. Beginning in the late 1890s, in fact, he questioned the manliness of those who did not support a naval build-up and who argued against the United States's rule of the Philippines. In "The Strenuous Life," his famous speech before a Chicago men's club in 1899, he insisted: "We do not admire the man of timid peace. We admire the man who embodies victorious effort; . . . who has those virile qualities necessary to win in the stern strife of actual life." He went on to argue that Americans must accept the new responsibilities incurred through victory in the Spanish-American War. With regard to the Philippines in particular, he argued that the United States must not allow the islands to rule themselves but rather must govern them. Otherwise, Roosevelt warned, "Some stronger, manlier power would have to step in and do the work, and we would have shown ourselves weaklings. . . ." Later in his speech, he reiterated that if the United States shirked governing the Philippines, then that rule would be instituted "by some stronger and more manful race."

Finally, Roosevelt waved away the concerns of those who believed it undemocratic for the United States to engage in imperial rule. He expressed only contempt for those "who cant about 'liberty' and the 'consent of the governed,' in order to excuse themselves for their unwillingness to play the part of men."

For Roosevelt, real men ruled other men, especially men of races he considered inferior. The racial component of his definition of manhood was clear in his Chicago speech. There, he reasoned that those who worried about extending liberty and consent of the governed to Filipinos, "would make it incumbent on us to leave the Apaches of Arizona to work out their own salvation, and to decline to interfere in a single Indian reservation." In another memorable passage, Roosevelt cautioned his audience that if they did not accept the responsibilities of imperial rule, then they could expect "to play the part of China, and be content to rot by inches in ignoble ease within our borders. . . ." The United States could then expect to discover in itself "what China has already found," which was that it had "lost the manly and adventurous qualities."

These were themes that Theodore Roosevelt would play out routinely until his death: American manhood required participation in rough sports, outdoor life, military adventures, and imperial rule. This combination of themes often went together among white progressive men who believed that the big corporations were here to stay. Albert Shaw, for instance, in a series of college commencement speeches delivered in the early twentieth century, insisted that capitalistic combinations were permanent and that, as a result, the U.S. was heading into a new, more "cooperative age."

Shaw identified the problem posed for middle-class American men as others had: "we have been so gravely and so incessantly warned about the crushing out of opportunities for young men through the growth of capitalistic combinations, that many of us find it hard to believe that we are not in some danger of being folded, stifled, and crushed within the tentacles of the octopus." He admitted that, if he had his druthers, he would prefer the older option of going into business or a profession in a small town where men of the nineteenth century had to "elbow their way to the front in law practice and in politics as persons of at least local importance." But, he insisted, those days were over: "a greatly increased proportion of young men must expect to work on salaries in large organizations." The conditions of America's "pioneering period," which created "a wonderful spirit of individuality, independence, and self-direction in the average man," were gone. They had "ended with the Spanish War." And now, America was in transition to "the intelligent, cooperative man of the future, as against the competitive man of the past." It was a manhood that, according to Shaw, would flourish not only within big corporations, but also in the military and among rulers of colonies. In his speeches to graduating college men, Shaw advocated a big navy and America's rule of the Philippines.

Critics of this new manhood agreed on its origins. In one scathing and satirical article titled "The Military Idea of Manliness," Ernest Howard Crosby— poet, reformer, and muckraker—explained: "As a nation of mere tradesmen and farmers we have never assimilated the ideals of honor, manliness and glory which distinguish the military peoples." Those ideals, he insisted, included picking on people weaker than oneself, a practice embodied in all of military/imperial life from hazing at West Point to the habit of imperial powers to move against the weakest states rather than against each other. Furthermore, he argued, this military/imperial manhood required "[a]bsolute obedience, readiness to obey orders. . . ." These Crosby insisted, "are necessary military qualities." They composed "the new manliness," belief in which required that American men say good-bye "to the ancient belief in freedom and independence which prevailed before the recent repeal of the Declaration [embodied in the decision to rule the Philippines]."

Crosby thus castigated those who supported a Rooseveltian attempt to set American manhood on a new footing that ordered men within a hierarchy where the strong seemed to prey on the weak and the higher ups demanded deference. To some turn-of-the-century observers, that was precisely what corporate and military life shared: an acceptance of men as dependents within a hierarchy in which only a few could move up and the rest must be satisfied to learn the rules and obey them. They construed this as an enormous shift from nineteenth-century manhood, resting as it had on independence of thought and action.

Roosevelt's laying out alternatives to Victorian manhood made it possible for him to achieve tremendous popularity while *supporting* governmental regulation of big business. In fact, William Allen White, a renowned Progressive, also understood the centrality of manliness in the election of 1912. In a letter to losing presidential candidate, Theodore Roosevelt, the Kansas newspaperman explained that many of Roosevelt's votes were "votes of men who had confidence in you personally without having any particular intelligent reason to give why; except that you were a masculine sort of a person with extremely masculine virtues and palpably masculine faults for which they loved you."

CONCLUSION

This essay has argued that race-specific gender structured the trustbusting debate in two ways. First, it identified who participated in the debate. Sometimes represented as the crux of Progressivism, the battle over big business was largely confined to the community of white men. While such issues as women's suffrage and juvenile justice animated discussions among men and women, black and white, the issue of trusts was overwhelmingly a white man's issue. In view of this, we need to find a way to represent it in textbooks and other general considerations of the early twentieth century as the sharply race- and gender-specific issue that it was. Otherwise, we misunderstand Progressivism by misidentifying its central themes and causes, and we obscure the experience of African Americans and women by presenting the concerns of white men as those of reformers as a whole.

Another aspect of Progressivism revealed in the trustbusting debate was the belief that manhood and womanhood were created rather than natural. Some turn-of-the-century commentators believed that historically changing institutions and beliefs imbued men and women with the particular qualities associated with each sex in a given era. If, therefore, they wanted to create particular kinds of women and men, they believed they had to build particular kinds of institutions and popularize particular beliefs. These writers assumed that politics and public policy touched areas so intimate as personal identity: in the battle over the trusts, they self-consciously struggled over the form that white manhood should take in the twentieth century.

And this was the second way in which gender structured the debate over trusts: the controversy was in part *about* the form that white American manhood would take in the twentieth century. Gender, in this case, the meaning of white manhood, wove through arguments about the appropriate response to corporate capitalism at the turn of the century. Many Americans believed that the decision to break up the trusts or to regulate them had implications for the form that white American manhood would take in the decades to come, and they sometimes formed their arguments for busting or regulating explicitly in terms of the effect on manliness. Thus, we have come to see another previously unrecognized element of the trustbusting debate.

According to many middle-class thinkers at the turn of the century, American manhood had, during the nineteenth century, rested in large part on the independence presumably afforded a man by owning his own farm, business, or professional practice. American men's citizenship was premised on precisely that independence, which was supposed to give each man the freedom to vote his own mind. The emergence of corporate capitalism seemed to these commentators to mean that increasing percentages of American men would never achieve the requisite independence. They would instead spend all of their working lives as employees of someone else—as workers, managers, or salesmen for large corporations. Trustbusting seemed to recuperate the possibility of a nineteenth-century form of economic self-sufficiency while regulation seemed to surrender that foundation of manhood.

Unlike middle-class trustbusters, working-class white men did not look nostalgically to the nineteenth century for their ideal of independent manhood. Leaders of organized labor redefined independence to mean the ability of male workers to unite and through unity to gain some control over the conditions of their labor and levels of compensation. Though different from the middle-class version, this notion of independence was very much tied to manhood for commentators of the working class, and they, too, saw some trusts as a threat to their independence and thus to American manhood.

The debate over trusts was in part, then, a debate between those who welcomed the "cooperative man of the future" and those who championed "the competitive man of the past." But "cooperative man" took more than one form in the imaginations of these debaters. In the minds of some, the American manhood implicitly promoted by corporate combinations regulated by governmental agencies was economically dependent insofar as he was not his own boss but an employee; not an autonomous decision-maker but one of many woven into decision-making bodies, be they boards of directors, governmental commissions, or committees of managers; embedded in various hierarchies within individual companies, within larger corporate structures, and between business and government. At his best, "the cooperative man of the future" was an unselfish and competent team player satisfied to play his small part in the economic life of the country; at his worst, he was a bureaucratic drudge.

For other thinkers, however, big business—if regulated—promised increased wealth and comfort for everyone; it might usher in the day of men truly free and devoted to community rather than competition. In the minds of those like Jack London, finer kinds of men might finally materialize when men no longer had to dedicate all of their energies to brute survival in a cut-throat economic system. Genuine equality, democracy, and individuality might be the result of increased economic cooperation.

Ernest Thompson Seton

BECOMING A MAN: THE BOY SCOUTS

Founded in England in 1908, the Boy Scouts was incorporated in the United States in 1910. English-born Ernest Thompson Seton had established an American precedent with his Woodcraft Indians, organized in 1902. As the following selections from the Boy Scouts' handbook (1910) reveal, scouting was very much concerned with masculinity. According to the handbook, what historical circumstances had contributed to the decline of the masculine? What kind of boy—and what kind of man—did Seton wish to foster through his organization? Would Seton have agreed with Woodrow Wilson and others like him, who sought to restore the economy to greater competitiveness?

INTRODUCTION

Every American boy, a hundred years ago, lived either on a farm or in such close touch with farm life that he reaped its benefits. He had all the practical knowledge that comes from country surroundings; that is, he could ride, shoot, skate, run, swim; he was handy with tools; he knew the woods; he was physically strong, self-reliant, resourceful, well-developed in body and brain. In addition to which, he had a good moral training at home. He was respectful to his superiors, obedient to his parents, and altogether the best material of which a nation could be made.

We have lived to see an unfortunate change. Partly through the growth of immense cities, with the consequent specialization of industry, so that each individual has been required to do one small specialty and shut his eyes to everything else, with the resultant perpetual narrowing of the mental horizon.

Partly through the decay of small farming, which would have offset this condition, for each mixed farm was a college of handicraft.

From Ernest Thompson Seton, *Boy Scouts of America: A Handbook of Woodcraft, Scouting, and Lifecraft* (New York: Doubleday, Page, 1910), pp. xi, xii, 2–4.

And partly through the stereotyped forms of religion losing their hold, we see a very different type of youth in the country to-day.

It is the exception when we see a boy respectful to his superiors and obedient to his parents. It is the rare exception, now, when we see a boy that is handy with tools and capable of taking care of himself under all circumstances. It is the very, very rare exception when we see a boy whose life is absolutely governed by the safe old moral standards.

The personal interest in athletics has been largely superseded by an interest in spectacular games, which, unfortunately, tend to divide the nation into two groups—the few overworked champions in the arena, and the great crowd content to do nothing but sit on the benches and look on, while indulging their tastes for tobacco and alcohol.

It is this last that is turning so many thoughtful ones against baseball, football, etc. This, it will be seen, is a reproduction of the condition that ended in the fall of Rome. In her days of growth, every man was a soldier; in the end, a few great gladiators were in the arena, to be watched and applauded by the millions who personally knew nothing at all of fighting or heroism.

Degeneracy is the word.

To combat the system that has turned such a large proportion of our robust, manly, self-reliant boyhood into a lot of flat-chested cigarette-smokers, with shaky nerves and doubtful vitality, I began the Woodcraft movement in America. Without saying as much, it aimed to counteract the evils attendant on arena baseball, football, and racing, by substituting the better, cleaner, saner pursuits of Woodcraft and Scouting. . . .

Nine leading principles are kept in view:

(1) This movement is essentially for *recreation.*
(2) *Camp-life.* Camping is the simple life reduced to actual practice, as well as the culmination of the outdoor life.

     Camping has no great popularity to-day, because men have the idea that it is possible only after an expensive journey to the wilderness; and women that it is inconvenient, dirty, and dangerous.

     These are errors. They have arisen because camping as an art is not understood. When intelligently followed camp-life must take its place as a cheap and delightful way of living, as well as a mental and physical saviour of those strained and broken by the grind of the over-busy world.

     The wilderness affords the ideal camping, but many of the benefits can be got by living in a tent on a town lot, piazza, or even house-top.
(3) *Self-government.* Control from without is a poor thing when you can get control from within. As far as possible, then, we make these camps self-governing. Each full member has a vote in affairs.
(4) *The Magic of the Camp-fire.* What is a camp without a camp-fire?—no camp at all, but a chilly place in a landscape, where some people happen to have some things.

When first the brutal anthropoid stood up and walked erect—was man, the great event was symbolized and marked by the lighting of the first camp-fire.

For millions of years our race has seen in this blessed fire the means and emblem of light, warmth, protection, friendly gathering, council. All the hallow of the ancient thoughts, hearth, fireside, home, is centered in its glow, and the home-tie itself is weakened with the waning of the home-fire. Not in the steam radiator can we find the spell; not in the water coil; not even in the gas-log: they do not reach the heart. Only the ancient sacred fire of wood has power to touch and thrill the chords of primitive remembrance. When men sit together at the camp-fire, they seem to shed all modern form and poise, and hark back to the primitive—to meet as man and man—to show the naked soul. Your camp-fire partner wins your love, or hate, mostly your love; and having camped in peace together, is a lasting bond of union,—however wide your worlds may be apart.

The camp-fire, then, is the focal centre of all primitive brotherhood. We shall not fail to use its magic powers. . . .

(6) *Honors by Standards.* The competitive principle is responsible for much that is evil. We see it rampant in our colleges to-day, where every effort is made to discover and develop a champion, while the great body of students is neglected. That is, the ones who are in need of physical development do not get it, and those who do not need it are overdeveloped. The result is much unsoundness of many kinds. A great deal of this would be avoided if we strove to bring all the individuals up to a certain standard. In our non-competitive tests the enemies are not *"the other fellows,"* but *time and space,* the forces of Nature. We try *not to down the others,* but *to raise ourselves.* A thorough application of this principle would end many of the evils now demoralizing college athletics. Therefore, all our honors are bestowed according to worldwide standards. (Prizes are not honors.)

(7) *Personal Decoration for Personal Achievements.* The love of glory is the strongest motive in a savage. Civilized man is supposed to find in high principle his master impulse. But those who believe that the men of our race, not to mention boys, are civilized in this highest sense, would be greatly surprised if confronted with figures. Nevertheless, a human weakness may be good material to work with. I face the facts as they are. All have a chance for glory through the standards, and we blazon it forth in personal decorations that all can see, have, and desire.

(8) *A Heroic Ideal.* The boy from ten to fifteen, like the savage, is purely physical in his ideals. I do not know that I ever met a boy that would not rather be John L. Sullivan than Darwin or Tolstoy. Therefore, I accept the fact, and seek to keep in view an ideal that is physical, but also clean, manly, heroic, already familiar, and leading with certainty to higher things.

(9) *Picturesqueness in Everything.* Very great importance should be attached to this. The effect of the picturesque is magical, and all the more subtle

and irresistible because it is not on the face of it reasonable. The charm of titles and gay costumes, of the beautiful in ceremony, phrase, dance, and song, are utilized in all ways. . . .

NATIONAL DETERIORATION

In the first place we have to recognize that our nation is in need of help, from within, if it is to maintain its position as a leading factor for peace and prosperity among the other nations of the earth.

History shows us, that with scarcely an exception, every great nation, after climbing laboriously to the zenith of its power, has then apparently become exhausted by the effort, and has settled down in a state of repose, relapsing into idleness and into indifference to the fact that other nations were pushing up to destroy it, whether by force of arms or by the more peaceful but equally fatal method of commercial strangulation. In every case the want of some of that energetic patriotism which made the country has caused its ruin; in every case the verdict of history has been, "Death through bad citizenship."

Signs have not been wanting of recent years that all is not right with our citizenship in Britain. Ominous warnings have been heard from many authorities and many sources, in almost every branch of our national life. These have been recently summed up by one of our public men in the following words:—

"The same causes which brought about the fall of the great Roman Empire are working to-day in Great Britain."

THE UNEMPLOYED

One sign of the disease (which was also one of the signs of decay in Rome before her fall) is the horde of unemployed leading miserable, wasted lives in all parts of the country—the great army of drones in our hive.

It is no longer a mere temporary excrescence, but is a growing tumor pregnant with evil for the nation.

These people, *having never been taught to look after themselves, or to think of the future or their country's good,* allow themselves to become slaves by the persuasive power of a few professional agitators whose living depends on agitating (whether it is needed or not); and blinded by the talk of these men they spurn the hand which provides the money, till they force employers to spend fortunes either in devising machinery that will take their place and will not then go on strike, or in getting in foreign labor, or in removing their business to other countries, leaving the agitators fat, but the mass of their deluded followers unemployed and starving and unable to provide for the crowds of children which they still continue improvidently to bring into the world.

Jane Addams

HULL-HOUSE: THE SOFTER SIDE OF PROGRESSIVE REFORM?

Jane Addams (1860–1935) was the most prominent of a generation of women who committed their lives to the cause of social reform. Born in 1860, Addams returned from Europe in the 1880s convinced of the need to take action against the ills of urban America. In 1889, she established the social settlement of Hull-House—a mansion in the heart of Chicago's Italian and eastern European immigrant community that would assist the area's people in liberating themselves from their Old World cultures and customs, in overcoming their ignorance, in adjusting to modern, urban life, and in securing needed changes in the neighborhood. By 1900, there were over 100 social settlements in cities across the nation, nearly all of them managed by women.

In the first section of the following account, published in 1910, Addams presents some of the ideas and attitudes she observed in the Italian immigrant community, and she explains how the immigrants' adjustment to American industrial conditions might be facilitated by a labor museum. In the second section, she describes her efforts to deal with conditions in a nearby "slum." What do you think of Addams's labor museum? Of her solution to the tenement conditions? What did area residents think of her work? According to Addams, why did the problems she uncovered exist, and, speaking generally, what needed to be done to solve them? Is there anything particularly female about Addams's approach to social reform?

This tendency upon the part of the older immigrants to lose the amenities of European life without sharing those of America, has often been deplored by keen observers from the home countries. When Professor Masurek of Prague gave a course of lectures in the University of Chicago, he was much distressed over the materialism into which the Bohemians of Chicago had fallen. The early immigrants had been so stirred by the opportunity to own real estate, an appeal perhaps to the Slavic land hunger, and their energies had become so completely absorbed in money-making that all other interests had apparently dropped away. And yet I recall a very touching incident in connection with a lecture Professor Masurek gave at Hull-House, in which he had appealed to his countrymen to arouse themselves from this tendency to fall below their home civilization and to forget the great enthusiasm which had united them into the Pan-Slavic Movement. A Bohemian widow who supported herself and her two children by scrubbing, hastily sent her youngest child to purchase, with the twenty-five cents which was to have supplied them with food the next day, a

Jane Addams, *20 Years at Hull-House* (New York: Macmillan, 1910).

bunch of red roses which she presented to the lecturer in appreciation of his testimony to the reality of the things of the spirit.

An overmastering desire to reveal the humbler immigrant parents to their own children lay at the base of what has come to be called the Hull-House Labor Museum. This was first suggested to my mind one early spring day when I saw an old Italian woman, her distaff against her homesick face, patiently spinning a thread by the simple stick spindle so reminiscent of all southern Europe. I was walking down Polk Street, perturbed in spirit, because it seemed so difficult to come into genuine relations with the Italian women and because they themselves so often lost their hold upon their Americanized children. It seemed to me that Hull-House ought to be able to devise some educational enterprise, which should build a bridge between European ·and American experiences in such wise as to give them both more meaning and a sense of relation. I meditated that perhaps the power to see life as a whole, is more needed ·in the immigrant quarter of a large city than anywhere else, and that the lack of this power is the most fruitful source of misunderstanding between European immigrants and their children, as it is between them and· their American neighbors; and why should that chasm between fathers and sons, yawning at the feet of each generation, be made so unnecessarily cruel and impassable to these bewildered immigrants? Suddenly I looked up and saw the old woman with her distaff, sitting in the sun on the steps of a tenement house. She might have served as a model for one of Michael Angelo's Fates, but her face brightened as I passed and, holding up her spindle for me to see, she called out that when she had spun a little more yarn, she would knit a pair of stockings for her goddaughter. The occupation of the old woman gave me the clew that was needed. Could we not interest the young people working in the neighboring factories, in these older forms of industry, so that, through their own parents and grandparents, they would find a dramatic representation of the inherited resources of their daily occupation. If these young people could actually see that the complicated machinery of the factory had been evolved from simple tools, they might at least make a beginning towards that education which Dr. Dewey defines as "a continuing reconstruction of experience." They might also lay a foundation for reverence of the past which Goethe declares to be the basis of all sound progress.

My exciting walk on Polk Street was followed by many talks with Dr. Dewey and with one of the teachers in his school who was a resident at Hull-House. Within a month a room was fitted up to which we might invite those of our neighbors who were possessed of old crafts and who were eager to use them.

We found in the immediate neighborhood, at least four varieties of these most primitive methods of spinning and three distinct variations of the same spindle in connection with wheels. It was possible to put these seven into historic sequence and order and to connect the whole with the present method of factory spinning. The same thing was done for weaving, and on every Saturday evening a little exhibit was made of these various forms of labor in the textile industry. Within one room a Syrian woman, a Greek, an Italian, a Russian, and an Irishwoman enabled even the most casual observer to see that there is no break in orderly evolution if we look at history from the industrial standpoint; that industry develops similarly and peacefully year by year among the workers of each nation, heedless of differences in language, religion, and political experiences.

And then we grew ambitious and arranged lectures upon industrial history. I remember that after an interesting lecture upon the industrial revolution in England and a portrayal of the appalling conditions throughout the weaving districts of the north, which resulted from the hasty gathering of the weavers into the new towns, a Russian tailor in the audience was moved to make a speech. He suggested that whereas time had done much to alleviate the first difficulties in the transition of weaving from hand work to steam power, that in the application of steam to sewing we are still in the first stages, illustrated by the isolated woman who tries to support herself by hand needlework at home until driven out by starvation, as many of the hand weavers had been.

The historical analogy seemed to bring a certain comfort to the tailor as did a chart upon the wall, showing the infinitesimal amount of time that steam had been applied to manufacturing processes compared to the centuries of hand labor. Human progress is slow and perhaps never more cruel than in the advance of industry, but is not the worker comforted by knowing that other historical periods have existed similar to the one in which he finds himself, and that the readjustment may be shortened and alleviated by judicious action; and is he not entitled to the solace which an artistic portrayal of the situation might give him? I remember the evening of the tailor's speech that I felt reproached because no poet or artist had endeared the sweaters' victim to us as George Eliot has made us love the belated weaver, Silas Marner. The textile museum is connected directly with the basket weaving, sewing, millinery, embroidery, and dressmaking constantly being taught at Hull-House, and so far as possible with the other educational departments; we have also been able to make a collection of products, of early implements, and of photographs which are full of suggestion. Yet far beyond its direct educational value, we prize it because it so often puts the immigrants into the position of teachers, and we imagine that it affords them a pleasant change from the tutelage in which all Americans, including their own children, are so apt to hold them. I recall a number of Russian women working in a sewing-room near Hull-House, who heard one Christmas week that the House was going to give a party to which they might come. They arrived one afternoon when, unfortunately, there was no party on hand and, although the residents did their best to entertain them with impromptu music and refreshments, it was quite evident that they were greatly disappointed. Finally it was suggested that they be shown the Labor Museum—where gradually the thirty sodden, tired women were transformed. They knew how to use the spindles and were delighted to find the Russian spinning frame. Many of them had never seen the spinning wheel, which has not penetrated to certain parts of Russia, and they regarded it as a new and wonderful invention. They turned up their dresses to show their homespun petticoats; they tried the looms; they explained the difficulty of the old patterns; in short, from having been stupidly entertained, they themselves did the entertaining. Because of a direct appeal to former experiences, the immigrant visitors were able for the moment to instruct their American hostesses in an old and honored craft, as was indeed becoming to their age and experience.

In some such ways as these have the Labor Museum and the shops pointed out the possibilities which Hull-House has scarcely begun to develop, of demonstrating that culture is an understanding of the long-established occupations and thoughts of men, of the arts with which they have solaced their toil. A yearning to recover for the household arts something of their early sanctity and meaning, arose strongly within me one evening when I was attending a Passover Feast to which I had been invited by a Jewish family in the neighborhood, where the traditional and religious significance of woman's daily activity was still retained. The kosher food the Jewish mother spread before her family had been prepared according to traditional knowledge and with constant care in the use of utensils; upon her had fallen the responsibility to make all ready according to Mosaic instructions that the great crisis in a religious history might be fittingly set forth by her husband and son. Aside from the grave religious significance in the ceremony, my mind was filled with shifting pictures of woman's labor with which travel makes one familiar; the Indian women grinding grain outside of their huts as they sing praises to the sun and rain; a file of white-clad Moorish women whom I had once seen waiting their turn at a well in Tangiers; south Italian women kneeling in a row along the stream and beating their wet clothes against the smooth white stones; the milking, the gardening, the marketing in thousands of hamlets, which are such direct expressions of the solicitude and affection at the basis of all family life.

There has been some testimony that the Labor Museum has revealed the charm of woman's primitive activities. I recall a certain Italian girl who came every Saturday evening to a cooking class in the same building in which her mother spun in the Labor Museum exhibit; and yet Angelina always left her mother at the front door while she herself went around to a side door because she did not wish to be too closely identified in the eyes of the rest of the cooking class with an Italian woman who wore a kerchief over her head, uncouth boots, and short petticoats. One evening, however, Angelina saw her mother surrounded by a group of visitors from the School of Education, who much admired the spinning, and she concluded from their conversation that her mother was "the best stick-spindle spinner in America." When she inquired from me as to the truth of this deduction, I took occasion to describe the Italian village in which her mother had lived, something of her free life, and how, because of the opportunity she and the other women of the village had to drop their spindles over the edge of a precipice, they had developed a skill in spinning beyond that of the neighboring towns. I dilated somewhat on the freedom and beauty of that life—how hard it must be to exchange it all for a two-room tenement, and to give up a beautiful homespun kerchief for an ugly department store hat. I intimated it was most unfair to judge her by these things alone, and that while she must depend on her daughter to learn the new ways, she also had a right to expect her daughter to know something of the old ways.

That which I could not convey to the child but upon which my own mind persistently dwelt, was that her mother's whole life had been spent in a secluded spot under the rule of traditional and narrowly localized observances, until her very religion clung to local sanctities,—to the shrine before which she had always prayed, to the pavement and walls of the low vaulted church,—and then suddenly she was torn from it all and literally put out to sea, straight away from the solid habits of her religious and domestic life, and she now walked timidly but with poignant sensibility upon a new and strange shore.

It was easy to see that the thought of her mother with any other background than that of the tenement was new to Angelina and at least two things resulted; she allowed her mother to pull out of the big box under the bed the beautiful homespun garments which had been previously hidden away as uncouth; and she openly came into the Labor Museum by the same door as did her mother, proud at least of the mastery of the craft which had been so much admired.

. . . Our experience in inspecting [the ward's garbage disposal facilities] only made us more conscious of the wretched housing conditions over which we had been distressed from the first. It was during the World's Fair summer that one of the Hull-House residents in a public address upon housing reform used as an example of indifferent landlordism a large block in the neighborhood occupied by small tenements and stables unconnected with a street sewer, as was much similar property in the vicinity. In the lecture the resident spared neither a description of the property nor the name of the owner. The young man who owned the property was justly indignant at this public method of attack and promptly came to investigate the condition of the property. Together we made a careful tour of the houses and stables and in the face of the conditions that we found there, I could not but agree with him that supplying South Italian peasants with sanitary appliances seemed a difficult undertaking. Nevertheless he was unwilling that the block should remain in its deplorable state, and he finally cut through the dilemma with the rash proposition that he would give a free lease of the entire tract to Hull-House, accompanying the offer, however, with the warning remark, that if we should choose to use the income from the rents in sanitary improvements we should be throwing our money away.

Even when we decided that the houses were so bad that we could not undertake the task of improving them, he was game and stuck to his proposition that we should have a free lease. We finally submitted a plan that the houses should be torn down and the entire tract turned into a playground, although cautious advisers intimated that it would be very inconsistent to ask for subscriptions for the support of Hull-House when we were known to have thrown away an income of two thousand dollars a year. We, however, felt that a spectacle of inconsistency was better than one of bad landlordism and so the worst of the houses were demolished, the best three were sold and moved across the street under careful provision that they might never be used for junkshops or saloons, and a public playground was finally established. Hull-House became responsible for its management for ten years, at the end of which time it was turned over to the City Playground Commission although from the first the city detailed a policeman who was responsible for its general order and who became a valued adjunct of the House.

During fifteen years this public-spirited owner of the property paid all the taxes, and when the block was finally sold he made possible the playground equipment of a near-by school yard. On the other hand, the dispossessed tenants, a group of whom had to be evicted by legal process before their houses could be torn down, have never ceased to mourn their former estates. Only the other day I met upon the street an old Italian harness maker, who said that he had never succeeded so well anywhere else nor found a place that "seemed so much like Italy."

Festivities of various sorts were held on this early playground, always a May day celebration with its Maypole dance and its May queen. I remember that one year the honor of being queen was offered to the little girl who should pick up the largest number of scraps of paper which littered all the streets and alleys. The children that spring had been organized into a league and each member had been provided with a stiff piece of wire upon the sharpened point of which stray bits of paper were impaled and later soberly counted off into a large box in the Hull-House alley. The little Italian girl who thus won the scepter took it very gravely as the just reward of hard labor, and we were all so absorbed in the desire for clean and tidy streets that we were wholly oblivious to the incongruity of thus selecting "the queen of love and beauty."

It was at the end of the second year that we received a visit from the warden of Toynbee Hall and his wife, as they were returning to England from a journey around the world. They had lived in East London for many years, and had been identified with the public movements for its betterment. They were much shocked that, in a new country with conditions still plastic and hopeful, so little attention had been paid to experiments and methods of amelioration which had already been tried; and they looked in vain through our library for blue books and governmental reports which recorded painstaking study into the conditions of English cities.

They were the first of a long line of English visitors to express the conviction that many things in Chicago were untoward not through paucity of public spirit but through a lack of political machinery adapted to modern city life. This was not all of the situation but perhaps no casual visitor could be expected to see that these matters of detail seemed unimportant to a city in the first flush of youth, impatient of correction and convinced that all would be well with its future. The most obvious faults were those connected with the congested housing of the immigrant population, nine tenths of them from the country, who carried on all sorts of traditional activities in the crowded tenements. That a group of Greeks should be permitted to slaughter sheep in a basement, that Italian women should be allowed to sort over rags collected from the city dumps, not only within the city limits but in a court swarming with little children, that immigrant bakers should continue unmolested to bake bread for their neighbors in unspeakably filthy spaces under the pavement, appeared incredible to visitors accustomed to careful city regulations. I recall two visits made to the Italian quarter by John Burns,—the second, thirteen years after the first. During the latter visit it seemed to him unbelievable that a certain house owned by a rich Italian should have been permitted to survive. He remembered with the greatest minuteness the positions of the houses on the court, with the exact space between the front and rear tenements, and he asked at once whether we had been able to cut a window into a dark hall as he had recommended thirteen years before. Although we were obliged to confess that the landlord would not permit the window to be cut, we were able to report that a City Homes Association had existed for ten years; that following a careful study of tenement conditions in Chicago, the text of which had been written by a Hull-House resident, the association had obtained the enactment of a model tenement-house code, and that their secretary had carefully watched the administration of the law for years so that its operation might not be minimized by the granting of too many exceptions in the city council. Our progress still seemed slow to Mr. Burns because in Chicago the actual houses were quite unchanged, embodying features long since declared illegal in London. Only this year could we have reported to him, had he again come to challenge us, that the provisions of the law had at last been extended to existing houses and that a conscientious corps of inspectors under an efficient chief, were fast remedying the most glaring evils, while a band of nurses and doctors were following hard upon the "trail of the white hearse."

The mere consistent enforcement of existing laws and efforts for their advance often placed Hull-House, at least temporarily, into strained relations with its neighbors. I recall a continuous warfare against local landlords who would move wrecks of old houses as a nucleus for new ones in order to evade the provisions of the building code, and a certain Italian neighbor who was filled with bitterness because his new rear tenement was discovered to be illegal. It seemed impossible to make him understand that the health of the tenants was in any wise as important as his undisturbed rents.

Nevertheless many evils constantly arise in Chicago from congested housing which wiser cities forestall and prevent; the inevitable boarders crowded into a dark tenement already too small for the use of the immigrant family occupying it; the surprisingly large number of delinquent girls who have become criminally involved with their own fathers and uncles; the school children who cannot find a quiet spot in which to read or study and who perforce go into the streets each evening; the tuberculosis superinduced and fostered by the inadequate rooms and breathing spaces. One of the Hull-House residents, under the direction of a Chicago physician who stands high as an authority on tuberculosis and who devotes a large proportion of his time to our vicinity, made an investigation into housing conditions as related to tuberculosis with a result as startling as that of the "lung block" in New York.

THE PROGRESSIVE VISION OF LEWIS HINE: A PHOTO ESSAY

"I have heard their tragic stories," wrote Lewis Hine in 1914, *"watched their cramped lives and saw their fruitless struggles in the industrial game where the odds are all against them."* Hine spent a decade—from 1908 to 1918—taking thousands of photographs of an estimated 2 million children who worked in the nation's factories, fields, mines, and tenements. His employer was the National Child Labor Committee, a typical progressive-era organization in the Jane Addams mold, whose goal it was to survey and publicize the facts of child labor and get the states to pass laws against it. Hine and his fellow reformers had some success; between 1903 and 1917, most of the states outside the South regulated child labor. Most states limited workers under age sixteen to eight hours per day; a few—Rhode Island, New York, and Utah—prohibited the employment of children under sixteen in factories. By the mid-1930s, all states but Wyoming had set a minimum age limit of fourteen years for general factory work. A national child labor law, passed by Congress in 1916 to keep employers from playing one state against another, was declared unconstitutional in 1918.

The photographs that follow show how Hine's work was used in Survey magazine, a publication that advocated mothers' pensions, an end to child labor, and other social reforms. The photographs are documents, to be sure; they constitute a record of child labor in the early twentieth century. But Hine's vision is more complex than that. What attitude did Hine have toward these young workers? What did he think about work and the workplace? What was his opinion of the larger system of capitalism that employed children? When Hine wrote in 1932, "cities do not build themselves," what did he mean?

Child Workers in Shrimp and Oyster Canneries, Pass Christian, Mississippi, c. 1912.

1915. Original Caption: "Alfred, 13, who lost part of a finger in a spinning machine, has worked since he was 10."

1914. This Complex Tableaux Depicts City Children Pressed into Service to Pick Cotton. Hine wrote: "A group of children who go from a nearby city after school to pick cotton on a Texas farm. Ages range from 4 to 6 years. The enlarged picture is a four-year-old youngster who works regularly."

ILLITERATES IN MASSACHUSETTS

THE THREE YOUNGEST IN THIS GROUP AT A FALL RIVER MILL ARE PORTUGUESE CHILDREN WHO COULD NOT WRITE THEIR OWN NAMES. ONE COULD NOT SPELL THE NAME OF THE STREET HE LIVED ON. ALL THREE SPOKE ALMOST NO ENGLISH.

1914. The Print Below Reads: "The three youngest in this group at a Fall River [Massachusetts] Mill are Portuguese who could not write their own names. One could not spell the name of the street he lived on. All three spoke almost no English."

TIME EXPOSURES *by* HINE

THE INDUSTRIAL REVOLUTION UP TO DATE

The manufacturers of this cotton-picking machine believe that it will not only save time and money, but will drive the child pickers whose work was described and pictured in THE SURVEY for February 7. Large growers are adding it... plan is to arrange for co-operative ownership of machines among small cotton growers, much as north... and reapers in neighborhood groups. The power cotton-picker must be manned by skilled operat... directly to drive women and children from the long-drawn drudgery of the fields.

Cotton Pickers, and a Cotton-Picking Machine, 1914. The copy below reads: "The manufacturers of this cotton-picking machine believe that it will not only save time and money, but will eventually drive out the child pickers. . . ."

the big picture

The progressives are often described as "reformers," a label that implies that they acted out of altruism rather than self-interest. Were all progressives altruists? Do the motives of progressive reformers resemble those of the advocates of empire, discussed in Chapter 5?

chapter seven

FROM WAR TO "NORMALCY"

The generation that came of age in the 1920s did so in the shadow of World War I. A nation led to expect that the struggle would be morally satisfying—that had boldly announced in song that "the Yanks are coming"—would be reduced to seeking meaning in an unidentifiable soldier, buried in Arlington, Virginia. That a war of such short duration—direct American involvement lasted little more than eighteen months—could have had such an impact may seem surprising. But part of an explanation may be found by examining how Americans experienced the conflict and what they were led to believe it would achieve.

Several groups experienced the war years as a time of increased opportunity. Blacks—migrating from the South into Chicago, Detroit, New York, and other industrial cities—and women—heretofore denied most jobs open to men—found themselves suddenly employable. The same circumstances allowed organized labor to double its membership in the four years after 1914. Farmers prospered because of rising European demand and, after 1917, because of government price guarantees. Soldiers, however, experienced the typical wartime "tax" on income, and many lost their positions on promotional ladders.

Continued deficit spending fueled the economy during demobilization. In 1919, activity in automobile production and building construction, two industries held back by the war, helped the nation avoid a prolonged postwar tailspin. But economic crisis could be postponed for only so long. By mid-1921, the economy was mired in a serious depression that cut industrial output by some 20 percent. It seems likely that a downturn in the postwar economy, deeply affecting a people who had no history of planning for such events, helped to dissolve the aura of economic progress and personal success that had been part of the war and to inaugurate a decade of conflict between young and old, employer and employee, country and city, religion and science, nation and locality. In the minds of many Americans, depression was inseparably linked to demobilization and the peace settlement.

Unlike World War II, World War I was not an especially popular conflict with Americans. It had to be sold, systematically and unabashedly, like any other product. The government's advertising agency was the Committee on Public Information, headed by journalist George Creel. The Creel Committee employed an elaborate publicity apparatus to educate Americans on proper wartime values. In one advertisement, a smiling American soldier clenched a White Owl cigar between his teeth and said, "Did I bayonet my first hun? Sure! How did it feel? It *doesn't* feel! There *he* is. There *you* are. One of you has got to go. I preferred to stay."

Perhaps fighting a war—especially a war with which large numbers of the population disagreed—required a kind of artificially imposed unity. This would explain the Creel Committee propaganda. But when the fighting stopped—when the great crusade was over—a new crusade, called the Red Scare, took the place of wartime coercion of dissidents. When this latest hysteria subsided in the spring of 1920, hundreds of radicals of every persuasion—socialists, communists, even ordinary union members—had been arrested, beaten, lynched, tried, or deported.

Just as wartime coercion had yielded to the Red Scare, so was the Red Scare reincarnated in the politics of Warren Harding. In May 1920, emphasizing that "too much has been said about bolshevism in America," Harding coined the word that would capture his appeal and win him the presidency, urging return to "not heroism, but healing, not nostrums, but normalcy." With "normalcy," Harding and the American people seemed to be rejecting the world that Woodrow Wilson had sought to create—the world in which words replaced concrete realities, in which dreams of world government (the League of Nations) transcended political facts. The Creel Committee had described the war as "a Crusade not merely to re-win the tomb of Christ, but to bring back to earth the rule of right, the peace, goodwill to men and gentleness he taught." When it proved much less than this, Americans beat an emotional retreat to the comfort of Harding's slogans.

By mid-decade, when prosperity had returned and "normalcy" was in full swing, it was clear that the economy was undergoing a gradual change of enormous importance: the old economy of "production" was yielding, decade by decade, to a new economy of "consumption." This change occurred partly because many of the problems of production appeared to have been solved; the moving assembly line and Frederick W. Taylor's scientific management had made possible a new level of productive efficiency. Now the roadblock to abundance seemed to be at the level of the consumer. One approach, decidedly unpopular with business and with the Republican presidents who held office in the decade, was to encourage consumption by using the tax system to distribute money to those who would spend rather than save it. Another approach was to teach (some would say condition) people to desire, and then to buy, the available products. This teaching or conditioning was the function of advertising, which grew by leaps and bounds during the 1920s. Many advertising agencies were staffed by people who had honed their skills at the Creel Committee. Indeed, the ad agencies of the twenties were simply applying what appeared to be the great lesson of wartime propaganda: that the "masses" could be manipulated—made to go to war, or to buy—using the techniques of modern psychology.

The 1920s had powerful currents of individualism, of course. In fact, the decade has been rightly famed for its affection for jazz, for its compulsion for mah-jongg and flagpole sitting, for the flapper, and for the iconoclast H. L. Mencken (for whom every group, even the New England town meeting, was a mob run by demagogues). Harding's "normalcy," however, seemed to center on a program of cultural conformity, and it was to infect the entire decade. The Ku Klux Klan, revived at a Georgia meeting in 1915, grew rapidly in the early 1920s through campaigns against blacks, Catholics, Jews, and immigrants. National prohibition, which required millions to give up deeply ingrained drinking habits or evade the law, was in effect throughout the decade. The first law establishing immigration quotas was passed in 1921; a second measure passed three years later was designed to reduce immigration of peoples from eastern and southern Europe—the later immigrants discussed in Chapter 4. If "normalcy" is broad enough to encompass these aspects of the 1920s, then perhaps wartime coercion, the Red Scare, the new economy of consumption, and "normalcy" were all variations on a theme—a theme perhaps placed in bold relief by the war, demobilization, and postwar economic crisis, but ultimately one set more deeply in the nation's character and its institutions than any of these events.

interpretive essay

William M. Tuttle, Jr.

RED SUMMER, RED SCARE

As William M. Tuttle, Jr. reminds us in the following selection, the race riot that took place on Chicago's South Side in the summer of 1919 was only one of more than two dozen such episodes that shook the nation's cities and towns in the aftermath of the Great War. It was not even the most deadly. Chicago's toll of thirty-eight blacks and whites was not much more than a tenth of the number who died in Tulsa, Oklahoma's, racial upheaval two years later.

In its analysis of the riot, completed in 1921 after two years of testimony, Chicago's biracial Commission on Race Relations gave the event a sociological spin, examining the role of gangs, crowds, and mobs; the migration of African Americans from the South; the distribution and density of black neighborhoods; housing problems in the African-American community; black employment opportunities; and rumor, myth, and propaganda in the city's race relations. Instead, Tuttle offers us a historian's perspective, setting the Chicago riot—and others like it—in the context of a national war and postwar climate of conformity and intolerance. What connections does Tuttle make between the war and the postwar riots? Between the riots and the political anxiety of the Red Scare? Did it matter that blacks had fought in the war, albeit in segregated units?

"The parks and bathing beaches," Chicago's leading black newspaper, the *Defender*, reminded its readers in July 1919, "are much more inviting these warm days than State Street. A hint to the wise should be sufficient." Specifically, the *Defender* recommended Lake Michigan's 25th Street beach, where there were free towels and lockers and where "every precaution is being taken to safeguard the interests of the bathers." The *Whip*, another of the city's black newspapers, also boosted the attractions to be found at the 25th Street beach. There were not only bathing beauties there but even a black lifeguard, who, unlike some of his white counterparts, was courteous and helpful. So

William M. Tuttle, Jr., *Race Riot: Chicago in the Red Summer of 1919,* 2nd edition (Urbana: University of Illinois Press, 1996). © 1970 by William M. Tuttle, Jr.

come to 25th Street, the *Whip* urged, and help Chicago's black people "make this beach [their] Atlantic City."

For teenage boys, however, such advice was superfluous, especially as the temperature on Sunday, July 27, soared into the nineties. Fourteen-year-old John Harris was an energetic teenager, as were his companions that day, four boys named Williams. Charles and Lawrence Williams were brothers, who with Harris and Paul Williams, unrelated, all lived on Chicago's South Side in the vicinity of Harris' house at 53rd and State, while Eugene Williams lived in another neighborhood, about fifteen blocks to the north. The four lads from farther south in the city had met Eugene at the beach.

The heat was already stifling by early afternoon when the boys hopped onto a produce truck driving north on Wabash Avenue. It was an Autocar, "a real speed wagon." At 26th Street, the truck slowed down again, this time to cross the streetcar tracks, and the boys alighted. They walked east and they walked fast, practically jogging the seven blocks to the lake. Perspiring freely and carrying their rolled-up swimming trunks, they were naturally eager to get to the cooling water and to the homemade raft that awaited them at the beach. But they also moved hurriedly because the territory through which they were passing was the domain of an Irish gang that had attacked them several times before with rocks.

The boys were not headed for the black-patronized 25th Street beach; nor did they intend to try to swim at the white beach at 29th Street, behind the Michael Reese Hospital. They were going to their own, very private spot, which was located just in between. Familiar landmarks loomed up as they walked east on 26th Street—the Burnham Park Police Station, the Hydrox Ice Cream Company, the tracks of the Illinois Central, and finally, at the lake front, a little island which the boys called the "hot and cold." Located behind the Keeley Brewery and Consumers Ice, the "hot and cold" got its name from the effluence discharged by these companies. The waters of Lake Michigan could be as cold as the melting ice from Consumers, yet the run-off from the vats at the brewery was not only hot but chemically potent as well. It could even temporarily bleach a black person white. "It was hot," John Harris recalled, "and Jesus, I would be as white [as a white man] when I got done—so actually no women or nothing ever come through, so we [often] didn't even wear a suit, just take our clothes off and go down to the bank. . . ."

Tied up at the "hot and cold" was the raft. The product of several weeks of work by a dozen-and-a-half teenagers, the raft was "a tremendous thing," fully fourteen by nine feet, with a "big chain with a hook on one of the big logs, and we'd put a rope through it and tie it." Harris and his friends were far from being expert swimmers, but they could hang onto the raft and propel it forward by kicking; and, occasionally, "we could swim under water and dive under water and come up," always making sure, however, that they were within easy distance of the raft. "As long as the raft was there," Harris noted, "we were safe." The goal of the youths that Sunday was a marker nailed on a post several hundred yards from shore. At about two o'clock, the boys pushed off, angling their raft south toward the post—and toward 29th Street.

Meanwhile, at the 29th Street beach, the fury of racial hatred had just erupted. Defying the unwritten law which designated that beach as exclusively white, several black men and women had strolled to 29th Street determined to enter the water. Curses, threatening gestures, and rocks had frightened the intruders away. Minutes later, however, their numbers re-inforced, the blacks reappeared, this time hurling rocks. The white bathers fled. But the blacks' possession of the beach was only temporary; behind a barrage of stones white bathers and numerous sympathizers returned. The battle that ensued was frightening in its violence but it merely anticipated Chicago's long-feared race war. Sparked by the conflict at the beach, all the racial fears and hates of the past months and years in Chicago would explode in bloody warfare.

Innocently unaware of the savage exchange of projectiles and angry words at 29th Street, the five boys continued to "swim, kick, dive, and play around." Passing by the breakwater near 26th Street, the youths noticed a white man. He was standing on the end of the breakwater about seventy-five feet from the raft, and he was hurling rocks at them. It was simply "a little game," the boys thought. "We were watching him," said Harris. "He'd take a rock and throw it, and we would duck it—this sort of thing. . . . As long as we could see him, he never could hit us, because after all a guy throwing that far is not a likely shot. And you could see the brick coming . . . ." For several minutes he hurled rocks; and "one fellow would say, 'Look out, here comes one,' and we would duck. It was a game that we would play." It is not clear whether the rock thrower was playing the same game as the boys, or whether he was acting in angry retaliation against the black intrusion at 29th Street. One thing is certain, though: the next act in this drama brought pure tragedy.

Eugene Williams' head had just bobbed out of the water when one of the other boys diverted his attention. "And just as he turned his head this fellow threw [the rock] and it struck him . . . on the . . . forehead." John Harris could tell that Eugene was injured, for he slid back into the water; not diving, "he just sort of relaxed." Harris dived down to try to help, but, as he remembered, Eugene "grabbed my right ankle, and, hell, I got scared. I shook him off." By that time the boys were in about fifteen feet of water. Gasping for breath and panic-stricken, Harris surfaced and "began to shudder." "I shook away from him to come back up, and you could see the blood coming up, and the fellows were all excited. . . ." Groaning something like "Oh, my God," the man on the breakwater then ran toward 29th Street.

"Let's get the lifeguard," shouted Harris as he pushed off from the raft. Dog-paddling and swimming under water, Harris finally reached shore. Then he dashed to the 25th Street beach to tell the head lifeguard, Butch, who "blew a whistle and sent a boat around." But by that time there was nothing that anybody could do. Thirty minutes later, divers recovered Eugene's body.*

---

*It should be pointed out that Mr. Harris' relating of the events of July 27, 1919, conflicts at times with the coroner's version. The coroner contended, for example, that Williams was an excellent swimmer, but there is no indication of his source for this information, and the evidence seems to be to the contrary. He also held that "a superficial abrasion" on the decedent's body could not of itself have caused death; true, but a rock hitting one's body, however slightly, could cause panic and result in drowning. It is possible, too, that had the coroner had an opportunity to interview Mr. Harris, his findings might have been quite different.

Also by that time, anger had begun to replace the panic and the awe of the black boys. With the black policeman from 25th Street, they marched to 29th Street and pointed out the man they believed to be the rock thrower to the white policeman on duty, Officer Daniel Callahan. But Callahan would not only not arrest the man; he even refused to permit the black policeman to arrest him. As the policemen argued, Harris and his friends ran back to 25th Street and "told the colored people what was happening, and they started running this way," to 29th Street.

Panic had again overtaken the black youths. Hastily gathering up their clothes, they sprinted along 26th Street "all the way to Wabash." "We were putting our clothes on as fast as we were running." Boarding the first bus that appeared, they rode to the 55th Street beach, where they collapsed on the sand, thoroughly shaken and still panting. "I wasn't going home [right away]," said Harris, "because I knew I had better cool myself down. . . ." Also, he had left his cap and shoes at 26th Street, and he had to think of a way to explain their disappearance to his mother.

The argument at 29th Street raged on. And in the midst of it, Officer Callahan, while continuing to ignore the exhortations of blacks to arrest the alleged murderer, arrested a black man on the complaint of a white. In the meantime, distorted rumors of the drowning and the brawl had assumed exaggerated proportions on the South Side. Whites told each other in alarmed voices that a white swimmer had drowned after being struck with a rock thrown by a black. A rumor in the nearby "black belt" was that Officer Callahan had not

Whites and Blacks Leaving 29th Street Beach After the Drowning of Eugene Williams.
The Chicago Commission on Race Relations.

only caused Williams' death by preventing expert swimmers from rescuing him, but that he had even "held [his] gun on [the] colored crowd and permitted white rioters to throw bricks and stones at [the] colored." Hundreds of angry blacks and whites swarmed to the beach. The crowd was tumultuous when a patrol wagon pulled up at 29th Street to put the arrested black man in custody. Volleys of bricks and rocks were exchanged. Then a black man, James Crawford, drew a revolver and fired into a cluster of policemen, wounding one of them. A black officer returned the fire, fatally injuring Crawford. Suddenly other pistol shots reverberated. The restless onlookers, many of them armed, had their cue. The gunfire had signaled the start of a race war.

Once ignited on July 27, the rioting raged virtually uncontrolled for the greater part of five days. Day and night white toughs assaulted isolated blacks, and teenage black mobsters beat white peddlers and merchants in the black belt. As rumors of atrocities circulated throughout the city, members of both races craved vengeance. White gunmen in automobiles sped through the black belt shooting indiscriminately as they passed, and black snipers fired back. Roaming mobs shot, beat, and stabbed to death their victims. The undermanned police force was an ineffectual deterrent to the waves of violence which soon overflowed the environs of the black belt and flooded the North and West Sides and the Loop, Chicago's downtown business district. Only several regiments of state militiamen and a cooling rain finally quenched the passions of the rioters, and even then sporadic outbursts punctuated the atmosphere for another week. The toll was awesome. Police officers had fatally wounded seven black men during the riot. Vicious mobs and lone gunmen had brutally murdered an additional sixteen blacks and fifteen whites, and well over 500 Chicagoans of both races had sustained injuries.

The bloodshed inflicted an ineradicable scar on the city's reputation, and it outraged the sensibilities of countless Americans, black and white. But the Chicago race riot of 1919 should not have been altogether surprising to men and women who had read the chronicle of America's past, with its history, if not its tradition, of racial violence. Racial bloodshed struck New York City in the 1830's and in 1863; race riots erupted in Cincinnati in 1829 and 1841; in Utica and Palmyra, New York, in the 1830's; in Philadelphia in 1819 and at least five separate times in the 1830's and 1840's; various northern cities experienced interracial labor conflict during the Civil War; the races clashed in numerous places during Reconstruction, and at Wilmington, North Carolina, in 1898. Add to these outbreaks the violence of the traffic in slaves and of oppressive slaveholders, revolts by slaves, vigilante tactics of the Ku Klux Klan, election riots in various Southern states in the 1880's and 1890's, and thousands of lynchings, and one can begin to understand this history.

The advent of the twentieth century brought no surcease to racial bloodshed in America. The North as well as the South saw a burgeoning of racial violence in the first decades of the new century. Monuments to this fact were the riots in New York City in 1900, Springfield, Ohio, in 1904, Atlanta, Georgia, and Greensburg, Indiana, in 1906, and Springfield, Illinois, in 1908.

Original Caption: "Whites stoning Negro to death."
The Chicago Commission on Race Relations.

Clearly, urban racial violence was a national problem. White Northerners could no longer scoff at the barbarity of their Southern countrymen. "I'm not sure," the well-known satirist Mr. Dooley wrote at the turn of the century, "that I'd not as lave be gently lynched in Mississippi as baten to death in New York." The North had no corner on racial justice, he added; quite the contrary. "I'm not so much throubled about th' naygur whim he lives among his opprissors as I am whin he falls into the hands iv his liberators. Whin he's in th' south he can make up his mind to be lynched soon or late an' give his attintion to his other pleasures iv . . . wurrukin' f'r th' man that used to own him an' now on'y owes him his wages. But 'tis th' divvle's own hardship f'r a coon to . . . be pursooed be a mob iv abolitionists till he's dhriven to seek polis protection, which . . . is th' polite name f'r fracture iv th' skull."

East St. Louis, Illinois, stands as corroboration of Mr. Dooley's observation. Fueled by bigoted and alarmist trade unionists, self-centered corporate managers, strikebreaking black migrants from the South, corrupt white politicians, inflammatory news reporters, and biased and lax police officials, the smoldering fires of antagonism between blacks and whites exploded into furious rioting in July 1917. When the smoke from burning boxcars and houses lifted, nine whites and about forty blacks were dead, many of them the victims of unspeakable horror. A white reporter counted six black corpses lying near the corner of Fourth and Broadway. "I think every one I saw killed had both hands above his head begging for mercy." He had heard one moan, "My God, don't kill me, white man." Whites put torches to the homes of black people, leaving them with the choice of burning alive or fleeing to risk death by gunfire. Black women and children died along with their men; clubbed, shot, and stabbed, wounded and dying blacks lay in the streets. Others were lynched, including some who were already practically dead from other injuries. One black man had suffered severe head wounds; but, as he was not dead yet, the mob decided to hang him. "To put the rope around the negro's neck," noted a reporter, "one of the lynchers stuck his fingers inside the gaping scalp and lifted the negro's head by it, literally bathing his hand in the man's blood." Whites did not allow their black victims "to die easily"; when "flies settled on their terrible wounds the dying blacks [were warned not] to brush them off." Law enforcement was worse than nonexistent. Many police and militiamen, rather than try to quell the violence, worked in collusion with the white mobs in their quest to "get a nigger." State troops fraternized and joked with lawbreaking whites, and many were seen helping in the murders and arson.

Disgust and anger stirred many people in the nation after East St. Louis, though some whites in the Deep South praised the riot as just one more example of the "dauntless spirit of the white man" who would not bow before a "congenitally inferior race." Some blacks, on the other hand, called for revenge and retaliatory violence; and disconsolate words marked the conversations of black people regarding their future in America. Some asked how white America, in good conscience, could tolerate the enormous gulf between its professed ideals and the reality of race relations in its native land. Such was the import of a cartoon in the *New York Evening Mail* showing a black woman kneeling before President Woodrow Wilson, pleading for mercy. Huddling next to the woman were her two young children. In the background, East St. Louis was on fire. Wilson held a document asserting that "The World Must be Made Safe for Democracy." The simple entreaty of the black woman was, "Mr. President, Why Not Make America Safe for Democracy?"

The factors that had caused East St. Louis to explode were evident in varying degrees in other American cities in 1919, two years later. It seemed, in fact, that the atmosphere during the first year of peace after World War I was even more conducive to racial violence than that during the war itself. When black intellectual and civil rights leader James Weldon Johnson spoke of "the Red Summer," he was talking about the race riots that bloodied the streets of twenty-five towns and cities in the six-month period from April to early October 1919. One of these riots was a massacre, with an undetermined number of people slaughtered in rural Arkansas, and it is impossible to know exactly how many died in race riots that summer. But the number of blacks and whites killed must exceed 120.

The Red Summer was obviously consistent with the nation's history of racial violence. Yet the accentuated climate of violence in 1919 helps to account for the exorbitant number of race riots that year. It is not coincidental that the summer of 1919 also marked the beginning of the xenophobic and hysterically antiradical "Red Scare." Both phenomena were the ugly offspring of some of the same unrest, anxieties, and dislocations that plagued the United States and, indeed, most of the world in the immediate postwar years. Mankind's values, attitudes, and expectations were in disarray in 1919, and the resultant violence was worldwide.

In Europe, for example, the new states that had emerged from the dismantled Hapsburg Empire or had seceded from Russia clashed in the various regions of mixed nationality to which two or more laid claim. The Poles waged pitched battles with the Lithuanians over the Jewish city of Vilna and with the Czechs over the Teschen district; while Hungary clashed with Austria over Burgenland and with Rumania over Transylvania. Yugoslavia and Italy contended for Fiume; Rumania and Czechoslavakia vied for Bukovina; and Italy and Turkey wanted part of Anatolia. Greece and Turkey and Ireland and England vented their ancient hatred for each other. Nationalists in India and Egypt rebelled against British rule. In addition to these and other disputes, there was the Great Civil War, with the Bolshevik Red Army struggling to reconquer the territories that had proclaimed their independence from Russia, and with Allied armies intervening to contain Bolshevism. Despite these efforts, revolution swept briefly into Germany and Hungary in 1919. In January, the Spartacists in Germany sought to duplicate the events of 1917 in Russia. Although the Spartacists failed in Germany, Communists in Hungary established a short-lived government in March. But the Bolshevik undertaking which provoked widespread anxiety in the United States was the formation in March of the Third International, or Comintern. The Comintern's manifesto urged the workers to arm and seize governmental power. People in the United States looked around suspiciously. Even the most innocuous events began to suggest class revolution.

The world unrest was not confined to territorial disputes or the specter of revolutionary communism. Indeed, Hannah Arendt has written, the "magnitude of the violence let loose in the First World War," certainly one of the bloodiest conflicts in history, might "have been enough to cause revolutions in its aftermath even without any revolutionary tradition and even if no revolution had ever occurred before." Much of the distress was economic. The war had disjointed the prewar economy in which industrial Western Europe had prospered by trading with Eastern Europe and overseas nations. The value of many currencies in 1919 was uncertain, and several nations faced bankruptcy. In addition, demobilization had dumped millions of soldiers and war workers on the labor market. Unemployment was widespread, and the unemployed were hungry and restless. General strikes paralyzed Winnipeg and Havana, while riots and hunger strikes broke out in Spain, Germany, and Italy. "Bread and Peace" was the strikers' angry protest slogan.

A final manifestation of the acute disorder that plagued the world in 1919 was racial violence. Riots between black and white workers disrupted Johannesburg, South Africa; and in London and Liverpool, in Cardiff and

Barry, Wales, demobilized soldiers bitterly assaulted blacks imported from Jamaica during the war.

The United States' isolation from this unrest did not immunize it against similar domestic disorders. Indeed, in one field of violence, race riots and lynchings, America set the pattern. In the United States, as elsewhere in the world, 1919 was a year of transition. The Germans had been vanquished, yet the immediate fruits of victory disappointed those Americans who were unwilling to relinquish the moral idealism that the war had exuded, or whose desire for unified national purpose had gone unfulfilled. The nation was in transit between the passions of war and "normalcy"; in the meantime, it was also a battlefield for domestic conflict.

The nation had faced a common foe in April 1917, and Americans of diverse national origins, races, economic strata, and religions had united to defeat it. They did so not only by answering the appeal for troops, but also by flocking to factories to turn out the tools of war, purchasing Liberty Bonds, adhering to meatless days and breadless meals, and contributing services and funds to the YMCA and Red Cross. The singular purpose of these enterprises established intense national unity. Such unity demanded an unquestioning loyalty, intolerant of nonconforming ideas and behavior or even of suspected nonconformity. Yet in a significant way the wartime cohesion also served to restrain aggression. Heterogeneous elements of the population had united, and involvement in the war effort accorded to even the lowest strata of society a degree of status. With the Armistice, however, this national unity dissolved, and with it the restraint emanating from common purpose. But the wartime zeal survived, and social schisms proliferated. One offspring of this environment was the Red Scare.

The Red Scare was an extension of the atmosphere of the war, with its cult of patriotism, its generalized climate of violence, and its need of an enemy. In fact, the anti-German and antiradical agitation of late 1918 and the early months of 1919 so overlapped that, as John Higham has noted, "no date marks the end of one or the beginning of the other." Yet, by midyear, the emotional opposition to the external threat had blurred into indiscriminate hatred of the "inner enemy," aliens and dissenters. So widespread had become this inability to discriminate that *The Fleet Review* could ask: "Wonder if Berlin Bill is raising a scrubby beard so as to join the Bolsheviki? He'd doubtless feel at home with his friends Trotsky and Lenin."

Although subversion and sabotage did crop up spectacularly in 1919, such as the springtime bombings of government officials' residences, critics of the radicals ascribed every sort of disorder to them, including the social and industrial unrest that trailed in the wake of the federal government's amorphous demobilization program. "The moment we knew the armistice to have been signed," President Wilson told Congress in December 1918, "we took the harness off." With few controls and little planning, armies dispersed, wartime regulations expired, and industries either shut down or underwent the task of retooling for peacetime consumption. By July, while government agencies had abruptly terminated war contracts, the army had issued 2,600,000 discharges, at the rate of 15,000 per day. Veterans thus glutted the labor market in the very months of decreasing employment.

Unemployment rose sharply in April and May, and with it the nation's industrial unrest. As a consequence, the United States suffered one of its worst years of labor strife since the 1890's. As the 181 strikes and lockouts in March soared to 262 in April and 413 in May, employers and politicians, some of them genuinely frightened, others perceiving advantage in allegations of radicalism, blamed these disruptions on radicals and traitors. Probably more than any other labor dispute of that year, the Seattle general strike of February reinforced the dread of a workers' revolution. Although conducted by craft unionists who were hardly revolutionaries, the strike helped to transform the anxiety of countless people into panic. It was not a labor dispute at all, claimed Seattle's Mayor Ole Hanson. It was an attempt by revolutionaries "to establish a Soviet Government and control and operate all enterprises and industries." Hanson and other publicists of the threat of radicalism also asserted that alien agitators were the masterminds behind the strike, thus linking the fear of revolution to the distrust and hatred of the foreign-born and accentuating the apprehension that immigrant laborers were inherently dangerous to internal security.

Politicians and industrialists were not alone in embracing the emotionalism of antiradicalism and xenophobia. Overzealous soldiers, sailors, and Marines continued to act according to the militant aims that had guided them during the war. The fear of a proletarian uprising evoked responses similar to those elicited earlier by the "Huns." When radical union members circumvented a red flag ordinance by sporting red neckties at a rally protesting the conviction of Tom Mooney, a fellow unionist sentenced to death for murder, the organ of the enlisted men of the Navy declared resolutely: "If regulated authority fails in its mission to suppress the 'Reds,' there is some hope in the prospect that there will be enough of the Navy and Marine Corps and Army in the vicinity of these revolutionary meetings to deal properly with the enemies of the country." On May Day, soldiers invaded the Russian People's House in New York City, confiscated radical literature, and forced the aliens there to sing the "Star Spangled Banner." Later that day, more soldiers and sailors stormed the offices of the New York *Call*, a Socialist newspaper, assaulting several May Day celebrants. Vigilante war veterans also disrupted demonstrations in Boston and Cleveland, and in each of these cities one person was mortally wounded.

By midyear, the balmy spring of 1919 had become a torrid summer, and the antiradical and xenophobic mania had clearly risen with the heat. In the hands of employers, politicians, and much of the press, the epithet "Bolshevism" had become an increasingly effective instrument for damning all sorts of opposition and contrary beliefs; Communism was a phantom that conjured up a myriad of demonic images, and these images inspired a host of aggressive impulses. By midyear, moreover, government at all levels had succumbed to this emotional tide. Several states had enacted red flag, criminal anarchy, syndicalist, and sedition laws; and the federal police powers, led by Attorney General A. Mitchell Palmer, were mounting the onslaught that would yield the grossest indignities of the Red Scare.

Emma Goldman, a Feisty and Determined Anarchist. Goldman was imprisoned in 1916 for publicly advocating birth control, and again in 1917 for obstructing the draft. She was deported to her native Russia in 1919, at the height of the Red Scare. Note the sign above her.
Library of Congress.

The Red Scare was functioning without reserve by late summer and early autumn. A visitor to the United States at that time, A.G. Gardiner, editor of *The London Daily News,* was dismayed by the irrationality he witnessed. He could not forget, he wrote a half-dozen years later, "the feverish condition of the public mind at that time. It was hag-ridden by the spectre of Bolshevism. It was like a sleeper in a nightmare, enveloped by a thousand phantoms of destruction. Property was in an agony of fear"; and dissent, and indeed most any kind of nonconformity, was in danger of being denounced as "radical." " 'Radical' covered the most innocent departure from conventional thought with a suspicion of desperate purpose. 'America,' as a wit of the time said, 'is the land of liberty— liberty to keep in step.' "

The structure of society in 1919 was thus as conducive to the Red Scare as to the Red Summer. Bolstered by the force of law and the nation's mores, the "search for the 'inner enemy,' " as the sociologist Georg Simmel observed, "became institutionalized after World War I; and then instead of being disapproved by members of one's group for being prejudiced, one was punished for not being prejudiced." Although the motives for and the manifestations of race prejudice in 1919 were somewhat different, this statement was as true of race relations as it was of antiradicalism and the treatment of the foreign-born. For the most highly susceptible objects of prejudice in postwar America were its black men and women, not because they were radicals, but because they threatened the accommodative race system of white superordination and black subordination. The white populace had long been inimical to the strivings of black people, and during World War I this hostility became markedly more intense as over 450,000 Southern blacks migrated to the North. There, in crowded cities, they met in bitter competition with whites over jobs, housing, political power, and facilities for education, transportation, and relaxation. Moreover, black people, visibly distinct and with behavior patterns ostensibly alien to whites, were convenient scapegoats, especially for whites who feared that their social status had dropped because of the influx of blacks from the South. The employment of a new black worker in a shop or the arrival of a black family on a block only heightened anxieties of status deprivation, often prompting whites to revive the ancient shibboleth that blacks were grasping, not for material improvement, but for "social equality." White hostility to individual black people became generalized into a categorical hatred of an entire race.

For their part, black men and women, North and South, entered 1919 with aspirations for a larger share of both the nation's democracy and its wealth. Tension mounted as these aspirations collided with a general white determination to reaffirm the black people's prewar status on the bottom rung of the nation's racial and economic ladder. In 1919 racial uneasiness was evident in cities and towns throughout the country. And there seemed to be a threshold of tension above which racial violence was almost bound to occur, if spurred by a precipitating incident and in the absence of external controls of law enforcement. These various factors coalesced time and time again in 1919, to provoke an unparalleled outburst of racial violence.

Blacks Under Protection of Police Leaving Wrecked House in Riot Zone.
The Chicago Commission on Race Relations.

Lynch mobs murdered seventy-eight black people in 1919, an increase of
fifteen over 1918 and thirty over 1917. Ten of the victims were war veterans,
several of them still in uniform. Throughout the South the hangings, shootings,
and burnings multiplied in frequency and brutality as summer followed
spring. March and April each saw four outrages, while nine blacks were
lynched in May and nine more in June. The National Association for the
Advancement of Colored People had expressed shock in 1918 when lynch
mobs had murdered two black men by fire; in 1919, eleven men were burned
alive at the stake.

Perhaps the most monstrous lynching of the summer occurred in
Mississippi in late June. The day before the lynching, a mob had severely
wounded an accused black rapist, John Hartfield, in the canebrakes near
Ellisville. Fearing that Hartfield might expire before the hanging and burning
scheduled for the next day at "the big gum tree," a doctor prolonged his life. In
the meantime, newspapers in Jackson and New Orleans advertised the forthcoming event. "3,000 WILL BURN NEGRO," proclaimed the *New Orleans States*
in bold red type across the top of the front page. Thousands of curiosity seekers
flocked to Ellisville, and Mississippi's Governor Theodore G. Bilbo gave the
lynching his official sanction. When asked if he planned to prevent it, Bilbo
replied: "I am utterly powerless. The State has no troops, and if the civil authorities at Ellisville are helpless, the State is equally so." Moreover, he added,
"excitement is at such a high pitch throughout South Mississippi that any attempt to interfere with the mob would doubtless result in the death of hundreds

of persons. The negro has confessed, says he is ready to die, and nobody can keep the inevitable from happening." White Mississippians evidently disagreed only about the method of executing Hartfield. The *New Orleans States* reported that "some of the angry citizens . . . wanted Hartfield lynched, while others wanted him burned." He was both hanged and burned, and also shot.

While the lynchings of the Red Summer were usually confined to the South, practically half of the epidemic of race riots burst forth in Northern and border states. Several proposed hangings, moreover, soon developed into riots when blacks retaliated.

Charleston, South Carolina, suffered the first of the major riots of the Red Summer. It was Saturday night, May 10, when the black man doubled up in pain and slumped to the street. There had been an argument, and the bullet wound inflicted by a white sailor had been fatal. Hundreds of other sailors were also on liberty that night; hearing rumors of a racial altercation involving a Navy man, they began to swarm angrily into the city's black district. Augustus Bonaparte was having his hair cut at the time. Looking out the barbershop window, he saw a mob of sailors dash into the nearby shooting gallery, which they proceeded to loot for rifles. Automobiles filled with sailors, many of them armed with rifles, clubs, and hammers, soon crowded the streets. "Get a nigger," was their cry. James Frayer, a black cobbler, saw frightened black men and boys running toward his shop, shouting that the sailors were coming. Quickly, Frayer shut his door and latched it. He hid behind the counter with three customers. "Open the door," yelled a voice. When nobody moved, the sailor outside fired his weapon at random through the door, wounding Frayer's apprentice in the lower part of his back. Unable to subdue the rioters, the city police asked for help from Navy officials, who promptly ordered sailors to return to ship and dispatched Marines with fixed bayonets to occupy the streets. Although the presence of Marines aided in restoring calm, certain of the troops continued the terror that the sailors had begun. T. B. Nelson, for example, darted from his house upon hearing moaning in the street. Lying there wounded was a black youth, who pleaded with the Marines who hovered over him. "What are you shooting me for? I was not doing anything." "Why didn't you halt when we told you to?" demanded one of the troops. The boy gasped that he had not been ordered to stop. "Hush your mouth or we'll give you some more." When Isaac Moses also told Marines that he had not heard their command to halt, they responded by calling him a "damned liar," knocking him in the head with a gun butt, stealing five dollars, and stabbing him through the left leg with a bayonet. The death toll from that night of rioting in Charleston was two black men. Wounded were seventeen blacks, seven sailors, and a white policeman.

Longview, the center of population of Gregg County, an east Texas county of 8,500 whites and 8,200 blacks, had been uneasy with racial tension during the spring and summer months of 1919. Members of the local chapter of the Negro Business League had established black cooperative stores that sold products at lower prices than the white merchants. Black leaders—men such as Dr. C. P. Davis, a physician, and S. L. Jones, a high school teacher—had urged black farmers to avoid the white cotton brokers in Longview by selling direct to the buyers in Galveston. On June 16, Lemuel Walters was discovered in a white woman's bedroom. The next day his nude body was found lying near the railroad tracks at a desolate spot known as Foote's Switch, four miles south of Longview. Fear and apprehension swept the black community, and a delegation of eleven men led by Davis and Jones made a call on the county judge, Erskine H. Bramlette. The judge advised silence, saying that "there [should] be no talking as talking would interfere with locating the culprits." Days passed, but no arrests were made, and it appeared to the men of the Negro Business League that law officials not only were not investigating the lynching but that they were even using this time to destroy evidence which would prove the guilt of the perpetrators of the crime. The black men returned to Judge Bramlette, who told them that he had informed the district attorney of their suspicions. Again the judge advised "no talking."

A Saturday morning event in Longview's black district, as in black sections in towns across the South, was the arrival on the train of the weekly *Chicago Defender.* That July 5 issue of the newspaper was of special interest, for it had a story about Longview. Lemuel Walters, read the article on page two, "was taken from the Longview jail by a crowd of white men when a prominent white woman declared she loved him, and if she were in the North would obtain a divorce and marry him." His only offense, the *Defender* added, was having had a white woman love him, and the penalty he had paid was death. No formal charges had been preferred against Walters, and the sheriff had "gladly welcomed the mob" that had dragged the black man from jail and "shot [him] to pieces."

Jones, who was also the local *Defender* agent, drove his automobile to the downtown business district the following Thursday, July 10. But when he returned to his car, he encountered three white men who brusquely demanded that he come with them. Jones refused and tried to pull away from one of the men who had seized him. Another of the men pulled a wrench out of his coat and struck Jones a heavy blow on the head. Other blows followed. Jones fell to the pavement, struggled to get up, but fell again. He had written the *Defender* article, his attackers charged, and it would be much easier if he simply admitted it. When Jones denied that he had, they beat him again. Finally, the pummeling stopped, and Jones dragged himself to Dr. Davis' office. Later, at home, Jones asked that J. J. Ross, secretary of the Chamber of Commerce, be brought to him. He told Ross what he had told his assailants—that he was not the author of the article; and if Ross did not believe him, Jones said, he should wire the *Defender* for confirmation. Ross said he would.

Meanwhile, there was talk in town of impending "trouble that night." If Jones were still in Longview by midnight, according to one rumor, he would be lynched. Mayor G. A. Bodenheim sent a messenger to Davis to warn him and Jones to leave town at once. But Davis sent word back that he was staying. Davis also learned that the mayor and other city officials were meeting in emergency session at city hall, and he decided to join them. When he arrived at city hall, however, all that the white authorities would tell him was to take off his hat. "Yes!" Davis replied heatedly. "That's all you all say to a colored man who comes to talk serious business to you: 'Take off your hat.' I am not going to do it. I want to know what protection we colored citizens are going to have tonight." "You will have to take your chances," the mayor replied.

As darkness settled on Longview, black volunteers met at Davis' house, "pledging their lives in his defense." The doctor assumed command of the men, posting them "where they could safeguard every side from which an attack could be made," and instructing them not to fire before he did and "under no circumstances to shoot into white people's houses." At about 11:00, Dr. Davis sneaked through alleys and dark streets to within eyeshot of the city hall. It was just as he had feared. There he saw armed men gathering, using the fire department as their command post. Returning to Jones' house, he told his troops what the prospects were, and "offered to allow any of them who did not feel like risking his life . . . to retire. . . . Every man stayed and said he was prepared to take what might come." "Soon afterward and approaching midnight," Davis and Jones recalled, "the mob came down through a back street." The black men crouched quietly, waiting in ambush until Jones' house was "approached or attacked. Four white men came on the back porch of the house and called to Jones to come out." There was no answer. "When it became evident that they intended to force their way in, Davis fired the first shot and the melee began." Between 100 and 150 shots were fired in a half hour, and four whites fell with fatal wounds. The rest of the mob of about a dozen whites retreated to the town square. Minutes later, and one at a time, automobiles sped down the street leading to Jones' house, white men hopped out, picked up the dead and wounded, and sped away.

Throughout the night, a fire bell was sounded, eventually summoning about 1,000 white men to the town square. The mayor, Judge Bramlette, and other town leaders also arrived, however, to make speeches urging the men to disperse and go home. Until almost daybreak the leaderless crowd simply milled around. Then, as if suddenly energized by the first shafts of daylight, men began smashing their way into the hardware store and helping themselves to rifles, pistols, and ammunition. Thus armed, a mob headed back to Jones' house. But by then Jones and Davis were in hiding, so the mob occupied itself by dousing their homes with kerosene and igniting them, along with the homes of four other of the "principal" black residents. The next day, police officers, aided by bloodhounds, tracked down Marion Bush, the 60-year-old father-in-law of Davis, and shot him dead in a corn field three miles south of town.

Davis and Jones succeeded in escaping from Longview. Dressed in a soldier's uniform and improvised leggings, Davis boarded a train a few miles from town. Knowing that authorities searching for him would be looking for a doctor, he "bought some popcorn, some red pop and some other refreshment and walked around . . . throwing the bottle in the air, drinking from it ostentatiously and eating and singing, like a simple 'darky.'" He also talked a white boy into shooting craps with him, and after making a special effort to lose fifteen cents, he muttered, "That cleans me. I ain't done got no more money. . . ." Fearing worse violence, the governor of Texas declared martial law in

Longview and ordered the state militia and Texas Rangers into the town. Yet there was no more bloodshed. Certain white citizens of the community even adopted a resolution deploring the vigilante actions of the white mob, after also deploring the "scurrilous [*Defender*] article" about "a respectable white lady." That day and night of rioting, however, had left five dead, a score wounded, and many homeless.

After Charleston and Longview, the third major riot of the Red Summer erupted in Washington, D.C., a city where lurid tales of black rapists had been rampant for weeks. In June and July, four women allegedly were assaulted in Washington, and three in the portion of Maryland contiguous to the District of Columbia. The press featured emotional accounts of these attacks, imputing them all, without substantive evidence, to blacks. One alleged victim claimed that she had been sexually assaulted by "two young negroes . . . wearing white shirts, no coats, tan or yellow hats." Two weeks later she admitted that she had not been attacked by black youths, or indeed attacked at all. But the denial received miniscule coverage compared to the initial accusation. Such inflammatory journalism aroused the ire of whites, especially of military personnel stationed in or near the Capital, and racial tension mounted. On Saturday, July 19, the *Washington Post* ran headlines telling of another sexual assault: "NEGROES ATTACK GIRL . . . WHITE MEN VAINLY PURSUE." The next night Washington exploded. Racial tempers flared after a minor dispute on Pennsylvania Avenue in the midst of the capital city. Roaming bands of soldiers, sailors, and Marines began to molest any black person in sight, hauling them off streetcars and out of restaurants, chasing them up alleys, and beating them mercilessly on street corners. With ineffectual police restraint, violence reigned for three days as white mobs ran amuck through the streets. Blacks retaliated on the fourth day when the whites threatened to burn their homes.

During the riot, further irresponsible journalism, by both the white and the black press, heightened the anger of the mobs. On the first day of bloodshed, for example, the *Bee,* a black newspaper, declared: "A RIOT IS ALMOST CREATED: A Texan in the War Risk Bureau Assaults a Colored Female." The article beneath the headline told that the "assault" was actually a verbal insult. Two days later the *Washington Post* notified the aroused armed servicemen of a "Mobilization for Tonight." "It was learned," the *Post* noted, "that a mobilization of every available service man . . . has been ordered for tomorrow evening near the Knights of Columbus hut. . . . The hour of assembly is 9 o'clock and the purpose is a 'clean-up' that will cause the events of the last two evenings to pale into insignificance." Thus the *Post* had not only inflamed the passions of the rioters, it had even furnished them with a battle plan.

The helplessness of the Washington police compelled Secretary of War Newton D. Baker to order in 2,000 regular Army soldiers. On the evening of July 22, with federal troops and a downpour of rain deterring would-be rioters, the violence finally subsided, having left six dead in the streets and upwards of 100 injured.

After the bloodshed in Washington, the *New York Times* consoled itself by noting that, "painful as it is to say," a race riot such as the one in the Capital "could not have arisen in any Northern city where the police had been trained to expect riot duty." The *Times* displayed little prescience on this occasion, however. For in a Northern city, just four days later, John Harris and his four young black friends hopped onto the back of a produce truck, dreaming about the Lake Michigan beach at the foot of Chicago's 26th Street, and about their homemade raft and all the excitement that awaited them in the water.

sources

AFRICAN-AMERICAN PERSPECTIVES

In the course of its investigation of the 1919 riot, the Chicago Commission on Race Relations collected examples of African-American opinion on black leadership, the war experience, Chicago race relations, and other issues. A few of these—some brief, some extensive—are printed below. The introductory remarks that precede each comment are by the Commission. What conclusions can you draw about the state of mind of Chicago's black community in the wake of the riot?

 This report merely sets out examples of those views in the hope of showing the beliefs that control the conduct of Negroes in Chicago. . . .

Not a race problem.—A Negro business man said:

There is no race problem; if the white people would only do as they would be done by we would not have need of commissions to better conditions. This won't be done, but an easier plan is to enforce the law. The laws are good enough but they are not enforced. Riots grow out of hate, jealousy, envy, and prejudice. When a man becomes a contented citizen there will be little chance of causing him to fight anyone. Give us those things that are due us—law, protection, and equal rights—then we will become contented citizens.

For better race relations in Chicago.—A Negro alderman said:

1. Pass a vagrancy law that will take the idle, shiftless and intolerant hoodlum off the streets. Put the burden of proof on the one so arrested.
2. Close all vicious poolrooms and dens of vice, and permit no boy under nineteen years of age to enter poolrooms.
3. Forbid loitering on the street corners, especially transfer points.
4. Prohibit vicious and race-antagonizing campaign speeches on the streets of the city and in public halls. Races must not be arrayed against each other.

Chicago Commission on Race Relations, *The Negro in Chicago: A Study of Race Relations and a Race Riot* (Chicago: The University of Chicago Press, 1922), pp. 478–86.

5. Make more rigid the habeas corpus act, tighten up on the parole and probation laws and enforcement of the truancy law.

6. Stop the newspapers from referring to the territory occupied by the colored people as the "Black Belt."

7. Inciting and inflammatory headlines in the newspapers must be stopped.

8. Open the gates of employment to all races in our public utilities, such as street-car and elevated-road service, Chicago Telephone Co. exchanges, Peoples Gas Light & Coke Co., and the Commonwealth Edison Co.

9. Better housing for the colored people and improvement of the district in which a vast majority of them reside by turning certain streets into boulevards, building small parks and playgrounds, and let the city or South Park Commissioners build a bathing-beach equal to any other for the benefit and comfort of all races along the water front, between Twenty-ninth and Thirty-ninth streets. This without lines or thought of segregation and for the benefit of a neglected part of our tax-paying community.

10. Apprehend and convict the bomb throwers by placing in command of our police-stations officers who will do their duty and place patrolmen on duty who will not sympathize with this lawless element of our citizenry. Greater still, insist that the state's attorney do his full duty in prosecuting the people who are responsible for inciting these criminal acts.

11. Safeguard the rights of all races in our public parks and on the public highways.

12. Give us a man's chance in the field of labor, and we will prove that we are no burden to any other race of people.

*   *   *

Ready for trouble.—A Negro ex-soldier said:

I went to war, served eight months in France; I was married, but I didn't claim exemption. I wanted to go, but I might as well have stayed here for all the good it has done me. . . . No, that ain't so, I'm glad I went. I done my part and I'm going to fight right here till Uncle Sam does his. I can shoot as good as the next one, and nobody better start anything. I ain't looking for trouble, but if it comes my way I ain't dodging.

*   *   *

A Negro and a mob.—How does a Negro feel when he is being hunted or chased by a mob? Few persons are able to analyze their emotions under such stress. It happens, however, that a Negro university student fell victim to the sportive brutality of a gang of white men in a clash in September, 1920, and after being chased and hunted for five hours and a half in an unfriendly neighborhood escaped uninjured. He recounted his experience in an effort at a purely objective study of his emotions.

While at work in a plant just outside Chicago he became ill and was forced to leave early. Unaware that a riot was in progress, he left a street car to transfer in a hostile neighborhood. As he neared the corner one of a group of about

twenty young white men yelled: "There's a nigger! Let's get him!" He boarded
a car to escape them. They pulled off the trolley and started into the car after
him. His story follows:

The motorman opened the door, and before they knew it I jumped out and ran up
Fifty-first Street as fast as my feet could carry me. Gaining about thirty yards on
them was a decided advantage, for one of them saw me and with the shout
"There he goes!" the gang started after me. One, two, three, blocks went past in
rapid succession. They came on shouting, "Stop him! Stop him!" I ran on the sidewalk and someone tried to trip me, but fortunately I anticipated his intentions and
jumped into the road. As I neared the next street intersection, a husky, fair-haired
fellow weighing about 180 pounds came lunging at me. I have never thought so
quickly in all my life as then, I believe. Three things flashed into my mind—to
stop suddenly and let him pass me and then go on; to try to trip him by dropping
in front of him; or to keep running and give him a good football straight arm. The
first two I figured would stop me, and the gang would be that much nearer, so I
decided to rely on the last. These thoughts flashed through my mind as I ran
about ten steps. As we came together, I left my feet, and putting all my weight and
strength into a lunge, shot my right hand at his chin. It landed squarely and by a
half-turn the fair-haired would-be tackler went flying to the road on his face.

That was some satisfaction, but it took a lot of my strength, for by this time
I was beginning to feel weak. But determination kept me at it, and I ran on.
Then I came to a corner where a drug-store was open and a woman standing
outside. I slowed down and asked her to let me go in there, that a gang was
chasing me; but she said I would not be safe there, so I turned off Fifty-first
Street and ran down the side street. Here the road had been freshly oiled and I
nearly took a "header" as I stepped in the first pool, but fortunately no accident
happened. My strength was fast failing; the suggestion came into my mind to
stop and give up or try to fight it out with the two or three who were still chasing me, but this would never do, as the odds were too great, so I kept on. My
legs began to wobble, my breath came harder, and my heart seemed to be
pounding like a big pump, while the man nearest me began to creep up on me.
It was then that an old athletic maxim came into my mind—"He's feeling as
tired as you." Besides, I thought, perhaps he smokes and boozes and his wind
is worse than mine. Often in the last hundred yards of a quarter-mile that
thought of my opponent's condition had brought forth the last efforts necessary for the final spurt. There was more than a medal at stake this time, so I
stuck, and in a few strides more they gave up the chase. One block further on,
when I had made sure that no one was following me on the other side of the
street, I slowed down to walk and regained my breath. Soon I found myself on
Forty-sixth Street just west of Halsted where the street is blind, so I climbed up
on the railroad tracks and walked along them. But I imagined that in crossing
a lighted street I could be seen from below and got down off the tracks, in-
tending to cross a field and take a chance on the street. But this had to be abandoned, for as I looked over the prospect from the shadow of a fence I saw an
automobile held up at the point of a revolver in the hands of one member of a
gang while they searched the car apparently looking for colored men.

This is no place for a minister's son, I thought, and crept back behind a
fence and lay down among some weeds. Lying there as quietly as could be I reflected on how close I had come to a severe beating or the possible loss of my

life. Fear, which had caused me to run, now gave place to anger, and a desire to fight, if I could fight with a square deal. I remembered that as I looked the gang over at Fifty-first and Ashland I figured I could handle any of them individually with the possible exception of two, but the whole gang of blood-thirsty hoodlums was too much. Anger gave place to hatred and a desire for revenge, and I thought if ever I caught a green-buttoned "Ragen's Colt" on the South Side east of State that one of us would get a licking. But reason showed me such would be folly and would only lead to reprisals and some other innocent individual getting a licking on my account. I knew all "Ragen's" were not rowdies, for I had met some who were pretty decent fellows, but some others— ye gods!

My problem was to get home and to avoid meeting hostile elements. Temporarily I was safe in hiding, but I could not stay there after daybreak. So I decided to wait a couple of hours and then try to pass through "No Man's Land"—Halsted to Wentworth. I figured the time to be about 11:30 and so decided to wait until 1:30 or 2:00 A.M., before coming out of cover. Shots rang out intermittently; the sky became illumined; the fire bells rang, and I imagined riot and arson held sway as of the previous year. It is remarkable how the imagination runs wild under such conditions.

Then the injustice of the whole thing overwhelmed me—emotions ran riot. Had the ten months I spent in France been all in vain? Were those little white crosses over the dead bodies of those dark-skinned boys lying in Flanders fields for naught? Was democracy merely a hollow sentiment? What had I done to deserve such treatment? I lay there experiencing all the emotions I imagined the innocent victim of a southern mob must feel when being hunted for some supposed crime. Was this what I had given up my Canadian citizenship for, to become an American citizen and soldier? Was the risk of life in a country where such hatred existed worth while? Must a Negro always suffer merely because of the color of his skin? "There's a Nigger; let's get him!" Those words rang in my ears—I shall never forget them. . . .

*   *   *

A Negro resident of Chicago for fourteen years, formerly of Louisiana, said:

I went to Wilson's last inauguration in Washington and tried to talk to the President. I got in the gate, but the guard would not let me go farther without a pass. I went into every place that men were allowed to enter and found no "Jim-Crowing" in any public place. The nearest approach to it was in the printing department of the government. There were several colored girls all working at the same table. In other departments I had seen white and colored together. I went into every washroom on every floor of one building and must have washed my hands twenty times.

Negroes, real Americans.—A letter from a Negro workman to Governor Lowden said:

Why is it that intelligent colored people, the real Americans and the most humble and purest nation that ever trod the soil of America since they have been here—we have never thrown any bombs; we have never written a black-hand letter and what disgrace and shameful things we do it was learned to us by our foreparents' masters down south because they taught them to steal and murder and do all other most disgraceful things. We have never bombed any white people's homes, but I cannot see into it why it is that all nations such as the Polish, Japan, Chinaman, Mexican, German and Russ and now you see what they have done to this country; they have done everything to overthrow this Government and have got the I.W.W. and the Red. Where have we done such dirty deeds? We have enriched this soil of America with our blood in every war for this country and then cannot live where we want to as an American citizen. We even shed our blood in France to save someone else money and their homes, and the thanks we got when we come back was a big race riot which I do believe was started by southern white men to put a disgrace on the North because the North do not lynch and burn as they do. Of course I know you cannot do anything by yourself. But if you can get enough men who have got a backbone to protect the ones who have always protected them this outrage could be stopped. I read a piece in the *Herald-Examiner* that it would be a riot here; that has poisoned the minds of so many people. So now I hope you will try to stop such trouble.

THE NEW WOMAN: A PHOTO ESSAY

Just as African-American soldiers returned from the Great War with a new sense of self-worth, many middle-class and upper-middle-class women emerged from wartime work experiences, and from the atmosphere of democracy that permeated the conflict, invigorated and self-confident. Under these circumstances, woman suffrage was inevitable, and it came in 1920, with the Nineteenth Amendment to the Constitution. By mid-decade, black self-assurance had blossomed into the idea of a "New Negro," liberated from genteel culture, free to explore African-American identities. Similarly, many women embraced the concept of a "New Woman," freed from Victorian social and physical restraints— the corset, floor-length gowns, a full figure, and long hair. In contrast, the "flapper" look of the 1920s featured knee-length (or shorter) skirts; a thin, boyish figure; and short, bobbed hair.

The New Woman seemed poised to engage the world in a new way. But was that new way truly significant? Was the New Woman one aspect of a serious assault on the citadel of male power? Or something less meaningful, even trivial? Based on the photographs on the following pages, how would you describe the values and preoccupations of the New Woman?

Miss Suzette Dewey, Daughter of Assistant Secretary of the Treasury and Mrs. Chas. Dewey, Beside Her Roadster, 1927.
Library of Congress.

Margaret Gorman, Miss America, 1921.
Library of Congress.

Tybee Beach No. 6, Savannah, Georgia.
Library of Congress.

Girls Dancing During Noon Hour at Armour & Company Plant, 1927.
National Archives.

"The Gay Northeasterners" Strolling on 7th Avenue, c. 1927.
Schomburg Collection, New York Public Library.

the big picture

The nation experienced an unusual level of social upheaval, conflict, and change in the years immediately following the end of the Great War. Did the war cause this conflict, or would it have occurred even if the war had never happened?

chapter eight

THE GREAT DEPRESSION AND
THE NEW DEAL

The economic decline that followed the stock market crash of October 1929 was unparalleled in the nation's history. Over 4 million people were unemployed in 1930, 8 million in 1931, and almost 13 million, or close to one-quarter of the total civilian labor force, in 1933. Detroit, a city symbolic of the high-flying consumer economy of the 1920s, suffered in proportion to its earlier prosperity. Of the city's 690,000 gainful workers in October 1930, 223,000 were without jobs in March 1931. Because millions of small farmers reacted to falling prices by continuing to produce full crops, agricultural production fell little; farm income, however, was halved in the four years after 1929.

Work for wages was the heart of the economy of the early 1930s, and when it faltered, the effects rippled through every area of American life. In one sixty-day period in Detroit, for example, some 50,000 homeowners lost the equity in their property—the banks foreclosed on their mortgages and took their homes. Children went to school without food. Throughout that city, people of all races rummaged through garbage cans in the city's alleys, stole dog biscuits from the pound, and even tried to dig homes in the ground.

Herbert Hoover was not a do-nothing president. His attempts to persuade business to maintain wage rates were moderately successful for more than two years. Through the Agricultural Marketing Act, passed four months prior to the crash, the national government sought to maintain agricultural prices. National expenditures on public works increased. The Reconstruction Finance Corporation lent funds to banks, railroads, building and loan associations, and insurance companies. It saved a number from bankruptcy.

Perhaps Hoover's greatest failure was his firm opposition to national expenditures for relief. Private charity and city government, the primary agencies of relief, soon proved inadequate. Even in Philadelphia, where philanthropic traditions ran deep, the city's Community Council described its situation in July 1932 as one of "slow starvation and progressive deterioration of family life." Detroit, with its highly developed *public* welfare system, in 1931 debated whether to cut its welfare rolls in half or reduce payments by 50 percent—whether to "feed half the people or half-feed the people."

As people gradually became aware just how deep the crisis went, and as the government under Hoover failed to deal with it, it became obvious that fundamental change of one kind or another might be the only solution. One possible direction of change was dictatorship. The Great Depression was not a domestic crisis only. European nations were hit just as severely as the United States. And there, turning to an authoritarian figure—a Hitler in Germany or a Mussolini in Italy—at least promised to restore order and a sense of purpose. Europe's dictators frightened many Americans. But they also led many to think of strong leadership as a necessary phenomenon of the age, a prerequisite to the restoration of international order and domestic prosperity.

Another possible direction—a threat or a promise, depending on where one stood politically—was revolution. To many, some sort of socialist or communist transformation of the economic and political order seemed the only answer. Early in the decade, the Communist Party did make some gains. The party tried to organize unemployed urban workers into "councils," built around neighborhoods, blocks, or even apartment houses. In 1930, these Unemployed Councils managed a series of demonstrations in major cities, drawing crowds ranging from 5,000 to 35,000. Later, after they deemphasized their talk of immediate revolution, the Communists had some substantial successes within the Congress of Industrial Organizations (CIO), a new and powerful labor union. Large numbers of intellectuals—writers, scientists, teachers, and bureaucrats—also joined the party. The Socialist Party, too, began a vigorous program of recruitment and political campaigning, with the very popular Norman Thomas as its presidential candidate.

Into this atmosphere of uncertainty came Franklin Delano Roosevelt. A master at capturing the national mood in his speeches, Roosevelt talked of action, of advance, of what he called a New Deal for the American people.

It was not all talk, of course. Within three months of his inauguration in March 1933—the so-called Hundred Days—Roosevelt had signed into law a bewildering variety of legislation, much of it designed either to restructure the economy or to bring recovery. In the Emergency Banking Act, Congress gave the president broad discretionary powers over financial transactions. The Government Economy Act cut government employees' salaries and veterans' pensions in an attempt to balance the federal budget. The Agricultural Adjustment Act (AAA) granted subsidies to farmers who voluntarily reduced acreage or crops. In an act of boldness not to be repeated, development of the Tennessee River Valley was turned over to a public corporation.

Akin to the policy toward agriculture but more comprehensive, the National Industrial Recovery Act (NIRA) attempted to promote recovery by granting businesses the right to cooperate. Each industry wrote its own code of fair competition— setting minimum wages and maximum workweeks, limiting construction of new capacity, even fixing prices by prohibiting sales below cost. In addition, section 7(a) of the NIRA appeared to give workers the right to bargain collectively with employers. (The NIRA is perhaps the best evidence that the New Deal sought to strengthen capitalism rather than replace it with socialism.)

Relief efforts went well beyond those of the Hoover administration. To absorb the unemployed, Congress created the Civilian Conservation Corps (CCC) and set up the Public Works Administration to promote construction in the public interest. In 1935, the Works Progress Administration (WPA) was established to coordinate public works. The Emergency Relief Act directed Hoover's Reconstruction Finance Corporation to make relief funds available to the states and signaled the shift away from Hoover's opposition to using federal money for relief. The Social Security Act of 1935 brought the national government into old-age assistance and insurance and unemployment compensation.

For all its accomplishments, the New Deal made no commitment to remedying even the worst aspects of race relations: racial segregation, racial discrimination, denial of suffrage in the South, the lynching of black Americans. Fearful that a strong stand on racial issues would alienate the southern wing of his Democratic Party and bring an end to the New Deal, Roosevelt refused to use the Fourteenth Amendment to help blacks, and although sympathetic to the cause, he failed to support the growing movement for a federal antilynching statute. Because they were poor (rather than because they were black), many black Americans benefited from New Deal relief programs. For example, although blacks made up 10 percent of the population, they filled 18 percent of the WPA rolls. Yet some New Deal programs actually made life worse for blacks. When, for example, southern farmers took land out of production under the AAA, some 200,000 rural black farmworkers were left jobless. Moreover, numerous New Deal programs gave blacks less than they should have received. Many NIRA wage codes allowed businesses to pay lower wages to black than to white workers. Federal public housing programs often amounted to "Negro clearance." And the showy New Deal model communities, like Greenbelt, Maryland, had no black residents.

Historians have long debated whether the New Deal had any significant effect on the depression, and there is no more agreement on the New Deal's legacy for black Americans. But of one thing there can be little doubt. Roosevelt did manage to steal the rhetorical thunder from *both* the advocates of dictatorship and the proponents of revolution and to convince most blacks that the New Deal was worthy of their support. When he presented his legislative program to Congress, he could sound as though he meant to do everything that any European leader could, asking for "broad executive power to wage a war against the emergency, as great as the power that would be given to me if we were in fact invaded by a foreign foe." And he could now and then sound like a bit of a socialist, lambasting the "economic royalists" who controlled the nation's wealth. Most of the Rooseveltian rhetoric designed to appeal to blacks came from the lips of Eleanor rather than Franklin, but significantly, in 1936, to his famous phrase "forgotten man" he added "forgotten races."

Historians have also argued about whether Roosevelt's New Deal "saved" American capitalism or fundamentally altered it. What he was probably most anxious to save, however, was not the economic system, or even the political structure, but the faith of his constituents in the system. The nation did not respond to calls for revolution. The actual power of the Communist Party probably declined after Roosevelt's election. Blacks affirmed their commitment to a political party—the Democratic Party—with an influential southern, racist component. The "deal" Roosevelt offered the people may not have been as "new" as he made it sound, but he did convince most Americans—and most black Americans—that he was in charge of the only game in town.

interpretive essay

Cheryl Lynn Greenberg

MEAN STREETS: BLACK HARLEM IN THE GREAT DEPRESSION

On the eve of the Great Depression, the area of upper Manhattan known as Harlem was two very different places. For white, middle- and upper-class Americans, who did not live there, it was a symbol of the "jazz age," the antithesis of Main Street, a place where "expressive," "primitive," and "exotic" Negroes sang and danced and laughed and otherwise rebelled against the materialism and monotony of American life. For many of its black residents, Harlem was a slum, albeit a newly created one. As late as 1910, Harlem was a racially and ethnically diverse and reasonably prosperous community. During the 1910s and 1920s, massive in-migration of blacks from the rural South and from the West Indies, along with the out-migration of Italians, Jews, and other whites, created a community that was mostly black and very poor—in some respects, today's Harlem. Thus even before the stock market crash of October 1929 triggered economic decline, life in Harlem was difficult. Blacks paid high rents, did the menial and unskilled tasks regarded as "Negro jobs," and suffered from the highest rates of infant mortality and tuberculosis of any New York City neighborhood.

Cheryl Lynn Greenberg's essay can help us understand some of the ways in which the black people of Harlem understood and dealt with their basic poverty and with the additional burdens imposed by the Great Depression. It is a complex story, involving federal, state, and local governments, private agencies, and community organizations, as well as some creative family management. Having read Greenberg's account, do you think Harlem blacks survived the Great Depression with dignity, or were they demeaned by the crisis? What evidence is there that black economic problems were significantly exacerbated by race? And how might Greenberg's essay lead one to be more critical of the inactivity of the New Deal on racial issues (chronicled in the introduction to this chapter)?

Whether on relief or employed in private industry (and most black families experienced both at some point in the depression), few managed to make ends meet without some sort of extra income. People with little helped those with less; ties of family and community proved strong and durable. Men and women picked up temporary work whenever possible. Families took in lodgers or boarders or moved into the homes of relatives. Many borrowed money from friends or kin or bought groceries on credit from local merchants. Some engaged in illegal activities. A large proportion of Harlem arrests during the depression were for possession of policy slips, prostitution, and illegal distilling, all income-producing rather than violent crimes. These activities were certainly not new to the 1930s; blacks had been poor before this. But more families resorted to them in the years of the depression.

One woman's experiences illustrate the available choices—and their limitations. Thirza Johnson was twenty-one years old with three young children. Her husband had worked for the WPA for eighteen months. Despite that income the family could not pay its bills, and Mr. Johnson "tampered with the gas meter." For this he received sixty days in jail. The family had been receiving $5.40 every two weeks to supplement Mr. Johnson's paycheck, but without the WPA income that amount was completely inadequate. The utility companies cut off the gas and the electricity and Mrs. Johnson fell a month behind in paying the rent. When all three children fell ill, she asked her mother to come in from New Jersey to help. Her mother told her employer she needed a few days off to tend to her grandchildren. He fired her. This brought the number in the house to five, but the relief agency refused to increase the family's relief allotment because Mrs. Johnson's mother was not a New York resident. The grocery store gave her no more credit. Completely desperate, Mrs. Johnson turned to the Universal Negro Improvement Association (UNIA) for aid, and the Home Relief Bureau at last agreed to help.

Families like the Johnsons were so poor they were often forced to choose among necessities. Consumption patterns of Harlem families reveal both their real poverty and the constraints of living in a segregated community. Because of low incomes, African-Americans lived in poor, overcrowded housing, with high disease and death rates and high crime. Yet, . . . the New Deal programs had brought some progress to Harlem as well: health care, for example, improved in the depression decade, and for a few, new public housing became available.

Certainly black Harlem was not one homogeneous neighborhood. Within it lived population clusters divided by income and nativity. On some blocks only a few families received relief; on others, a majority did. Particular streets hosted the grocery stores, benefit societies, or restaurants of different national groups. As Vernal Williams, lawyer for the Consolidated Tenants League, explained:

> Why, every one of us have our own standards of living. We don't all live together. Just as you have Riverside, West End and Park Avenues, we have the same standard among our people, and you won't find that doctors [are] willing to go to the cheaper quarters along where the longshoremen live. . . . [To

live in the Dunbar apartments, for example] you had to be a doctor or a wealthy business man or work in the Post Office.

Nevertheless, virtually no family was immune from the depression's ravages, and all shared both the burdens of life in a discriminatory society and the strengths found in networks of support within the black community.

MAKING ENDS MEET

The most important first step for impoverished Harlem families was to supplement their earnings. Many families in the New Deal era turned to the long-standing practice in black communities of taking in lodgers. Perhaps because everyone was poor, the number of lodgers in black families in this period did not appear to bear a relation to any economic consideration. In the Harlem sample of the 1935 Bureau of Labor Statistics study, neither the family's earnings nor its expenditures provided a reliable predictor of whether or not that family would take in lodgers. The decision did depend on family size to some extent; families with many children seldom had lodgers. . . .

Black families in Harlem as elsewhere also turned to nonfinancial solutions, such as swapping and borrowing, and relied on the generosity of those temporarily better off. Evidence of these sorts of alternative economic strategies comes from many sources. Relief agencies, for example, demanded from applicants an accounting of expenses and income for the previous twelve months. Other agencies, such as the Bureau of Labor Statistics, investigated current earnings of nonrelief families. Private organizations conducted their own studies. Of the eighty-one Harlem families in the BLS sample, sixteen reported receiving gifts, and one a loan, from friends or relatives. Three others had picked up odd jobs and thirteen received "other income" from interest, "pool game," or sickness benefits from a lodge. If the number of families receiving money from gifts, loans, insurance, winnings, odd jobs, and lodgers were added together, over half the BLS survey families supplemented their earnings over the year, with an average of $153 per family with such added income. Families turning to the Unemployed Unit of the UNIA for help in obtaining relief also reported a heavy reliance on such means of supplementing their incomes.

Several families told of moving in with friends or relatives or receiving economic help from them. Both Nathan Campbell and Sarah Johnson told the UNIA that their family received money from friends. Minnie Jones complained she had to borrow money from her employer for food. In every income category, almost twice as many blacks as whites in New York City reported contributing to the support of relatives in 1935. Many men and women worked in exchange for free rent. Madeline Bright served as superintendent of an apartment building in return for lodgings. This, too, was common practice; one-fifth of single black women not living with families surveyed in Philadelphia, and two-fifths of such women in Chicago, engaged in this sort of exchange as well.

The proportion of all black families relying on these practices cannot be precisely documented. But impressionistic evidence suggests such interactions were commonplace. Francie, the protagonist of Louise Meriwether's Harlem-based novel, *Daddy Was a Number Runner,* borrows from her neighbor:

> [Mother] gave me a weak cup of tea.
> "We got any sugar?"
> "Borrow some from Mrs. Caldwell."
> I got a chipped cup from the cupboard and going to the dining-room window, I knocked at our neighbor's window-pane. The Caldwells lived in the apartment next door and our dining rooms faced each other . . . . Maude came to the window.
> "Can I borrow a half cup of sugar?" I asked.
> She took the cup and disappeared, returning in a few minutes with it almost full. "Y'all got any bread?" she asked. "I need one more piece to make a sandwich."
> "Maude wants to borrow a piece of bread," I told Mother.
> "Give her two slices," Mother said.

Loften Mitchell remembered: "In this climate [Harlem] the cooking of chitterlings brought a curious neighbor to the door. Mrs. Mitchell, you cooking chitterlings? I thought you might need a little cornbread to go with em'. A moment later a West Indian neighbor appeared with rice and beans. Another neighbor followed with some beer to wash down the meal. What started as a family supper developed into a building party." As another contemporary wrote, "The people [of Harlem] are the kindest and most sympathetic people that can be found. They will take one into the home and share everything there except the mate or sweetheart."

Some turned to illegal activities such as bootlegging and numbers running. Between 1931 and 1935, over half of all black arrests in Harlem were for "possession of policy slips," and police charged three-quarters of all black females arrested with vagrancy and prostitution. One woman included in a Welfare Council study explained that she earned money from "rent parties and home brew sales" and rented out rooms in her apartment for "immoral" purposes. The investigator suspected another family of earning money in this fashion as well, but that family did not admit it. Several people reported altering gas pipes and electrical wiring to avoid paying utilities; arrests for "tampering with gas meter" or similar offenses dotted the Harlem precinct records.

> Our electricity had been cut off for months for nonpayment . . . [explained Francie] so Daddy had made the jumper. . . . I took the metal wire from behind the box where we hid it, and opening the box, I inserted the two prongs behind the fuse the way Daddy had showed me. . . . Daddy said almost everybody in Harlem used a jumper.

Lillian Holmes, to document her need for relief, told the UNIA how she earned money in the past. For several years, she reported, she had been "engaged in the illegitimate business of *manufacturing liquor*" (UNIA's emphasis): six gallons of 100-proof alcohol a week. Her living costs, including manufacturing, came to $199.90 a month, while she earned approximately $208. In April 1937, however, there was a *"RAID"* (UNIA emphasis), at which time she applied for relief but was rejected. Paroled, the UNIA record concludes, she "return[ed] to making 'hot stuff.'" The record does not reveal whether the UNIA persuaded the relief agency in question to accept Ms. Holmes or whether she continued her life of crime.

Income-producing strategies did not add enough income for most families to live comfortably. They had to budget carefully and often deprive themselves of one necessity to afford another. The widespread poverty of Harlem and its character as a segregated community were reflected in consumption decisions made by black families. High rents required large portions of family earnings, and family size determined the amount spent on food and other household goods. The amount families set aside for such items as recreation and personal care, by contrast, varied according to personal decision. Consumption decisions therefore depended on many factors, some beyond the control of the family. How Harlemites chose to spend their money reflected all these considerations and demonstrates the extreme poverty of the area.

The average family in the Harlem sample of the Bureau of Labor Statistics study spent $548 per person for the year. Both income and the size of the family, of course, affected this figure. Not unexpectedly, the poorer the family, the more per-person expenditures depended on the number of members; as more people sit down to eat a small pie, each slice becomes smaller. At higher income levels, families spent with fewer constraints; a larger family could spend as much per person as a smaller family and simply save less.

The typical blue-collar and clerical nonrelief black family earned $1446 and spent $1459, compared with white earnings of $1745 and expenditures of $1839. On average, black families spent just under a third of their total expenditures, $450, on food and almost as much, $417, on rent. White families, by contrast, spent approximately 40 percent of their budget on food and 20 percent on rent. Controlling for income yields similar results. Black families at each economic and occupational level spent a lower proportion of their total income on food, and a higher proportion on rent, than did comparable whites. Blacks at each level spent more than whites on other housing costs, personal care, and clothing, but less on medical care. . . .

Blacks spent less of their total income on food than whites at the same economic level, in part because their families were smaller and in part because so much of their income was used for rent. But food was costly; food prices did rise during the depression, and they were higher in Harlem. Between 1934 and 1935, for example, food prices rose 11 percent. In the later year, a dozen eggs cost approximately 40 cents in most city neighborhoods, and 42 cents in Harlem. Flour cost 6 cents a pound; cornmeal 7 cents; again slightly higher in Harlem. Milk cost 13 cents a quart, potatoes 2 cents a pound, and carrots 6 cents a bunch. Meat was more expensive. Bacon cost 37 cents a pound; ham 29 cents citywide, and more in Harlem. *Amsterdam News* columnist Roi Ottley noted that food prices in Harlem were "considerably higher" than elsewhere in the city during the depression. "For every dollar spent on food the Negro housewife has to spend at least six cents in excess of what the housewife in any other comparable section is required to pay." Adam Clayton Powell, Jr., claimed "foodstuffs were 17 percent above the general level." The Reverend Mr. Garner of Grace Church complained: "Our food in Harlem is higher than the food we can get elsewhere. Food on the east side is much cheaper than food in the immediate neighborhood." The Department of Markets received more complaints from Harlem than from anywhere else about unfair costs and "shortweight practices."

Black families spent slightly more on clothing, household furnishings, and personal care than comparably impoverished whites possibly because, poor for a longer time, they could not continue to defer those needs. For medical care, white spending exceeded black in both amount and percentage of income. For both races, families with lower incomes were less likely to have annual medical exams or to go to a private doctor rather than a free clinic. Many poor families deferred dental visits.

The poorest spent less on every item in the budget than the general pool of blacks did. In fact, in the Harlem sample the poorest blacks had so little disposable income that the amount allotted for food did not change, regardless of family size. With more members a family might vary the quality of food it bought (less meat, for example, and more vegetables), but it could not afford to increase its overall food budget. . . .

This family was by no means unique. Most of the Harlem families in the [BLS] survey did not break even; fully three-quarters of them ended the year with some small deficit. Interestingly, the percentage of families with deficits did not decline as income rose. Rather, most families appeared to live at a level slightly above their actual income. Presumably, these families had all suffered a decline in their usual earnings and had not yet adjusted completely.

Still, for each income level, the average deficit of white families far exceeded that of black. Ninety-five percent of all Harlem black families in the survey either overspent by less than 5 percent of their total income or actually saved money. Only two families exceeded their income by more than 10 percent. The average debt for whites who had debts was $265, or 15 percent of their total expenditures, according to the BLS citywide study of wage earners; while for blacks it was $115, or 8 percent. . . .

Poverty alone could not account for indebtedness, since, according to the Harlem sample, black families at all income levels were equally likely to fall into debt. Nor could family size: among nonrelief families, those with deficits were no larger than those without. In other words, families of all types used debt as one way to stretch tight budgets. This did not imply extravagance, however, since those families with surpluses and those with debts spent approximately the same amount for food, rent, and all other items. In practical terms, then, any wage-earning family could find itself in the red. An emergency need would probably force a family into debt since virtually all lived close to the edge of their income level. As Myrtle Pollard explained, impoverished

Harlemites got along by buying one thing at a time. If someone needed a new coat, the rent would have to go unpaid that month. When this strategy failed, a family could find itself forced to turn to relief.

The Bennett family illustrates the preceding discussion: the all-too-common pattern of economic decline, a cut in consumption, debt, and finally application for relief. David Bennett, a thirty-three-year-old laborer, and his wife and two children lived on his WPA wages until January 1937, when he received his last $14.46 check. He had found work as a longshoreman and earned $88 that month. He also supplemented this with $32 in tips he received as a "helper" at the Washington Market. That month, despite $15 in medical bills, the family met all its obligations, paying $24 in rent, $37 on food, and an $8 insurance premium. After these costs, plus clothing, utilities, and carfare, there was still something left over for cigarettes and "entertainment." The following month David earned only $66 at the docks and $14 at the market, but the family still managed by cutting food purchases down to $30, paying only half the insurance, and foregoing clothing and "entertainment." The family struggled on this way for a while; David earning between $80 and $110 a month, and everyone spending less.

The third week in August, however, David lost his longshoreman's job, and his wife hired herself out as a domestic worker to two families. One paid her $7 a week, the other $4. By skimping on food they managed again, but September was much worse. With only Mrs. Bennett's wages of $44 and the $12 David earned shining shoes, they eliminated all spending but rent and food (which they had cut again). In October they decided to take in a lodger who paid $3.50 a week. They broke even only by pawning a watch and eight pairs of shoes.

In November, David's wife lost her previous jobs and hired on with two new families. She now earned $4 from one, and $3 from the other. That month the Bennetts went into debt. Food, rent, and utilities cost $65, while David's $12 from shoeshining, his wife's $28, and the lodger's $14 came to only $54. They withdrew money from their Christmas fund in December, but still could pay only half their rent that month. By the new year, they had to accept a loan of $10 and a gift of $3.50 from friends because Mrs. Bennett had again lost her jobs. Now able to afford only $22 for food, and paying no rent or utilities, they applied for public relief. Rejected with no explanation, they took another loan of $15, and turned to the UNIA for help. The file ended with the notation "no food."

CONSEQUENCES

The constant choosing between necessities or going without, the struggle to maintain a livable income, and the weight of discrimination and segregation resulted in poor housing and health, high crime, and inadequate public facilities in Harlem.

Neither the depression nor the New Deal lessened the segregation that trapped black families in substandard housing. Rental costs for Harlem residents remained high in the depression, although absolute costs fell slightly. In

1933, the City Affairs Committee reported Harlem to have "the worst housing conditions in the city. . . . Negro tenants pay from one percent to twenty percent more of their income for rent than any other group, despite the fact that the income of the Negro family is about 17 percent lower than that of the typical family in any other section of the city." This committee in fact understated the problem. The Neighborhood Health Committee surveyed rental costs in Manhattan in the depression's early years. It found that while the average Manhattan apartment rented for $44 a month, most in poor areas paid significantly less. In East Harlem, for example, where poor Italians and Puerto Ricans lived, rents averaged $30. In Central Harlem, however, rents never fell below $31 a month, and often ran as high as $70. The average resident of Central Harlem paid $52. The League of Mothers' Clubs found tenement-house blacks paid almost $1 more per room, per month, than comparably poor whites. Thus, for most Harlem residents, rents had not declined much; they were in some cases even higher than pre-depression rates. Even the Brotherhood of Sleeping Car Porters was forced to resort to rent parties to pay for its offices.

The policies of relief agencies aggravated housing problems. The enormous demand on their limited funds led several to provide no rent payments until eviction was threatened. Landlords learned that the sooner they made such threats the sooner they received overdue rent. Families who did not qualify for aid therefore faced eviction earlier than they otherwise might have. The Communist party, which fought eviction notices in the courts and carried the furniture of evicted families back into their apartments in an effort to stop the process, reported that hundreds of successful evictions occurred each week. . . .

Some black families economized by moving to smaller apartments of lesser quality or by moving in with relatives. The biggest problem in Harlem, the Welfare Council reported, was "the changes . . . in living conditions. . . . 'Doubling up' of families was common." Previously independent children returned to their parents' homes. The Charity Organization Society reported that, of families receiving care, twice as many families lived with relatives in 1931 as two years earlier; three times as many took in lodgers. A study of city slums found the average number of persons per room had risen in Harlem since the beginning of the depression because of such changes in household composition.

All was due not only to poverty but also to segregation. As the New York State Temporary Commission on the Condition of the Urban Colored Population pointed out, blacks gained access to apartments only when conditions there deteriorated and white tenants could not be found. In other words, blacks inherited bad conditions that simply got worse. Landlords neglected these apartments, but charged high rents because blacks could not find housing elsewhere. Mrs. S. Jecter of 16 West 136th Street, who supported her three children on her part-time earnings, complained that her landlord refused to make any repairs. She reminded him often of the fact that her gas stove was broken and she had no doorknobs, making the apartment impossible to lock. She paid her rent every month, nonetheless. She came home one day to find an eviction notice. Her landlord had grown tired of her complaints, and she was left without recourse. . . .

The cost of the housing did not reflect its quality. Of the thirty-one inhabited buildings on two blocks studied by the Housing Commission, nine had been officially condemned. The Housing Authority concluded after a survey of Harlem that "due to circumstances over which they have no control, many families are compelled to accept the old law tenement accommodations [buildings erected before 1901 and therefore not subject to the health and safety codes passed that year]. These houses are usually without heat, hot water and bathrooms together with improper plumbing, inadequate light and air, and have hall party lavatories." The Citywide Citizens' Committee on Harlem found that of 2191 occupied Class B buildings they examined in West Harlem in 1941, 1979 had major violations. Over 29,000 people lived in them. (Housing was classified by the type and number of facilities—heat, hot water, toilet, bath—provided, with A as the best and F as the worst.) The Mayor's Commission estimated that 10,000 blacks lived in cellars and basements with no toilets or running water. A former manager of Harlem apartments, an "agent for one of Harlem's largest real estate concerns," the New York Life Insurance Company, informed the Mayor's Commission:

> Do you know that apartments in my houses reeked with filth through no fault of the tenant? Bad plumbing—rats—mice—bugs—no dumbwaiters—no paint—heat—water and would you believe it I have been in apartments where young children lived and the toilet of the floor above flushed upon them. In fact things were so bad that I even appropriated money from the rents to help make the dumps livable much to the chagrin of my superiors.

Because Harlem had been built more recently than many areas in Manhattan, some of the housing there did provide modern conveniences. A higher proportion of Harlem apartments had private bathrooms, hot water, and heat than did apartments elsewhere in Manhattan, one study found, although these amenities did not always work. It listed approximately the same proportion of Harlem as non-Harlem Manhattan apartments in "good," "fair," and "poor" condition. That these newer apartments did not receive a "good" rating more often than the rest of the borough supports the conclusion that landlords in Harlem did less to maintain properties than they did elsewhere. . . .

The Harlem River houses on Seventh Avenue between 151st and 155th streets, built by the Public Works Administration (PWA) in 1937, offered modern, clean, spacious apartments at rents of $19 to $31 a month. The Houses also provided playgrounds, a nursery school, a health clinic, and laundry facilities. The United Tenants' League of Greater New York chose it as "the cleanest and most beautifully kept project in the city." But 20,000 families applied for the 574 spots.

As a result, more people lived in a smaller area in Harlem than anywhere else in the city. As Langdon Post, commissioner of housing, testified:

> A recent survey of . . . Harlem . . . [revealed] the average family income is $17.14. Forty percent of that went for rent. . . . In other parts of the city it is 20 to 25 percent for rent. . . . There are of course violations . . . but the problem of Harlem is not so much the bad housing, although there are plenty of them, it is the congestion to which they are forced through high rents.

On the block of 133d and 134th streets between Seventh and Lenox avenues, 671 people per acre crowded together, the highest density in the city. The block of 138th and 139th streets between the same avenues held 620 per acre. The Mayor's Commission on City Planning found 3871 people living between Lenox and Seventh avenues on 142d and 143d streets in 1935: "the city's most crowded tenement block." As the *Herald Tribune* reported, this block

> is tenanted exclusively by Negroes. On its four sides the area presents a front of gray and red brick fire escapes broken only by dingy areaway entrances to the littered backyard about which the rectangle of tenements had been built. . . . Half of all the tenants are on relief and pass their days and nights lolling in the dreary entrances of the 40 apartments which house them or sitting in the ten by fifteen foot rooms which many of them share with a luckless friend or two. Unless they are fortunate their single windows face on narrow courts or into a neighbor's kitchen and the smell of cooking and the jangle of a dozen radios is always in the air. . . .

Black nationalists and the Communist and Socialist parties all tried to mobilize tenants to protest these inexcusable conditions, and occasionally took landlords to court. While they won some victories, segregation proved stronger than activism in Harlem. At the Harlem River Houses, for example, the long waiting list proved too great an intimidation to those lucky enough to have an apartment there. There was nowhere else to move. In any building, tenants who made trouble could be evicted, but in Harlem there were low vacancy rates, and outside Harlem, few would rent to blacks. Thus, blacks expelled from their apartments faced homelessness as their most likely fate. Segregation, then, inhibited the emergence of black activism on housing, despite efforts of the Consolidated Tenants League and others.

Every housing report of the period linked Harlem's poor housing to other social ills, especially poor health. The existing situation, argued the Housing Authority, "spells many evils the most salient of which are disease, immorality, crime and high mortality. But the vast amount of unemployment is the greatest of all evils for that and that alone is the propelling force which drives the populace to seek cheaper rentals and into dilapidated homes." Harlem housing conditions constituted a "serious menace . . . not only to the health of the residents but to the welfare of the whole city," argued the Mayor's Committee on City Planning. It concluded that "large areas are so deteriorated and so unsuited to present needs that there is no adequate solution but demolition."

Certainly health statistics in Harlem did not compare favorably with those in the rest of the city, because of both substandard housing and inadequate incomes. In 1934 in Central Harlem, fourteen people died per thousand, compared with ten per thousand in the city as a whole. The area's tuberculosis rate was over four times higher. Of every one thousand live births, ninety-four Central Harlem babies died, almost double the city's rate. Black women died in childbirth twice as often as whites; in part because over one-third of the black deaths compared with one-seventh of the white came as a result of an illegal abortion. For every cause of death, and virtually all health problems, Central Harlem had the highest rate of all Manhattan Health Districts. Of 1921 students registered in P.S. 157 at 327 St. Nicholas Avenue, only 248 had no "observable" health defects in 1934. With the exception of bad teeth (942 with dental problems), the largest problem was "nutrition," with 641 students suffering from inadequate diets. While citywide rates of malnutrition among school children ranged between 17 and 20 percent in the years after 1929, a 1936 study claimed that fully 63 percent of Harlem school children "suffer[ed] from malnutrition."

On the other hand, these mortality and morbidity rates, though worse than those for the rest of the city, had declined since the 1920s and the pre-New Deal years. A comparison of health statistics for these earlier periods suggests that both races had seen dramatic improvement in the quality of health care. While medical advances contributed to the mortality decline, of course, the improvement also resulted from the increased availability of free health clinics. . . . At all income levels but one, black reliance on free clinics exceeded white. (For both races these rates were comparable to those of other cities.) In many cases this meant a lessening of the gap between black and white because of a substantial improvement in black access to health care and a slowing of improvements in white health as depression conditions worsened.

Mortality statistics continued to drop during the rest of the decade. In 1940, the general death rate in Central Harlem had dropped to 12.4 per thousand, the Manhattan rate to 11.5, and, for the first time, the mortality rate in another health district surpassed Harlem's. Harlem's tuberculosis deaths and infant mortality rates declined. Because the black community had been so destitute before the depression, in some ways conditions for them had improved with the advent of New Deal programs.

Relief programs correlated with some health improvements as well. While those on relief—the poorest—had a higher overall death rate, according to E. Franklin Frazier, they had lower rates of infant mortality. Probably relief babies were healthier because caseworkers advised their parents about prenatal and child care, and because of the medical care available to them. Pregnant women also received higher home relief food allotments. Thus, in terms of public services, the depression worsened conditions in Harlem while the New Deal improved them.

Poverty, poor housing, and poor health intensified other problems in Harlem. The Citywide Citizens' Committee on Harlem argued that "the poverty, the difficulties of home life and overcrowding, and the suffering of the adult population as a result of the unemployment in [Harlem] have . . . made educational needs greater than that of the average neighborhood of the city." Yet old buildings, scarce playgrounds, and overcrowded schools worsened the educational situation, demoralizing both teachers and students. The Mayor's Commission heard testimony from the executive secretary of the Central Committee of the Harlem Parents' Associations expressing her "great distress" about overcrowding and the poor facilities in Harlem. She politely "beg[ged] and petition[ed]" the commission to "do something about this because we, the parents of the children, are suffering because our children are involved." Mrs. William Burroughs of the Harlem Teachers' and Students' Association echoed these remarks, demanding that the city

> remedy overcrowding . . . safeguard life and health of pupils—immediate abandonment of old unsanitary firetraps, four in . . . Harlem . . . clinics in schools. . . . Retardation . . . is a vital problem in Harlem. . . . Many pupils come from an area with small educational facilities. In addition to this, the scandalous conditions here, inadequate staff, crowded classes, outmoded buildings, skimpy supplies, frequent lack of sympathy, lifeless curriculum, do not help; but hinder a slow pupil.

Ira Kemp forthrightly tied these conditions to racial discrimination and advocated the nationalist position he had articulated in the "Don't Buy" campaign.

> . . . We believe that the various school institutions in Harlem are overpopulated with teachers who aren't our people. . . . We feel a considerable percentage of teachers [in Harlem] should be colored.
> Q. Do you mean to insinuate that there is discrimination?
> A. I do. . . .
> Q. The specific question is whether you know of any instances where there is a violation of the law. Do you know of any girl [teacher] that has been discriminated against?
> A. My answer is that the system of keeping colored girls off the rolls who are on the eligible lists is so systematic that you can't get at it.
> Q. We are asking for proof. . . .
> A. I explained before that it is impossible to get facts from the authorities. We have had many complaints.

Ultimately, the Mayor's Commission on Conditions in Harlem concluded:

> The school plant as a whole is old, shabby . . . in many instances not even sanitary or well-kept and the fire hazards . . . are great. The lack of playgrounds and recreational centers . . . is all the more serious when it is considered that some of the schools are surrounded by . . . corrupt and immoral resorts of which the police seem blissfully unaware. Four of the schools lack auditoriums; one endeavors to serve luncheons to 1,000 children when there are seats for only 175. Most of all, no elementary school has been constructed in Harlem in 10 years. . . .
>   Prejudicial discrimination appears from the fact that the Board of Education, asking funds from the federal government for 168 school buildings, asked for but one annex for Harlem. . . .

The Teachers Union, Local 5 of the American Federation of Teachers, endorsed the Mayor's Commission's findings of poor school facilities in Harlem and cited "overcrowded classes, dangerous lack of adequate recreational facilities, antiquated and unsanitary school plant, 'horrifying' moral conditions, inadequate handling of the over-age child, and shortage of teaching staff." It concluded: "The conditions described . . . make proper teaching and proper receptivity to the teaching process impossible." The union's proposals—reducing class size, funding new school buildings, modernizing the old, hiring unemployed teachers to take children to nearby parks for recreation, staffing school playgrounds until six o'clock, and providing free lunches and winter clothing to the children of the unemployed—were endorsed by, among others, the Mayor's Committee on Harlem Schools, Father Divine's Peace Mission, the Joint Conference Against Discriminatory Practices, the Adam Clayton Powells, William Lloyd Imes and other ministers, YWCA and YMCA representatives, and Countee Cullen. To spur government action, the union reminded the mayor of the link between these problems and the 1935 riot: "The unhealthful and inadequate school buildings in Harlem had much to do with the unrest which led to the disorders of March 19."

Harlem residents added their voices, circulating petitions to the Board of Education:

> Public education in Harlem has been . . . long and grossly neglected. The facts are notorious.
>
> Dirt and filth and slovenliness have no more educational value for our children than for yours. . . . New school-houses with ample grounds and appropriate modern facilities are urgently needed to supplement or replace overcrowded and outmoded structures, to provide for the large increase in our population during the past decade or more. . . .
>
> Teachers, principals and superintendents are needed who have abiding faith in our children and genuine respect for the loins and traditions from which they have sprung. . . .
>
> So far as public education is concerned, we beg you to dispel by concrete action the widespread conviction that this region is neglected because its people are comparatively poor in this world's goods and in social and political influence, because many of them are of African descent.

In March 1936, Harlem organizations, including the Communist party and several black churches, created a Permanent Committee for Better Schools in Harlem, meeting in the New York Urban League building "with 400 delegates representing every phase of social, political, religious, cultural and civic activity in Harlem." These efforts, the commission report, and the memory of the Harlem riot brought some improvements within the year: the city budget included appropriations for four new school buildings, some repairs were made at most Harlem schools, and "many individual cases of discriminatory zoning have been satisfactorily settled." That year for the first time students could take a course in black history.

Of course Harlem's educational problems were by no means solved. In 1941, the Citizens' Committee reported that overcrowding forced many Harlem schools to run on a three-shift school day. From West 114th Street to West 191st, there was not a single public vocational or secondary school. One junior high school served the entire area from 125th Street to 155th, between the Harlem River and St. Nicholas Avenue. In one elementary school, ten classes lacked classrooms; in another, six did.

Still, educational levels among blacks did rise in the 1930s. Whether because Harlem's schools provided a better education than those of the south, because jobs were scarce in the depression, or because relief eased families' desperation, black children from both relief and nonrelief families attended school for longer during the depression than they had before. The proportion of black children aged fourteen to twenty-four remaining in school rose through the 1930s until it approached the figures for whites. . . .

Unlike delinquency, adult crimes rose. While most death rates declined in Harlem during the depression, homicides rose from nineteen per 100,000 in 1925 to twenty-four in 1937, while city rates fell. A 1931 investigation of the relationship between housing and crime found, not unexpectedly, that Manhattan's slum areas had higher rates of arrests of all types and a higher rate of convictions than the borough's average. The top two areas were both in Central Harlem. The same held for later years. Still, like delinquency, by and large, Harlem crimes by adults were more often income-producing than violent. As already noted, arrests for prostitution, operating illegal stills, and playing the numbers rose. Of a random sample of Harlem arrests in the first six months of 1935, all types of theft, from shoplifting to grand larceny, constituted only an eighth of the total, despite the fact that the period surveyed included the riot, with its many burglary arrests. Possession of policy slips, by contrast, accounted for about a third of all Harlem arrests. Except for the rise of arrests for policy slips and the decline for other gambling offenses since the early years of the depression, the rates for the different sorts of crimes remained fairly constant.

Of those arrested statewide, a smaller proportion of blacks than whites were charged with homicide or with theft of any sort, which suggests that whites were less often arrested for minor crimes than blacks were. The black rate for these more serious crimes proportional to their population, however, was greater than the white. Statewide, the ratio of whites arrested to their total population was 140 to 100,000, compared with 853 for blacks.

As we have seen, crime statistics are not foolproof indicators of community behavior. As with delinquency, discrimination or racism may have led to selective arrest, prosecution, and conviction. Perhaps police cared less about black crime and therefore acted less vigorously on Harlem cases. This would mean that arrest rates were lower than actual criminal behavior. Similarly, the rise in Harlem homicide deaths may have been due to a new vigilance by police rather than a real rise in the number of murders. An alternative possibility is that racism provoked officers to arrest blacks more readily than whites. The greater poverty of blacks might further skew their arrest rates, since the rich are generally more able to avoid arrest for minor crimes such as disturbing the peace than the poor are. Racist juries and judges might be similarly disposed to distrust blacks. Thus high black arrest and conviction rates may reflect factors other than strictly higher rates of criminality. Nevertheless, whatever the actual rates, criminal behavior in Harlem offers hints of the problems faced by a poor black community. Criminality reflected not only black behavior, but white as well.

Police corruption led to selective and discriminatory enforcement of the laws in Harlem. An NAACP memorandum argued that Harlem's high rate of arrests for prostitution and illegal sale of alcohol was attributable to police corruption: "We are made to look more immoral, less decent than anyone else and the environment of prostitution is being fostered [*sic*] on our women and young girls by the Harlem police officials in their scheme and business of tribute." A second memorandum estimated "perhaps forty to fifty percent of [prostitutes] . . . (colored) are forced or semi-forced and the rest act voluntarily." This memorandum cited the Cotton Club and several Italian-owned saloons as central "clearing house[s]" for these women. While the memo noted that the NAACP did not advocate illegal activity, it pointed out that it hardly seemed fair that black women were arrested for prostitution more often than white. The NAACP was convinced police arrested black women more often because they feared public outcry if they arrested too many whites. . . .

COMMUNITY

Yet while blacks in Harlem recognized the harsh conditions they lived under and the pernicious effects of their poverty, few believed the solution was wholesale abandonment of the area. Living together offered resources and strengths unavailable to dispersed individuals. Rather, African-Americans demanded better services where they lived, recognizing the positive power of community. The Reverend Mr. Garner, minister of the Grace Congregational Church, testified before the Mayor's Commission: "We find that our rents are higher than anywhere else in the city in proportion to what we get. Our food in Harlem is higher." But he refused to consider the suggestion that blacks move elsewhere to find less expensive housing:

> Our industrial life and social and economic and religious lives are centered in Harlem at the present time. We object to the beating up of our community on those grounds. . . . To break up the community in small segregated groups gives no opportunity for the friends to develop themselves on and among themselves [sic].

Street surveys of the Mayor's Commission and the "Negroes in New York" study of the Federal Writers' Project documented the large numbers of storefront churches, billiard halls, social clubs, dance halls, and mutual welfare lodges that provided social space throughout the depression decade. Over two thousand social, political, and mutual aid societies flourished in Harlem, including the United Aid for Peoples of African Descent, the Tuskeegee Alumni Association, Iota Phi Lambda (a sorority for business women), the King of Clubs (half of whose members were black police officers), the Hampton Alumni Club, the Bermuda Benevolent Organization, the Southern Aristocrats, the Trinidad Benevolent Association, the Anguilla Benevolent Society, the St. Lucia United Association, California #1, the New Englanders, the Hyacinths Social

Club, the Montserrat Progressive Society, St. Helena's League and Benefit Club, and hundreds of others.

Both poverty and community, then, shaped Harlem family and social life. As Loften Mitchell recalled,

> [T]he child of Harlem had the will to survive, to "make it." . . . This Harlem child learned to laugh in the face of adversity, to cry in the midst of plentifulness, to fight quickly and reconcile easily. He became a "backcapping" signifying slicker and a suave, sentimental gentleman. From his African, Southern Negro and West Indian heritage, he knew the value of gregariousness and he held group consultations on street corners to review problems of race economics, of politics.
>
> He was poor but proud. He hid his impoverishment with clothes, pseudo-good living, or sheer laughter.
>
> . . . In the nineteen thirties we had our own language, sung openly, defiantly. . . .
>
> We celebrated, too—our biggest celebrations were on nights when Joe Louis fought. . . . When he won a fight I went into the streets with other Negroes and I hollered until I was hoarse. . . . We had culture too. The Schomburg collection, a mighty fortress . . . three theaters, Louis Armstrong, Cab Calloway . . . Bill "Bojangles" Robinson . . . Bessie Smith . . . Langston Hughes . . . Romare Bearden . . . Augusta Savage. . . .

Richard Wright explained the energy and joy in black culture as rooted in poverty and anger:

> Our music makes the whole world dance. . . . But only a few of those who dance and sing with us suspect the rawness of life out of which our laughing-crying tunes and quick dance steps come; they do not know that our songs and dances are our banner of hope flung desperately up in the face of a world that has pushed us to the wall.

Others offered even less sanguine pictures. Alfred Smith of the FERA [Federal Emergency Relief Administration], a black man, discussed the African-American family in terms that today might be viewed as racist, but that nonetheless raised important questions about the impact of dire poverty on family life:

> The comparatively unstable family life of the Negro in urban areas may be ascribed to poor living conditions. Illegitimacy, illiteracy and a lack of a sense of responsibility or obligation all have their roots in the Negroes' unfortunate past, but are nurtured and fostered in city slums. Negroes are required to pay a larger proportion of their income for rent than any other group and they get less for their expenditure. The landlord who rents to the Negro mass in urban areas has no sense of responsibility to his renters. Negroes are forced to live in proscribed areas of the city, and in quarters where their health and morals suffer. They get little attention, little notice (other than being occasionally photographed in his slums as examples of need for "better housing") and much sympathy.

One part of his equation, "unstable family life," deserves some attention. Black and white leaders lamented the frequency of female-headed households. Clayton Cook of the Children's Aid Society reported 20 percent of Harlem black children "come from 'broken homes'—that is—families that have only a woman at the head. At one school in 699 families out of 1,600 . . . the father was either dead or had deserted." Certainly the high number of widows attests to the evil effects of poverty on adult (particularly male) longevity. Some social problems such as juvenile delinquency occurred more often in families without fathers according to contemporary studies (although, interestingly, the effects were more pronounced for girls than for boys). Yet other measures of "social disorganization," such as reliance on relief, seemed to bear no relationship to whether or not a man was present at home.

Many feared an absent male would ensure that these families would live in poverty, since black women had even lower earning potential than black men did. In fact, ironically, these economic liabilities were mitigated by the depression. While black working women did earn less, on average, than working men, female-headed families more often had additional earners. Thus, in the BLS sample, for example, families without a husband present earned no less per person than those with both husband and wife. Nor were black families with women at the head more likely than others to be on relief: the figure for black female-headed families on relief, 20 percent in New York City, was no higher than the proportion of female-headed families in the black population. A study of 675 Harlem families done by the Mayor's Commission found families on different blocks had very different average incomes. But in both high-income and low-income blocks, the proportion of female-headed families was identical.

Thus, while the likelihood of some social problems (such as juvenile delinquency) seemed correlated with the presence or absence of a father, other measures of "social disorganization" (such as reliance on relief) seemed to bear no relationship to that question. It may be that the depression threw so many men out of work that their absence made little economic difference to the family. When employment opportunities improved in the next decade, two-headed families would fare better than single-parent households, on the whole. But in an era of high unemployment and highly fluid household structures in which a family's income came from a variety of contributors, the presence of a male mattered less economically than one might expect.

Making ends meet was a difficult business in depression Harlem, and families used a variety of financial and nonfinancial, legal and illegal methods to do so. No one starved, but few in Harlem prospered, and the consequences of such grinding poverty reached into all areas of life. Housing and health were poor, mortality and crime rates high. Strong kin and community networks prevented much of the worst from occurring, and New Deal programs provided some help. Harlem itself, though, remained a ghetto and a slum and its people trapped in the conditions brought on by poverty and discrimination. As the New York State Temporary Commission on the Condition of the Urban Colored Population concluded in 1939:

While the Commission has no desire to indulge in dramatic over-statement it does earnestly wish to impress upon your honorable bodies the extreme seriousness of the conditions which it has studied. The conditions often seem almost incredible in so advanced a commonwealth as the State of New York, and they cannot remain uncorrected without general danger to the public welfare of the State as a whole.

sources

LETTERS FROM THE "FORGOTTEN MAN"

New York Governor Franklin Delano Roosevelt coined the term "forgotten man" during the presidential campaign of 1932. "These unhappy times," he said, "call for the building of plans . . . that build from the bottom up and not the top down, that put their faith once more in the forgotten man at the bottom of the economic pyramid."

Forgotten, perhaps. But this was no "silent majority" of the sort imagined by Richard Nixon in the late 1960s. The forgotten men (and women) were an opinionated bunch. They wrote letters by the thousands to the president, the first lady, and other public officials. A few of those letters—illustrative of the broad spectrum of voices captured by the term "forgotten man," are printed below. What is the theme of each letter? If you were handling correspondence for the Roosevelts, how, in each case, would you have responded?

 [New York, N. Y.
May 1936]

Mr Hopkins
Dear Sir: When you opened that "Sewing Project" at 18 St N.Y.C. did you forget that there are still a few "white Americans left. Its the worst thing as far as placing is concerned. Nothing but colored, Spanish, West Indies, Italians + a hand ful of white   Every colored that comes in is placed as "clerk, head or boss over tables + Knocking other people around. Well, if you dont see a race riot there its a surprise. If its colored + foreign your so interested in place them to themselves + not amongst "Humane" people—You just making the whites take a back seat. Its a very good useful project + hospitals + poor need the things that are made   But the system is rotten Just like a lot of cattle Being driven around when its time to go home they all rush no matter who they bump into. Too many bosses + no one seems to Know whats to be done—Maybe a few of us <u>whites</u> would like to be placed in something else but a "Sweat shop" work 6 days a week its a wonder they let you have

From *Down and Out in the Great Depression: Letters from the Forgotten Man* by Robert S. McElvaine. Copyright © 1983 by the University of North Carolina Press. Used by permission of the publisher.

Sunday off. If you dont give American people more of a Show we will
take up with President Roosevelt who did this good act so Americans dont
starve.

A disgusted
American

[New York, N.Y.
March 1936]

Dear President,
       why is it that it is the work-man that is always kicked when things go
wrong with the officials   my Husband has worke on W.P.A. for some time
a carpenter @ 85 dols per month + this morning he was reduced to timber-
man @ 60 per month   I know there was a mistake as he is a good carpenter.
I am sorry to trouble you but please Dear President I need that 25 dols he is
cut Do you know what it is to have money then find yourself broke, next
children, + finally live in a cold water Dump get up to two children at
night and find them nearly frozen from lack of clothing well I do, +
struggled along although I very often thought of suicide as the best way
out. I am not a coward but good Lord it is awful to stand helpless when you
need things.
       When that letter came from Project Labor officer Frank C. Hunt W.P.A.
N.Y.C. this morning informing him that he was reduced to 60 per month. well
I hate to think of what will happen. Please, get him replaced as carpenter
again his tag number is "123986" + he works at 125 St. N.Y.C. I am sorry I
cannot give you my name as I do not want publicity though I see no way of
avoiding it if things do not pick up. Thanking you for favours + forgive
scribbling as am all nerves.

[Anonymous]

Detroit, Mich.
Oct 2—1935

Mr. Franklin D. Roosevelt.
       Dear Mr. President.
       In this letter I'm asking you if you are kind enough to help me out. I'm a
girl of 18 years old. And I need a coat. I have no money to buy a coat   I need
about $25.00   Dear President are you kind to help me and send me the
money so I can buy my self the coat.
       My father isnt working for 5 yrs. He has a sore leg they wont take him to
work any place because of that sore leg. He cant buy me a coat. Were on welfare
       Dear Mr. President my father voted for you   he also told lot of his
friends to vote for you. He help you so please help us now.
       I know that you have a kind heart and wont refuse a girl that needs help
Others are dressed but me with out a coat   If I wont get any help from you
Dear Mr. President than I will take my life away. I can't stand it no longer. We
were thrown out on the street few times   I hate to live the way I'm living now.

Again please be kind and help me. I'll be waiting for your answer.

Yours Truly

M. L. [female]

Detroit, Mich.

My father reads the Bible and he has a picture of you in the bible.

Sept. 21, 1935.

Mr. Hopkins,

Relief Administrator,

Washington, D. C.

Dear Sir:—

Why are the Relief Projects being help up in St. Louis? The Projects that have already been started and are being help up for no one knows why, but you and I do not think you know. They could be continued and at least put some of our men to work right away and not wait until all the rest are ready, for if that is done and you fool around and pass the buck like you have none will be started at all.

We are not getting the allowances we did and our children are suffering for lack of food. And some have no clothes where with to attend school. Now is that right? And we will soon need coal and will not receive the funds for it, then what about that?

Of course, you are getting yours, and never have suffered like our people have, therefore you do not care. You have never been hungry and without all the luxuries of life, let alone the bare necessities. It is not the fault of our people that this condition exzists here, for they have tried and worked at anything at all to make a few pennies, but there is not the work to be had here.

Now there is work waiting here for some of our men and you are responsible for them not getting it. How can you answer to these people for that. They demand some consideration. And I am afraid they will soon tire of this delay and take some action themselves. They have been held down long enough through your petty Political Playing. That is all it is. The red tape could have been cut long ago. But what is your excuse. We know it is not true. Petty Politics is the answer. You will never get yours later by such actions.

Your plate at the table is full. Your family can enjoy life from the peoples money, and not have a care where this and that is coming from.

You were put in that position to do a real job and now you find you cannot fulfill it, and are playing around to the interests of the most moneyed men and starve the real working people of the country. God rights everything. And I hope to live to see the day that you and yours will have a little taste of what you are giving us daily for your food. NOTHING.

The Press all over the Country is razzing you and you think you are doing a swell job. Well people are something like elephants, they never forget. And the year 1936 is not far off.

You may not take this seriously but I have heard so many comments from people who have waited and waited for you to do something and the time is not far off when they will take action themselves. No one will be to blame but you. And now you want to pass the Buck to the State Administrators and in the next word you say they cannot pass finally on these unless they are O.K'd by Washington, which is BIG YOU. Well get busy and learn how to do something for some one besides your self.

Roosevelt is a coward like you are, he was afraid to come to St. Louis to the Legion Convention and you would be afraid to come too at an invitation. You are so yellow, but it is your type that holds such positions and should be put out. If you are afraid to fulfill your duties, why resign. there are many better and nobler men who are not afraid to do the right thing by the working people.

The women are the real ones that have to suffer when they see their children underfeed. And then they advocate to eat more food. Yes we would gladly eat more feed and give more to our children if we had work where we could earn them money to purchase more food.

Please take this situation seriously and grant these men work right away. Start them on the work that is laying waiting for them to take up. The Winter is going to be hard enough, when we are all needing so much and nothing to get it with and we are being cut here and there on our allowances. The children have to suffer.

Put a small amount of men to work and by doing that it will take that much burden off of the Relief Rolls and give more for those that have to remain on.

In the name of GOD, Start our men to work NOW. There is plenty for them to do.

A distracted Mother.

I have tried to get work and there is nothing for a woman of my age to do. There are too many young married women allowed to keep their positions after they marry and in that way throw men out of work and our young single girls who have just finished college and should be allowed to hold a position are prevented from getting one on this account. That is something else that should be taken up all over the country. Preventing young married women from continuing in their positions after marrying in order to lay up a large sum of money and there-fore keeping men out of work. When you have nothing more to do than you are doing now you might try a hand at trying to remedy this situation.

Apr. 10, 1936
N.Y.C.

Harry Hopkins
W.P.A. Administrator
Wash. D.C.
Dear Sir,

I am a W.P.A. worker—I have heard of your plans to lay off the W.P.A. workers and I am very much opposed to it. I come from an old American family who pioneered this country—They did not build this country so that their posterity should starve in it. I believe that this country owes a living to every man woman and child and if it cant give us this living thru private industry it

<u>must</u> provide for us thru government means—I am ready to fight for what I believe to be an inalianable right of every person living under this govt.

A. B. [female]

Toledo ohio
Feb 11-1936

Dear Mother

Of the Greatest country on god earth allso the father of the greatest I am one of the least and hope I am Doing Right and truely mean no Wrong by Writeing these few line   I am just a voter But I Dont mean any thing all that much But Just the same I am saying this I think the President is Doing alright But what a Pull Back we have got. so many vote for him and do Difference when it com to suporting him   I would call you som other Big Name But there is No other Name More Better than Mother and I Do think you and the President is the Mother and father of this Great USA   Well this is What I Want to say Would it hurt to Do a little investigating lot of the People is Kicking about any and every thing the father of the house hold is Done Well far as I can see the Middle class is trying to Poison the Mind of the lower class Making it as tough as they can without you noing it althou this May be so small that you may Not Pay it No Mind But little thing som time like that help a lot. . . .

[Anonymous]

IMAGES FROM THE 1930s: A VISUAL ESSAY

The works of art reproduced on the following pages were among hundreds of paintings and frescoes produced under the Federal Art Project of the Works Progress Administration and other, similar programs. The New Deal found itself in the art business partly because subsidies to artists did not bring the government into competition with private enterprise; and partly because government officials understood that post office murals might have a certain public relations value.

The artists who produced these works had to pay attention to the needs of their patron, the national government; to the desires of the local community in which the finished work would reside; and to the voices of the "people" in an era of depression. While these multiple demands on the artists make it impossible to isolate any single source for a work of art, the same multiplicity ensures that the artworks have some broad, social meaning.

What do you see in the following works of art? What do they tell us about how Americans understood and coped with the Great Depression? What ideas of gender do they present? Do they suggest that Americans feared technology or welcomed it? What balance is struck between urban and rural values? What would Harlem blacks think of any one of these murals if they encountered it at their local post office?

Allan Thomas, *"Extending the Frontier in Northwest Territory,"* Crystal Falls, Michigan.
(From: "Engendering Culture," by Barbara Melosh, pg. 35, fig. 2.2, Smithsonian Institution Press, Washington, DC, © 1991). Photo © National Archives and Records Administration.

Xavier Gonzalez, *"Pioneer Saga,"* Kilgore, Texas.
(From: "Engendering Culture," by Barbara Melosh, pg. 44, fig. 2.10, Smithsonian Institution Press, Washington, DC, © 1991). Photo © National Archives and Records Administration.

Paul Meltsner, *"Ohio,"* Bellevue, Ohio.
(From: "Engendering Culture," by Barbara Melosh, pg. 65, fig. 3.13, Smithsonian Institution Press, Washington, DC, © 1991). Photo © National Archives and Records Administration.

These illustrations appear in Barbara Melosh, *Engendering Culture: Manhood and Womanhood in New Deal Public Art and Theater,* Smithsonian Institution Press, Washington, D.C., 1991. We are grateful to Professor Melosh for making the prints available for use in *The American Record.*

Caroline S. Rohland, *"Spring"* (Sketch), Sylvania, Georgia.
(From: "Engendering Culture," by Barbara Melosh, pg. 74, fig. 3.20, Smithsonian Institution Press, Washington, DC, © 1991). Photo © National Archives and Records Administration.

Howard Cook, *"Steel Industry,"* Pittsburgh, Pennsylvania.
(From: "Engendering Culture," by Barbara Melosh, pg. 87, fig. 4.4, Smithsonian Institution Press, Washington, DC, © 1991). Photo © National Archives and Records Administration.

MIGRANT MOTHER

Between 1935 and 1942, photographers for the New Deal's Farm Security Administration Photographic Project took some 80,000 photographs of depression-era America. Together, they constitute a remarkable record of rural and small-town life—truly one of the great achievements of "documentary" photography. Dorothea Lange's Migrant Mother *is the best known of all the FSA photographs and one of the most famous photographs of the twentieth century.*

But what does it "document"? According to historian James Curtis's account of the evolution of this photograph, Migrant Mother *was the sixth and last of a series. The early photos in the series were taken from a distance and encompassed migrant mother's tent and four children, including a teenage daughter. The third photo was of the mother alone, breastfeeding her baby. Photos four and five brought one young child back into the frame, looking over the mother's shoulder toward the camera. To achieve the undeniable power of* Migrant Mother, *Lange asked the two young children to turn away from the camera, and she told the mother to bring her hand to her face. The whole process took only minutes.*

Does Lange's manipulation of the mother, her children, and the scene change your mind about the photograph? Does it mean that the photograph is somehow less truthful, less "a document"?

Dorothea Lange, *Migrant Mother* (no. 6), Nipomo, California, March 1936 (FSA).
Library of Congress.

t h e   b i g   p i c t u r e

This chapter is about some of the ways that Americans experienced and, in most cases, survived, the catastrophic economic downturn of the 1930s. How would you describe, characterize, or categorize their responses? According to the sources in this chapter, was government a great help?

chapter nine

WORLD WAR II:
OPTIMISM AND ANXIETY

When older Americans reflect on the 1940s, they recall the decade in halves: the first half, dominated by World War II, a difficult time when men and women fought for democracy against the forces of tyranny; and the second half, remembered as the beginning of a long period of prosperity and opportunity that would reach into the 1960s. There is much to be said for this view of the decade. Although Americans had been reluctant to go to war (the United States remained formally neutral when France was invaded by Germany in 1940), the Japanese attack on Pearl Harbor in December 1941 brought a flush of patriotism that temporarily buried most remaining doubts. A Virginia politician announced that "we needed a Pearl Harbor—a Golgotha—to arouse us from our self-sufficient complacency, to make us rise above greed and hate." Vice President Henry Wallace was one of many who revived Wilsonian idealism. "This is a fight," he wrote in 1943, "between a slave world and a free world. Just as the United States in 1862 could not remain half slave and half free, so in 1942 the world must make its decision for a complete victory one way or another." When the United States ended the war in the Pacific by exploding atomic bombs over Hiroshima and Nagasaki, many Americans considered the act appropriate retribution for the attack at Pearl Harbor by a devious and immoral enemy.

In many ways, the war justified idealism, for it accomplished what the New Deal had not. Organized labor prospered. The name "Rosie the Riveter" described the new American woman who found war-related opportunities in the factories and shipyards. Black people—segregated by New Deal housing programs, injured as tenant farmers by New Deal farm policies, and never singled out as a group worthy of special aid—found skilled jobs in the wartime economy. They also received presidential assistance—in the form of the Fair Employment Practices Commission—in their struggle to end racially discriminatory hiring practices. A growing military budget in 1941 produced the nation's first genuinely progressive income tax legislation. Despite a serious and disruptive wave of postwar strikes that was triggered by high unemployment, for the most part the prosperity and economic growth generated by the war carried over into the late 1940s and 1950s.

Yet this *good war/good peace* view of the 1940s leaves too much unexplained and unaccounted for. It does not explain that the very patriotism that made Americans revel in wartime unity also had negative consequences. For example, on the Pacific coast, more than 100,000 Japanese Americans, including many American citizens, were taken from their homes and removed to distant relocation centers, where they remained for the "duration." *Good war/good peace* does not explain the popularity between 1942 and 1958 of *film noir,* a gloomy black-and-white film style that pictured a world in which ordinary, decent people were regularly victimized by bad luck. And *good war/good peace* does not reveal how thoroughly the war disrupted existing gender and race relations, setting the stage for the silly and absurd things postwar Americans did to try to restore the prewar status quo.

Beneath the surface of 1940s America was a pervasive anxiety. Some of this anxiety was economic; those who had experienced the Great Depression could never quite believe that another one wasn't around the corner. But far more important were anxieties linked to the use of the atomic bomb on the Japanese, the killing of 6 million Jews by the Nazis, the war-related deaths of 60 million people worldwide, and the increasing seriousness of the Cold War. These extraordinary facts and events created the most elemental form of insecurity: the knowledge that any human life could end senselessly and without warning. And many thoughtful Americans began to question—in a way they had not before, even during the Great Depression—whether history was still the story of civilization and progress, or a sad tale of moral decline. The concepts *good war* and *good peace* remained vital to Americans' understanding of their world, but they could not encompass the haunting feeling, so much a part of the late 1940s, that something very important had gone wrong.

interpretive essay

Valerie Matsumoto

JAPANESE-AMERICAN WOMEN DURING WORLD WAR II

The beginning of the war in the Pacific on December 7, 1941, was a nightmare come true for many Japanese Americans. Americans were angry, even hysterical, and the press gave voice to their anger and fears, referring to the Japanese as "yellow men," "Nips," "vermin," and even "Mad dogs." Concerns were particularly acute on the Pacific coast, where the presence of substantial Japanese communities raised the possibility (it was never more than that) of subversive activity that could, conceivably, disrupt the war effort and endanger American lives. Within three days, the U.S. Army had proposed a mass evacuation of Japanese Americans, and by August of the following year, all West Coast Japanese Americans—some 120,000 men, women, and children—had been rounded up and put in camps of one sort or another, for the "duration." With scant regard for the Constitution, this policy was applied uniformly to those born in Japan (the Issei) and to the American-born generation (the Nisei).

Valerie Matsumoto's account of this experience focuses on the lives of the Nisei women who lived in the relocation centers and, between 1943 and 1945, relocated to cities in the Midwest and East. How does Matsumoto characterize what happened to those women? Using the historical information she provides, how would you explain the decision to relocate Japanese Americans? Consider, too, the possibility that this strange and shameful episode may offer insights into the larger American wartime experience. That is, to what extent was the Japanese-American experience of relocation a bizarre version of what was happening to millions of Americans in a world disrupted, and irrevocably changed, by the war of the century?

The life here cannot be expressed. Sometimes, we are resigned to it, but when we see the barbed wire fences and the sentry tower with floodlights, it gives us a feeling of being prisoners in a "concentration camp." We try to be happy

Valerie Matsumoto, "Japanese American Women During World War II," *Frontiers*, 8 (1984).

and yet oftentimes a gloominess does creep in. When I see the "I'm an American" editorial and write-ups, the "equality of race etc."—it seems to be mocking us in our faces. I just wonder if all the sacrifices and hard labor on [the] part of our parents has gone up to leave nothing to show for it?

—Letter from Shizuko Horiuchi,
Pomona Assembly Center, May 24, 1942

Thirty years after her relocation camp internment, another Nisei woman, the artist Miné Okubo, observed, "The impact of the evacuation is not on the material and the physical. It is something far deeper. It is the effect on the spirit." Describing the lives of Japanese American women during World War II and assessing the effects of the camp experience on the spirit are complex tasks: factors such as age, generation, personality, and family background interweave and preclude simple generalizations. In these relocation camps Japanese American women faced severe racism and traumatic family strain, but the experience also fostered changes in their lives: more leisure for older women, equal pay with men for working women, disintegration of traditional patterns of arranged marriages, and, ultimately, new opportunities for travel, work, and education for the younger women.

I will examine the lives of Japanese American women during the trying war years, focusing on the second generation—the Nisei—whose work and education were most affected. The Nisei women entered college and ventured into new areas of work in unfamiliar regions of the country, sustained by fortitude, family ties, discipline, and humor. My understanding of their history derives from several collections of internees' letters, assembly center and relocation camp newspapers, census records, and taped oral history interviews that I conducted with eighty-four Nisei (second generation) and eleven Issei (first generation). Two-thirds of these interviews were with women.

The personal letters, which comprise a major portion of my research, were written in English by Nisei women in their late teens and twenties. Their writing reflects the experience and concerns of their age group. It is important, however, to remember that they wrote these letters to Caucasian friends and sponsors during a time of great insecurity and psychological and economic hardship. In their struggle to be accepted as American citizens, the interned Japanese Americans were likely to minimize their suffering in the camps and to try to project a positive image of their adjustment to the traumatic conditions.

PREWAR BACKGROUND

A century ago, male Japanese workers began to arrive on American shores, dreaming of making fortunes that would enable them to return to their homeland in triumph. For many, the fortune did not materialize and the shape of the dream changed: they developed stakes in small farms and businesses and, together with wives brought from Japan, established families and communities.

The majority of Japanese women—over 33,000 immigrants—entered the United States between 1908 and 1924. The "Gentlemen's Agreement" of 1908 restricted the entry of male Japanese laborers into the country but sanctioned the immigration of parents, wives, and children of laborers already residing in the United States. The Immigration Act of 1924 excluded Japanese immigration altogether.

Some Japanese women traveled to reunite with husbands; others journeyed to America as newlyweds with men who had returned to Japan to find wives. Still others came alone as picture brides to join Issei men who sought to avoid army conscription or excessive travel expenses; their family-arranged marriages deviated from social convention only by the absence of the groom from the *miai* (preliminary meeting of prospective spouses) and wedding ceremony. Once settled, these women confronted unfamiliar clothing, food, language, and customs as well as life with husbands who were, in many cases, strangers and often ten to fifteen years their seniors.

Most Issei women migrated to rural areas of the West. Some lived with their husbands in labor camps, which provided workers for the railroad industry, the lumber mills of the Pacific Northwest, and the Alaskan salmon canneries. They also farmed with their husbands as cash or share tenants, particularly in California where Japanese immigrant agriculture began to flourish. In urban areas, women worked as domestics or helped their husbands run small businesses such as laundries, bath houses, restaurants, pool halls, boarding houses, grocery stores, curio shops, bakeries, and plant nurseries. Except for the few who married well-to-do professionals or merchants, the majority of Issei women unceasingly toiled both inside and outside the home. They were always the first to rise in the morning and the last to go to bed at night.

The majority of the Issei's children, the Nisei, were born between 1910 and 1940. Both girls and boys were incorporated into the family economy early, especially those living on farms. They took care of their younger siblings, fed the farm animals, heated water for the *furo* (Japanese bath), and worked in the fields before and after school—hoeing weeds, irrigating, and driving tractors. Daughters helped with cooking and cleaning. In addition, all were expected to devote time to their studies: the Issei instilled in their children a deep respect for education and authority. They repeatedly admonished the Nisei not to bring disgrace upon the family or community and exhorted them to do their best in everything.

The Nisei grew up integrating both the Japanese ways of their parents and the mainstream customs of their non-Japanese friends and classmates—not always an easy process given the deeply rooted prejudice and discrimination they faced as a tiny, easily identified minority. Because of the wide age range among them and the diversity of their early experiences in various urban and rural areas, it is difficult to generalize about the Nisei. Most grew up speaking Japanese with their parents and English with their siblings, friends, and teachers. Regardless of whether they were Buddhist or Christian, they celebrated the New Year with traditional foods and visiting, as well as Christmas and Thanksgiving. Girls learned to knit, sew, and embroider, and some took lessons in *odori* (folk dancing). The Nisei, many of whom were adolescents during the 1940's, also listened to the *Hit Parade,* Jack Benny, and *Gangbusters* on the radio, learned to jitterbug, played kick-the-can and baseball, and read the same popular books and magazines as their non-Japanese peers.

The Issei were strict and not inclined to open displays of affection towards their children, but the Nisei were conscious of their parents' concern for them and for the family. This sense of family strength and responsibility helped to sustain the Issei and Nisei through years of economic hardship and discrimination: the West Coast anti-Japanese movement of the early 1920's, the Depression of the 1930's, and the most drastic ordeal—the chaotic uprooting of the World War II evacuation, internment, and resettlement.

EVACUATION AND CAMP EXPERIENCE

The bombing of Pearl Harbor on December 7, 1941, unleashed war between the United States and Japan and triggered a wave of hostility against Japanese Americans. On December 8, the financial resources of the Issei were frozen, and the Federal Bureau of Investigation began to seize Issei community leaders thought to be strongly pro-Japanese. Rumors spread that the Japanese in Hawaii had aided the attack on Pearl Harbor, fueling fears of "fifth column" activity on the West Coast. Politicians and the press clamored for restrictions against the Japanese Americans, and their economic competitors saw the chance to gain control of Japanese American farms and businesses.

Despite some official doubts and some differences of opinion among military heads regarding the necessity of removing Japanese Americans from the West Coast, in the end the opinions of civilian leaders and Lieutenant General John L. DeWitt—head of the Western Defense Command—of Assistant Secretary of War John McCloy and Secretary of War Henry Stimson prevailed. On February 19, 1942, President Franklin Delano Roosevelt signed Executive Order 9066, arbitrarily suspending the civil rights of American citizens by authorizing the removal of 110,000 Japanese and their American-born children from the western half of the Pacific Coastal States and the southern third of Arizona.

During the bewildering months before evacuation, the Japanese Americans were subject to curfews and to unannounced searches at all hours for "contraband" weapons, radios, and cameras; in desperation and fear, many people destroyed their belongings from Japan, including treasured heirlooms, books, and photographs. Some families moved voluntarily from the Western Defense zone, but many stayed, believing that all areas would eventually be restricted or fearing hostility in neighboring states.

Involuntary evacuation began in the spring of 1942. Families received a scant week's notice in which to "wind up their affairs, store or sell their possessions, close up their businesses and homes, and show up at an assembly point for transportation to an assembly center." Each person was allowed to bring only as many clothes and personal items as he or she could carry to the temporary assembly centers that had been hastily constructed at fairgrounds, race tracks, and Civilian Conservation Corps camps: twelve in California, one in Oregon, and one in Washington.

The rapidity of evacuation left many Japanese Americans numb; one Nisei noted that "a queer lump came to my throat. Nothing else came to my mind, it was just blank. Everything happened too soon, I guess." As the realization of leaving home, friends, and neighborhood sank in, the numbness gave way to bewilderment. A teenager at the Santa Anita Assembly Center wrote, "I felt lost after I left Mountain View [California]. I thought that we could go back but instead look where we are." Upon arrival at the assembly centers, even the Nisei from large urban communities found themselves surrounded by more Japanese than they had ever before seen. For Mary Okumura, the whole experience seemed overwhelming at first:

> Just about every night, there is something going on but I rather stay home because I am just new here & don't know very much around. As for the people I met so many all ready, I don't remember any. I am not even going to try to remember names because its just impossible here.

A Nisei from a community where there were few Japanese felt differently about her arrival at the Merced Assembly Center: "I guess at that age it was sort of fun for me really [rather] than tragic, because for the first time I got to see young [Japanese] people. . . . We signed up to work in the mess hall—we got to meet everybody that way."

Overlying the mixed feelings of anxiety, anger, shame, and confusion was resignation. As a relatively small minority caught in a storm of turbulent events that destroyed their individual and community security, there was little the Japanese Americans could do but shrug and say, *"Shikala ga nai,"* or, "It can't be helped," the implication being that the situation must be endured. The phrase lingered on many lips when the Issei, Nisei, and the young Sansei (third generation) children prepared for the move—which was completed by November 1942—to the ten permanent relocation camps organized by the War Relocation Authority: Topaz, Utah; Poston and Gila River, Arizona; Amache, Colorado; Manzanar and Tule Lake, California; Heart Mountain, Wyoming; Minidoka, Idaho; Denson and Rohwer, Arkansas. Denson and Rohwer were located in the swampy lowlands of Arkansas; the other camps were in desolate desert or semi-desert areas subject to dust storms and extreme temperatures reflected in the nicknames given to the three sections of the Poston Camp: Toaston, Roaston, and Duston.

The conditions of camp life profoundly altered family relations and affected women of all ages and backgrounds. Family unity deteriorated in the crude communal facilities and cramped barracks. The unceasing battle with the elements, the poor food, the shortages of toilet tissue and milk, coupled with wartime profiteering and mismanagement, and the sense of injustice and frustration took their toll on a people uprooted, far from home.

The standard housing in the camps was a spartan barracks, about twenty feet by one hundred feet, divided into four to six rooms furnished with steel army cots. Initially each single room or "apartment" housed an average of eight persons; individuals without kin nearby were often moved in with smaller families. Because the partitions between apartments did not reach the ceiling, even the smallest noises traveled freely from one end of the building to the other. There were usually fourteen barracks in each block, and each block had its own mess hall, laundry, latrine, shower facilities, and recreation room.

Because of the discomfort, noise, and lack of privacy, which "made a single symphony of yours and your neighbors' loves, hates, and joys," the barracks often became merely a place to "hang your hat" and sleep. As Jeanne Wakatsuki Houston records in her autobiography, *Farewell to Manzanar,* many family members began to spend less time together in the crowded barracks. The even greater lack of privacy in the latrine and shower facilities necessitated adjustments in former notions of modesty. There were no partitions in the shower room, and the latrine consisted of two rows of partitioned toilets "with nothing in front of you, just on the sides. Lots of people were not used to those kind of facilities, so [they'd] either go early in the morning when people were not around, or go real late at night. . . . It was really something until you got used to it."

The large communal mess halls also encouraged family disunity as family members gradually began to eat separately: mothers with small children, fathers with other men, and older children with their peers. "Table manners were forgotten," observed Miné Okubo. "Guzzle, guzzle, guzzle; hurry, hurry, hurry. Family life was lacking. Everyone ate wherever he or she pleased." Some strategies were developed for preserving family unity. The Amache Camp responded in part by assigning each family a particular table in the mess hall. Some families took the food back to their barracks so that they might eat together. But these measures were not always feasible in the face of varying work schedules; the odd hours of those assigned to shifts in the mess halls and infirmaries often made it impossible for the family to sit down together for meals.

Newspaper reports that Japanese Americans were living in luxurious conditions angered evacuees struggling to adjust to cramped quarters and crude communal facilities. A married woman with a family wrote from Heart Mountain:

> Last weekend, we had an awful cold wave and it was about 20° to 30° below zero. In such a weather, it's terrible to try going even to the bath and latrine house. . . . It really aggravates me to hear some politicians say we Japanese are being coddled, for *it isn't so!!* We're on ration as much as outsiders are. I'd say welcome to anyone to try living behind barbed wire and be cooped in a 20 ft. by 20 ft. room. . . . We do our sleeping, dressing, ironing, hanging up our clothes in this one room.

After the first numbness of disorientation, the evacuees set about making their situation bearable, creating as much order in their lives as possible. With blankets they partitioned their apartments into tiny rooms and created benches, tables, and shelves as piles of scrap lumber left over from barracks construction vanished; victory gardens and flower patches appeared. Evacuees also took advantage of the opportunity to taste freedom when they received temporary permits to go shopping in nearby towns. These were memorable occasions. A Heart Mountain Nisei described what such a trip meant to her in 1944:

> for the first time since being behind the fences, I managed to go out shopping to Billings, Montana—a trip about 4 hours ride on train and bus. . . . It was quite a mental relief to breathe the air on the outside. . . . And was it an undescribable sensation to be able to be dressed up and walk the pavements with my high heel shoes!! You just can't imagine how full we are of pent-up emotions until we leave the camp behind us and see the highway ahead of us. A trip like that will keep us from becoming mentally narrow. And without much privacy, you can imagine how much people will become dull.

Despite the best efforts of the evacuees to restore order to their disrupted world, camp conditions prevented replication of their prewar lives. Women's work experiences, for example, changed in complex ways during the years of internment. Each camp offered a wide range of jobs, resulting from the organization of the camps as model cities administered through a series of departments headed by Caucasian administrators. The departments handled everything from accounting, agriculture, education, and medical care to mess hall service and the weekly newspaper. The scramble for jobs began early in the assembly centers and camps, and all able-bodied persons were expected to work.

Even before the war many family members had worked, but now children and parents, men and women all received the same low wages. In the relocation camps, doctors, teachers, and other professionals were at the top of the pay scale, earning $19 per month. The majority of workers received $16, and apprentices earned $12. The new equity in pay and the variety of available jobs gave many women unprecedented opportunities for experimentation, as illustrated by one woman's account of her family's work in Poston:

> First I wanted to find art work, but I didn't last too long because it wasn't very interesting . . . so I worked in the mess hall, but that wasn't for me, so I went to the accounting department—time-keeping—and I enjoyed that, so I stayed there. . . . My dad . . . went to a shoe shop . . . and then he was block gardener. . . . He got $16. . . . [My sister] was secretary for the block manager; then she went to the optometry department. She was assistant optometrist; she fixed all the glasses and fitted them. . . . That was $16.

As early as 1942, the War Relocation Authority began to release evacuees temporarily from the centers and camps to do voluntary seasonal farm work in neighboring areas hard hit by the wartime labor shortage. The work was arduous, as one young woman discovered when she left Topaz to take a job plucking turkeys:

> The smell is terrific until you get used to it. . . . We all wore gunny sacks around our waist, had a small knife and plucked off the fine feathers.
>
> This is about the hardest work that many of us have done—but without a murmur of complaint we worked 8 hours through the first day without a pause.
>
> We were all so tired that we didn't even feel like eating. . . . Our fingers and wrists were just aching, and I just dreamt of turkeys and more turkeys.

Work conditions varied from situation to situation, and some exploitative farmers refused to pay the Japanese Americans after they had finished beet topping
or fruit picking. One worker noted that the degree of friendliness on the employer's part decreased as the harvest neared completion. Nonetheless, many
workers, like the turkey plucker, concluded that "even if the work is hard, it is
worth the freedom we are allowed."

Camp life increased the leisure of many evacuees. A good number of Issei
women, accustomed to long days of work inside and outside the home, found
that the communally prepared meals and limited living quarters provided them
with spare time. Many availed themselves of the opportunity to attend adult
classes taught by both evacuees and non-Japanese. Courses involving hand-
crafts and traditional Japanese arts such as flower arrangement, sewing, painting, calligraphy, and wood carving became immensely popular as an overwhelming number of people turned to art for recreation and self-expression.
Some of these subjects were viewed as hobbies and leisure activities by those
who taught them, but to the Issei women they represented access to new skills
and a means to contribute to the material comfort of the family.

The evacuees also filled their time with Buddhist and Christian church
meetings, theatrical productions, cultural programs, athletic events, and visits
with friends. All family members spent more time than ever before in the company of their peers. Nisei from isolated rural areas were exposed to the ideas,
styles, and pastimes of the more sophisticated urban youth; in camp they had
the time and opportunity to socialize—at work, school, dances, sports events,
and parties—in an almost entirely Japanese American environment. Gone were
the restrictions of distance, lack of transportation, interracial uneasiness, and
the dawn-to-dusk exigencies of field work.

Like their noninterned contemporaries, most young Nisei women envi-
sioned a future of marriage and children. They—and their parents—anticipated
that they would marry other Japanese Americans, but these young women also
expected to choose their own husbands and to marry "for love." This mainstream American ideal of marriage differed greatly from the Issei's view of love
as a bond that might evolve over the course of an arranged marriage that was
firmly rooted in less romantic notions of compatibility and responsibility. The
discrepancy between Issei and Nisei conceptions of love and marriage had
sturdy prewar roots; internment fostered further divergence from the old customs of arranged marriage.

In the artificial hothouse of camp, Nisei romances often bloomed quickly.
As Nisei men left to prove their loyalty to the United States in the 442nd
Combat Team and the 100th Battalion, young Japanese Americans strove to
grasp what happiness and security they could, given the uncertainties of the future. Lily Shoji, in her "Fem-a-lites" newspaper column, commented upon the
"changing world" and advised Nisei women:

> This is the day of sudden dates, of blind dates on the up-and-up, so let the flash
> of a uniform be a signal to you to be ready for any emergency. . . . Romance is
> blossoming with the emotion and urgency of war.

In keeping with this atmosphere, camp newspaper columns like Shoji's in *The Mercedian, The Daily Tulean Dispatch*'s "Strictly Feminine," and the *Poston Chronicle*'s "Fashionotes" gave their Nisei readers countless suggestions on how to impress boys, care for their complexions, and choose the latest fashions. These evacuee-authored columns thus mirrored the mainstream girls' periodicals of the time. Such fashion news may seem incongruous in the context of an internment camp whose inmates had little choice in clothing beyond what they could find in the Montgomery Ward or Sears and Roebuck mail-order catalogues. These columns, however, reflect women's efforts to remain in touch with the world outside the barbed wire fence; they reflect as well women's attempt to maintain morale in a drab, depressing environment. "There's something about color in clothes," speculated Tule Lake columnist "Yuri"; "Singing colors have a heart-building effect. . . . Color is a stimulant we need—both for its effect on ourselves and on others."

The evacuees' fashion columns addressed practical as well as aesthetic concerns, reflecting the dusty realities of camp life. In this vein, Mitzi Sugita of the Poston Sewing Department praised the "Latest Fashion for Women Today—Slacks," drawing special attention to overalls; she assured her readers that these "digging duds" were not only winsome and workable but also possessed the virtues of being inexpensive and requiring little ironing.

The columnists' concern with the practical aspects of fashion extended beyond the confines of the camps, as women began to leave for life on the outside—an opportunity increasingly available after 1943. Sugita told prospective operatives, "If you are one of the many thousands of women now entering in commercial and industrial work, your required uniform is based on slacks, safe and streamlined. It is very important that they be durable, trim and attractive." Women heading for clerical positions or college were more likely to heed Marii Kyogoku's admonitions to invest in "really nice things," with an eye to "simple lines which are good practically forever."

RESETTLEMENT: COLLEGE AND WORK

Relocation began slowly in 1942. Among the first to venture out of the camps were college students, assisted by the National Japanese American Student Relocation Council, a nongovernmental agency that provided invaluable placement aid to 4,084 Nisei in the years 1942–46. Founded in 1942 by concerned educators, this organization persuaded institutions outside the restricted Western Defense zone to accept Nisei students and facilitated their admissions and leave clearances. A study of the first 400 students to leave camp showed that a third of them were women. Because of the cumbersome screening process, few other evacuees departed on indefinite leave before 1943. In that year, the War Relocation Authority tried to expedite the clearance procedure by broadening an army registration program aimed at Nisei males to include all adults. With this policy change, the migration from the camps steadily increased.

Many Nisei, among them a large number of women, were anxious to leave the limbo of camp and return "to normal life again." With all its work, social events, and cultural activities, camp was still an artificial, limited environment. It was stifling "to see nothing but the same barracks, mess halls, and other houses, row after row, day in and day out, it gives us the feeling that we're missing all the freedom and liberty." An aspiring teacher wrote: "Mother and father do not want me to go out. However, I want to go so very much that sometimes I feel that I'd go even if they disowned me. What shall I do? I realize the hard living conditions outside but I think I can take it." Women's developing sense of independence in the camp environment and their growing awareness of their abilities as workers contributed to their self-confidence and hence their desire to leave. Significantly, Issei parents, despite initial reluctance, were gradually beginning to sanction their daughters' departures for education and employment in the Midwest and East. One Nisei noted:

> [Father] became more broad-minded in the relocation center. He was more mellow in his ways. . . . At first he didn't want me to relocate, but he gave in. . . . I said I wanted to go [to Chicago] with my friend, so he helped me pack. He didn't say I could go . . . but he helped me pack, so I thought, "Well, he didn't say no."

The decision to relocate was a difficult one. It was compounded for some women because they felt obligated to stay and care for elderly or infirm parents, like the Heart Mountain Nisei who observed wistfully, "It's getting so more and more of the girls and boys are leaving camp, and I sure wish I could but mother's getting on and I just can't leave her." Many internees worried about their acceptance in the outside world. The Nisei considered themselves American citizens, and they had an allegiance to the land of their birth: "The teaching and love of one's own birth place, one's own country was . . . strongly impressed upon my mind as a child. So even though California may deny our rights of birth, I shall ever love her soil." But evacuation had taught the Japanese Americans that in the eyes of many of their fellow Americans, theirs was the face of the enemy. Many Nisei were torn by mixed feelings of shame, frustration, and bitterness at the denial of their civil rights. These factors created an atmosphere of anxiety that surrounded those who contemplated resettlement: "A feeling of uncertainty hung over the camp; we were worried about the future. Plans were made and remade, as we tried to decide what to do. Some were ready to risk anything to get away. Others feared to leave the protection of the camp."

Thus, those first college students were the scouts whose letters back to camp marked pathways for others to follow. May Yoshino sent a favorable report to her family in Topaz from the nearby University of Utah, indicating that there were "plenty of schoolgirl jobs for those who want to study at the University." Correspondence from other Nisei students shows that although they succeeded at making the dual transition from high school to college and from camp to the outside world, they were not without anxieties as to whether they could handle the study load and the reactions of the Caucasians around them. One student at Drake University in Iowa wrote to her interned sister about a professor's reaction to her autobiographical essay, "Evacuation":

> Today Mr.—, the English teacher that scares me, told me that the theme that I wrote the other day was very interesting. . . . You could just imagine how wonderful and happy *I* was to know that he liked it a little bit. . . . I've been awfully busy trying to catch up on work and the work is *so* different from high school. I think that little by little I'm beginning to adjust myself to college life.

Several incidents of hostility did occur, but the reception of the Nisei students at colleges and universities was generally warm. Topaz readers of *Trek* magazine could draw encouragement from Lillian Ota's "Campus Report." Ota, a Wellesley student, reassured them: "During the first few days you'll be invited by the college to teas and receptions. Before long you'll lose the awkwardness you might feel at such doings after the months of abnormal life at evacuation centers." Although Ota had not noticed "that my being a 'Jap' has made much difference on the campus itself," she offered cautionary and pragmatic advice to the Nisei, suggesting the burden of responsibility these relocated students felt, as well as the problem of communicating their experiences and emotions to Caucasians.

> It is scarcely necessary to point out that those who have probably never seen a nisei before will get their impression of the nisei as a whole from the relocated students. It won't do you or your family and friends much good to dwell on what you consider injustices when you are questioned about evacuation. Rather, stress the contributions of [our] people to the nation's war effort.

Given the tenor of the times and the situation of their families, the pioneers in resettlement had little choice but to repress their anger and minimize the amount of racist hostility they encountered.

In her article "a la mode," Marii Kyogoku also offered survival tips to the departing Nisei, ever conscious that they were on trial not only as individuals but as representatives of their families and their generation. She suggested criteria for choosing clothes and provided hints on adjustment to food rationing. Kyogoku especially urged the evacuees to improve their table manners, which had been adversely affected by the "unnatural food and atmosphere" of mess hall dining:

> You should start rehearsing for the great outside by bringing your own utensils to the dining hall. Its an aid to normality to be able to eat your jello with a spoon and well worth the dishwashing which it involves. All of us eat much too fast. Eat more slowly. All this practicing should be done so that proper manners will seem natural to you. If you do this, you won't get stagefright and spill your water glass, or make bread pills and hardly dare to eat when you have your first meal away from the centers and in the midst of scrutinizing caucasian eyes.

Armed with advice and drawn by encouraging reports, increasing numbers of women students left camp. A postwar study of a group of 1,000 relocated students showed that 40 percent were women. The field of nursing was particularly attractive to Nisei women; after the first few students disproved the hospital administration's fears of their patients' hostility, acceptance of Nisei into nursing schools grew. By July 1944, there were more than 300 Nisei women in over 100 nursing programs in twenty-four states. One such student wrote from the Asbury Hospital in Minneapolis: "Work here isn't too hard and I enjoy it very much. The patients are very nice people and I haven't had any trouble as yet. They do give us a funny stare at the beginning but after a day or so we receive the best compliments."

The trickle of migration from the camps grew into a steady stream by 1943, as the War Relocation Authority developed its resettlement program to aid evacuees in finding housing and employment in the East and Midwest. A resettlement bulletin published by the Advisory Committee for Evacuees described "who is relocating":

> Mostly younger men and women, in their 20s or 30s; mostly single persons or couples with one or two children, or men with larger families who come out alone first to scout opportunities and to secure a foothold, planning to call wife and children later. Most relocated evacuees have parents or relatives whom they hope and plan to bring out "when we get re-established."

In early 1945, the War Department ended the exclusion of the Japanese Americans from the West Coast, and the War Relocation Authority announced that the camps would be closed within the year. By this time, 37 percent of the evacuees of sixteen years or older had already relocated, including 63 percent of the Nisei women in that age group.

For Nisei women, like their non-Japanese sisters, the wartime labor shortage opened the door into industrial, clerical, and managerial occupations. Prior to the war, racism had excluded the Japanese Americans from most white-collar clerical and sales positions, and, according to sociologist Evelyn Nakano Glenn, "the most common form of nonagricultural employment for the immigrant women (issei) and their American-born daughters (nisei) was domestic service." The highest percentage of job offers for both men and women continued to be requests for domestic workers. In July 1943, the Kansas City branch of the War Relocation Authority noted that 45 percent of requests for workers were for domestics, and the Milwaukee office cited 61 percent. However, Nisei women also found jobs as secretaries, typists, file clerks, beauticians, and factory workers. By 1950, 47 percent of employed Japanese American women were clerical and sales workers and operatives; only 10 percent were in domestic service. The World War II decade, then, marked a turning point for Japanese American women in the labor force.

Whether they were students or workers, and regardless of where they went or how prepared they were to meet the outside world, Nisei women found that leaving camp meant enormous change in their lives. Even someone as confident as Marii Kyogoku, the author of much relocation advice, found that reentry into the Caucasian-dominated world beyond the barbed wire fence was not a simple matter of stepping back into old shoes. Leaving the camps—

like entering them—meant major changes in psychological perspective and self-image.

> I had thought that because before evacuation I had adjusted myself rather well in a Caucasian society, I would go right back into my former frame of mind. I have found, however, that though the center became unreal and was as if it had never existed as soon as I got on the train at Delta, I was never so self-conscious in all my life.

Kyogoku was amazed to see so many men and women in uniform and, despite her "proper" dining preparation, felt strange sitting at a table set with clean linen and a full set of silverware.

> I felt a diffidence at facing all these people and things, which was most unusual. Slowly things have come to seem natural, though I am still excited by the sounds of the busy city and thrilled every time I see a street lined with trees, I no longer feel that I am the cynosure of all eyes.

Like Kyogoku, many Nisei women discovered that relocation meant adjustment to "a life different from our former as well as present way of living" and, as such, posed a challenge. Their experiences in meeting this challenge were as diverse as their jobs and living situations.

"I live at the Eleanor Club No. 5 which is located on the west side," wrote Mary Sonoda, working with the American Friends Service Committee in Chicago:

> I pay $1 per day for room and two meals a day. I also have maid service. I do not think that one can manage all this for $1 unless one lives in a place like this which houses thousands of working girls in the city. . . . I am the only Japanese here at present. . . . The residents and the staff are wonderful to me. . . . I am constantly being entertained by one person or another.
>
> The people in Chicago are extremely friendly. Even with the Tribune screaming awful headlines concerning the recent execution of American soldiers in Japan, people kept their heads. On street cars, at stores, everywhere, one finds innumerable evidence of good will.

Chicago, the location of the first War Relocation Authority field office for supervision of resettlement in the Midwest, attracted the largest number of evacuees. Not all found their working environment as congenial as Mary Sonoda did. Smoot Katow, a Nisei man in Chicago, painted "another side of the picture":

> I met one of the Edgewater Beach girls. . . . From what she said it was my impression that the girls are not very happy. The hotel work is too hard, according to this girl. In fact, they are losing weight and one girl became sick with overwork. They have to clean about fifteen suites a day, scrubbing the floors on their hands and knees. . . . It seems the management is out to use labor as labor only. . . . The outside world is just as tough as it ever was.

These variations in living and work conditions and wages encouraged—and sometimes necessitated—a certain amount of job experimentation among the Nisei.

Many relocating Japanese Americans received moral and material assistance from a number of service organizations and religious groups, particularly the Presbyterians, the Methodists, the Society of Friends, and the Young Women's Christian Association. One such Nisei, Dorcas Asano, enthusiastically described to a Quaker sponsor her activities in the big city:

> Since receiving your application for hostel accommodation, I have decided to come to New York and I am really glad for the opportunity to be able to resume the normal civilized life after a year's confinement in camp. New York is really a city of dreams and we are enjoying every minute working in offices, rushing back and forth to work in the ever-speeding sub-way trains, counting our ration points, buying war bonds, going to church, seeing the latest shows, plays, operas, making many new friends and living like our neighbors in the war time. I only wish more of my friends who are behind the fence will take advantage of the many helpful hands offered to them.

The Nisei also derived support and strength from networks—formed before and during internment—of friends and relatives. The homes of those who relocated first became way stations for others as they made the transition into new communities and jobs. In 1944, soon after she obtained a place to stay in New York City, Miné Okubo found that "many of the other evacuees relocating in New York came ringing my doorbell. They were sleeping all over the floor!" Single women often accompanied or joined sisters, brothers, and friends as many interconnecting grapevines carried news of likely jobs, housing, and friendly communities. Ayako Kanemura, for instance, found a job painting

Racist Hostility to the Japanese Was Not Limited to the West Coast. *This billboard was in Louisville, Kentucky.*
Royal Photo Company Collection, Special Collections: Photographic Archives, University of Louisville.

Hummel figurines in Chicago; a letter of recommendation from a friend enabled her "to get my foot into the door and then all my friends followed and joined me." Although they were farther from their families than ever before, Nisei women maintained warm ties of affection and concern, and those who had the means to do so continued to play a role in the family economy, remitting a portion of their earnings to their families in or out of camp, and to siblings in school.

Elizabeth Ogata's family exemplifies several patterns of resettlement and the maintenance of family ties within them. In October 1944, her parents were living with her brother Harry who had begun to farm in Springville, Utah; another brother and sister were attending Union College in Lincoln, Nebraska. Elizabeth herself had moved to Minneapolis to join a brother in the army, and she was working as an operative making pajamas. "Minn. is a beautiful place," she wrote, "and the people are so nice. . . . I thought I'd never find anywhere I would feel at home as I did in Mt. View [California], but I have changed my mind." Like Elizabeth, a good number of the 35,000 relocated Japanese Americans were favorably impressed by their new homes and decided to stay.

The war years had complex and profound effects upon Japanese Americans, uprooting their communities and causing severe psychological and emotional damage. The vast majority returned to the West Coast at the end of the war in 1945—a move that, like the initial evacuation, was a grueling test of flexibility and fortitude. Even with the assistance of old friends and service organizations, the transition was taxing and painful; the end of the war meant not only long-awaited freedom but more battles to be fought in social, academic, and economic arenas. The Japanese Americans faced hostility, crude living conditions, and a struggle for jobs. Few evacuees received any compensation for their financial losses, estimated conservatively at $400 million, because Congress decided to appropriate only $38 million for the settlement of claims. It is even harder to place a figure on the toll taken in emotional shock, self-blame, broken dreams, and insecurity. One Japanese American woman still sees in her nightmares the watchtower searchlights that troubled her sleep forty years ago.

The war altered Japanese American women's lives in complicated ways. In general, evacuation and relocation accelerated earlier trends that differentiated the Nisei from their parents. Although most young women, like their mothers and non-Japanese peers, anticipated a future centered around a husband and children, they had already felt the influence of mainstream middle-class values of love and marriage and quickly moved away from the pattern of arranged marriage in the camps. There, increased peer group activities and the relaxation of parental authority gave them more independence. The Nisei women's expectations of marriage became more akin to the compassionate ideals of their peers than to those of the Issei.

As before the war, many Nisei women worked in camp, but the new parity in wages they received altered family dynamics. And though they expected to contribute to the family economy, a large number did so in settings far from the family, availing themselves of opportunities provided by the student and worker relocation programs. In meeting the challenges facing them, Nisei women drew not only upon the disciplined strength inculcated by their Issei parents but also upon firmly rooted support networks and the greater measure of self-reliance and independence that they developed during the crucible of the war years.

sources

CAREER WOMAN, OR HOMEMAKER?

 **DEBATES** *With hindsight, it is possible to see the origins of modern feminism in the optimistic, adventuresome self-confidence of the Nisei women leaving the relocation centers for college or jobs in Minneapolis, Chicago, or New York. To be sure, most were not feminists, and would not have regarded themselves as such; they did not think much about gender equality and, although many had to deal with fathers who would have preferred they stay "home," they probably experienced that fatherly preference as the advice of another generation, rather than as the demand of a misguided patriarchy. But they had been liberated—by the opportunities of wartime, ironically—and their daughters (the Sansei generation), learning from their mothers, would raise the feminist banner.*

The same thing happened to millions of women who were not of Japanese ancestry, and who had not been in camps. Virtually overnight, the wartime demand for labor opened up the world of work to middle-class women who, during the Great Depression, had been satisfied with domesticity. It was just the beginning of one of the most significant economic and social trends of the late twentieth century: except for a brief downturn after the war, women have worked outside the home in increasing numbers and percentages in every decade.

Whether middle-class women should work (working-class women had always worked in large numbers) on anything but an emergency basis was controversial. In January 1944, Ladies' Home Journal *aired some of the issues in a pair of articles that took opposing stands. The anti-work side was argued by an anonymous "career wife"; the pro-work side was defended by Leslie B. Hohman, a Johns Hopkins University psychiatrist (and next to that piece was one of those ubiquitous* Ladies' Home Journal *advertisements, this one featuring a smiling woman, bent over her washing machine, smelling the suds made by Fels-Naptha, a popular laundry soap of the day).*

In examining the debate, look for similarities as well as differences; that is, to what extent does Hohman share the assumptions of the career wife? What is the goal of each author? Does Hohman suggest anything resembling the liberation of women? What is each author's perception of men, and of how men would respond to a household with a working woman?

Leslie B. Hohman, M.D.
WORKING WIVES MAKE THE BEST WIVES

When I talked to young Mr. and Mrs. Robert Walker in Hollywood, they were regarded as being deeply in love. "This is a career marriage that is working beautifully," the movie colony was saying with affectionate admiration for an achievement all too rare there. The rumors of disagreement which drifted to me were dismissed by the friends who should have known best as spiteful gossip. Bob Walker, who gained his first motion-picture fame as the boyish sailor in Bataan, and Jennifer Jones, who rose simultaneously to stardom in the title role of The Song of Bernadette, seemed to be as assured of success in their marriage as in their profession.

As this article went to press, the rumors of trouble had been superseded by verified reports of a separation, without a divorce—at least for the time being. It still remained undecided whether the rift would be final or whether there would be a reconciliation and a resumption of happiness. Whatever the ultimate outcome, when the bad news of the marital stumble of this highly publicized couple flies around, many sincere and intelligent persons throughout America will cite the case of Bob and Jennifer as another example of the harm in outside jobs for wives.

Let's state frankly and fairly the most effective arguments of those who are honestly convinced that marriage—and especially a marriage with children, like Bob and Jennifer's—is doomed to complete or partial failure when the wife has other work. They assert that other work brings other interests, which inevitably lessen the wife's interest for and in her husband, her children and her home. They believe that the wife who has another job is too tired and irritable at the end of the day to fulfill her family duties. She usually is subjected to the risks of casual friendship with other men besides her husband, they point out, and she is more likely to seek excitement than the stay-at-home wife. Her personal vanity, so the argument goes, increases with her earning capacity, while her husband's self-respect is damaged by his partial economic dependence on her.

All the arguments have a ring of truth. Yet all of them have basic flaws as applied to the average job for the average wife. They usually tend to be true only in a super-glamorous "career" situation such as that in which Bob and Jennifer have been placed; and the trouble then is in the extraordinary situation rather than the mere fact that the wife works. The arts, the stage, the films and some of the higher-bracket business and executive positions for women attract strongly individualistic and gifted persons of a type which frequently is emotionally unstable in some respects. These gifted ones are thrown into markedly artificial environments. Only the rarest, rock-sound characters can keep a marriage whole in Hollywood, for instance, against the career drive, the fabulous money drive, the publicity build-up, the public adulation and all the other forces against marital happiness.

Unfortunately, the wide notice attracted by any marriage troubles of noted career women confuses the issues while stimulating the debate about women working. If Bob and Jennifer, at twenty-four, cannot keep on living happily together, it will be because at least one of them has "gone Hollywood," not because they did not start right. They did start right. They started with deep affection and they started with the building of alert interests. In years of the practice of psychiatry I have listened to many heart-warming stories of marriage success and many heart-breaking stories of failure. What husbands and wives themselves reveal, sometimes unwittingly, refutes the argument that there is grave danger of loss of interest in husbands, children and homes by wives who have other work. Exactly the opposite is true. The greatest danger to marriages in everyday situations is in not remaining intelligently alive. The greatest danger is boredom.

The American tradition which urges us, quite sensibly, to marry for romantic love tricks us often, also, into the notion that romantic love can go on glowing endlessly—love alone, without any additional support. There is an especial threat to wives in this notion. At the critical age when their physical attractiveness begins to fade with the passing of youth, wives with dull time on their hands frequently become somewhat dull. And there is an increasing amount of dull time for wives as modern conveniences multiply and families become smaller. The tragedy of war has brought at least one compensation by luring a multitude of women into more stimulating tasks.

Jennifer and Bob told me their romance developed slowly out of a friendship inspired by mutual enthusiasm for the theater. Whether their romance is strong enough to withstand the many unfavorable factors or not, Jennifer's work, in my belief, was a valuable influence toward preventing them from losing the attraction which drew them together originally.

As a typical example, I can cite a former stenographer who came to me for advice because her marriage appeared to be going bankrupt. During her husband's courtship and their early married years, she said, they could talk for hours with the keenest zest. Now nothing worth talking about every seemed to happen. Their three children were away at school most of the day, and generally played out-of-doors after school hours. The housework and the children did not keep her busy. She became bored nearly every afternoon, and was still bored in the evenings. She and her husband rarely exchanged more than a few brief and listless remarks—except when they snappishly disagreed.

"What made your conversations so much more absorbing while you were engaged," I asked, "besides, of course, the fresh bloom of romance?"

She insisted at first that romance was the only difference, but as I pressed for detailed recollections there slowly emerged a description of a much more alert woman than she had become after a decade of marriage. Although her former work as a stenographer might not have been regarded as exciting, the material which crossed her desk had ideas in it. She had been determined then to be successful in business. She read rather widely, because she saw she needed to be reasonably well informed to make a good impression. When her fiancé spoke of his job, his ambitions or some news event, he got a quick flash of intelligent response. She conceded that this was more than he had received from her since they had let their home life drift into humdrum routine.

As a result of our conference, she arranged for a sister who lived near her to look after the children at noon and from 4 to 5:30 o'clock, and took a stenographic job in a war plant. She recently reported to me that she and her husband were more companionable now than they had been for years.

Most of the wives with a problem like hers, who ask my opinion, are fairly easy to convince of their need for a broader horizon. Still, it is hard to persuade some of them that they should tie themselves down to a regular paid job or to definitely specified and pledged hours and days of volunteer work for one of the many civic, charitable or service organizations which could use them. They resolve to read more, to visit art galleries, to do some social work, to do any number of splendid things; and nearly always their resolutions fail. The good luck of those who have regular jobs is that they are forced to wake up and keep busy.

In addition to the inner aliveness that is one of the best possible safeguards against unhappiness in middle age, a job supplies two substantial outward advantages. The first is stimulation of pride in personal appearance through the necessity of dressing to go out every day. The second, and most important, is training in remaining likable, being good-natured with associates, not showing irritation over every minor mishap. It would be as ridiculous to insist that the training always performs miracles on looks and temperament as to assert that outside jobs would save all marriages. But rather extensive observation has convinced me that employed wives, as a general rule—far from being tired and irritable invariably at the end of the day—make more successful and sustained efforts on both appearance and disposition than those whose only activities are in their homes.

The most enthusiastic believer in daily outside contacts as a disposition improver whom I happen to know is a husband who once opposed his wife's taking her present office position. He was against it, he admits, because he was a little afraid of the competition of men with whom she would be working. He now recognizes that the gain from filling a place which can be lost by loss of temper far outweighs the possible risks.

Another potent factor which he does not yet recognize fully is also worth serious attention from other husbands who object to their wives' working. Part of the disappearance of his wife's bad temper was unquestionably due to the relief by her added salary of their worry over expenses—a tension which puts a strain on countless marriages in this era of high living costs. Illness, unexpected bills, the thought that a husband may die, perhaps leaving children to support, are not so overwhelming to a woman with proved earning capacity as to one without it. A feeling of financial security makes marriages more secure emotionally.

Since the prejudice of husbands against "taking money from a woman" is often based on their interpretation of masculine independence, it is amusing to notice how a wife's earnings can contribute to a husband's manly freedom. I could name several who were able to quit unpromising jobs and take a chance for a better future only because their wives' incomes liberated them from fear of what might happen if the new venture failed. In the lean days in New York when Bob Walker was trying to get started by occasional bit parts in radio, the money earned by Jennifer helped him to hold to his determination to be an actor. Jennifer was a Powers model for hat photographs whenever she could get an assignment, until the approaching arrival of their first son.

Jennifer and Bob were wise, too, in planning, even then when money was extremely scarce, to have their children promptly so that they could continue their careers later. The more usual plan in America of the wife's continuing to work "only until a house is paid for and there is a little something in the bank" ends too often in postponement of babies through the best years of parenthood, and in vain regrets for a childless marriage after it is too late.

My strong belief in regular outside jobs for women is coupled with an equally strong belief that children are among the greatest blessings of marriage. I simply do not see that the admitted difficulties of combining wifehood and motherhood with outside jobs are as insurmountable as they generally are believed to be. Mothers certainly cannot have jobs outside the home during childbearing and their children's infancy. Yet with the increase in nursery schools and the acceptance of children in private and public schools at earlier ages, mothers surely can return to jobs after having several children and starting them well in their training.

For those who are firmly determined, some method of solving the combination can always be found. Arrangements can be made to have a relative or a competent neighbor woman care for the children in the hours when the mother is away, for a fee generally commensurate with the financial ability of the family or the neighborhood. I am aware that cases of neglect of children by working mothers have been reported in war-boom areas. In all such cases that I have been able to learn about directly, the fault was in crowded living conditions and the social and economic upheavals of war, rather than the mere fact that the mothers were working. From experience in conducting a nursery school and advising mothers on the training of children in their own homes, I know that, as a rule to which there are few exceptions, the mother who has outside contacts brings home to her children a breadth of vision and a stimulating companionship which frequently are lacked by mothers who have no outside interests, or only such frittering ones as luncheons or afternoon bridge. Deep concern for children and good training of children are far more a question of the quality of the association between them and their parents than of its quantity.

What specific rules can be laid down for avoiding the admitted difficulties of the average working wife in representative American communities?

First, to combat the danger that the job will be permitted to dwarf home considerations, a much more careful and exact budgeting of time and energy is essential for the wife with outside work than for wives who do not have extra demands. Whenever a question arises whether she is pushing herself to excessive fatigue or loss of interest in her marriage, the answer should be dictated invariably by what is best for her marriage.

Second, the husbands of working wives should face the fact that their home responsibilities are increased by the wives' added responsibilities. To do their fair share, they have to give more attention to helping with the housework and with the children. Comments I have heard from wives indicate that, in general, husbands actually do offer to help more when they have no basis for the husbandly idea, unjust or not, that their wives "haven't been doing a thing all day." The more help husbands give at home, the more their home interest will grow. Wives, children, homes, and the husbands themselves, will be the gainers.

A third rule is that a definite charting of expenses is necessary if the wife works. The rule should be emphasized for the very reason that budgeting usually is relaxed when the wife makes money. It is easy to look upon her salary as so much extra mileage and speed up the standard of living accordingly. Instead of saving against the possibility of illness or unexpected misfortunes and adding financial security to the marriage, habits of extravagance can be acquired which are a threat to plans to have children or even to marriage happiness. Jennifer and Bob, like many Hollywood stars, have been spared the details of budgeting by having a financial agent who managed all their affairs. They have not been freed, however, from such universal problems as, "How much of the show of success do we want?"

Because family expenditures which exceed too greatly the typical American husband's income are likely to give him a feeling of failure, our third rule leads directly into our fourth—which is that there should be an emotional charting along with a charting of time, energy and finances. No matter how silly the idea is intellectually, the average American's sense of importance may be endangered if his wife rivals him, not to mention surpasses him, in career achievement or income. To offset this competitive danger, working women must deliberately keep in mind the truth that marriage success is not measured in dollars, but in intangibles of affection, evidences of thoughtfulness and confidences shared. Vast numbers of wives who don't work fail here, too, but the prevailing sensitivenesss of husbands demands the greatest effort from working wives. As an exact suggestion, indicative of others too numerous to list, the working wife should be particularly careful to consult her husband's opinion on business and financial problems. She should avoid like poison, which they are, such remarks as "my house," "my money," "my children." One of the symbols of authentic partnership in marriage is the frequency with which the word "our" is used by the partners.

If the rules of success seem difficult, remember that the necessity of more conscious planning is made easier because outside work tends to build—and force—a more conscious way of living. In a word, the employed woman is often more efficient. She has a gauge of her efficiency in the income she earns. As to the threat of increased personal vanity from any job except a glittering career position, if she knows the difficulties she will be less inclined to underestimate her husband, or even to nag him, because he doesn't make more money. By keeping alert and interesting to herself and to her husband, and by contributing financially to marriage security, she can help to establish a partnership of deep love and understanding which will endure long after the first romantic glow of the engagement and honeymoon.

A Successful Career Wife

YOU CAN'T HAVE A CAREER AND BE A GOOD WIFE

It is not startling to hear that Jennifer Jones Walker and Bob Walker have come to a parting of the ways. Always in double-career marriages there is terrific strain. With two strong personalities thrusting forward to success, not all the pull can be smoothly co-operative. There is crowding, and sometimes conflict. It could not be otherwise.

A marriage that survives twin careers is the exception; one that can *thrive* on a dual setup is a miracle. Many marriages, it is true, continue to be endured under these circumstances, for not everyone has the courage to face the situation as the Walkers are doing, admitting they no longer have a going concern, and taking steps to rectify matters. "Successful career couples," so-called, try to keep up a glossy surface, hoping it will not crack and expose the disappointing makeshifts underneath.

What is the matter with this dream of a man and a woman, both workers out in the world, making a solid home together? Why shouldn't two people, each with an outside job to do, unite all the more firmly to build a rich setting for their private lives? Why shouldn't such a partnership be unusually full of understanding, and mutual respect, and lively ideas—twice as many of the last, in fact, as when only one partner goes afield to garner them? Why shouldn't the children of such progressive parents, with doubly wide horizons, be especially privileged and happy?

Unfortunately, it rarely works out that way. The picture of this ideal partnership has a deceptive and meretricious brightness. It is only after years of observation and experience that one realizes how superficial that brightness is; realizes, too, that the best marriages do not necessarily glitter on the surface at all, but are solid affairs built on time-tested foundations. The reasons for this go very far back in human history, and have not been too much changed by household inventions or woman's suffrage or nursery schools or diaper services.

Most women want to keep on working after marriage for one of three reasons: 1. Because they want extra money; 2. Because they are lonely and want something to fill their days besides the care of a three-room apartment; 3. Because they feel they have something to express and have an honest urge toward work they really like.

Each of these reasons brings its own peculiar danger. The woman who works to supplement her husband's income is setting up financial habits which she will find increasingly hard to change. His money promotions, which would be important cause for celebration if he alone were the breadwinner, become less impressive. There is less sharp incentive to fight ahead. The double income becomes a pleasantly accepted fact. The baby they were going to have "someday" becomes a more and more distant prospect, involving too much rearrangement of their lives, too much sacrifice of comfort. After all, who wants to settle down to washing dishes—and baby things—when the extra money makes it possible to live more easily?

The wife who works to defeat loneliness is only postponing, or side-stepping in cowardly fashion, the period of adjustment necessary to make her new life successful. Marriage and home building should bring special interests of their own, not be simply an extension of the pattern of girlhood. The bride who continues to build her daily living around familiar office activities, friends and gossip, instead of starting to develop additional friends and interests compatible with her changed condition, is as shortsighted as the young wife who wants to continue eating at mother's because she doesn't want to learn how to cook. Marriage requires rearrangement of many previous attitudes, and the best possible time to do that is right in the beginning.

Most insidious of all is the danger threatening the girl who really finds her work stimulating. A good job is a demanding job. The young woman who is giving her best to her work cannot give her husband and home all they deserve. As anyone who has fought forward in the world of commerce and careers knows, success comes from ideas, and ideas cannot be turned off and on by the clock. They arrive disturbingly at daybreak, or on Sunday afternoon, or when Aunt Minnie is coming to dinner. Often they call for an audience, or at least a pad, a stub of pencil and a few uninterrupted minutes.

Now every family is the better for *one* person who is throwing off ideas and creative steam in general. And "creative" in this instance applies just as much to schemes for selling plumbing supplies, or an improved system of bookkeeping, as to more colorful efforts in art and literature. It's good to have one partner vigorously emitting ideas and challenging the imagination with plans for the future. And that person needs an audience who is wholeheartedly interested, and who will put everything else aside to give him encouragement in critical moments. Because inside the heart of even the bravest fighter there is always a little loneliness and unsureness, and a great need of warm words. It is fine and sobering, too, for that fighter when he is out in front to know that the welfare of his family unit depends entirely on him and that he is backed by complete faith.

But when the front action is divided? When there are *two* fighters, each needing encouragement; two performers, each demanding an audience? What then?

If they could alternate their needs, that would help, but too often life, with devilish ingenuity, piles everything up at once. Caleb has a row with the boss and comes home to find Sylvia in tears because they have hired a new young woman in the department and given her the very work they promised Sylvia. Even worse is the New Year's when Caleb's raise doesn't come through on schedule and he comes wearily through the front door to be met by a joyful Sylvia shouting over an unexpected bonus. A man wants comfort and someone to share his grousing at the boss at a low moment like that, and no matter how many articles are written to prove it shouldn't be so, it hurts his male pride to have his woman winning, on her own, the business laurels he had hoped to lay at her feet. If this experience is repeated too often, he may become chronically embittered, or he may relax his own effort and become one of those subdued husbands often seen in the wake of successful businesswomen. In either case, the marriage is thrown off balance. An aggressive husband and an apologetic wife do not make a satisfactory couple, but it is even more against nature when the positions are reversed.

The problems of the children of a business couple deserve a whole volume. Presuming that a liberal financial setup, good health and flexible working hours for the mother have assured the arrival of a baby without too desperate accounting of time and pennies, the home life still takes on an incredible intricacy. Even the steadiest marriages, involving only a couple of adults, can be full of the unexpected; and when a baby—or more—is added to a household run by a working wife, things really begin to happen!

In spite of competent nurses, housekeepers and kindly relatives, there will be crises, arising from illness, minor accidents or the collapse of household personnel. In no time at all the career mother finds herself trying to be at least two people: an efficient, smartly turned out professional woman, and a devoted and conscientious mother. There is obviously little time left for being a wife.

There are inevitable penalties for this. Husbands become discontented as they feel themselves neglected; for no matter how much a business wife may be contributing to a mutual household in the way of an alert mind, an enriched personality and a wider circle of interests—quite apart from mere money—the husband who can't find his clean laundry considers himself abused and puts it all down to his unnatural home setup. It is of no use to point out to him that clean collars have been known to get mislaid by full-time wives. The real trouble, of course, is that in his heart, whether he himself knows it or not, he has an age-old male resentment of the fact that his woman is out in the world about her own business instead of staying safely in the cave he provides for her.

Conscious of her husband's feeling of not having an entirely normal home, his wife redoubles her efforts, tries to be a satisfactory mate as well as a harassed young mother and ambitious career girl. Something gives: nerves fray, health gives way. The tired businessman is merely suffering from mild fatigue compared with the tired business wife and mother. If her income is considerable, she can hire secretaries, cooks, nurses and maids, but the whole staff put together cannot take over the fundamental job of being the heart of her household, with the responsibilities of emotion and imagination which belong to a wife and mother. Was there ever a husband in the world who would prefer a hard-driven professional "success woman" to a relaxed, laughter-loving wife?

Yes, home wives work hard too. But they do not work at a stiff, competitive pace, with someone else calling the turn. They are their own directors. They are in business for themselves, and it doesn't take a psychologist to tell you that you can do twice the work, happily, under your own steam that you can be driven to do by outside forces.

Why, then, do women have this suicidal hunger for success outside the home? Why do they crave so deeply to "go out to business," instead of making a business of their homes? This does not apply to those women with rare abilities who will forge ahead and express themselves, and should, no matter what their environment. Most of the career-hungry girls would do much better as wives and mothers than as businesswomen. Arriving at middle age, and stopping to count the cost, they themselves wonder what they have attained that seemed so worth struggling for at twenty. Even the old argument that women in business stay more alert and hold youth longer is not true now—if it ever was. The modern happy wife and mother in her forties is apt to look like a better-adjusted and younger woman than her successful professional contemporary in thirty-dollar hat!

Who, then, is to blame for this exodus of women from the home? Mostly, *the men themselves.* The very men who would prefer to have their women stay by their own firesides have been extraordinarily inept in selling them the idea. And this in a nation of supersalesmen!

Take that heavy-handed, man-made phrase, "Woman's place is in the home," which men have kept repeating for generations. In that repetition, indeed, lies the trouble. It is not the lack of truth in the statement, but its terrible monotony. It sounds like a sentence, as though the woman—any woman—were going to be locked in a safe, and completely dull, place for life. You can almost hear the key turning in the lock. Any woman with spunk resents this attitude. Why should any man, even her beloved husband, assume the right to shackle her to a spot, or to a set of obligations? Even though he promises to treat her kindly, if she pleases him!

Oh, what a poor selling job the males have done all these years! They, whose selling ability has become legendary, have fallen down on the biggest job of all, the job of making the little woman feel that she is so extraordinarily lucky just to be a woman, and a potential wife and mother, that she really ought to hug the knowledge to her heart in a kind of secret joy lest she be accused of vulgar boasting.

Instead, the obtuse male sets about destroying his own future peace of mind, as far as marriage is concerned, while he is still short-trousered. The first time he growls patronizingly to a feminine schoolmate, "Aw, you're just a girl. Whadda *you* know anyway?" he is planting seeds of discontent. At that instant there may be born in his pig-tailed mate a determination to "show him someday." The *why* of that determination will vanish, but the feeling of resenting male belittlement may be carried on and translated into powerful activity ten years later.

There is no perfect solution, of course, but if the men who are complaining about what seems to them a topsy-turvy arrangement today, and the younger men who are worrying about an even greater invasion of women in business tomorrow, will *stop scolding and start selling*—well, women have always been a responsive buying audience!

In the meantime, in spite of the serious handicaps involved, some couples will make a good job of double-career marriages by being willing to work extra hard and to learn the great law of compromise. But it takes an exceptional woman—and an even more exceptional husband.

Harry S. Truman

Truman on Hiroshima (August 6, 1945)

One can only imagine the emotions of Japanese Americans as they heard that the Enola Gay *had released an atomic bomb over the city of Hiroshima, or read the following statement by President Harry Truman, released by the White House. It is an extraordinary document, full of the twists and turns that were perhaps inevitable at this moment when the public was first introduced to the atomic bomb, told about its use at Hiroshima, and informed of its atomic future. How did Truman justify the use of this weapon? What aspects of the atomic bomb did Truman emphasize? What should or might he have said that he did not?*

Sixteen hours ago an American airplane dropped one bomb on Hiroshima, an important Japanese Army base. That bomb had more power than 20,000 tons of T.N.T. It had more than two thousand times the blast power of the British "Grand Slam" which is the largest bomb ever yet used in the history of warfare.

The Japanese began the war from the air at Pearl Harbor. They have been repaid many fold. And the end is not yet. With this bomb we have now added a new and revolutionary increase in destruction to supplement the growing power of our armed forces. In their present form these bombs are now in production and even more powerful forms are in development.

It is an atomic bomb. It is a harnessing of the basic power of the universe. The force from which the sun draws its power has been loosed against those who brought war to the Far East.

Before 1939, it was the accepted belief of scientists that it was theoretically possible to release atomic energy. But no one knew any practical method of doing it. By 1942, however, we knew that the Germans were working feverishly to find a way to add atomic energy to the other engines of war with which they hoped to enslave the world. But they failed. We may be grateful to Providence that the Germans got the V-1s and the V-2s late and in limited quantities and even more grateful that they did not get the atomic bomb at all.

The battle of the laboratories held fateful risks for us as well as the battles of the air, land and sea, and we have now won the battle of the laboratories as we have won the other battles.

Foreign Relations of the United States, *Potsdam,* vol. 2, Washington, D.C., 1960, pp. 1380–1381.

Beginning in 1940, before Pearl Harbor, scientific knowledge useful in war was pooled between the United States and Great Britain, and many priceless helps to our victories have come from that arrangement. Under that general policy the research on the atomic bomb was begun. With American and British scientists working together we entered the race of discovery against the Germans.

The United States had available the large number of scientists of distinction in the many needed areas of knowledge. It had the tremendous industrial and financial resources necessary for the project and they could be devoted to it without undue impairment of other vital war work. In the United States the laboratory work and the production plants, on which a substantial start had already been made, would be out of reach of enemy bombing, while at that time Britain was exposed to constant air attack and was still threatened with the possibility of invasion. For these reasons Prime Minister Churchill and President Roosevelt agreed that it was wise to carry on the project here. We now have two great plants and many lesser works devoted to the production of atomic power. Employment during peak construction numbered 125,000 and over 65,000 individuals are even now engaged in operating the plants. Many have worked there for two and a half years. Few knew what they have been producing. They see great quantities of material going in and they see nothing coming out of these plants, for the physical size of the explosive charge is exceedingly small. We have spent two billion dollars on the greatest scientific gamble in history—we won.

But the greatest marvel is not the size of the enterprise, its secrecy, nor its cost, but the achievement of scientific brains in putting together infinitely complex pieces of knowledge held by many men in different fields of science into a workable plan. And hardly less marvelous has been the capacity of industry to design, and of labor to operate, the machines and methods to do things never done before so that the brain child of many minds came forth in physical shape and performed as it was supposed to do. Both science and industry worked under the direction of the United States Army, which achieved a unique success in managing so diverse a problem in the advancement of knowledge in an amazingly short time. It is doubtful if such another combination could be got together in the world. What has been done is the greatest achievement of organized science in history. It was done under high pressure and without failure.

We are now prepared to obliterate more rapidly and completely every productive enterprise the Japanese have above ground in any city. We shall destroy their docks, their factories, and their communications. Let there be no mistake; we shall completely destroy Japan's power to make war.

It was to spare the Japanese people from utter destruction that the ultimatum of July 26 was issued at Potsdam. Their leaders promptly rejected that ultimatum. If they do not now accept our terms they may expect a rain of ruin from the air, the like of which has never been seen on this earth. Behind this air attack will follow sea and land forces in such numbers and power as they have not yet seen and with the fighting skill of which they are already well aware.

The secretary of war, who has kept in personal touch with all phases of this project, will immediately make public a statement giving further details.

His statement will give facts concerning the sites of Oak Ridge near Knoxville, Tennessee, and at Richland near Pasco, Washington, and an installation near Santa Fe, New Mexico. Although the workers at the sites have been making materials to be used in producing the greatest of destructive force in history they have not themselves been in danger beyond that of many other occupations, for the utmost care has been taken of their safety.

The fact that we can release atomic energy ushers in a new era in man's understanding of nature's forces. Atomic energy may in the future supplement the power that now comes from coal, oil, and falling water, but at present it cannot be produced on a basis to compete with them commercially. Before that comes there must be a long period of intensive research.

It has never been the habit of the scientists of this country or the policy of this government to withhold from the world scientific knowledge. Normally, therefore, everything about the work with atomic energy would be made public.

But under present circumstances it is not intended to divulge the technical processes of production or all the military applications, pending further examination of possible methods of protecting us and the rest of the world from the danger of sudden destruction.

I shall recommend that the Congress of the United States consider promptly the establishment of an appropriate commission to control the production and use of atomic power within the United States. I shall give further consideration and make further recommendations to the Congress as to how atomic power can become a powerful and forceful influence towards the maintenance of world peace.

Edwin Rosskam

CELEBRATING WAR'S END (AUGUST 14, 1945)

The bombing of Hiroshima did not bring an end to the war. Three days later, another atomic bomb was dropped, this one on Nagasaki. On August 14, the Japanese accepted the Allied terms of surrender, and World War II came to an end. Photographer Edwin Rosskam was in New Orleans on that day. In a letter to his friend and colleague, Roy Stryker, Rosskam described the celebration he saw, and what he felt, capturing the curious combination of idealism and dread that was at the heart of the decade.

Letter from Edwin Rosskam to Roy Stryker, August 14, 1945, Standard Oil of New Jersey Papers, file "Rosskam Correspondence," University of Louisville Photographic Archives, Louisville, Kentucky.

 **VOICES**

Dear Roy,

I am beginning this letter on August 14th, though I may not be ready to send it for several days. It will turn out to be, I have no doubt, the last of our regular letters from this assignment, which we might as well call the "water assignment". The river story is the main monument of this trip, and I feel certain that it is nothing to be ashamed of. The Humble Oil story in this area is no less aqueaous. By now, ready to leave for Puerto Rico by freighter, we are beginning to detect the webs forming between our toes. Or is it heat rash?

This has been the damnedest experience: *V.E. day in Pittsburgh,* the labor party victory of the British in New Orleans, Atom Bombs in Potash, La. and now painfully, the uncertain dawn of possible peace over the little radio in our room at the Pontchartrain hotel. And always with us the great river and the canals and the bayous and the marsh, and the wet heat.

It has come.

We were in town when it came. We heard the first announcement over a blaring, indistinct loudspeaker in front of a clothing store on St. Charles Street. We were in the crowd which grew as flash-floods grow, without visible origin, overwhelmingly.

That was the moment. All the wild, hysterical celebration which came later, was nothing more than an attempt to escape from the impact of this sudden intelligence, sudden even after the many false starts, too big to grasp and to recognize, so big and strange and immeasurable that it became like the witnessing of a birth or a death—a pulling in the throat and tears barely contained.

This was before the kissing started and the noise-making and the drinking out of bottles hoarded against this instant. The people in the crowd were quiet. They looked at each other and they said nothing. Everyone of them was, for a moment, alone. And over them the loud fuzzy electrical voice thundered.

An individual does'nt often get the chance to be in on one of the big climaxes. Usually you're asleep when it happens, or busy with something else, or merely looking the other way; and what you see afterwards, even ten minutes later, is no longer the thing at all, but only its subversion, the hilarity and the roaring rumpus that people dive into to get away from the big news, too big to share quickly, too strong to bear for long without screaming and yelling and parading.

We, in that crowd in front of the boarded-up furniture store on St. Charles street were present not only when The Moment happened; we were in on its dissolution. I dont know how long it took, five minutes, maybe eight. By that time the loudspeaker was repeating. The crowd had grown out into the street from the sidewalks, and the cars, trying to get through, made much noise with their horns, over-riding the words, the words which, repetitions though they were, still held the standing people to them and would not let them go. And then, out of a little bar next to the clothing store a fat sweating man in a soaked-through shirt, pushed a juke box out on the street. On the jukebox he had fastened an old headline of that morning "JAPS SURRENDER STILL DELAYED." Only he had ripped off the STILL DELAYED so that now it read JAPS SURRENDER. And the fat sweating man pulled up the electric cord and attached the jukebox, and the jukebox started playing. It played softly, and its music was hidden under the brass words repeating themselves on the loudspeaker. The fat sweating man looked around at the faces in the crowd and he looked up at the loudspeaker, once. Then he turned up the volume button on the jukebox, and suddenly the jukebox became the loud thing and the words, the words on the loudspeaker, were drowned out so that they were indistinguishable. The jukebox was playing "Bell-bottom Trousers."

The fat sweating man grinned. People grinned back. And that was the breaking point.

What followed was loud, drunken and commonplace. Everybody crowded out on Canal Street and did everything that was expected of them. Sailors roamed through the mob, kissing girls. Bottles passed. Noisemakers were sold and widely used, though the biggest noise came from the automobile horns which never stopped bellowing. American flags were sold too, but here business was not so good. Flags, after all, are connected with war, and people didn't want to be reminded of war. They were celebrating peace rather than victory.

The big drunk went on in the pink evening sun and into the dusk and into the night. By eleven o'clock Canal Street was emptying. By twelve thirty it looked as it always looks, a broad, undistinguished, rather empty street waiting for morning. Except for the paper which lay ankle thick on the pavement, rustling softly. . . .

[Edwin Rosskam]

DARK VICTORY: A VISUAL ESSAY

Three of the illustrations in this grouping feature Americans dealing in ordinary ways with the fact of World War II. The fourth is an illustration from a high school yearbook for 1946 (a year of transition: the war was over, the Cold War not yet recognizable). What does each illustration reveal about the era? About the war? About relations between men and women?

Soldier Home on Furlough, Brown Summit, North Carolina, May 1944.
Standard Oil Collection, Special Collections: Photographic Archives, University of Louisville.

The Tanner Family—Velma, Jimmie, and Their Son—at Home in the Humble Oil Company "Poor Boy" Camp, Tomball, Texas, 1945.
Standard Oil Collection, Special Collections: Photographic Archives, University of Louisville.

A Barmaid in Great Falls, Montana, 1944.
Standard Oil Collection, Special Collections: Photographic Archives, University of Louisville.

Riverside High School Skipper, *Buffalo, New York, 1946.*

the big picture

Many of the items in this chapter deal with war as a gendered experience. How did the war affect men and women differently? What tensions did World War II produce between the sexes, and why?

chapter ten

COLD WAR, COLD WAR AT HOME

*T*he end of World War II marked a clear American military and economic success. But it also created a power vacuum in Europe and a sense of insecurity about the immediate future in Washington. Some prominent Americans, like Henry Luce, the publisher of *Life* magazine, welcomed the opportunity to inaugurate an "American Century," an era where the United States was challenged to embrace world leadership and create an environment conducive to American commercial growth and development. Should the nation fail to grasp this opportunity, Luce argued, it might find itself, as it had after World War I, hostage to the fortunes of fascist, totalitarian, or communist nations that were less keen on peace, commercial development, and democracy.

Throughout World War II, Washington's major policies were consistent with Luce's vision of an American Century. At the Bretton Woods Conference in April 1944, the World Bank, the International Monetary Fund, and a system of currency exchange were created, all aimed at facilitating and stabilizing the free flow of trade. A further American diplomatic priority was world stability, addressed through the renewed commitment to collective security as defined by the United Nations, another agency given new life by the Allies' military success.

America held one other high card in its hand, in addition to its immense military and economic and financial establishments. In August 1945, American technology and science were proved superior when the first atomic bomb was exploded over Hiroshima. In sole possession of a startling new weapon that re-defined warfare, Americans felt they had a sure winner. It was, however, frus-tratingly difficult to find combat situations where the bomb could be profitably employed, especially since it took months to build each one. The preponder-ance of the American contribution in funding the war, in ending the conflict in the Pacific, and in creating the monetary environment of the future seemed to indicate that the American Century had commenced.

Yet August 1945 did not immediately usher in a secure, stable world for American workers. The problems inherent in converting the American econ-omy to peacetime production, the demobilization of millions of servicemen, and the shift in the labor force as returning servicemen displaced recently hired women and minorities meant a period of inflation and insecurity for a nation only too familiar with the economic hardships of the recent depression. Americans became aware, once again, that they could win the war and lose the peace. The clear military victory of 1945 was followed by inconclusive diplo-macy, as the Allies were unable to agree on the structure of postwar Germany; American factories were in danger of cutting production for lack of clients; and the shared goals and ideals of wartime were giving way to socialism and state economies among the Allies.

As these concerns grew and multiplied, President Truman took action. In March 1947, he boldly asked Congress for $400 million in aid to Greece and Turkey. The general anxiety and sense of crisis among the American public re-garding recent world events coalesced into active fear of the Soviet Union and communist regimes. The Cold War had officially begun.

Within two months, the Truman administration would call for the largest foreign aid program in the history of the United States: the Marshall Plan. The intent was to save the economies of Europe and indirectly to provide markets to sustain America's production. In 1948, the first arguments for American de-fense of Europe were heard; in 1949, the North Atlantic Treaty Organization was formed, and military containment was born. The American decision to re-construct Western Europe led the Soviet Union to retaliate by forming its own east European bloc. Truman's response to the crisis of 1947 institutionalized a military, economic, and diplomatic contest between the United States and the Soviet Union.

The 1952 election of Dwight D. Eisenhower redefined the problem. Republicans accused Truman of misunderstanding the nature of the fight; what Democrats called a relatively short-term crisis was, the Republicans ar-gued, a long-term, ideological struggle between the forces of communism and capitalism—a struggle that threatened, if not dealt with correctly, to destroy the very foundations of American society. In this contest to the death, America's fu-ture lay in maintaining budgetary balance, military superiority, and a clear moral definition of its goals. If a "clear and present danger" existed in America's future, then all of America's promises of freedom, democracy, and individualism had to be placed on hold until security was won.

The acute insecurity expressed in the elections of 1950 and 1952 blurred the lines between foreign policy and domestic policy. Once the concept of America under siege became political consensus, dissension in actions or thoughts could easily be seen as treason, offering aid and comfort to the enemy, deeds worthy of prosecution and punishment. This was the climate that spawned the second Red Scare.

interpretive essay

Walter LaFeber

TWO HALVES OF THE SAME WALNUT (1947–1948)

The origins of the Cold War have been widely debated by historians and politicians. A central controversial question remains: who was to blame? The Soviet Union, for its aggressive, imperial, military activities in Eastern Europe after World War II? Or, the United States, anxious about its economic future and insecure about Soviet ideology, seeking to preemptively contain Soviet power? Were both countries driven by domestic imperatives, each blind to the security and economic needs of the other?

The enunciation of the Truman Doctrine stands as the opening salvo and the defining ethos of the Cold War. Alone, it defines an altruistic American response to Soviet aggression "to support free peoples who are resisting attempted subjugation by armed minorities or by outside pressures." But, when Walter LaFeber, an eminent historian of the revisionist school, analyzes the Truman Doctrine in combination with the Marshall Plan, the overall intent of the policy is less humanitarian, more economically self-interested, and infinitely more complicated. Although criticized by many as a great giveaway program, the Marshall Plan provided huge markets for American products, especially munitions.

America's economic picture in 1945 was muddled. The sudden, early end of the war brought about by the atomic explosions at Hiroshima and Nagasaki ended all chances of a gradual conversion to a peacetime economy. Instead, policies originally expected to develop over months were approved over a weekend. The Office of War Mobilization and Reconversion reported that unemployment might reach 8 million by 1946. Demobilization ran at a precipitous rate, as Truman himself announced that 2 million men would be home by Christmas 1945. The biggest economic problem of all was inflation, which reached 18.2 percent in 1946. America's gross national product was growing,

America, Russia, and the Cold War: 1945–1972, 7th edition, McGraw-Hill, Inc., New York, 1993, pp. 49–73. © 1993. Used with the permission of The McGraw-Hill Companies.

but American workers could not afford to purchase American products. American exports in 1947 accounted for one-third of the world's exports, and many worried that unless trade continued to expand, another depression would descend. But Europe, America's best customer and historic trading partner, was not recovering, and some governments were actually espousing socialist and communist programs. Was it time for America to stake out a new policy and take on responsibility for Europe's economic health? And if so, how could Congress and the people be convinced to indulge such an expensive, entangling endeavor?

On March 12, 1947, President Truman finally issued his own declaration of cold war. Dramatically presenting the Truman Doctrine to Congress, he asked Americans to join in a global commitment against communism. The nation responded. A quarter of a century later, Senator J. William Fulbright declared, "More by far than any other factor the anti-communism of the Truman Doctrine has been the guiding spirit of American foreign policy since World War II.

An odd circumstance, however, must be explained if the Truman Doctrine is to be understood. The Soviet Union had been less aggressive in the months before the president's pronouncement than at any time in the postwar period. Stalin consolidated his hold over Rumania and Poland through manipulated elections, and at home Soviet propagandists encouraged Western socialists and other "proletarians" to undertake revolutionary action. But throughout the winter of 1946–1947, the Soviet [leaders] acted cautiously. State Department officials privately believed that "the USSR is undergoing serious economic difficulties," which have led to "the less aggressive international attitude taken by Soviet authorities in recent weeks." This policy was only "a temporary retreat." Nonetheless, the problems seemed so great that the Russians gave military discharges to "hundreds of thousands of young men [who] will now become available for labor force in industry, agriculture and construction." Stalin reduced his 12 million military men of 1945 to between 3 and 4 million in 1947. (American forces dropped from 10 million to 1.4 million, but Americans enjoyed a monopoly of atomic weapons.) Russian military levels would go no lower, for the Red Army was Stalin's counter to Truman's atomic bomb. Poised in Eastern Europe, the troops threatened to take the continent hostage in case of atomic attack on Russia. Stalin had no navy capable of long-range offensive strikes. The fleet depended on 300 submarines geared for defensive purposes.

Truman's immediate problem was not the threat of a Russian invasion. As Dean Acheson privately remarked, the Russians would not make war with the United States "unless they are absolutely out of their minds."* The greater danger was that Stalin might be proven correct when he indicated the Communists could bide their time since a "general crisis" was becoming so "acute" in the West that it would sweep away "atom-dollar" diplomacy. Communist party power rose steeply in Europe, particularly in France, where the first cabinet of the new Fourth Republican contained four Communists, including the minis-

*Undersecretary Dean Acheson would be secretary of state from 1949 to 1953.

ter of defense. Chaotic conditions in former colonial areas also opened exceptional opportunities to revolutionaries. The two gems of the British crown, India and Egypt, shattered the empire with drives for independence. They were soon joined by Pakistan, Burma, Ceylon [Sri Lanka], and Nepal. France began a long, futile, eight-year war to regain Indochina. The Dutch faced full-scale revolution in Indonesia. The Middle East was in turmoil over the determination of a half-dozen countries to be totally independent, as well as over the influx of 100,000 Jews who hoped to establish a homeland in Palestine.

In late 1946 and early 1947, American officials gave increasing attention to these newly emerging areas. Europe could not be fully stabilized until England, France, and the Netherlands settled their colonial problems. The State Department also assumed that the American economy, as well as the economy of the western community, which depended upon American prosperity, demanded a proper settlement of these conflicts. In a speech in November 1946, [Assistant Secretary of State] Will Clayton explained that the expansion in the domestic economy and the "depletion of our natural resources" would make the United States much more dependent on the importation of raw materials and minerals. Many of these came from the newly emerging areas. "No nation in modern times," the assistant secretary of state warned, "can long expect to enjoy a rising standard of living without increased foreign trade." Adolf Berle, economist, adviser to Roosevelt and Truman, and State Department official, declared in late 1946 that the Soviet [Union] and the United States had begun a battle for the allegiance of the less industrialized nations. "Within four years the world [will] be faced with an apparent surplus in production beyond any previously known," Berle explained. If American surpluses were used to "take the lead in material reconstruction" of the newly emerging countries, the United States could level off those "cycles of 'boom and bust' which disfigured our prewar economy."

"Boom and bust" already threatened. The American economy sagged, and unemployment rose in early 1946 before some expansion began. State Department experts worried that the improvement was temporary, for it rested on a $15 billion American export trade, nearly four times the level of the 1930s. Most of these exports were rebuilding western Europe, but the Europeans were rapidly running out of dollars to pay for the goods. When its remaining dollars and gold were spent, Europe would stagnate, then perhaps grasp at socialism to save itself. Americans would face the loss of their most vital market and probably the return of the 1930s with all the attendant political consequences. Truman understood this by early 1947, but a tax-cutting Republican Congress and his own low popularity seemed to block any action.

The turn came on Saturday morning, February 21, 1947, when a British embassy official drove to the near-deserted State Department building. He informed Acheson that because of its own economic crisis (more than half its industry was quiet), England could not provide the $250 million of military and economic support needed by Greece and Turkey. As Secretary of State George Marshall later observed, "It was tantamount to British abdication from the Middle East with obvious implications as to their successor."

American officials were not taken by surprise. From 1944 until early 1947 they had closely watched the British attempt to regain control of Greece become bogged down in a Greek civil war. On one side was a conservative-monarchical group supported by London. On the other was the National Liberation Front (NLF), with Communist leadership, which had gained popularity and power by leading resistance efforts against the Nazis. By 1947 the NLF received support from Yugoslav Communist leader Josep Broz (Marshal Tito). The Yugoslav was not motivated by affection for his fellow Communists in Greece. Rather, he hoped to annex parts of Greece to a large Yugoslav federation. Stalin was not directly involved and indeed developed a strong dislike for Tito's ambitions.

But as NLF strength grew, the United States did become involved. Throughout 1946 it sent special missions, poured in $260 million of aid, and sided with the British. Drawing on this experience, the State Department was able to work out a detailed proposal for assistance within a week after Acheson received the British message. After only nineteen days, Truman could appear before Congress with a complete program. Clearly, the president's request on March 12 for $400 million in Greek and Turkish aid (the Truman Doctrine speech) was not a sudden, drastic departure in American foreign policy.

But the reasoning in Truman's speech was radically new. That reasoning was worked out by American officials who had long been waiting for this opportunity. As they developed the speech, "they found release from the professional frustrations of years," as one later declared. "It seemed to those present that a new chapter in world history had opened and they were the most privileged of men." Those words help explain why the officials made certain choices. For example, they could have determined simply that Greece was in a civil war and therefore the United States had no business intervening. Or they could quietly have asked Congress to continue aid to Greece and Turkey while transferring to those nations weapons left from the war. The administration, however, rejected those alternatives, choosing instead to appear dramatically before Congress to request support for a global battle against communism. A White House adviser remarked that the message would be "the opening gun in a campaign to bring people up to [the] realization that the war isn't over by any means."

As State Department officials prepared drafts of the speech, Truman, Secretary of State Marshall, and Acheson met with congressional leaders. It was not a warm audience. The Republicans were busily cutting taxes 20 percent and chopping $6 billion from Truman's already tight budget. The legislators remained unmoved until Acheson swung into the argument that the threat was not a Greek civil war but Russian communism; its aim was the control of the Middle East, South Asia, and Africa; and this control was part of a communist plan to encircle and capture the ultimate objective, Germany and Europe. It was a struggle between liberty and dictatorship. By defending Greece and Turkey, therefore, Americans were defending their own freedoms. "The Soviet Union was playing one of the greatest gambles in history at minimal cost," Acheson concluded. "We and we alone are in a position to break up the play."

The congressmen were stunned. Silence followed until Arthur Vandenberg (now chairman of the Senate Foreign Relations Committee) told Truman that the message must include Acheson's explanation. As the senator advised, the president "scared hell" out of the American people. Insofar as public opinion was concerned, this tactic worked well for Truman (at least until three years later when Senator Joseph McCarthy and others turned the argument around and accused the administration of too gently handling such a horrible danger). The president also won over Congress with assurances that the United States would not only control every penny of America's aid to Greece but run the Greek economy by controlling foreign exchange, budget, taxes, currency, and credit.

Inside the State Department, however, Acheson ran into opposition. George Kennan, the top expert on Soviet affairs, objected bitterly to sending military assistance to nations such as Turkey that had no internal Communist problems and bordered the Soviet Union. Unlike economic help, military aid could be provocative. Acheson rejected the argument. The opportunity to build Turkey's military strength was too good to miss. Thus in the words of one official, "Turkey was slipped into the oven with Greece because that seemed the surest way to cook a tough bird." Kennan also protested against the harsh ideological tone and open-ended American commitment in the speech drafts. He was joined by Secretary of State Marshall and Charles Bohlen, another expert on Russia, who told Acheson that "there was a little too much flamboyant anticommunism in the speech." Acheson stood his ground. Marshall was informed that Truman believed the Senate would not approve the doctrine "without the emphasis on the Communist danger."

Acheson, however, carefully kept the central economic factors out of the speech. He and Truman wanted a simple ideological call to action that all could understand, not a message that might trigger arguments over American oil holdings in the Middle East. The economic interests were nevertheless crucial. As State Department official Joseph Jones noted, if Greece and similar key areas "spiral downwards into economic anarchy, then at best they will drop out of the United States orbit and try an independent nationalistic policy; at worst they will swing into the Russian orbit," and the result would be a depression worse than that of the 1930s.

Jones's insight was incorporated into a major speech made by Truman at Baylor University on March 6. The address provided the economic dimension to the Truman Doctrine pronounced six days later. The president frankly declared that if the expansion of state-controlled economies (such as the Communists') was not stopped, and an open world marketplace restored for private businessmen, depression would occur and the government would have to intervene massively in the society. Americans could then bid farewell to both their traditional economic and personal freedoms. "Freedom of worship—freedom of speech—freedom of enterprise," Truman observed. "It must be true that the first two of these freedoms are related to the third." For "Peace, freedom and world trade are indivisible." He concluded, "We must not go through the thirties again." The president had given the economic reasons for pronouncing the Truman Doctrine. The Baylor speech (written by Acheson and Will Clayton) explained why Americans, if they hoped to preserve their personal freedom, had to rebuild the areas west of the iron curtain before these lands collapsed into anarchy, radical governments, or even communism.

The Truman Doctrine speech itself laid out the ideological and political reasons for the commitment. The president requested $400 million for military and economic aid, but he also asked for something else. Truman warned Congress that the world must now "choose between alternative ways of life." He urged Americans to commit themselves to helping "free peoples" and to opposing "totalitarian regimes." This request, plus Truman's failure to place any geographical limits on where Americans must commit themselves (Africa as well as Germany? Southeast Asia as well as western Europe?), raised criticism.

Robert Taft of Ohio, the Senate's Republican leader, accused Truman of dividing the world into communist and anticommunist zones, then said flatly, "I do not want war with Russia." On the left, Henry Wallace, traveling in Europe, accused Truman of "reckless adventure" that would cost the world "a century of fear." Senator Vandenberg rushed to the president's defense by calling Wallace an "itinerant saboteur." But such fear was not only on Taft's and Wallace's minds. Shortly before the speech, Acheson told J. Robert Oppenheimer, a leading scientist in the atomic weapons field, "We are entering an adversary relationship with the Soviet [Union]," and "we should bear that in mind" while making atomic plans.

Congress wriggled uncomfortably. As Senator Vandenberg began closed-door hearings on what he called "the most fundamental thing that has been presented to Congress in my time," Acheson hedged on whether the Truman Doctrine had any limitations. "If there are situations where we can do something effective, then I think we must certainly do it." But he was clear on one issue: "I think it is a mistake to believe that you can, at any time, sit down with the Russians and solve questions." Only when the West built insuperable bastions of strength would Stalin listen to American terms. Acheson assumed Russia was primarily responsible for the Greek revolution. After all, said Lincoln MacVeagh, United States ambassador to Greece, "Any empire that bases itself on revolution always has expansionist tendencies." (The ambassador was alluding to the revolution of 1917, not 1776.) This view of Soviet involvement was wrong. The Greek problem was caused by internal forces and fueled by Tito for his own purposes. But this point made little difference. The administration asked for a commitment against communism anywhere, not just against the Soviet [Union].

That caused a special problem in Greece, for as MacVeagh admitted, "the best men" in Greece "are the heads of the Communist movement. . . . That is the sad part of it." But Americans had to keep on "trying to make bricks without straw . . . or you are going to lose the country." The Greek government became so brutal that the State Department privately warned it must stop torturing its political prisoners or "the president's program" would be damaged. When criticized for helping the Greek and Turkish right-wing parties, however, Truman could simply ask Americans whether they preferred "totalitarianism" or "imperfect democracies." This settled that question.

The president and Acheson mousetrapped those in Congress who wanted to be both anticommunist and penny pinchers. As a leading Democrat chuckled privately, of course the Republicans "didn't want to be smoked out. . . . They don't like Communism but still they don't want to do anything to stop it. But they are all put on the spot now and they all have to come clean." The president, moreover, had moved so quickly that Congress had no choice but to give him increased powers. "Here we sit," mourned Vandenberg, "not as free agents," but dealing with something "almost like a Presidential request for a declaration of war." "There is precious little we can do," the senator concluded, "except say 'yes.' " Vandenberg was correct. Congress's acceptance of Truman's definition of crisis marked the point in the cold war when power in foreign policy formulation began shifting rapidly from Capitol Hill to the White House.

Nine days after his speech, Truman helped ensure his victory by announcing a loyalty program to ferret out security risks in government. The first such peacetime program in American history, it was so vaguely defined that political ideas and long-past associations were suddenly made suspect. Most ominously, the accused would not have the right to confront the accuser. Truman thus strikingly dramatized the communist issue, exerting new pressure on Congress to support his doctrine. By mid-May Congress had passed his request by large margins.

The Truman Doctrine was a milestone in American history for at least four reasons. First, it marked the point at which Truman used the American fear of communism both at home and abroad to convince Americans they must embark upon a cold war foreign policy. This consensus would not break apart for a quarter of a century. Second, as Vandenberg knew, Congress was giving the president great powers to wage this cold war as he saw fit. Truman's personal popularity began spiraling upward after his speech. Third, for the first time in the postwar era, Americans massively intervened in another nation's civil war. Intervention was justified on the basis of anticommunism. In the future, Americans would intervene in similar wars for supposedly the same reason and with less happy results. Even Greek affairs went badly at first, so badly that in late 1947 Washington officials discussed sending as many as two divisions of Americans to save the situation. That proved unnecessary, for when Yugoslavia left the Communist bloc in early 1948, Tito turned inward and stopped aiding the rebels. Deprived of aid, the Greek left wing quickly lost ground. But it had been close, and Americans were nearly involved massively in a civil war two decades before their Vietnam involvement. As it was, the success in Greece seemed to prove that Americans could, if they wished, control such conflicts by defining the problem as "Communist" and helping conservatives remain in power.

Finally, and perhaps most important, Truman used the doctrine to justify a gigantic aid program to prevent a collapse of the European and American economies. Later such programs were expanded globally. The president's arguments about anticommunism were confusing, for the western economies would have been in grave difficulties whether or not communism existed. The complicated problems of reconstruction and the United States dependence on world trade were not well understood by Americans, but they easily comprehended anticommunism. So Americans embarked upon the cold war for the good reasons given in the Truman Doctrine, which they understood, and for real reasons, which they did not understand. Thus, as Truman and Acheson intended, the doctrine became an ideological shield behind which the United States marched to rebuild the western political-economic system and counter the radical left. From 1947 on, therefore, any threats to that western system could be easily explained as communist inspired, not as problems that arose from difficulties within the system itself. That was the most lasting and tragic result of the Truman Doctrine.

The president's program evolved naturally into the Marshall Plan. Although the speech did not limit American effort, Secretary of State Marshall did by concentrating the administration's attention on Europe. Returning badly shaken from a foreign ministers conference in Moscow, the secretary of state insisted in a nationwide broadcast that western Europe required immediate help. "The patient is sinking," he declared, "while the doctors deliberate." Personal conversations with Stalin had convinced Marshall that the Russians believed Europe would collapse. Assuming that the United States must lead in restoring Europe, Marshall appointed a policy planning staff under the direction of George Kennan to draw up policies.

Kennan later explained the basic assumption that underlay the Marshall Plan and, indeed, the entire range of America's postwar policies between 1947 and the mid-1950s. Excluding the United States, Kennan observed,

> there are only four aggregations which are major ones from the standpoint of strategic realities [that is, military and industrial potential] in the world. Two of those lie off the shores of the Eurasian land mass. Those are Japan and England, and two of them lie on the Eurasian land mass. One is the Soviet Union and the other is that of central Europe. . . .
>
> Viewed in absolute terms, I think the greatest danger that could confront the United States security would be a combination and working together for purposes hostile to us of the central European and the Russian military-industrial potentials. They would really create an entity . . . which could overshadow in a strategic sense even our own power. It is not anything, I think, which would be as easy of achievement as people often portray it as being here. I am not sure the Russians have the genius for holding all that together. . . . Still, they have the tendency of political thought, of Communist political expansion.

Building on this premise, round-the-clock conferences in May 1947 began to fashion the main features of the Marshall Plan. Kennan insisted that any aid, particularly military supplies, be limited and not given to just any area where Communists seemed to be enjoying some success. The all-important question then became how to handle the Russians. Ostensibly, Marshall accepted Kennan's advice to "play it straight" by inviting the Soviet bloc. In reality, the State Department made Russian acceptance improbable by demanding that economic records of each nation be open to scrutiny. For good measure Kennan also suggested that the [Soviet Union's] devastated economy, weakened by war and at that moment suffering from drought and famine, participate in the plan by shipping Soviet goods to Europe. Apparently no one in the State Department wanted the Soviet [Union] included. Russian participation would vastly multiply the costs of the program and eliminate any hope of its acceptance by a purse-watching Republican Congress, now increasingly convinced by Truman that Communists had to be fought, not fed.

Acheson's speech at Cleveland, Mississippi, in early May and Marshall's address at Harvard on June 5 revealed the motives and substance of the plan. In preparing for the earlier speech, Acheson's advisers concluded that American exports were rapidly approaching the $16 billion mark. Imports, however, amounted to only half that amount, and Europe did not have sufficient dollars to pay the difference. Either the United States would have to give credits to Europeans or they would be unable to buy American goods. The president's Council of Economic Advisers predicted a slight business recession, and if, in addition, exports dropped in any substantial amount, "the effect in the United States," as one official wrote, "might be most serious." Acheson underlined these facts in his Mississippi speech.

At Harvard, Marshall urged Europeans to create a long-term program that would "provide a cure rather than a mere palliative." On June 13 British Foreign Minister Ernest Bevin accepted Marshall's suggestion that Europeans take the initiative. Bevin traveled to Paris to talk with French Foreign Minister Georges Bidault. The question of Russian participation became uppermost in their discussions. *Pravda* had labeled Marshall's speech as a Truman Doctrine with dollars, a useless attempt to save the American economy by dominating European markets. Bidault ignored this; pressured by the powerful French Communist party and fearful that Russia's absence might compel France to join the Anglo-Saxons in a divided Europe dominated by a resurrected Germany, he decided to invite [Soviet Foreign Minister Vyacheslao] Molotov. The Russian line immediately moderated.

On June 26 Molotov arrived in Paris with eighty-nine economic experts and clerks, then spent much of the next three days conferring over the telephone with Moscow officials. The Russians were giving the plan serious consideration. Molotov finally proposed that each nation individually establish its own recovery program. The French and British proposed instead that Europe as a whole create the proposal for American consideration. Molotov angrily quit the conference, warning that the plan would undermine national sovereignty, revive Germany, allow Americans to control Europe, and, most ominously, divide "Europe into two groups of states . . . creating new difficulties in the relations between them." Within a week after his return to Moscow, the Soviet [Union] set [its] own "Molotov Plan" in motion. The Poles and the Czechs, who had expressed interest in Marshall's proposal, now informed the Paris conference that they could not attend because it "might be construed as an action against the Soviet Union."

As the remaining sixteen European nations hammered out a program for Marshall to consider, the United States moved on another front: it determined to revive Germany quickly. In late 1946 the Americans and British had overridden French opposition to merge economically the United States and British zones in Germany. Administrative duties were given to Germans. By mid-July 1947 Washington officials so rapidly rebuilt German industry that Bidault finally pleaded with Marshall to slow down or else the French government would never survive to carry through the economic recovery program. The United States nevertheless continued to rebuild German nonmilitary industry to the point where the country would be both self-sufficient and able to aid the remainder of western Europe. On September 22, the Paris meeting completed its work, pledging increased production, tariff reductions, and currency convertibility in return for American aid. The State Department could view its successes in Germany during the summer as icing on the cake.

The European request for a four-year program of $17 billion of American aid now had to run the gauntlet of a Republican Congress, which was dividing its attention between slashing the budget and attacking Truman, both in anticipation of the presidential election only a year away. In committee hearings in late 1947 and early 1948, the executive presented its case. Only large amounts of government money that could restore basic facilities, provide convertibility of local currency into dollars, and end the dollar shortage would stimulate private investors to rebuild Europe, administration witnesses argued. Then a rejuvenated Europe could offer many advantages to the United States: eradicate the threat of continued nationalization and socialism by releasing and stimulating the investment of private capital; maintain demand for American exports; encourage Europeans to produce strategic goods, which the United States could buy and stockpile; preserve European and American control over Middle Eastern oil supplies from militant nationalism, which might endanger the weakened European holdings; and free Europeans from economic problems so they could help the United States militarily. It would all be like magic.

George Kennan summarized the central problem in a note to Acheson. "Communist activities" were not "the root of the difficulties of Western Europe" but rather "the disruptive effects of the war on the economic, political, and social structure of Europe." So in the final plan Italy, with Europe's largest Communist party, received less aid than other, more economically important nations. In this sense the plan revolved around a rebuilt and autonomous Germany. As Secretary of State Marshall told Congress, "The restoration of Europe involved the restoration of Germany. Without a revival of German production there can be no revival of Europe's economy. But we must be very careful to see that a revived Germany can not again threaten the European community." The Marshall Plan offered a way to circumvent allied restrictions on German development, for it tied the Germans to a general European program and then offered vast sums to such nations as France that might otherwise be reluctant to support reconstructing Germany.

The Marshall Plan served as an all-purpose weapon for Truman's foreign policy. It charmed those who feared a slump in American exports and who believed, communist threat or no communist threat, that American and world prosperity rested on a vigorous export trade. A spokesman for the National Association of Manufacturers, for example, appeared considerably more moderate toward communism than some government officials when he argued that

Europe suffered not from "this so-called communistic surge," but from a "production problem" that only the Marshall Plan could solve. Appropriately, Truman named as administrator of the plan Paul Hoffman, a proven entrepreneur who, as Acheson once observed, preached a "doctrine of salvation by exports with all the passion of an economic Savonarola." The plan also attracted a group, including Reinhold Niebuhr, which placed more emphasis upon the containment of communism. The plan offered all things to all people. Or almost all, for Henry Wallace decided to oppose it in late 1947 on the grounds that only by channeling aid through the United Nations could calamitous relations between the United States and the Soviet Union be avoided.

The Marshall Plan now appears not the beginning but the end of an era. It marked the last phase in the administration's use of economic tactics as the primary means of tying together the Western world. The plan's approach, that peaceful and positive approach which Niebuhr applauded, soon evolved into military alliances. Truman proved to be correct in saying that the Truman Doctrine and the Marshall Plan "are two halves of the same walnut." Americans willingly acquiesced as the military aspects of the doctrine developed into quite the larger part.

Why such programs could so easily be transformed into military commitments was explained by George Kennan in a well-timed article appearing in July 1947 under the mysterious pseudonym Mr. "X." Washington's most respected expert on Soviet affairs, Kennan (who once called Niebuhr "the father of us all") had warned throughout the early 1940s against any hope of close postwar cooperation with Stalin. In early 1946 he sent a long dispatch to Washington from Moscow suggesting that at the "bottom of the Kremlin's neurotic view of world affairs is the traditional and instinctive Russian sense of insecurity." In post-1917 Russia, this became highly explosive when mixed with Communist ideology and "Oriental secretiveness and conspiracy." This dispatch brought Kennan to the attention of Secretary of the Navy James Forrestal, who helped bring the diplomat back to Washington and then strongly influenced Kennan's decision to publish the "X" article.

The article gave the administration's view of what made the Russians act like Communists. The analysis began not by emphasizing "the traditional Russian sense of insecurity" but by assuming that Stalin's policy was shaped by a combination of Marxist-Leninist ideology, which advocated revolution to defeat the capitalist forces in the outside world, and the dictator's determination to use "capitalist encirclement" as a rationale to regiment the Soviet masses so that he could consolidate his own political power. Kennan belittled such supposed "encirclement," although he recognized Nazi-Japanese hatred of the Soviet [Union] during the 1930s. (He omitted mentioning specifically the American and Japanese intervention in Russia between 1918 and 1920 and the United States attempt to isolate the Soviet [Union] politically through the 1920s.) Mr. "X" believed Stalin would not moderate communist determination to overthrow the western governments. Any softening of the Russian line would be a diversionary tactic designed to lull the west. For in the final analysis Soviet diplomacy "moves along the prescribed path, like a persistent toy automobile wound up and headed in a given direction, stopping only when it meets some unanswerable force." Endemic Soviet aggression could thus be "contained by the adroit and vigilant application of counterforce at a series of constantly shifting geographical and political points." The United States would have to undertake this containment alone and unilaterally, but if it could do so without weakening its prosperity and political stability, the Soviet party structure would undergo a period of immense strain climaxing in "either the break-up or the gradual mellowing of Soviet power."

The publication of this article triggered one of the more interesting debates of the cold war. Walter Lippmann was the dean of American journalists and one of those who did not accept the "two halves of the same walnut" argument. He condemned the military aspects of the Truman Doctrine while applauding the Marshall Plan because he disagreed with Kennan's assessment of Soviet motivation. And that, of course, was a crucial point in any argument over American policy. In a series of newspaper articles later collected in a book entitled *The Cold War*, Lippmann argued that Soviet policy was molded more by traditional Russian expansion than by Communist ideology. "Stalin is not only the heir of Marx and of Lenin but of Peter the Great, and the Czars of all the Russians." Because of the victorious sweep of the Red Army into Central Europe in 1945, Stalin could accomplish what the czars for centuries had only hoped to obtain. This approach enabled Lippmann to view the Soviet advance as a traditional quest for national security and, in turn, allowed him to argue that Russia would be amenable to an offer of withdrawal of both Russian and American power from central Europe. The fuses would thus be pulled from that explosive area.

Lippmann outlined the grave consequences of the alternative, the Mr. "X"—Truman Doctrine policy: "unending intervention in all the countries that are supposed to 'contain' the Soviet Union"; futile and costly efforts to make "Jeffersonian democrats" out of eastern European peasants and Middle Eastern and Asian warlords; either the destruction of the United Nations or its transformation into a useless anti-Soviet coalition; and such a tremendous strain on the American people that their economy would have to be increasingly regimented and their men sent to fight on the perimeter of the Soviet bloc. The columnist warned that if Mr. "X" succeeded in applying counterforce to the "constantly shifting geographical and political points," the Soviet [Union] would perforce be allowed to take the initiative in the cold war by choosing the grounds and weapons for combat. Finally, Lippmann, like the administration, emphasized Germany's importance, but he differed by observing that Russia, which controlled eastern Germany, could, at its leisure, outmaneuver the west and repeat the 1939 Nazi-Soviet pact of offering the ultimate reward of reunification for German cooperation. "The idea that we can foster the sentiment of German unity, and make a truncated Germany economically strong," Lippmann wrote, "can keep her disarmed, and can use her in the anti-Soviet coalition is like trying to square the circle."

Lippmann was profound, but he had no chance of being persuasive. By the end of August 1947, the State Department rejected Lippmann's proposals for disengagement in Germany. American officials instead assumed that the "one world" of the United Nations was "no longer valid and that we are in political fact facing a division into two worlds." The "X" article also indicated the administration was operating on another assumption: economic development could not occur until "security" was established. This increasing concern with things military became evident in late 1947 when Kennan suggested that the United States change its long-standing hostility to Franco's government in Spain in order to cast proper military security over the Mediterranean area. A year earlier the United States had joined with Britain and France in asking the Spanish people to overthrow Franco by political means because his government was pro-Nazi and totalitarian. Kennan's suggestion marked the turn in Spanish-American relations, which ended in close military cooperation after 1950.

The quest for military security also transformed American policy in Asia. With Chiang Kai-shek's decline, the State Department searched for a new partner who could help stabilize the far east. The obvious candidate was Japan, which from the 1890s until 1931 had worked closely with Washington. It was also the potential industrial powerhouse of the area, the Germany of the Orient. Since 1945 the United States had single-handedly controlled Japan. The Soviet [Union] had been carefully excluded. Even Australia was allowed to send occupation forces only after promising not to interfere with the authority of General Douglas MacArthur, head of the American government in Japan. MacArthur instituted a new constitution (in which Japan renounced war for all time), then conducted elections that allowed him to claim that the Japanese had overwhelmingly repudiated communism. To the general, as to Washington officials, this was fundamental. In 1946 MacArthur privately compared America in its fight against communism to the agony of Christ at Gethsemane, for "Christ, even though crucified, nevertheless prevailed."

He added that Japan was becoming "the western outpost of our defenses." In 1947–1948 Japan received the "two halves of the same walnut" treatment. The State Department decided to rebuild Japanese industry and develop a sound export economy. At the same time, American bases on the islands were to be expanded and maintained until, in one official's words, "the at present disarmed soldiers of Japan are provided with arms and training to qualify them to preserve the peace." As in Europe, economic development and security moved hand in hand as Americans buttressed the Pacific portion of their system. . . .

Of special importance to Truman's "security" effort, the president transformed what he termed "the antiquated defense setup of the United States" by passing the National Security Act through Congress in July 1947. This bill provided for a single Department of Defense to replace the three independently run services, statutory establishment of the Joint Chiefs of Staff, a National Security Council to advise the president, and a Central Intelligence Agency to correlate and evaluate intelligence activities. James Forrestal, the stepfather of Mr. "X" and the leading advocate among presidential advisers of a tough military approach to cold war problems, became the first secretary of defense. Forrestal remained until he resigned in early spring 1949. Two months later on the night of May 22, Forrestal, suffering from mental and physical illness, jumped or accidentally fell to his death from the twelfth floor of the Bethesda Naval Hospital.

The military and personal costs of the Truman Doctrine—Mr. "X" policy would be higher than expected. And the cost became more apparent as Truman and J. Edgar Hoover (director of the Federal Bureau of Investigation) carried out the president's Security Loyalty program. Their search for subversives accelerated after Canadians uncovered a Soviet spy ring. During hearings in the Senate on the appointment of David E. Lilienthal as chairman of the Atomic Energy Commission, the first major charges of "soft on communism" were hurled by Robert Taft [in part] because of Lilienthal's New Deal background. . . .

Since the Iranian and Turkish crises of 1946, the Soviet [Union] had not been active in world affairs. But Molotov's departure from the Marshall Plan conference in Paris during July 1947 marked the turn. Russian attention was riveted on Germany. The Politburo interpreted the Marshall Plan to mean the American "intention to restore the economy of Germany and Japan on the old basis [of pre-1941] provided it is subordinated to interests of American capital." Rebuilding Europe through the plan and tying it closer to American economic power threatened Stalin's hope of influencing west European policies. Incomparably worse, however, was linking that Europe to a restored western Germany. This not only undercut Soviet determination to keep this ancient enemy weak, as well as divided, but vastly increased the potential of that enemy, tied it to the forces of "capitalist encirclement," and revived the memories of two world wars.

Molotov quickly initiated a series of moves to tighten Soviet control of the bloc. A program of bilateral trade agreements, the so-called Molotov Plan, began to link the bloc countries and Russia in July 1947. The final step came in January 1949, when the Council for Mutual Economic Assistance (COMECON) provided the Soviet answer to the Marshall Plan by creating a centralized agency for stimulating and controlling bloc development. As a result of these moves, Soviet trade with the east European bloc, which had declined in 1947 to $380 million, doubled in 1948, quadrupled by 1950, and exceeded $2.5 billion in 1952. Seventy percent of east European trade was carried on with either the Soviet Union or elsewhere within the bloc.

Four days after his return from Paris, Molotov announced the establishment of the Communist Information Bureau (Cominform). Including Communists from Russia, Yugoslavia, France, Italy, Poland, Bulgaria, Czechoslovakia, Hungary, and Rumania, the Cominform provided another instrument for increasing Stalin's control. This was his answer to the Czech and Polish interest in joining the Marshall Plan. In late August, a month before the first Cominform meeting, Soviet actions in Hungary indicated the line that would be followed. After a purge of left-wing anticommunist political leaders, the Soviet [Union] directly intervened by rigging elections. All anticommunist opposition disappeared. Three weeks later at the Cominform meeting in Warsaw, [Cominform leader Andrei] Zhdanov formally announced new Soviet policies in a speech that ranks next to Stalin's February 9, 1946, address as a Russian call to cold war.

Zhdanov's analysis of recent international developments climaxed with the announcement that American economic power, fattened by the war, was organizing western Europe and "countries politically and economically dependent on the United States, such as the Near-Eastern and South-American countries and China" into an anticommunist bloc. The Russians and the "new democracies" in eastern Europe, Finland, Indonesia, and Vietnam meanwhile formed another bloc, which "has the sympathy of India, Egypt and Syria." In this way, Zhdanov again announced the rebirth of the "two-camp" view of the world, an attitude that had dominated Russian policy between 1927 and 1934 when Stalin bitterly attacked the west, and a central theme in the dictator's speech of February 1946. In some respects Zhdanov's announcement resembled the "two-world" attitude in the United States. The mirror image was especially striking when Zhdanov admonished the socialist camp not to lower its guard. "Just as in the past the Munich policy united the hands of the Nazi aggressors, so today concessions to the new course of the United States and the imperialist camp may encourage its inspirers to be even more insolent and aggressive."

Following Zhdanov's call to action, the Cominform delegates sharply criticized French and Italian Communists, who seemed to want a more pacific approach, and, once again following the disastrous practices of the 1927–1934 era, ordered all members to foment the necessary strikes and internal disorder for the elimination of independent socialist, labor, and peasant parties in their countries. The meeting was the high-water mark of the tough Zhdanov line in Soviet foreign policy. Its effect was soon felt not only in bloc and west European countries but inside Russia as well. Stalin cleansed Soviet economic thinking by discrediting and removing from public view Eugene Varga, a leading Russian economist who had angered the Politburo by warning that Marxists were wrong in thinking that the western economies would soon collapse.

American officials fully understood why the Soviet [Union was] trying these new policies. As Secretary of State Marshall told Truman's cabinet in November 1947, "The advance of Communism has been stemmed and the Russians have been compelled to make a reevaluation of their position." America was winning its eight-month cold war. But the [Soviet Union's] difficulties provided an excuse for Congress, which was not anxious to send billions of dollars of Marshall Plan aid to Europe if the Russians posed no threat. Congress dawdled as the plan came under increased criticism. Taft urged that good money not be poured into a "European TVA." On the other side of the political spectrum, Henry Wallace labeled it a "Martial Plan." In speeches around the country, Marshall tried to sell the program for its long-term economic and political benefits. His arguments fell on deaf ears. The American economy seemed to be doing well. Just weeks before the 1948 presidential campaign was to begin, Truman faced a major political and diplomatic defeat.

And then came the fall of Czechoslovakia. The Czechs had uneasily coexisted with Russia by trying not to offend the Soviet [Union] while keeping doors open to the west. This policy had started in late 1943, when Czech leaders signed a treaty with Stalin that, in the view of most observers, obligated Czechoslovakia to become a part of the Russian bloc. President Eduard Beneš and Foreign Minister Jan Masaryk, one of the foremost diplomatic figures in Europe, had nevertheless successfully resisted complete communist control. Nor had Stalin moved to consolidate his power in 1946 after the Czech Communist party emerged from the parliamentary elections with 38 percent of the vote, the largest total of any party. By late 1947 the lure of western aid and internal political changes began to pull the Czech government away from the Soviet [Union]. At this point Stalin, who like Truman recalled the pivotal role of Czechoslovakia in 1938, decided to put the 1943 treaty into effect. Klement Gottwald, the Czech Communist party leader, demanded the elimination of independent parties. In mid-February 1948 Soviet armies camped on the border as Gottwald ordered the formation of a wholly new government. A Soviet mission of top officials flew to Prague to demand Beneš's surrender. The Communist assumed full control on February 25. Two weeks later Masaryk either committed suicide or, as Truman believed, was the victim of "foul play."

Truman correctly observed that the coup "sent a shock throughout the civilized world." He privately believed, "We are faced with exactly the same situation with which Britain and France was faced in 1938–9 with Hitler." In late 1947 Hungary had been the victim of a similar if less dramatic squeeze. Within two months, new opportunities would beckon to the Cominform when the Italian election was held. On March 5 a telegram arrived from General Clay in Germany. Although "I have felt and held that war was unlikely for at least ten years," Clay began, "within the last few weeks, I have felt a subtle change in Soviet attitude which . . . gives me the feeling that it may come with dramatic suddenness." For ten days, government intelligence worked furiously investigating Clay's warnings and on March 16 gave Truman the grim assurance that war was not probable within sixty days. Two days before, on March 14, the Senate had endorsed the Marshall Plan by a vote of 69 to 17. As it went to the House for consideration, Truman, fearing the "grave events in Europe [which] were moving so swiftly," decided to appear before Congress.

In a speech remarkable for its repeated emphasis on the "increasing threat" to the very "survival of freedom," the president proclaimed the Marshall Plan "not enough." Europe must have "some measure of protection against internal and external aggression." He asked for Universal Military Training, the resumption of Selective Service (which he had allowed to lapse a year earlier), and speedy passage of the Marshall Plan. Within twelve days the House approved authorization of the plan's money.

With perfect timing and somber rhetoric, Truman's March 17 speech not only galvanized passage of the plan but accelerated a change in American foreign policy that had been heralded the previous summer. Congress stamped its approval on this new military emphasis by passing a Selective Service bill. Although Universal Military Training, one of Forrestal's pet projects, found little favor, a supposedly penny-proud Congress replaced it with funds to begin a seventy-group Air Force, 25 percent larger than even Forrestal had requested.

Perhaps the most crucial effect of the new policy, however, appeared in the administration's determination to create great systems that would not only encourage military development but would also compel the western world to accept political realignments as well. The first of these efforts had been the Rio Pact and the new policies toward Japan. The next, somewhat different, and vastly more important effort would be the North Atlantic Treaty Organization (NATO).

THE SEARCH FOR COMMUNISTS: HUAC INVESTIGATES HOLLYWOOD

In the fall of 1947, only months after the Truman doctrine and the Marshall Plan had announced a deepening Cold War, the House Un-American Activities Committee (HUAC) opened hearings designed to probe communist infiltration of the Hollywood film industry. The inquiry was only one of several attacks on communism taking place at the time. The United States Attorney General had distributed a list of "subversive" organizations with presumed communist ties; and in March, 1947, President Truman had issued an order requiring investigations of all federal employees.

HUAC called dozens of witnesses, many of them famous actors, directors, screenwriters, and studio heads. Ronald Reagan, then a movie actor and a member of the Screen Actors Guild, offered rather vague testimony about a "small clique" that had made an effort to be a "disruptive influence" in the guild, while admitting that he had no knowledge that the group included communists. Novelist and screenwriter Ayn Rand described at length the contents of the film Song of Russia, *a wartime production that Rand, and many members of the committee, considered deceitful and propagandistic. Other witnesses echoed and amplified Rand's concerns, but the HUAC hearings did not uncover much solid evidence of communist influence in Hollywood.*

Even so, the inquiry had an impact. In November, studio executives announced a "blacklist" of people who would no longer be allowed to work in the industry, and the House of Representatives held ten "unfriendly" witnesses in contempt and sent them to jail. More important, the pressure on producers, directors and screenwriters to avoid anything that smacked of radicalism shaped the content of Hollywood films for about fifteen years.

In reading the following testimony, consider the possibility that the purpose of the inquiry may have been something other than the discovery of com-

U.S. Congress, House, Committee on Un-American Activities, *Hearings Regarding the Communist Infiltration of the Motion Picture Industry,* 80th Cong., 1st Sess., October 20–30, 1947 (Washington: GPO, 1947).

munism or communists. How did witnesses define activities or values they deemed un-American? What people, events, or organizations were understood to be dangerous? What is the meaning of John Charles Moffitt's story of the "Sleepy Lagoon" case?

Besides those testifying, those speaking include Robert E. Stripling, Chief Investigator of the Committee on Un-American Activities; Richard M. Nixon, Republican congressman from California; and H. A. Smith, investigator for the committee.

TESTIMONY OF JACK L. WARNER, VICE-PRESIDENT OF WARNER BROTHERS STUDIO

MR. STRIPLING. Mr. Warner, you are here before the Committee on Un-American Activities in response to a subpena served upon you on September 29, 1947; is that correct?

MR. WARNER. Yes, sir.

MR. STRIPLING. What is your occupation?

MR. WARNER. In charge of production of Warner Bros. studios at Burbank, Calif.

MR. STRIPLING. Are you a vice president of Warner Bros.?

MR. WARNER. I am.

Statement of Jack L. Warner

It is a privilege to appear again before this committee to help as much as I can in facilitating its work.

I am happy to speak openly and honestly in an inquiry which has for its purpose the reaffirmation of American ideals and democratic processes. As last May, when I appeared before a subcommittee of this group in Los Angeles, my testimony is based on personal opinions, impressions, and beliefs created by the things I have heard, read, and seen. It is given freely and voluntarily.

Our American way of life is under attack from without and from within our national borders. I believe it is the duty of each loyal American to resist those attacks and defeat them.

Freedom is a precious thing. It requires careful nurturing, protection, and encouragement. It has flourished under the guaranties of our American Constitution and Bill of Rights to make this country the ideal of all men who honestly wish to call their souls their own.

I believe that I, as an individual, and our company as an organization of American citizens, must watch always for threats to the American way of life. History teaches the lesson that liberties are won bitterly and may be lost unwittingly.

We have seen recent tragic examples of national and personal freedoms destroyed by dictator-trained wrecking crews. The advance guards of propagandists and infiltrationists were scarcely noticed at first. They got in their first licks quietly, came into the open only when they were ready to spring the trap. Heedless peoples suddenly woke up to find themselves slaves to dictatorships imposed by skillful and willful groups.

I believe the first line of defense against this familiar pattern is an enlightened public. People aware of threats to their freedom cannot be victimized by the divide-and-conquer policies used by Hitler and his counterparts.

It is my firm conviction that the free American screen has taken its rightful place with the free American press in the first line of defense.

Ideological termites have burrowed into many American industries, organizations, and societies. Wherever they may be, I say let us dig them out and get rid of them. My brothers and I will be happy to subscribe generously to a pest-removal fund. We are willing to establish such a fund to ship to Russia the people who don't like our American system of government and prefer the communistic system to ours.

That's how strongly we feel about the subversives who want to overthrow our free American system.

If there are Communists in our industry, or any other industry, organization, or society who seek to undermine our free institutions, let's find out about it and know who they are. Let the record be spread clear, for all to read and judge. The public is entitled to know the facts. And the motion-picture industry is entitled to have the public know the facts.

Our company is keenly aware of its responsibilities to keep its product free from subversive poisons. With all the vision at my command, I scrutinize the planning and production of our motion pictures. It is my firm belief that there is not a Warner Bros. picture that can fairly be judged to be hostile to our country, or communistic in tone or purpose.

Many charges, including the fantasy of "White House pressure" have been leveled at our wartime production Mission to Moscow. In my previous appearance before members of this committee, I explained the origin and purposes of Mission to Moscow.

That picture was made when our country was fighting for its existence, with Russia as one of our allies. It was made to fulfill the same wartime purpose for which we made such other pictures as Air Force, This Is the Army, Objective Burma, Destination Tokyo, Action in the North Atlantic, and a great many more.

If making Mission to Moscow in 1942 was a subversive activity, then the American Liberty ships which carried food and guns to Russian allies and the American naval vessels which convoyed them were likewise engaged in subversive activities. The picture was made only to help a desperate war effort and not for posterity.

The Warner Bros. interest in the preservation of the American way of life is no new thing with our company. Ever since we began making motion pictures we have fostered American ideals and done what we could to protect them.

Not content with merely warning against dangers to our free system, Warner Bros. has practiced a policy of positive Americanism. We have gone, and will continue to go, to all possible lengths to iterate and reiterate the realities and advantages of America. . . .

TESTIMONY OF ADOLPH MENJOU, ACTOR

MR. STRIPLING. Mr. Menjou, will you please state your name and address?

MR. MENJOU. My name is Adolph Menjou, and my address is 722 North Bedford Drive, Beverly Hills, Calif. . . .

MR. STRIPLING. Mr. Menjou, what is your occupation?

MR. MENJOU. I am a motion-picture actor, I hope.

MR. STRIPLING. When and where were you born, Mr. Menjou?

MR. MENJOU. I was born in Pittsburgh, Pa., February 18, 1890.

MR. STRIPLING. How long have you been in the motion-picture industry?

MR. MENJOU. Thirty-four years.

MR. STRIPLING. And how long have you been in Hollywood?

MR. MENJOU. Twenty-seven years.

MR. STRIPLING. Mr. Menjou, were you in the First World War?

MR. MENJOU. Yes, sir.

MR. STRIPLING. In the armed services?

MR. MENJOU. Yes, sir. I served abroad for 2 years. I was in the Army 3 years, 1 year in America. I served in Italy, with the Italian Army, being attached to the Italian Army; attached to the French Army; and with the Fifth Division until the surrender on November 11, 1918.

MR. STRIPLING. Were you in World War II?

MR. MENJOU. I served 6 months with the U.S. Camp Shows, Inc., entertaining troops—for 4 months in England, 2 months in North Africa, Sicily, Tunisia, Algeria, Morrocco, Brazil, and the Caribbean.

MR. STRIPLING. Mr. Menjou, have you made a study of the subject of communism, the activities of the Communists, in any particular field in the United States?

MR. MENJOU. I have. I have made a more particular study of Marxism, Fabian socialism, communism, Stalinism, and its probable effects on the American people, if they ever gain power here.

MR. STRIPLING. Based upon your study, have you observed any Communist activity in the motion-picture industry or in Hollywood, as we commonly refer to it?

MR. MENJOU. I would like to get the terminologies completely straight. Communistic activities—I would rather phrase it un-American or subversive, antifree enterprise, anticapitalistic. I have seen—pardon me.

MR. STRIPLING. Have you observed any Communist propaganda in pictures, or un-American propaganda in pictures which were produced in Hollywood?

MR. MENJOU. I have seen no communistic propaganda in pictures—if you mean "vote for Stalin," or that type of communistic propaganda. I don't think that the Communists are stupid enough to try it that way. I have seen in certain pictures things I didn't think should have been in the pictures.

MR. STRIPLING. Could you tell the committee whether or not there has been an effort on the part of any particular group in the motion-picture industry to inject Communist propaganda into pictures or to leave out scenes or parts of stories which would serve the Communist Party line?

MR. MENJOU. I don't like that term "Communist propaganda," because I have seen no such thing as Communist propaganda, such as waving the hammer and sickle in motion pictures. I have seen things that I thought were against what I considered good Americanism, in my feeling. I have seen pictures I thought shouldn't have been made—shouldn't have been made, let me put it that way. . . .

MR. NIXON. In answer to a question by Mr. Stripling you indicated that although you might not know whether a certain person was a Communist, I think you said he certainly acted like a Communist.

MR. MENJOU. If you belong to a Communist-front organization and you take no action against the Communists, you do not resign from the organization when you still know the organization is dominated by Communists, I consider that a very, very dangerous thing.

MR. NIXON. Have you any other tests which you would apply which would indicate to you that people acted like Communists?

MR. MENJOU. Well, I think attending any meetings at which Mr. Paul Robeson* appeared and applauding or listening to his Communist songs in America, I would be ashamed to be seen in an audience doing a thing of that kind.

MR. NIXON. You indicated you thought a person acted like a Communist when he stated, as one person did to you, that capitalism was through.

MR. MENJOU. That is not communistic per se, but it is very dangerous leaning, it is very close. I see nothing wrong with the capitalistic system, the new dynamic capitalism in America today. Mr. Stalin was very worried when he talked to Mr. Stassen. He asked him four times when the great crash was coming in America. That is what they are banking on, a great crash, and I do not think it is coming.

MR. NIXON. You indicated that belonging to a Communist-front organization, in other words, an association with Communists, attending these planned meetings, making statements in opposition to the capitalistic system are three of the tests you would apply.

MR. MENJOU. Yes, sir.

TESTIMONY OF JOHN CHARLES MOFFITT, FILM CRITIC FOR *ESQUIRE* MAGAZINE, SCREENWRITER

MR. STRIPLING. Mr. Moffitt, will you please state your name for the record?

MR. MOFFITT. John Charles Moffitt.

MR. STRIPLING. That is M-o-f-f-i-t-t?

MR. MOFFITT. That is correct.

MR. STRIPLING. You are here in response to a subpena served on you on September 29, Mr. Moffitt?

MR. MOFFITT. Yes sir.

MR. STRIPLING. What is your present address?

---

*African-American actor and singer Paul Robeson was associated with communist causes in the 1930s. —Ed.

MR. MOFFITT. 463 South McAddam Place, Los Angeles 5.

MR. STRIPLING. Please state when and where you were born.

MR. MOFFITT. I was born in Kansas City, Mo., on May 8, 1901. . . .

MR. STRIPLING. You have been employed by the motion-picture industry as a writer in the past; have you not?

MR. MOFFITT. Many times. . . .

MR. STRIPLING. Did you ever join any organizations while you were in Hollywood in connection with being a writer for the motion-picture industry?

MR. MOFFITT. Yes, sir; I did. In 1937, shocked by the conduct of the Fascists in Spain, I joined an organization known as the Hollywood Anti-Nazi League. Both my wife and I became members of that organization. We contributed considerable sums of money—for us—to what we supposed was the buying of ambulances and medical supplies for the assistance of the Loyalists in Spain.

MR. STRIPLING. Will you relate to the committee your experiences with the Anti-Nazi League, so far as they deal with any Communist activity?

MR. MOFFITT. Well, fascinated by the subtlety of this approach, fascinated and, I may say, horrified by the way an innocent liberal was induced to give money to a Communist front and induced to lend what little prestige his name might have professionally to a communist activity, I remained in about 6 weeks before I resigned, in order to try to see how they worked. I think I learned considerable of their technique in that time.

MR. STRIPLING. Would you give the committee an account of the activities that you observed as a member during those 6 weeks?

MR. MOFFITT. Well, the most significant activity I observed came out in a conversation with Mr. John Howard Lawson——

MR. STRIPLING. Would you identify Mr. Lawson?

MR. MOFFITT. Yes, sir.

MR. STRIPLING. He is a writer, is he not?

MR. MOFFITT. John Howard Lawson is a writer. He was the first president of the Screen Writers Guild.

It has been testified before the Tenney committee of the California Legislature that Mr. Lawson was sent to Los Angeles by the Communist Party for the purpose of organizing Communist activities in Hollywood. It was testified by a former secretary of the Communist Party for Los Angeles County.

Mr. Lawson has this record, as far as I know, with front organizations. He was a sponsor of the American Youth for Democracy, which was formerly the Young Communist League. He was a speaker at the California Labor School. He was sponsor of the City Committee for the Defense of American Youth in what was known as the Sleepy Lagoon case.*

---

*The "Sleepy Lagoon" case began in 1942, when the body of Jose Diaz was found on a city road in Los Angeles, near a swimming hole known as "Sleepy Lagoon" to Hispanic youngsters who lived nearby. The body was found near a ranch where Hispanic teenagers had tangled the night before, and police overreacted, rounding up and questioning some 600 Hispanic youngsters. In a trial that revealed the deep prejudice of judge and jury, seventeen Mexican-American youths were convicted of murder and jailed for the crime. The conviction led to the creation of the Sleepy Lagoon Defense Committee, whose sponsors and representatives included the Screen Artist's Guild, film director Orson Welles, and actors Anthony Quinn and Rita Hayworth. —Ed.

I would like to point out that the Sleepy Lagoon case was an attempt to raise a racial issue in Los Angeles.

As I understand it, the actual case had no racial implications whatever. It was a murder case in which the victim was a Mexican, the accused was Mexican, and the arresting officer was a Mexican. I use the term "Mexican" as meaning persons of Mexican descent. I do not mean to imply any discrimination against persons of Spanish or Mexican origin when I say that.

The victim in the case was an elderly, reputable hard-working good citizen. He, with some of his friends who were also of the same racial heritage, celebrated his birthday at a little farm. They had a little wine, some food, and a concrete slab on which they danced.

During the entertainment a group of what we later came to call "zoot suiters," according to the testimony of the arresting officers, loaded with marihuana, drove up, broke up the party, beat the old man to death with a tire chain and chased another of his friends into a pool or a rock quarry where, I believe, the man was drowned. I am not sure whether they saved him.

My impression is that there were two deaths.

The arresting officers were men from the Los Angeles Mexican detail and from the sheriff's office. There was absolutely no racial discrimination issue involved there until the Communist Party took it over and endeavor to reframe it, recast it, and publicize it as the effort of the American courts to railroad innocent youths because they were of Mexican origin.

MR. STRIPLING. Mr. Lawson was affiliated with that front effort to the Communist Party?

MR. MOFFITT. He was sponsor of the city committee for the defense of these men.

TESTIMONY OF WALTER E. DISNEY, HEAD OF THE WALT DISNEY STUDIO

MR. STRIPLING. Mr. Disney, will you state your full name and present address please?

MR. DISNEY. Walter E. Disney, Los Angeles, Calif.

MR. STRIPLING. When and where were you born, Mr. Disney?

MR. DISNEY. Chicago, Ill., December 5, 1901.

MR. STRIPLING. December 5, 1901?

MR. DISNEY. Yes, sir.

MR. STRIPLING. What is your occupation?

MR. DISNEY. Well, I am a producer of motion-picture cartoons.

MR. STRIPLING. Mr. Chairman, the interrogation of Mr. Disney will be done by Mr. Smith.

THE CHAIRMAN. Mr. Smith.

MR. SMITH. Mr. Disney, how long have you been in that business?

MR. DISNEY. Since 1920.

MR. SMITH. You have been in Hollywood during this time?

MR. DISNEY. I have been in Hollywood since 1923.

MR. SMITH. At the present time you own and operate the Walt Disney Studio at Burbank, Calif.?

MR. DISNEY. Well, I am one of the owners. Part owner.

MR. SMITH. How many people are employed there, approximately?

MR. DISNEY. At the present time about 600.

MR. SMITH. And what is the approximate largest number of employees you have had in the studio?

MR. DISNEY. Well, close to 1,400 at times. . . .

MR. SMITH. Aside from those pictures you made during the war, have you made any other pictures, or do you permit pictures to be made at your studio containing propaganda?

MR. DISNEY. No; we never have. During the war we thought it was a different thing. It was the first time we ever allowed anything like that to go in the films. We watch so that nothing gets into the films that would be harmful in any way to any group or any country. We have large audiences of children and different groups, and we try to keep them as free from anything that would offend anybody as possible. We work hard to see that nothing of that sort creeps in.

MR. SMITH. Do you have any people in your studio at the present time that you believe are Communist or Fascist, employed there?

MR. DISNEY. No; at the present time I feel that everybody in my studio is 100 percent American.

MR. SMITH. Have you had at any time, in your opinion, in the past, have you at any time in the past had any Communists employed at your studio?

MR. DISNEY. Yes; in the past I had some people that I definitely feel were Communists.

MR. SMITH. As a matter of fact, Mr. Disney, you experienced a strike at your studio, did you not?

MR. DISNEY. Yes.

MR. SMITH. And is it your opinion that that strike was instituted by members of the Communist Party to serve their purposes?

MR. DISNEY. Well, it proved itself so with time, and I definitely feel it was a Communist group trying to take over my artists and they did take them over.

THE CHAIRMAN. Do you say they did take them over?

MR. DISNEY. They did take them over.

During the Army-McCarthy hearings of 1954, McCarthy (*far right*) blocked an attempt by Army Counsel Joseph Welch (*far left*) to obtain names of McCarthy's office staff. McCarthy charged "a smear campaign" was under way against "anyone working with exposing communists."

Harris & Ewing/Washington Star Collection, Courtesy Washingtoniana Division, Public Library.

TAIL GUNNER JOE: THE WHEELING ADDRESS

Joseph McCarthy

McCarthyism is the name applied to the second Red Scare, a period of political repression in America, epitomized by the career of Senator Joseph McCarthy. "Tail gunner Joe" was elected as the junior senator from Wisconsin in 1946 and received little recognition until his speech in Wheeling, West Virginia, on February 9, 1950. For the next four years, he chaired Senate committee meetings where he accused first the Truman administration, and later the Eisenhower administration, of harboring known communists and probable spies in the government. He was censured by his colleagues in the Senate in 1954 and faded into obscurity.

McCarthy did not create the atmosphere of suspicion and anticommunism given his name. Indeed, years before McCarthy came on the scene, the Truman administration had instituted its own loyalty-security program (1947) and stepped up the use of the Smith Act throughout 1948 to prosecute Americans suspected of subversive thinking. Congress also contributed with the hearings of the House Un-American Activities Committee (HUAC) and the Alger Hiss investigation and trials (1948). Yet McCarthy was surely the most notorious opportunist of the era. His tactics of demagoguery, insinuation, and guilt by association defined the means by which thousands of Americans were denied their civil rights. Worse still, a public insecure about the postwar world accepted his vision of conspiracy and sanctioned his attacks.

The following is a sample of McCarthy's tactics against the State Department. How does Senator McCarthy define the threat to American security? What proof does he offer that the State Department is filled with known Communists? What were the elements of his success? Was his failure inevitable? Or could he have become more powerful than he was?

Ladies and gentlemen, tonight as we celebrate the one hundred and forty-first birthday of one of the greatest men in American history, I would like to be able to talk about what a glorious day today is in the history of the world. As we celebrate the birth of this man who with his whole heart and soul hated war, I would like to be able to speak of peace in our time, of war being outlawed, and of worldwide disarmament. These would be truly appropriate things to be able to mention as we celebrate the birthday of Abraham Lincoln.

Five years after a world war has been won, men's hearts should anticipate a long peace, and men's minds should be free from the heavy weight that comes with war. But this is not such a period—for this is not a period of peace. This is a time of the "cold war." This is a time when all the world is split into two vast, increasingly hostile armed camps—a time of a great armaments race.

Today we can almost physically hear the mutterings and rumblings of an invigorated god of war. You can see it, feel it, and hear it all the way from the hills of Indochina, from the shores of Formosa, right over into the very heart of Europe itself.

The one encouraging thing is that the "mad moment" has not yet arrived for the firing of a gun or the exploding of the bomb which will set civilization about the final task of destroying itself. There is still a hope for peace if we finally decide that no longer can we safely blind our eyes and close our ears to those facts which are shaping up more and more clearly. And that is that we are now engaged in a showdown fight—not the usual war between nations for land areas or other material gains, but a war between two diametrically opposed ideologies.

The great difference between our western Christian world and the atheistic Communist world is not political, ladies and gentlemen, it is moral. There are other differences, of course, but those could be reconciled. For instance, the

From U.S., Congress, Senate, *Congressional Record,* 81st Cong., 2d sess., 1950, 96, 1954, 1946, 1957.

Marxian idea of confiscating the land and factories and running the entire economy as a single enterprise is momentous. Likewise, Lenin's invention of the one-party police state as a way to make Marx's idea work is hardly less momentous.

Stalin's resolute putting across of these two ideas, of course, did much to divide the world. With only those differences, however, the east and the west could most certainly still live in peace.

The real, basic difference, however, lies in the religion of immoralism—invented by Marx, preached feverishly by Lenin, and carried to unimaginable extremes by Stalin. This religion of immoralism, if the Red half of the world wins—and well it may—this religion of immoralism will more deeply wound and damage mankind than any conceivable economic or political system. . . .

Today we are engaged in a final, all-out battle between communistic atheism and Christianity. The modern champions of communism have selected this as the time. And, ladies and gentlemen, the chips are down—they are truly down. . . .

Ladies and gentlemen, can there be anyone here tonight who is so blind as to say that the war is not on? Can there be anyone who fails to realize that the Communist world has said, "The time is now"—that this is the time for the showdown between the democratic Christian world and the Communist atheistic world?

Unless we face this fact, we shall pay the price that must be paid by those who wait too long.

Six years ago, at the time of the first conference to map out the peace—Dumbarton Oaks—there was within the Soviet orbit 180 million people. Lined up on the antitotalitarian side there were in the world at that time roughly 1,625,000,000 people. Today, only six years later, there are 800 million people under the absolute domination of Soviet Russia—an increase of over 400 percent. On our side, the figure has shrunk to around 500 million. In other words, in less than six years the odds have changed from 9 to 1 in our favor to 8 to 5 against us. This indicates the swiftness of the tempo of Communist victories and American defeats in the cold war. As one of our outstanding historical figures once said, "When a great democracy is destroyed, it will not be because of enemies from without, but rather because of enemies from within."

The truth of this statement is becoming terrifyingly clear as we see this country each day losing on every front.

At war's end we were physically the strongest nation on earth and, at least potentially, the most powerful intellectually and morally. Ours could have been the honor of being a beacon in the desert of destruction, a shining living proof that civilization was not yet ready to destroy itself. Unfortunately, we have failed miserably and tragically to arise to the opportunity.

The reason why we find ourselves in a position of impotency is not because our only powerful potential enemy has sent men to invade our shores, but rather because of the traitorous actions of those who have been treated so well by this nation. It has not been the less fortunate or members of minority groups who have been selling this nation out, but rather those who have had all the benefits that the wealthiest nation on earth has had to offer—the finest homes, the finest college education, and the finest jobs in government we can give.

This is glaringly true in the State Department. There the bright young men who are born with silver spoons in their mouths are the ones who have been worst.

Now I know it is very easy for anyone to condemn a particular bureau or department in general terms. Therefore, I would like to cite one rather unusual case—the case of a man who has done much to shape our foreign policy.

When Chiang Kai-shek was fighting our war, the State Department had in China a young man named John S. Service. His task, obviously, was not to work for the communization of China. Strangely, however, he sent official reports back to the State Department urging that we torpedo our ally Chiang Kai-shek and stating, in effect, that communism was the best hope of China.

Later, this man—John Service—was picked up by the Federal Bureau of Investigation for turning over to the Communists secret State Department information. Strangely, however, he was never prosecuted. However, Joseph Grew, the under secretary of state, who insisted on his prosecution, was forced to resign. Two days after Grew's successor, Dean Acheson, took over as under secretary of state, this man—John Service—who had been picked up by the FBI and who had previously urged that communism was the best hope of China, was not only reinstated in the State Department but promoted. And finally, under Acheson, placed in charge of all placements and promotions.

Today, ladies and gentlemen, this man Service is on his way to represent the State Department and Acheson in Calcutta—by far and away the most important listening post in the far east. . . .

This, ladies and gentlemen, gives you somewhat of a picture of the type of individuals who have been helping to shape our foreign policy. In my opinion the State Department, which is one of the most important government departments, is thoroughly infested with Communists.

I have in my hand fifty-seven cases of individuals who would appear to be either card-carrying members or certainly loyal to the Communist party, but who nevertheless are still helping to shape our foreign policy. . . .

This brings us down to the case of one Alger Hiss who is important not as an individual any more, but rather because he is so representative of a group in the State Department. It is unnecessary to go over the sordid events showing how he sold out the nation which had given him so much. Those are rather fresh in all of our minds.

However, it should be remembered that the facts in regard to his connection with this international Communist spy ring were made known to the then Under Secretary of State Berle three days after Hitler and Stalin signed the Russo-German alliance pact. At that time one Whittaker Chambers—who was also part of the spy ring—apparently decided that with Russia on Hitler's side, he could no longer betray our nation to Russia. He gave Under Secretary of State Berle—and this is all a matter of record—practically all, if not more, of the facts upon which Hiss's conviction was based.

Under Secretary Berle promptly contacted Dean Acheson and received word in return that Acheson (and I quote) "could vouch for Hiss absolutely"—at which time the matter was dropped. And this, you understand, was at a time when Russia was an ally of Germany. This condition existed while Russia and Germany were invading and dismembering Poland, and while the Communist groups here were screaming "warmonger" at the United States for their support of the allied nations.

Again in 1943, the FBI had occasion to investigate the facts surrounding Hiss's contacts with the Russia spy ring. But even after that FBI report was submitted, nothing was done.

Then late in 1948—on August 5—when the Un-American Activities Committee called Alger Hiss to give an accounting, President Truman at once issued a presidential directive ordering all government agencies to refuse to turn over any information whatsoever in regard to the Communist activities of any government employee to a congressional committee.

Incidentally, even after Hiss was convicted—it is interesting to note that the president still labeled the exposé of Hiss as a "red herring."

If time permitted, it might be well to go into detail about the fact that Hiss was Roosevelt's chief advisor at Yalta when Roosevelt was admittedly in ill health and tired physically and mentally. . . .

Of the results of this conference, Arthur Bliss Lane of the State Department had this to say: "As I glanced over the document, I could not believe my eyes. To me, almost every line spoke of a surrender to Stalin."

As you hear this story of high treason, I know that you are saying to yourself, "Well, why doesn't the Congress do something about it?" Actually, ladies and gentlemen, one of the important reasons for the graft, the corruption, the dishonesty, the treason in high government positions—one of the most important reasons why this continues is a lack of moral uprising on the part of the 140 million American people. In the light of history, however, this is not hard to explain.

It is the result of an emotional hangover and a temporary moral lapse which follows every war. It is the apathy to evil which people who have been subjected to the tremendous evils of war feel. As the people of the world see mass murder, the destruction of defenseless and innocent people, and all of the crime and lack of morals which go with war, they become numb and apathetic. It has always been thus after war.

However, the morals of our people have not been destroyed. They still exist. This cloak of numbness and apathy has only needed a spark to rekindle them. Happily, this spark has finally been supplied.

As you know, very recently the secretary of state proclaimed his loyalty to a man guilty of what has always been considered as the most abominable of all crimes—of being a traitor to the people who gave him a position of great trust. The secretary of state in attempting to justify his continued devotion to the man who sold out the Christian world to the atheistic world, referred to Christ's Sermon on the Mount as a justification and reason therefor, and the reaction of the American people to this would have made the heart of Abraham Lincoln happy.

When this pompous diplomat in striped pants, with a phony British accent, proclaimed to the American people that Christ on the Mount endorsed communism, high treason, and betrayal of a sacred trust, the blasphemy was so great that it awakened the dormant indignation of the American people.

He has lighted the spark which is resulting in a moral uprising and will end only when the whole sorry mess of twisted, warped thinkers are swept from the national scene so that we may have a new birth of national honesty and decency in government.

SELLING AMERICA

The two photographs that follow are idealizations of American life, created by the United States Information Agency, the international propaganda arm of the American government. In a sense, they were weapons in the Cold War. According to the first photograph, what apparent relationship exists between technology and domestic bliss and harmony? What idealized notions of youth culture are present in the second photograph? What does it mean to identify someone or some group as "typical"?

Original Caption: "Takoma Park, Maryland—In the living room of their home, the A. Jackson Cory family and some friends watch a television program. Some sociologists claim the growing popularity of television will tend to make family life stronger and make the home the center of the family's recreation. 1950."
United States Information Agency photo, National Archives.

Original Caption: "Washington, D.C.—Brennan Jacques, a typical
American teenager, has his own orchestra, the 'Fabulous Esquires,'
composed of youngsters aware of what their schoolmates like and do
not like in current music. Here, young Jacques plays the piano for a
group of young people, who have gathered around him. 1957."
United States Information Agency photo, National Archives.

the big picture

In retrospect, the dangers of internal communist subversion in the postwar era seem to have been minor. Why, then, was the Cold War played out at home, as well as overseas? What forces were at work?

chapter eleven

THE EISENHOWER CONSENSUS

Reason, objectivity, dispassion—these were the qualities and values that twice elected Dwight Eisenhower to the presidency. His appeal was bipartisan. In 1948 and 1952, politicians of both major parties sought to nominate this man with the "leaping and effortless smile" who promised the electorate a "constitutional presidency"—immune from the ideological harangues of European dictators, American demagogues, and New Deal presidents—and a secure economy—immune from major dislocations.

To replace the disjointed and unpredictable insecurity of depression, war, and ideological struggle, Eisenhower offered Americans a society based on consensus. In the consensual society, major disagreements over important issues such as race, class, and gender were presumed not to exist. Conflict—serious conflict, about who had power and who did not—was considered almost un-American.

By 1960, it was clear that Eisenhower, and the nation at large, had not sought to create or maintain the consensual society through any radical departures from the past. The Cold War, anticommunism, the welfare state—all inherited from his Democratic predecessor, Harry Truman—were not so much thrown aside as modulated or refined.

Anticommunism was central to the consensus, for the existence of a powerful enemy helped define the consensus and to deflect attention from the economic and social issues on which there could be no easy agreement. Joseph McCarthy would cease to be a factor after 1954, but otherwise, anticommunism was almost as much a part of the Eisenhower years as it had been of the Truman years. The purges that cleansed most labor unions of communist influence were completed when Ike took office, but Cold War attitudes permeated the labor movement throughout the decade. The House Un-American Activities Committee (HUAC) would never know the acclaim it had mustered in the late 1940s, but each year it received more money from Congress and continued to function. In 1959, the Supreme Court refused to declare HUAC in violation of the First Amendment. New Organizations—Robert Welch's John Birch Society and the Christian Anti-Communist Crusade, for example—emerged to carry on the struggle against internal subversion. Welch labeled Eisenhower a "dedicated, conscious agent of the Communist conspiracy."

Those who feared that the first Republican president since Herbert Hoover would grasp the opportunity to dismantle the welfare state had misunderstood both Eisenhower and the function of government at midcentury. If only intuitively, Eisenhower knew that what was left of the New Deal could not be eliminated without risking serious social and economic disruption. Countercyclical programs like old-age insurance and unemployment insurance were maintained or expanded; the Council of Economic Advisers, created in the Employment Act of 1946 to provide the president with his own planning staff, remained; spending for military hardware and interstate highways was expected to create jobs. Republicans did manage a rollback of New Deal policies in the areas of taxation and agriculture.

There was in much of this a pervasive element of acceptance—acceptance of American institutions as they were or as Americans wished they were. The power of the large corporation was accepted, its influence invited. Many agreed with General Motors president Charles E. Wilson, who during Senate hearings to confirm his nomination as secretary of defense said, "I thought what was good for our country was good for General Motors, and vice versa." Effective government was often conceptualized as the product of big business, big labor, and big government, each checking and balancing the others. The antitrust emphasis of the later New Deal was all but forgotten.

Instead, Americans took comfort in economist John Kenneth Galbraith's theory of countervailing power. While Galbraith acknowledged that many sectors of the American marketplace were dominated by just a few firms and therefore were no longer competitive by the usual standard, he argued that power on one side of the market (among sellers of a product, such as steel) usually produced a "countervailing" power on the other side of the market (among buyers of the product, such as automobile makers). Similarly, the market power of a very big seller of consumer durable goods, such as General Electric, was limited by the existence of equally powerful buyers of those goods, including Sears, Roebuck and Montgomery Ward. Because countervailing power was usually "self-generating," the role of government was limited to fine-tuning an economic system whose basic structure was understood to be reasonably competitive.

It followed that a wide variety of social problems—racism, unemployment, poverty, urban life, and the cult of domesticity, which suffocated women—were ignored, denied, accepted, or left in abeyance to be handled by some future generation. Throughout the 1950s, social commentators affirmed that America's central problems were ones of boredom, affluence, and classlessness. *The Midas Plague,* a science-fiction novel, described a world in which goods were so easily produced and so widely available that consuming had become a personal duty, a social responsibility, and an enormous and endless burden. David Riesman's *Lonely Crowd,* an influential study published in 1950, argued that the age of scarcity had ended; Americans would henceforth be concerned with leisure, play, and the "art of living."

According to Riesman, these new conditions had created a new American character type that he labeled "other-directed": gregarious, superficially intimate, deeply conformist. For many analysts of American society, the new conditions of life had eliminated old conflicts between capital and labor and ushered in what sociologist Daniel Bell referred to as "the end of ideology." In a 1960 book by that title, Bell described how most postwar intellectuals had given up on the class-based, ideological radicalism of the 1930s and adopted a new, more accommodating stance toward social and economic conditions. Economic growth—so some pundits believed—would increase the size of the total product to be distributed and soon result in a society consisting mainly of white-collar workers, who were unlikely to be critical of their circumstances or to demand profound social or economic change.

Beneath the surface of the consensual society, there were some currents that disturbed many Americans. Despite a landmark Supreme Court decision in 1954 ordering the racial integration of public schools with "all deliberate speed," black Americans remained outside the American system, gathering energies for a spectacular assault on the traditions of prejudice and exploitation. Women did not resist so overtly, but a growing body of scholarly literature suggests that many women were at best ambivalent about the June Cleaver *(Leave It to Beaver)* and Margaret Anderson *(Father Knows Best)* images that were television's contribution to the consensual society. Everyone was concerned about an apparent alienation among many young people, an alienation that expressed itself sometimes frighteningly as juvenile delinquency, sometimes just as a mystifying lack of energetic affirmation, most often in an affinity for a new music called rock 'n' roll. Following the launch of the Soviet satellite *Sputnik* in 1957, Americans began to ask whether this technological defeat reflected a general withering of national purpose (a theme taken up by Eisenhower's successor, John Kennedy). As the decade wore on, it became obvious, too, that millions of Americans were not participating in the prosperity the administration proclaimed. Eisenhower's farewell address would be silent on most of these issues; but its discussion of the military-industrial complex was perhaps Eisenhower's way of acknowledging that the consensus he had tried so hard to preserve—indeed, to create—was fundamentally unstable. If so, the next decade would prove him right.

Beth Bailey

REBELS WITHOUT A CAUSE?
TEENAGERS IN THE 1950S

Against images of Elvis Presley's contorted torso, of Little Richard's scream-
ing black sexuality, of Cleveland disc jockey Alan Freed introducing a gener-
ation of eager young people to the erotic pleasures of rhythm and blues, Beth
Bailey offers a very different perspective on American youth in the 1950s.
Using dating behavior to understand the emerging postwar youth culture,
Bailey suggests that young people were responding to a climate of insecurity
that had deep historical roots. Furthermore, she identifies the quest for secu-
rity with a revised, "'50s" version of the American dream that also encom-
passed family and suburbia. In short, Bailey seems to suggest that the youth
of the 1950s were as attuned to consensual values as any other group.

While reading the essay, consider some of these questions: Does Bailey's
argument apply to most American youths, or only to those who were white
and middle class? What did parents find objectionable in this youth behavior,
and why? Might "going steady" be understood as both *a form of acquiescence*
in dominant values and *a kind of resistance? And how can one square Bailey's*
perspective with the Presley, Little Richard, and Freed images mentioned
above?

The United States emerged from the Second World War the most powerful and affluent nation in the world. This statement, bald but essentially accurate, is the given foundation for understanding matters foreign and domestic, the cold war and the age of abundance in America. Yet the sense of confidence and triumph suggested by that firm phrasing and by our images of soldiers embracing women as confetti swirled through downtown streets obscures another postwar reality. Underlying and sometimes overwhelming both bravado and complacency were voices of uncertainty. America at war's end was not naively optimistic.

Beth Bailey, "Rebels Without a Cause? Teenagers in the 1950s," *History Today* vol. 40, February 1990, pp. 25–31, without photographs.

The Great War had planted the seeds of the great depression. Americans wondered if hard times would return as the war boom ended. (They wouldn't.) The First World War had not ended all wars. Would war come again? (It would, both cold and hot.) And the fundamental question that plagued postwar America was, would American citizens have the strength and the character to meet the demands of this new world?

Postwar America appears in stereotype as the age of conformity—smug, materialistic, complacent, a soulless era peopled by organization men and their (house)wives. But this portrait of conformity exists only because Americans created it. Throughout the postwar era Americans indulged in feverish self-examination. Experts proclaimed crises, limned the American character, poked and prodded into the recesses of the American psyche. Writing in scholarly journals and for an attentive general public, theorists and social critics suggested that America's very success was destroying the values that had made success possible. Success, they claimed, was eroding the ethic that had propelled America to military and industrial supremacy and had lifted American society (with significant exceptions seen clearly in hindsight) to undreamed-of heights of prosperity.

At issue was the meaning of the American dream. Did the American dream mean success through individual competition in a wide-open free marketplace? Or was the dream only of the abundance the American marketplace had made possible—the suburban American dream of two cars in every garage and a refrigerator-freezer in every kitchen? One dream was of competition and the resulting rewards. The *making* of the self-made man—the process of entrepreneurial struggle—was the stuff of that dream. Fulfillment, in this vision, was not only through material comforts, but through the prominence, social standing, and influence in the public sphere one achieved in the struggle for success.

The new-style postwar American dream seemed to look to the private as the sphere of fulfillment, of self-definition and self-realization. Struggle was not desired, but stasis. The dream was of a private life—a family, secure, stable, and comfortable—that compensated for one's public (work) life. One vision highlighted risk; the other security. Many contemporary observers feared that the desire for security was overwhelming the "traditional" American ethic. In the dangerous postwar world, they asserted, the rejection of the public, of work and of risk would soon destroy America's prosperity and security.

The focus for much of the fear over what America was becoming was, not surprisingly, youth. Adult obsession with the new postwar generation took diverse forms—from the overheated rhetoric about the new epidemic of juvenile delinquency (too many rebels without causes) to astringent attacks on the conformity of contemporary youth. These critiques, though seemingly diametrically opposed, were based on the shared assumption that young people lacked the discipline and get-up-and-go that had made America great.

Perhaps nowhere in American culture do we find a richer statement of concern about American youth and the new American dream than in the debates that raged over "going steady," an old name for a new practice that was reportedly more popular among postwar teenagers than "bop, progressive jazz, hot rods and curiosity (slight) about atomic energy." The crisis over the "national problem" of going steady is not merely emblematic—an amusing way into a serious question. "Going steady" seemed to many adults the very essence of the problem, a kind of leading indicator of the privatization of the American dream. Social scientists and social critics saw in the new security-first courtship patterns a paradigm for an emerging American character that, while prizing affluence, did not relish the risks and hard work that made it possible.

Certainly the change in courtship patterns was dramatic. And it was not hard to make a connection between the primary characteristics of teenagers' love lives and what they hoped to get out of American life in general. Before the Second World War, American youth had prized a promiscuous popularity, demonstrating competitive success through the number and variety of dates they commanded. Sociologist Willard Waller, in his 1937 study of American dating, gave this competitive system a name: "the campus rating complex." His study of Pennsylvania State University detailed a "dating and rating" system based on a model of public competition in which popularity was the currency. To be popular, men needed outward, material signs: an automobile, proper clothing, the right fraternity membership, money. Women's popularity depended on building and maintaining a reputation for popularity. They had to *be seen* with popular men in the "right" places, indignantly turn down requests for dates made at the "last minute," and cultivate the impression they were greatly in demand.

In *Mademoiselle's* 1938 college issue, for example, a Smith college senior advised incoming freshmen to "cultivate an image of popularity" if they wanted dates. "During your first term," she wrote, "get 'home talent' to ply you with letters, invitations, telegrams. College men will think, 'She must be attractive if she can rate all that attention.'" And at Northwestern University in the 1920s, competitive pressure was so intense that co-eds made a pact not to date on certain nights of the week. That way they could preserve some time to study, secure in the knowledge they were not losing ground in the competitive race for success by staying home.

In 1935, the Massachusetts *Collegian* (the Massachusetts State College student newspaper) ran an editorial against using the library for "datemaking." The editors proclaimed: "The library is the place for the improvement of the mind and not the social standing of the student." Social standing, not social life: on one word turns the meaning of the dating system. That "standing" probably wasn't even a conscious choice shows how completely these college students took for granted that dating was primarily concerned with competition and popularity. As one North Carolina teenager summed it up:

> Going steady with one date
> Is okay, if that's all you rate.

Rating, dating, popularity, competition: catchwords hammered home, reinforced from all sides until they seemed a natural vocabulary. You had to rate in order to date, to date in order to rate. By successfully maintaining this cycle, you became popular. To stay popular, you competed. There was no end; the competitive process defined dating. Competition was the key term in the formula—remove it and there was no rating, dating, or popularity.

In the 1930s and 1940s, this competition was enacted most visibly on the dance floor. There, success was a dizzying popularity that kept girls whirling from escort to escort, "cut in" on by a host of popular men. Advice columns, etiquette books, even student handbooks told girls to strive to be "once-arounders," never be left with the same partner for more than one turn around the dance floor. On the dance floor, success and failure were easily measured. Wallflowers were dismissed out of hand. But getting stuck—not being "cut in" on—was taken quite seriously as a sign of social failure. Everyone noticed, and everyone judged.

This form of competitive courtship would change dramatically. By the early 1950s, "cutting in" had almost completely disappeared outside the deep south. In 1955, a student at Texas Christian University reported, "To cut in is almost an insult." A girl in Green Bay, Wisconsin, said that her parents were "astonished" when they discovered that she hadn't danced with anyone but her escort at a "formal." "The truth was," she admitted, "that I wasn't aware that we were supposed to."

This 180-degree reversal took place quickly—during the years of the Second World War—and was so compete by the early 1950s that people under eighteen could be totally unaware of the formerly powerful convention. It signaled not simply a change in dancing etiquette but a complete transformation of the dating system as well. Definitions of social success as promiscuous popularity based on strenuous competition had given way to new definitions, which located success in the security of a dependable escort.

By the 1950s, early marriage had become the goal for young adults. In 1959, 47 percent of all brides married before they turned nineteen, and up to 25 percent of students at many large state universities were married. The average age at marriage had risen to 26.7 for men and 23.3 for women during the lingering depression, but by 1951 the average age at marriage had fallen to 22.6 for men, 20.4 for women. And younger teens had developed their own version of early marriage.

As early as 1950, going steady had completely supplanted the dating-rating complex as the criterion for popularity among youth. A best-selling study of American teenagers, *Profile of Youth* (1949) reported that in most high schools the "mere fact" of going steady was a sign of popularity "as long as you don't get tied up with an impossible gook." The *Ladies' Home Journal* reported in 1949 that "every high school student . . . must be prepared to fit into a high-school pattern in which popularity, social acceptance and emotional security are often determined by the single question: does he or she go steady?" A 1959 poll found that 57 percent of American teens had gone or were going steady. And, according to *Cosmopolitan* in 1960, if you didn't go steady, you were "square."

The new protocol of going steady was every bit as strict as the old protocol of rating and dating. To go steady, the boy gave the girl some visible token, such as a class ring or letter sweater. In Portland, Oregon, steadies favored rings (costing from $17 to $20). In Birmingham, Michigan, the girl wore the boy's identity bracelet, but never his letter sweater. In rural Iowa, the couple wore matching corduroy "steady jackets," although any couple wearing matching clothing in California would be laughed at.

As long as they went steady, the boy had to call the girl a certain number of times a week or take her on a certain number of dates a week (both numbers were subject to local convention). Neither boy nor girl could date anyone else or pay too much attention to anyone of the opposite sex. While either could go out with friends of the same sex, each must always know where the other was and what he or she was doing. Going steady meant a guaranteed date for special events, and it implied greater sexual intimacy—either more "necking" or "going further."

In spite of the intense monogamy of these steady relationships, teenagers viewed them as temporary. A 1950 study of 565 seniors in an eastern suburban high school found that 80 percent had gone or were going steady. Out of that number, only eleven said they planned to marry their steady. In New Haven, Connecticut, high school girls wore "obit bracelets." Each time they broke up with a boy, they added a disc engraved with his name or initials on the chain. In Louisiana, a girl would embroider her sneakers with the name of her current steady. When they broke up, she would clip off his name and sew an X over the spot. An advice book from the mid-1950s advised girls to get a "Puppy Love Anklet." Wearing it on the right ankle meant that you were available, on the left that you were going steady. The author advised having "Going Steady" engraved on one side, "Ready, Willing 'n Waiting" on the other—just in case the boys could not remember the code. All these conventions, cheerfully reported in teenager columns in national magazines, show how much teenagers took it for granted that going steady was a temporary, if intense, arrangement.

Harmless as this system sounds today, especially compared to the rigors of rating and dating, the rush to go steady precipitated an intense generational battle. Clearly some adult opposition was over sex: going steady was widely accepted as a justification for greater physical intimacy. But more fundamentally, the battle over going steady came down to a confrontation between two generations over the meaning of the American dream. Security versus competition. Teenagers in the 1950s were trying to do the unthinkable—to eliminate competition from the popularity equation. Adults were appalled. To them, going steady, with its extreme rejection of competition in favor of temporary security, represented all the faults of the new generation.

Adults, uncomfortable with the "cult of happiness" that rejected competition for security, attacked the teenage desire for security with no holds barred. As one writer advised boys, "To be sure of anything is to cripple one's powers of growth." She continued, "To have your girl always assured at the end of a telephone line without having to work for her, to beat the other fellows to her is bound to lessen your powers of personal achievement." A male adviser, campaigning against going steady, argued: "Competition will be good for you. It sharpens your wits, teaches you how to get along well in spite of difficulties." And another, writing in *Esquire*, explained the going steady phenomenon this way: "She wants a mate; he being a modern youth doesn't relish competition."

As for girls, the argument went: "She's afraid of competition. She isn't sure she can compete for male attention in the open market: 'going steady' frees her from fear of further failures." The author of *Jackson's Guide to Dating* tells the story of "Judith Thompson," a not-especially-attractive girl with family problems, who has been going steady with "Jim" since she was fourteen. Lest we think that poor Judith deserves someone to care for her or see Jim as a small success in her life, the author stresses that going steady is one more failure for Judith. "Now that Judith is sixteen and old enough to earn money and help herself in other ways to recover from her unfortunate childhood, she has taken on the additionally crippling circumstance of a steady boyfriend. How pathetic. The love and attention of her steady boyfriend are a substitute for other more normal kinds of success." What should Judith be doing? "A good deal of the time she spends going steady with Jim could be used to make herself more attractive so that other boys would ask her for dates."

There is nothing subtle in these critiques of going steady. The value of competition is presumed as a clear standard against which to judge modern youth. But there is more here. There is a tinge of anger in these judgments, an anger that may well stem from the differing experiences of two generations of Americans. The competitive system that had emerged in the flush years of the 1920s was strained by events of the 1930s and 1940s. The elders had come of age during decades of depression and world war, times when the competitive struggle was, for many, inescapable. Much was at stake, the cost of failure all too clear. While youth in the period between the wars embraced a competitive dating system, even gloried in it, as adults they sought the security they had lacked in their youth.

Young people and their advocates made much of the lack of security of the postwar world, self-consciously pointing to the "general anxiety of the times" as a justification for both early marriage and going steady. But the lives of these young people were clearly more secure than those of their parents. That was the gift their parents tried to give them. Though the cold war raged it had little immediate impact on the emerging teenage culture (for those too young to fight in Korea, of course). Cushioned by unprecedented affluence, allowed more years of freedom within the protected youth culture of high school and ever-more-frequently college, young people did not have to struggle so hard, compete so ferociously as their parents had.

And by and large, both young people and their parents knew it and were genuinely not sure what that meant for America's future. What did it mean—that a general affluence, at least for a broad spectrum of America's burgeoning middle class, was possible without a dog-eat-dog ferocity? What did *that* mean for the American Dream of success? One answer was given in the runaway best seller of the decade, *The Man in the Gray Flannel Suit*, which despite the title was not so much about the deadening impact of conformity but about what Americans should and could dream in the postwar world.

The protagonist of the novel, Tom Rath (the not-so-subtle naming made more explicit by the appearance of the word "vengeful" in the sentence following Tom's introduction), has been through the Second World War, and the shadow of war hangs over his life. Tom wants to provide well for his family, and feels a nagging need to succeed. But when he is offered the chance at an old-style American dream—to be taken on as the protégé of his business-wise, driven boss, he says no. In a passage that cuts to the heart of postwar American culture, Tom tells his boss:

> I don't think I'm the kind of guy who should try to be a big executive. I'll say it frankly: I don't think I have the willingness to make the sacrifices. . . . I'm try-ing to be honest about this. I want the money. Nobody likes money better than I do. But I'm not the kind of guy who can work evenings and weekends and all the rest of it forever. . . . I've been through one war. Maybe another one's com-ing. If one is, I want to be able to look back and figure I spent the time between wars with my family, the way it should have been spent. Regardless of war, I want to get the most out of the years I've got left. Maybe that sounds silly. It's just that if I have to bury myself in a job every minute of my life, I don't see any point to it.

Tom's privatized dream—of comfort without sacrifice, of family and per-sonal fulfillment—might seem the author's attempt to resolve the tensions of the novel (and of postwar American society). But the vision is more complex than simply affirmative. Tom's boss responds with sympathy and understand-ing, then suddenly loses control. "Somebody has to do the big jobs!" he says passionately. "This world was built by men like me! To really do a job, you have to live it, body and soul! You people who just give half your mind to your work are riding on our backs!" And Tom responds: "I know it."

The new American Dream had not yet triumphed. The ambivalence and even guilt implicit in Tom Rath's answer to his boss pervaded American culture in the 1950s—in the flood of social criticism and also in parents' critiques of teenage courtship rituals. The attacks on youth's desire for security are reveal-ing, for it was in many ways the parents who embraced security—moving to the suburbs, focusing on the family. The strong ambivalence many felt about their lives appears in the critiques of youth. This same generation would find even more to criticize in the 1960s, as the "steadies" of the 1950s became the sexual revolutionaries of the 1960s. Many of the children of these parents came to recognize the tensions within the dream. The baby-boom generation ac-cepted wholeheartedly the doctrine of self-fulfillment, but rejected the guilt and fear that had linked fulfillment and security. In the turbulence of the 1960s, young people were not rejecting the new American Dream of easy affluence and personal fulfillment, but only jettisoning the fears that had hung over a generation raised with depression and war. It turns out the 1950s family was not the new American Dream, but only its nurturing home.

THE SUBURBS

Photographs like this one, of a housing development called Levittown, on Long Island, appear in most history textbooks, usually to offer evidence of the inherent sterility of life in the new American suburbs. Yet there are those who argue that this is only a superficial impression and that up-close investigation of particular houses would reveal the effort most homeowners made to customize their homes and distinguish their properties from those of their neighbors. What do you think?

Levittown, New York. UPI.
Corbis Images.

TEEN CULTURE

There have always been people in their teen years, but the modern under-standing of the teenager as a special group with its own values, needs, and in-terests, has been around for only about a century. This idea of the teenager de-veloped after 1900, when increasing numbers of youth found themselves gathered in high schools—and, therefore, spending time with other young people—rather than working on farms or in urban factories and offices. In the 1940s and 1950s, teenagers became important consumers, especially of cloth-ing, music, movies, and automobiles. The items in this section explore aspects of the postwar "youth culture" and adult responses to it.

ROCK 'N' ROLL

The musical style called "rock 'n' roll" dates from the early 1950s. It is usu-ally considered a sign of revolt, musical evidence that the generational rebel-lion that would sweep the 1960s was already under way even as Dwight Eisenhower was serving his first term. It was this. But rock 'n' roll was also essentially a white music, and a white music that was developed almost en-tirely from black musical styles.

The verses below—from the rock 'n' roll classic "Shake, Rattle and Roll" (1954)—allow us to inquire into the historical meaning of this new music. The verses on the left are from the original version, written by Charles Calhoun and recorded by Joe Turner for the black market. The verses on the right are from the more popular "cover" version by Bill Haley and the Comets. Both versions were hits in 1954.

Why did Haley change the words? Was rock 'n' roll part of the Eisenhower consensus, or its antithesis?

"Shake, Rattle and Roll" (1954)

**The Charles Calhoun/
Joe Turner Version**

The Bill Haley Version

Get out of that bed,
And wash your face and hands. (twice)

Get out in that kitchen,
And rattle those pots and pans. (twice)

Get into the kitchen
Make some noise with the pots and pans

Roll my breakfast
'Cause I'm a hungry man.

Well you wear those dresses,
The sun comes shinin' through. (twice)

You wear those dresses,
Your hair done up so nice. (twice)

I can't believe my eyes,
That all of this belongs to you.

I said over the hill,
And way down underneath. (twice)

You make me roll my eyes,
And then you make me grit my teeth.

You look so warm,
But your heart is cold as ice.

(the third verse of the Calhoun/Turner
version is not part of the Haley version)

DRESS RIGHT

Parents, school officials, and other adult authorities carefully monitored the behavior of 1950s youth. The Catholic Church published a list of films considered morally objectionable, and many radio stations refused to play rhythm and blues or rock 'n' roll. The schools had regulations too numerous to mention, among them dress codes like the one below. Called "Dress Right," this code was designed in part by student representatives from various schools. It was in force in Buffalo in the late 1950s and emulated nationally as The Buffalo Plan. What were the purposes of the code? On what assumptions was it based? What accounts for the distinction between academic and vocational schools? From the accompanying photograph of the lunchroom at one of the city's vocational schools (with a summary of the code on the wall), what can one conclude about student attitudes toward the code?

Board of Education
Buffalo, New York
School-Community Coordination
Recommendations of the Inter High School Student Council for Appropriate
    Dress of Students in High School

Boys
Academic High Schools and
Hutchinson-Technical High School

Recommended:
1. Dress shirt and tie or conservative sport shirt and tie with suit jacket, jacket, sport coat, or sweater.
2. Standard trousers or khakis; clean and neatly pressed
3. Shoes, clean and polished; white bucks acceptable

Not Recommended:
1. Dungarees or soiled, unpressed khakis
2. T-shirts, sweat shirts
3. Extreme styles of shoes, including hobnail or "motorcycle boots"

Vocational High Schools

Recommended:
1. Shirt and tie or sport shirt and tie
2. Sport shirt with sweater or jacket
3. Standard trousers or khakis; clean and neatly pressed
4. Shoes, clean and polished; white bucks acceptable

Not Recommended:
1. Dungarees or soiled, unpressed khakis.
2. T-shirts, sweat shirts
3. Extreme styles of shoes, including hobnail or "motorcycle boots"

Note: The apparel recommended for boys should be worn in standard fashion with shirts tucked in and buttoned, and ties tied at the neck. Standard of dress for boys, while in school shops or laboratories, should be determined by the school.

Girls
Academic and Vocational High Schools

Recommended:
1. Blouses, sweaters, blouse and sweater, jacket with blouse or sweater
2. Skirts, jumpers, suits or conservative dresses
3. Shoes appropriate to the rest of the costume.

Not Recommended:
1. V-neck sweaters without blouse
2. Bermuda shorts, kilts, party-type dresses, slacks of any kind
3. Ornate jewelry
4. T-shirts, sweat shirts

Note: All recommended wear for girls should fit appropriately and modestly. Standard of dress for girls, while in school shops or laboratories, should be determined by the school.

January 24, 1956

The Cafeteria at Buffalo's Burgard Vocational High School, with the "Dress Right"
Code on the Wall.
Burgard Craftsman, *1958.*

SCHOOL SAMPLER: AN ESSAY IN WORDS AND IMAGES

The items on these pages come from Buffalo, New York, school yearbooks. What does each tell us about coming of age in the 1950s—and, in the case of one of the photographs, in the early 1960s?

Bombs Away!

Seneca Vocational Chieftain, *1952.*

"We can't all be captains, we've got to be crew,
There's something for all of us here.
There's big work to do and there's lesser to do,
And the task we must do is the near.

If you can't be a highway then just be a trail,
If you can't be the sun be a star;
It isn't by size that you win or you fail--
Be the best of whatever you are !"

--Douglas Malloch

We Can't All Be Captains.
Riverside Skipper, *1950.*

The Board of the Buffalo Seminary Yearbook, *The Seminaria,* **Beneath the Image of the School's Former Headmistress.**
The Seminaria, *1950.*

A Home Economics Class at Newly Integrated East High, 1954.
Eastonian.

Bishop Timon Seniors, Enjoying Their Smoking Privileges in the School Cafeteria.
Talisman, *1962*.

CHALLENGING THE CONSENSUS: INTEGRATING THE PUBLIC SCHOOLS

Melba Pattillo Beals

In a 1954 decision in Brown v. Board of Education of Topeka, Kansas, *the Supreme Court ruled that segregated public schools were unconstitutional. The decision is usually understood to mark the beginning of the modern civil rights movement, and with good reason. But* Brown v. Board *was also the culmination of a series of legal and political struggles that began during World War II, when A. Philip Randolph, head of the Brotherhood of Sleeping Car Porters, threatened to lead a march on Washington, D.C. in protest against segregation in the armed forces and race discrimination in the issuing of government contracts. Although the march did not take place, Randolph's aggressive stance put the nation's leaders on notice. Pushed and prodded by legal actions facilitated by the NAACP and its chief counsel, Thurgood Marshall, the courts were especially active on behalf of civil rights. A 1944 decision in* Smith v. Allwright *required the southern wing of the Democratic Party to open its all-white primary elections to African-American voters; in* Shelley v. Kraemer *(1948), the Supreme Court struck down an important form of housing segregation—the restrictive covenants that limited sales to Caucasians; and in 1950, the decision in* Sweatt v. Painter *held that Texas's system of segregated and separate law schools did not produce equal facilities. The stage was set for* Brown.

In the early 1950s, when the several cases that would together constitute Brown v. Board of Education *were making their way through the courts, most public schools in the United States were racially segregated. In the South, the segregation was by law, underpinned by the 1896 decision in* Plessy v. Ferguson, *which held that separate railroad facilities (and hence schools) were lawful, as long as they were also equal. In the North, the segregation was de facto—simply a "fact"—caused, in this case, by the "fact" that blacks and whites lived in different neighborhoods and, therefore, attended different schools. The color line in the North was not absolute; many public schools in northern big cities were minimally integrated. Thus the change promised by* Brown v. Board *was enormous: the racial integration of all the nation's public schools.*

The Supreme Court set no firm deadline for implementing its decision, announcing only that schools should be integrated "with all deliberate speed." When school districts refused to present a reasonable plan for integration, they sometimes had to be forced to act. That was the situation in Little Rock, Arkansas, where, in September, 1957, Governor Orval Faubus, sustained by angry white mobs, tried to block integration on the grounds that it would lead to violence. Under Faubus's direction, the National Guard took up positions outside Little Rock's Central High School. On September 4, the guardsmen turned away nine African-American teenagers, presumably to forestall conflict. In late September, under Court order, the guardsmen were withdrawn and the black youths admitted, only to be forced from the school by antagonistic students. To prevent violence, President Dwight Eisenhower sent in troops of the 101st Airborne—which is where Melba Pattillo Beals's story begins. Later, Eisenhower withdrew the 101st and left the school in the hands of the Arkansas National Guard, now under federal control.

If you were Melba Pattillo, how would you have responded to these events? How would you characterize Eisenhower's response to the situation? Should the federal government have been stronger in demanding compliance with the Court's decision?

 I arrived at school Tuesday morning, fully expecting that I would be greeted by the 101st soldiers and escorted to the top of the stairs. Instead, we were left at the curb to fend for ourselves. As we approached the stairs, we were greeted by taunting catcalls and the kind of behavior students had not dared to exhibit in the face of the 101st.

Where were the disciplined ranks we had come to count on? I looked all round, but sure enough, there were no 101st guards in sight. Just then a boy blocked our way. What were we to do? My first thought was to retreat, to turn and go back down the stairs and detour around to the side door. But that escape route was blocked by those stalking us. A large crowd of jeering, pencil-throwing students hovered around us menacingly. We had no choice but to go forward.

"Where are your pretty little soldier boys today?" someone cried out.

"You niggers ready to die just to be in this school?" asked another.

Squeezing our way through the hostile group gathered at the front door, we were blasted by shouts of "Nigger, go home. Go back to where you belong." At every turn, we were faced with more taunts and blows. There were no 101st soldiers at their usual posts along the corridors.

And then I saw them. Slouching against the wall were members of the Arkansas National Guard, looking on like spectators at a sports event—certainly not like men sent to guard our safety.

I wanted to turn and run away, but I thought about what Danny had said: "Warriors survive." I tried to remember his stance, his attitude, and the courage of the 101st on the battlefield. Comparing my tiny challenge with what he must have faced made me feel more confident. I told myself I could handle whatever the segregationists had in store for me. But I underestimated them.

Early that morning, a boy began to taunt me as though he had been assigned that task. First he greeted me in the hall outside my shorthand class and began pelting me with bottle-cap openers, the kind with the sharp claw at the end. He was also a master at walking on my heels. He hurt me until I wanted to scream for help.

By lunchtime, I was nearly hysterical and ready to call it quits, until I thought of having to face Grandma when I arrived home. During the afternoon, when I went into the principal's office several times to report being sprayed with ink, kicked in the shin, and heel-walked until the backs of my feet bled, as well as to report the name of my constant tormenter, the clerks asked why I was reporting petty stuff. With unsympathetic scowls and hostile attitudes, they accused me of making mountains out of molehills.

Not long before the end of the school day, I entered a dimly lit rest room. The three girls standing near the door seemed to ignore me. Their passive, silent, almost pleasant greeting made me uncomfortable, and the more I thought about their attitude, the more it concerned me. At least when students were treating me harshly, I knew what to expect.

Once inside the stall, I was even more alarmed at all the movement, the feet shuffling, the voices whispering. It sounded as though more people were entering the room.

"Bombs away!" someone shouted above me. I looked up to see a flaming paper wad coming right down on me. Girls were leaning over the top of the stalls on either side of me. Flaming paper floated down and landed on my hair and shoulders. I jumped up, trying to pull myself together and at the same time duck the flames and stamp them out. I brushed the singeing ashes away from my face as I frantically grabbed for the door to open it.

"Help!" I shouted. "Help!" The door wouldn't open. Someone was holding it—someone strong, perhaps more than one person. I was trapped.

"Did you think we were gonna let niggers use our toilets? We'll burn you alive, girl," a voice shouted through the door. "There won't be enough of you left to worry about."

I felt the kind of panic that stopped me from thinking clearly. My right arm was singed. The flaming wads of paper were coming at me faster and faster. I could feel my chest muscles tightening. I felt as though I would die any moment. The more I yelled for help, the more I inhaled smoke and the more I coughed.

I told myself I had to stop screaming so I wouldn't take in so much smoke. My throat hurt—I was choking. I remembered Grandmother telling me all I had to do was say the name of God and ask for help. Once more I looked up to see those grinning, jeering faces as flaming paper rained down on me. Please, God, help me, I silently implored. I had to hurry. I might not be able to swat the next one and put it out with my hands. Then what? Would my hair catch fire? I had to stop them. I picked up my books and tossed one upward as hard as I could, in a blind aim to hit my attackers.

I heard a big thud, then a voice cry out in pain and several people scuffle about. I tossed another and then another book as fast and as hard as I could. One more of their number cursed at me. I had hit my target.

"Let's get out of here," someone shouted as the group hurried out the door. In a flash, I leaped out of the stall, trying to find my things. I decided I wouldn't even bother reporting my problem. I just wanted to go home. I didn't care that I smelled of smoke or that my blouse was singed. Later when my friends asked what happened, I didn't even bother to explain.

Much worse than the fear and any physical pain I had endured, was the hurt deep down inside my heart, because no part of me understood why people would do those kinds of things to one another. I was so stunned by my experience that during the ride home I sat silent and listened to reports from the others. They, too, seemed to have had a bigger problem that day with hecklers and hooligans.

The experiment of doing without the 101st had apparently been a fiasco. By the end of the day more than one of us had heard talk that the 101st had been brought back.

Still, despite all our complaints, there were a few students who tried to reach out to us with smiles or offers to sit at our cafeteria tables; some even accompanied us along the halls. Each of us noticed, however, that those instances of friendship were shrinking rather than growing. There was no doubt that the hard-core troublemakers were increasing their activities, and without the men of the 101st, they increased a hundredfold.

> President Eisenhower says he will remove the 101st soldiers if Governor Faubus agrees to protect the nine Negro children with federalized Arkansas National Guardsmen.

Those words from the radio announcer sent a chill down my spine as I sat doing my homework on Tuesday evening. I had hoped the rumors of the return of the 101st were true. But according to the report, the same Arkansas soldiers who had been dispatched by Governor Faubus to keep us *out* of Central High would become totally responsible for keeping us *in* school and protecting our lives.

"Sounds like the wolf guarding the henhouse to me," grandma said. "Thank God you know who your real protector is, 'cause you certainly won't be able to count on those boys for help." She was peeking at me over the pages of the newspaper.

I didn't know how to tell her how right she was. But then I couldn't tell her I had had the kind of day that was making me think about running away where nobody could find me.

"Did you see where Judge Ronald Davies will be going back to North Dakota?" Grandma continued. "He will still retain jurisdiction over your case, though."

"That really frightens me," I said. "I feel safer with Davies being here."

"He is being replaced by Judge Harper from St. Louis, it says."

"Bad news," I replied. I didn't know bad things about Harper, but I had come to trust Davies as an honest and fair man with the courage of his convictions. St. Louis bordered the South; that Judge Harper might not be as open-minded.

"Of course, there is good news here," Grandma said, rattling the newspaper. "Seems as if some moderate white businessmen are getting together to oppose that special session of the legislature Faubus wants to call."

"The one to enact laws that would make integration illegal?" I asked.
"Yes, I hope they can do something to slow him down."

Ike rejects Faubus's statement and agreement falls through
                              —*Arkansas Gazette*, Wednesday, October 2, 1957

The Wednesday morning *Gazette* reported that Governor Faubus and the President had come to the brink of an agreement to remove the federal troops from Little Rock the day before, but at the last minute the President called it off because he didn't believe the governor would act in good faith.

As we walked toward Central that day, I was looking forward to having the 101st come back to make my life inside school at least tolerable. But right away my hopes for a more peaceful day were dashed. Showers of loud insults greeted us. Straight ahead, in front of the school, I could see a group of about fifty boys waiting at the top of the stairs as they had the day before. This time, however, they descended on us like locusts.

"Get the coons! Get the coons!" The boys were brash and bold, behaving as though they feared no consequences. There were no parading 101st soldiers to stop them. Frantically, we looked around for someone in authority, but none was in sight.

Minnijean, Ernie, and I decided to retreat, but just then, vice-principal Huckaby made her presence known at the bottom of the stairs. Tiny, erect, and determined, she stood there all alone between us and our attackers, demanding they leave us alone. One by one she challenged the leaders, calling them by name, telling them to get to class or there would be hell to pay. I had to respect her for what she did. Whether or not she favored integration, she had a heck of a lot of guts.

We circled around to the Sixteenth and Park Street entrance. As I climbed the stairs, there was no sign of Danny—or the other 101st guards I knew. In fact, I didn't see any uniformed soldiers. Just inside of the front entrance, where Danny usually stood, I saw some of the same hooligans who had tried to block our entrance only moments before. They moved toward me, and I circled away from them and walked quickly down the hall. I was desperately trying to figure out why there weren't any teachers or school officials guarding the halls the way there usually were.

I panicked; I couldn't decide where to go or what to do next. I was being pounded on my arms, my back, and my legs by angry students. Their blows hurt so much that my desire to stop the pain and survive overpowered the fear that paralyzed me. I got hold of myself. No matter what, I knew I had to stand up to them even if I got kicked out of school for doing it.

"Dead niggers don't go to school," someone said, hitting me hard in the stomach. My first instinct was to double over. The pain burned my insides. But I stood still and stared at my attacker without flinching. He taunted me: "You ain't thinking of hitting me back?"

"I'm gonna cut your guts out," I said, standing my ground. There was a long pause while we stared each other down. It was a bluff, but it worked. Looking almost frightened and mumbling under his breath, he backed off.

Just then, I noticed the members of the Arkansas National Guard lounging against the walls like cats in sunlight. Gathered in small clusters with smug, grinning expressions on their faces, they had been watching my confrontation all along. I couldn't get used to the fact that our safety now depended on nonchalant, tobacco-chewing adolescents who were most likely wearing white sheets and burning crosses on the lawns of our neighbors after sundown.

I had walked only a few steps before I was knocked to the floor. I called out for help. Three men from the Guard gave further substance to my suspicions by taking their time to respond, moving toward me in slow motion. I scrambled to my feet.

How I longed to see Danny, standing on guard in his starched uniform, and hear the swift steps of the 101st. As I felt hot tears stinging my eyes, I heard Grandmother India's voice say, "You're on the battlefield for your Lord."

I was as frightened by the ineptness of the Arkansas soldiers as by the viciousness of the increased attacks on me. If the soldiers had been armed, I was certain they would either have shot me in the back or themselves in the foot. I watched as they stood in giggling clusters while a crowd of thugs attacked Jeff and Terry and kicked them to the floor in the hallway just outside the principal's office. A female teacher finally rescued the two.

Once I was seated in class, I felt I could take a deep breath. For the moment at least I was off the front line of battle in the hallway. But just as I was feeling a snippet of peace, a boy pulled a switchblade knife and pressed the point of the blade against my forearm. In a heartbeat, without even thinking about it, I leaped up and picked up my books as a shield to fend him off.

He responded to a half-hearted reprimand from the teacher but whispered that he would get me later. At the very first sound of the bell ending class, I ran for my life, only to encounter a group of students who knocked me down and hit me with their books. As I felt rage overtake me I recalled what Danny had told me: "When you're angry, you can't think. You gotta keep alert to keep alive."

It was still early in the day, and things were so bad that I decided I had no choice: I had to find somebody in authority who would listen to me. Outside the principal's office I found Minnijean looking as abused and angry as I was.

"We gotta get out of here!" she said breathlessly.

"You're right. They're gonna kill us today," I replied.

"Let's call our folks."

"Let's call Mrs. Bates. Maybe she can talk to the army or reporters or the President." I assumed calling the head of the NAACP would at least get some response. Merely reporting this kind of trouble to school officials might not get anything except more of the same denial that there was trouble, or perhaps reprimands for being "tattletales."

Since neither of us had change for a call, we reluctantly decided to go to Mrs. Huckaby, although we were afraid she would try and convince us to stick it out. Mrs. Huckaby greeted us in a matter-of-fact way until it dawned on her that we might be using the change we asked for to call for outside help.

"Wait a minute. What's going on?" she asked, trailing behind us.

"We're calling Mrs. Bates. We need help. Maybe she can talk to the reporters and get us some protection."

Just as we suspected, Mrs. Huckaby insisted we go to the principal's office to give him a chance to solve the problem. She assured us that he would be fair.

Principal Matthews began to speak in his slow plodding way, wearing his usual nervous smile. It was apparent he only wanted to stop us from making the call. I was in no mood to have him tell me I was imagining things, not with my leg aching and the steel flash of that switchblade knife fresh in my mind.

"Either you give us some protection so we can function without getting killed, or we go home." I heard the words come out of my mouth, but I could hardly believe it was me speaking. My knees were shaking. It was the first time in my life I had ever stood up to any adult—certainly to any white adult. But I was on the edge, ready to take the risk, because how could anything the adults might do to me be worse than the abuse I was already enduring?

"Wait here," the principal said, his tone of voice leaving no doubt he was annoyed with us. Shortly afterward, we saw the brass approaching: General Clinger and Colonel McDavid of the Arkansas National Guard, and a third military man I did not recognize.

Clinger pointed to the two of us, most especially to me, and said, "You'll sit over there where I can look you in the face." Right away, I didn't like him, but I was ready to deal with him.

The rest of our group was summoned to the office. Everyone was vocal about the severity of the attacks during the morning. Each one had a story about how the physical abuse had increased significantly. We told Clinger that his men were not protecting us, that they stood by, socializing and flirting while we were being beaten within an inch of our lives. "Those guards are turning their backs to attacks on us, and we demand you do something about it," I insisted.

Clinger didn't deny the charges. He explained that his men had to live in the community.

"We just wanna keep living . . . period," I said.

"Don't talk directly to the guards. Go to the office and report incidents," we were told.

I said, "With all due respect, sir, how can we run to the office every time we want help. Somebody could be beating one of us at the far end of the hall, and we'd have to wait until they finished and let us up so we could come here to report it."

I felt something inside me change that day. I felt a new will to live rise up in me. I knew I wasn't just going to roll over and die. I could take care of myself and speak up to white folks, even if my mother and father sometimes feared doing so. I discovered I had infinitely more guts than I had started the school year with. I had no choice. It was my life I was dickering for. I knew that Clinger didn't care about our welfare—not even a tiny bit.

"Young lady," Clinger said, eyeballing me, "you are turning our words. I didn't say—"

But I cut him off. "My friends and I will leave school if we don't get adequate protection. It's as simple as that," I told him. The others were obviously as angry as I was as they chimed in with their complaints. They voiced their agreement that something had to be done immediately.

"You'll have bodyguards." Clinger spoke with a definite edge to his voice. He summoned another soldier and told him to select eighteen men while we waited there. Those Arkansas guardsmen were the biggest, dumbest, most disheveled hayseeds I'd ever seen. They looked as if they had slept in their rumpled uniforms. We stood there not believing our eyes, dumbfounded by the sight of them.

"These clods will trip over their own shoelaces," I whispered to Minnijean.

"Or worse yet, get us in some dark corner and beat the living daylights out of us," she replied.

After about fifteen minutes we "moved out," or in their case, shuffled out. It was a sight to behold. There we were, followed by an absurd wall of not so mighty military green trailing us like a ridiculous wagging tail.

We found ourselves laughing aloud, and the white students were laughing with us. For just one moment we all realized the ridiculous situation we were caught up in.

Four of us went to our usual table in the cafeteria; the guards took up their posts, leaning against a nearby wall. When I got up to get in line for a sandwich, they fell over each other trying to see where I was going and which of them would follow me. Two stood in line with me, arms folded, tummies out, and shoulders rounded. Each time one of us rose to get anything, two of those clowns stumbled up to follow. It was a comedy of errors.

As we moved through the halls in our oddball group, I saw, just a few feet away, the boy who had pulled the knife on me earlier. The momentary terror I felt reminded me our situation wasn't funny after all.

I missed Danny. That was another feeling taking me over. Rumor had it that the 101st waited at Camp Robinson, just outside Little Rock. But I knew that even if he came back again and again, there would come the day when he would be gone for good.

Still, I was overjoyed when on Thursday we once again had our 101st bodyguards. Maybe they were forced to come back because the morning *Gazette* had reported the story of Terry and Jeff being kicked while Arkansas National Guardsmen looked on.

As we arrived at school that morning, I noticed right away that there was a different kind of tension, as though everyone was waiting for something awful to happen, only we didn't know what. We had heard rumors of a planned student protest. I could see groups of students standing in the halls instead of in class where they would normally have been.

Just before first period, more students began walking out of classes. Rumors about a big event reverberated throughout the school. I could see and feel a new level of restlessness and a deepening sense of hostility. I was on edge, waiting for disaster any moment, like dynamite or a group attack or I didn't know what. "They're hangin' a nigger, just like we're gonna hang you," someone muttered. That's when I learned that some of those who walked out had assembled at the vacant lot at Sixteenth and Park across from the school, where they hanged and burned a straw figure.

That demonstration set the tone of the day. Belligerent student protests were firing up the already hostile attitude inside the school. Danny broke the rules by coming closer and talking to me—warning that we had to stay alert, no matter what.

Near the end of the day I was walking down a dimly lit hallway, with Danny following, when I spotted a boy coming directly toward me on a collision course. I tried to move aside, but he moved with me. I didn't even have time to call for help.

The boy flashed a shiny black object in my face. The sudden pain in my eyes was so intense, so sharp, I thought I'd die. It was like nothing I'd ever felt before. I couldn't hear or see or feel anything except that throbbing, searing fire centered in my eyes. I heard myself cry out as I let go of everything to clutch at my face.

Someone grabbed me by my ponytail and pulled me along very fast, so fast I didn't have time to resist. The pain of being dragged along by my hair was almost as intense as that in my eyes. Hands grabbed my wrists and pried my hands from my face, compelling me to bend over. Then cold, cold liquid was splashed in my eyes. The water felt so good. My God, thank you! The pain was subsiding.

"Easy, girl, easy. You're gonna be fine." It was Danny's voice, his hands holding my head and dousing my eyes with water.

"I can't see," I whispered. "I can't see."

"Hold on. You will."

Over and over again, the cold water flooded my face. Some of it went into my nose and down the front of my blouse. Bit by bit I could see the sleeve of Danny's uniform, see the water, see the floor beneath us. The awful pain in my eyes had turned into a bearable sting. My eyes felt dry, as though there were a film drawn tight over them.

"What was that?"

"I don't know," Danny said, "maybe some kind of alkaline or acid. The few drops that got on your blouse faded the color immediately. Hey, let's get you to the office so we can report this. You gotta get to a doctor."

"No. No," I protested.

"Why not?"

"School's almost over, I wanna go home, right now. Please, please don't make me. . . ." I felt tears. I knew he hated me to cry, but the thought of going to the office made me crazy. I couldn't handle having some hostile clerk telling me I was making mountains out of molehills.

"Calm down. You can do what you want but—"

"No, home right now." I said, cutting Danny off.

A short time later, an optometrist examined my eyes and studied the spots on my blouse. He put some kind of soothing substance into my eyes and covered them with eye patches. As I sat there in the dark, I heard him say,

"Whoever kept that water going in her eyes saved the quality of her sight, if not her sight itself. She'll have to wear the patch overnight. She'll have to be medicated for a while. She'll need to wear glasses for all close work. I'd really like to see her wear them all the time. I'll need to see her once a week until we're certain she's all right."

Glasses, all the time, I thought. No boy wants to date a girl with glasses.

Despite the doctor's instructions to wear an eye patch for twenty-four hours, I had to take it off. I couldn't let the reporters see me with the patch because they would ask questions and make a big deal of it.

By the time we got home it was seven o'clock, and I wasn't very talkative for the waiting reporters. Once inside I fell into bed, too exhausted to eat dinner. "Thank you, God," I whispered, "thank you for saving my eyes. God bless Danny, always."

> The hanging, stabbing, and burning of a Negro effigy near Central High
> —*Arkansas Gazette,* Friday, October 4, 1957

The newspaper story contained several vivid pictures of Central High students gathered the day before, hanging the effigy, then burning it. They were smiling gleefully as though they were attending a festive party.

"You made it. It's Friday," Danny said, greeting me at the front of Central once more. "Your peepers okay?"

My eyes still felt very dry and tight. There were floating spots before them, but I could see. They only stung when I went too long without putting the drops in.

Later that afternoon there was a movie star—someone I'd never heard of—speaking before a pep rally: Julie Adams, a former student. She was there to boost spirits because, she said, Central High School's reputation was being tainted.

Over the weekend of October 5th, a great thing happened that took the Little Rock school integration from the front pages of the national news. The Russians launched their 184-pound satellite, Sputnik.

But as the next week began, local radio, television, and newspapers claimed that 101st guards were following us females to the lavatory and harassing white girls. GI'S IN GIRLS' DRESSING ROOMS, FAUBUS SAYS ran as a banner headline in the *Gazette* for Monday, October 7. Of course it wasn't true. However, it made the military tighten up rules about where soldiers could or could not go with us and prompted them to launch a massive internal investigation.

I could see a steady erosion in the quality of security in response to charges of interference by the soldiers. It was evident as the early days of October passed that whenever the 101st troops relaxed their guard or were not clearly visible, we were in great danger.

the big picture

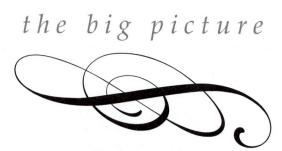

The 1950s and early 1960s are often described as a time of suffocating consensus, when the pressure to conform to mainstream values was especially intense,
when individualism was suppressed or not even highly valued, and when
change was negligible. Were the 1950s really like that?

chapter twelve

COMING APART:
THE 1960S

F or a time, the decade of the 1960s looked very much like its predecessor. John F. Kennedy, elected by a narrow margin over Richard Nixon in 1960, sought to pump up the nation with rhetoric while practicing a brand of consensus politics designed to avoid overt conflict. The problems of the 1960s, said Kennedy at Yale University's commencement in 1962, presented "subtle challenges, for which technical answers, not political answers, must be provided." Because he believed that basic problems of adequate food, clothing, and employment had been solved through economic growth and the evolution of the welfare state, Kennedy was not the reform activist that many expected him to be. Several of his policies and programs—the commitment to space exploration, the Peace Corps, the rollback of prices in the steel industry—were essentially symbolic gestures. In foreign affairs, Kennedy carried on the Cold War in grand fashion—deeper involvement in Vietnam; a CIA-sponsored invasion of Cuba in an attempt to depose Fidel Castro; a blockade to force the Soviet Union to remove its missiles from Cuba, when less bellicose but less satisfying alternatives were available.

There were signs of change and portents of turmoil in the early years of the decade—the gathering of political youth at Port Huron, Michigan, in 1962, to write and debate a manifesto; the assassination of John F. Kennedy; the assertive youth culture fostered by the English rock 'n' roll band the Beatles; the Berkeley Free Speech Movement in 1964. Yet the Eisenhower consensus was not irrevocably shattered until mid-decade. The cause was race. During the 1950s, black efforts to achieve integration had followed mainly legal channels. Gradually, though, black activists adopted the tactics of direct action. In February 1960, black and white college students conducted sit-ins at the segregated lunch counters of Woolworth dime stores in Durham and Greensboro, North Carolina; in 1961 and 1962, "freedom" rides took activists into segregated bus terminals across the Deep South. In August 1963, Martin Luther King, Jr., brought the civil rights movement north and sharpened its political content with an enormous march on the nation's capital.

Then, in 1965, a minor summer incident involving police in Watts, a black section of Los Angeles, set off five days of looting and rioting that left thirty-four people dead. Within two years, there were over a hundred major urban riots, all centered in black ghettos in cities like Newark and Detroit. It was in this setting that young black leaders began to question whether integration was an appropriate goal. They began to talk of black power. It was in this setting, too, that two of the most charismatic black leaders, Malcolm X and Martin Luther King, Jr., were shot to death.

The urban ghetto riots of the mid-1960s occurred during times of relatively low national rates of unemployment and inflation and within the context of Lyndon Johnson's Great Society—a liberal reform program that included the Voting Rights Act of 1965 and the War on Poverty. Comparable in importance to the Fifteenth Amendment to the Constitution (1870), the Voting Rights Act made illegal the literacy tests and other measures that southern states had used to keep African Americans from voting, and it gave the attorney general new powers to monitor registration and voting procedures. The law had an immediate impact. The War on Poverty was partly a response to a new wave of African-American activists who were more interested in reducing black poverty than in integrating the society. Focused on the inner cities, where the riots had occurred, this complex program included public works; job training for the poor; basic-skills training for preschool children (Head Start); VISTA, a domestic version of the Peace Corps; and the Community Action Program (CAP), which encouraged local antipoverty efforts that involved community participation. Despite billions in expenditures and a booming economy, the problems of the inner cities—problems that affected whites, Hispanics, and Asians as well as blacks—seemed intractable. "We fought a war on poverty," President Ronald Reagan later declared, "and poverty won."

If poverty won, it was in some measure because support for the Johnson agenda was being undermined by a growing backlash against the social unrest in the inner cities and on college campuses, and starved for money by the president's own policy of escalation in Vietnam. When Kennedy was killed in 1963, there were fewer than 20,000 American personnel in Vietnam; in 1968, there were more than 500,000. For Johnson, each new American commitment was absolutely necessary. Defeat or withdrawal, he believed, would only bring more aggression, new tests of the national and presidential will. Others, however, saw the conflict in Vietnam largely as a civil war and American involvement as an immoral and/or unlawful interference in a domestic dispute.

Protests against the war, centered on the college campuses and utilizing the tactics of the civil rights movement, began in earnest in early 1965 and grew in number and intensity through the decade. Almost every major campus in the United States was torn by rallies, teach-ins, and riots. One climax of the youth revolt was the massive demonstration—and the violent police response to it—centered on the Democratic National Convention in Chicago in 1968. The "protesters," as they had come to be called, could not prevent the nomination of the party's establishment candidate, Hubert Humphrey, but the event so clouded his candidacy that it almost ensured his defeat by Richard Nixon.

Nixon's widening of the Vietnam War in 1970, with an invasion of Cambodia, touched off the last major round of protest on the campuses. On May 4, panicky National Guardsmen, sent to quell a protest at Kent State University in Ohio, killed four students. Ten days later, two black youths were shot by police at Jackson State College in Mississippi.

By the end of the decade, the antiwar and civil rights movements had been joined and fueled by women seeking liberation from confining social roles and by a new group of environmental and consumer activists who saw that the nation had pursued economic growth at great cost to the quantity and quality of its remaining resources and the health of its citizens. Portions of this counterculture of protest were nonpolitical (Ken Kesey's San Francisco–based Merry Pranksters, for example, painted their faces with Day-Glo and inveigled protesters to "drop acid" and simply turn their backs on the war). But protest movements of the 1960s were by and large committed to making existing political frameworks responsive. Many believed that the Great Society could reconstruct the nation's cities, force corporations to clean up the air and water, provide for genuine equality of opportunity for all races, and even eliminate poverty. Others had faith that Ralph Nader and his "raiders" could mount and sustain a meaningful consumer movement and that Common Cause, an extensive liberal lobby established by former Department of Health, Education, and Welfare Secretary John Gardner, would significantly redress the balance in Congress. Not since the 1930s had Americans believed so mightily in the possibilities of change.

interpretive essay

Kenneth Cmiel

THE POLITICS OF CIVILITY

On the editorial page of this morning's newspaper, an essay by a local writer laments the decline of "civility" in American life. Hate crimes, student violence against teachers, nasty talk-show hosts, filthy sit-coms, gangsta rap, the indignities of the Clinton-Lewinsky scandal, politicians lacking in simple gentility—at every turn, evidence that the United States used to be a more courteous, more polite, and more gracious land. Critics on the right have been quick to locate the source of today's relative incivility in the decade of the 1960s, and to assign a special responsibility to the countercultural youth of the era, who seemed bent on eliminating refinement, formality, and good manners from the social order. Historian Kenneth Cmiel's subtle and nuanced account of the decline of civility in that decade confirms some aspects of that view, but it also offers a broader and more compelling interpretation of the phenomenon, while questioning the basic assumption that "civil is better." According to Cmiel, when did modern incivility emerge? Who was responsible? Would the nation have been better off had it remained a more civil society?

As the 1960s opened, civility was, quite literally, the law of the land. In 1942 the U.S. Supreme Court had declared that certain words were not protected by the First Amendment. Not only fighting words, but also the "lewd," "obscene," and "profane" were all excluded from protection. A statute declaring that "no person shall address any offensive, derisive or annoying word to any other person who is lawfully in any street" was upheld by the Court as perfectly legal. This decision, although modified in later years, was still law in 1960, and statutes like the one mentioned above continued to be on the books and enforced. They implied that free speech was possible only in what eighteenth-century writers had called "civil society." Civility, in other words, had to precede civil rights.

One part of the contentious politics of the sixties, however, was a fight over this notion. From a number of perspectives, prevailing attitudes toward social etiquette were attacked. African Americans argued that civil society as constructed by whites helped structure racial inequality. Counterculturalists insisted that civil politeness suppressed more authentic social relations. Some student radicals infused the strategic disruption of civility with political meaning. And finally, there was a moderate loosening of civil control at the center of society. Under this onslaught, the nation's courts struggled to redefine the relationship between law and civil behavior.

No regime is without an approach to social order, which means that none is without an attitude toward decorum. Many governments impose order from the top. Others allow huge pockets of disorder, passion, and even violence provided it all does not threaten the regime. A state ideologically committed to equal rights for all is especially hard-pressed to establish a standard of decorum, for any norm seems to undermine its deepest principles. Still, for nations with a professed belief in something resembling our First Amendment, there is more than one way to negotiate the contradiction between political principle and civil order. This essay charts the shift within the United States from one sense of order to another. In reaction to various social changes and pressures, federal courts, most importantly the Supreme Court, altered the law of decorum. From the belief that civility took precedence over civil rights, the Supreme Court decided that in public forums, incivility was protected by the First Amendment. But this major change was qualified. No incivility, the Court argued, could disrupt the normal workings of a school, workplace, or courtroom. Institutions had to function, the justices reasoned. Decorum there was mandatory.

BOURGEOIS FESTIVALS OF MISRULE

The civil rights movement's nonviolent efforts to alter the social order marked the first powerful sortie into the politics of civility during the 1960s. As the sixties opened, nonviolent direct action was the tactic of choice for organizations like the Congress of Racial Equality (CORE), the Southern Christian Leadership Conference (SCLC), and the Student Nonviolent Coordinating Committee (SNCC). To be sure, this tactic did not rise and fall with the sixties. It went back to the 1940s when CORE was founded, and it was under attack as early as 1961. Still, it played an important role in the first half of the decade and never entirely died out. Practitioners of direct action used an assertively polite decorum to upset social assumptions and topple the system of segregation.

Nonviolent resistance asked demonstrators to peaceably and lovingly call attention to the inequities of the social system. For those believing in direct nonviolent action, the path of protest was a complicated and patient one, moving through four distinct stages—the investigation of a problem, efforts to negotiate a solution, public protest, and then further negotiation. One never proceeded to the next stage without warrant. Henry David Thoreau's "Civil Disobedience" was often cited as a precursor to direct action. Another important source was

Mahatma Gandhi. Indeed, Gandhi's 1906 campaign in South Africa was seen as the first example of a mass direct nonviolent action.

But while Gandhi and Thoreau were sources, for both black and white activists committed to direct nonviolent action there was something far more important—the Gospel's injunction to love one's enemies. All the early leaders of CORE, SCLC, and SNCC were deeply influenced by the Christian message of hope and redemption. SNCC's statement of purpose on its founding in May 1960 called attention to those "Judaic-Christian traditions" that seek "a social order permeated by love." Martin Luther King, Jr., who post facto described the Montgomery boycott in terms of a Gandhian four-stage protest, was in fact only gradually becoming aware of Gandhi in the mid-1950s. As King put it to one reporter, he "went to Gandhi through Jesus."

These civil rights leaders placed great emphasis on orderly demonstrations. CORE's "Rules for Action" told members to "never use malicious slogans," to "make a sincere effort to avoid malice and hatred," and to "meet the anger of any individual or group in the spirit of good will and creative reconciliation." Similarly, Martin Luther King wanted activists to "protest courageously, and yet with dignity and Christian love." This was the "task of combining the militant and the moderate."

Civil rights protest took a number of characteristic forms—the boycott, the sit-in, the freedom ride, and the mass march. At all, efforts were made to keep the protest civil. In 1960, when four neatly dressed black college students sat down at a white-only lunch counter in a downtown Woolworth's in Greensboro, North Carolina, one began the protest by turning to a waitress and saying, "I'd like a cup of coffee, please." Although the students were not served, they continued to be well mannered, sitting "politely" at the counter for days on end. This first effort set off a wave of sit-ins to desegregate southern restaurants. Typical were the instructions given in Nashville: "Do show yourself friendly on the counter at all times. Do sit straight and always face the counter. Don't strike back or curse back if attacked." Candie Anderson, one of the students at the Nashville sit-in, recalled: "My friends were determined to be courteous and well-behaved. . . . Most of them read or studied while they sat at the counters, for three or four hours. I heard them remind each other not to leave cigarette ashes on the counter, to take off their hats, etc."

To be sure, especially when faced with taunts and violence, tempers were strained. There were breaks in decorum. But especially early in the sixties, leaders worked hard to maintain discipline and spoke out against even relatively mild disturbances. In 1962, when noisy foot stomping by local CORE activists interrupted a school board meeting in Englewood, New Jersey, the national president of CORE publicly declared that under "no condition" would the organization condone such behavior. "We would approve of a sit-in—quiet, peaceful, and orderly, but not a noisy disruption of the proceedings."

The meaning of the polite protests was complicated. Rosa Parks, who refused to move to the back of the bus in Montgomery, Alabama, the students integrating lunch counters in Greensboro, and the marchers at Selma were all not only acting with decorum, they were also all breaking the law, calling attention to the inadequacy of the present system, and violating long-standing white/black custom of the South. The southern caste system was reinforced through an elaborate etiquette. Blacks stepped aside on the street to let whites pass, they averted their eyes from whites, and even adult African Americans were called by a diminutive first name ("Charlie" or "Missie") while addressing all whites with the formal titles of "Sir," "Ma'am," "Mr.," or "Mrs." No distinctions in economic status changed this. Black ministers tipped their hats to white tradesmen. To the overwhelming majority of white southerners, the assertion of civil equality by civil rights protesters was in fact a radical *break* in decorum.

The protest, indeed, highlights some of the complexities of civility itself. On the one hand, politeness is a means of avoiding violence and discord. It is a way of *being nice.* One of sociologist Norbert Elias's great insights was to see that the introduction of civil etiquette in the early modern West was part of an effort to reduce the amount of interpersonal violence prevalent during the Middle Ages. At some time or other, all of us are polite to people we do not like simply because we do not want to live in an overly contentious world. On the other hand, however, civility *also* reaffirms established social boundaries. And when there are huge inequities in the social order, polite custom ratifies them in everyday life.

Direct nonviolent action attempted to undermine southern etiquette. It did so not by attacking civility pure and simple but by using polite behavior to challenge social inequality. More precisely, the first function of politeness (being nice) attacked the second (the caste system). The determined civility of the protesters dramatized the inequities of the South and at the same time signaled to the nation and world the "worthiness" (that is, civility) of African Americans.

Most southern whites did not see it this way. Even those who were called moderates in the early sixties often viewed the polite protests as an attack on civility. Sit-ins, boycotts, and marches openly challenged the caste system and, moderates argued, too easily slipped into violence. To the *Nashville Banner,* the sit-ins were an "incitation to anarchy." Such spokespeople understood civility to necessarily mean discussion instead of protest. In 1960 the *Greensboro Daily News* ran an editorial entitled "Of Civil Rights and Civilities" suggesting that the sit-ins were ill-conceived because civility had to take precedence over civil rights.

Such editorialists, at their best, were genuinely concerned with avoiding violence, even white violence against blacks. Yet in effect they were encouraging—even insisting on—passivity. And they misunderstood the more nuanced functions of the polite protests of SNCC, CORE, and SCLC. Direct action did a number of things at once. It protested the caste system. It also publicly displayed Negro civility. And finally, it demonstrated, again and again, the brutality lurking behind established southern etiquette.

In Greensboro, it was *white* children who were the first to be arrested for disorderly conduct, who harassed blacks at the lunch counter, who got angry. At Selma, it was the white police who waded into crowds of protesters and began clubbing them. Black activists, in fact, had expected this to happen. Martin Luther King was typical, noting that nonviolent resistance forced "the oppressor to commit his brutality openly—in the light of day—with the rest of the world looking on." The net effect, according to King, was that the social conscience of the nation would be stirred. Bob Moses of SNCC spoke of how activists had to bring the South to a "white heat" before change could come. Protest was a form of public drama. In 1962, when officials of Albany, Georgia, refused to beat protesters or make mass arrests, the protest was a bust.

Nonviolent resistance was designed to turn the world upside down. It can perhaps best be described as a bourgeois festival of misrule. Like the old carnivals of Europe, the boycotts, sit-ins, and marches were strategic dramas outside the purview of daily decorum that inverted the social order. Whereas the caste system of the South had been built on the supposed superior "civilization" of whites and the "backwardness" of blacks, the festivals of misrule turned this around. It was the protesters who displayed civility and the whites who did not.

Unlike the old festivals of misrule, however, which were raucous and wild, the sit-ins and boycotts were thoroughly civil and polite. They were utterly bourgeois. In this respect they appear to be directly related to the possibilities opened up by liberal democratic ideology of the nineteenth and twentieth century. Only under regimes where the notion that members of "civil society" should be full-fledged citizens has some weight do such protests make sense. Indeed, outside support for the protests often called attention to the inversion of social roles and the protection that civil protest must be accorded.

While Gandhi, leading thousands of peasants, might convey to British overlords the dignity of simple people, in the United States of America, with no public perception of a peasantry in its midst, mass direct action took on a different meaning. It demonstrated the bourgeois character of the dispossessed. The final goal was to establish an egalitarian civility. For these activists, the etiquette codes of the late 1950s and early 1960s were largely taken for granted. They only wanted them applied equally to African Americans. They were determined to create a truly all-encompassing civil society.

This style of protest was under assault almost as the sixties started. As early as 1961, and certainly by 1964, those partisans of "civil" protest were faced with a growing mass movement that was more assertive, less polite, and more willing to defend itself. A host of reasons explain this shift. The fiercely violent reaction of so many whites made nonviolent decorum extremely hard and dangerous to maintain. Black nationalism, grass roots activism, a growing sense of frustration, and burgeoning antiestablishment sentiment in the culture at large all helped throw bourgeois misrule on the defensive. It would be just a few more steps to the Black Panther party or the calls to violence by people like Stokely Carmichael and H. Rap Brown.

Civil disobedience never died out in the late sixties. And it did have an effect on southern society. By the end of the 1970s, especially in cities, the old etiquette had largely disappeared, although its residues persisted in the countryside and small towns. But nonviolent resistance did disappear from center stage. The rise of a more raucous, incivil disobedience, connected with elaborate attacks on the very idea of a civil society, pushed this peculiarly bourgeois form of carnival to the side.

THE COUNTERCULTURE

One place we can spot the erosion of polite protest is in the Freedom Summer of 1964. Among an important group of young SNCC activists there was a certain skepticism about Martin Luther King. For these civil rights workers, nonviolent resistance was understood to be a strategic tactic rather than a principled commitment. And there was a change in style. As sociologist Robert McAdam has noted, there was a feeling among these civil rights activists that they had to free themselves as much as the southern blacks they worked for. And that meant abandoning middle-class norms. Consequently, more rural dress (blue jeans and work shirt) became the mode. Movement slang also became prominent, as in "three of the white cats who bothered our guys have been picked up by the FBI. You dig it—they are in a Southern jail." While not particularly shocking when compared to what would soon come, these changes were one sign of an emerging attack on prevailing norms of polite behavior.

Another sign was the filthy speech movement at Berkeley. In the fall of 1964, the University of California at Berkeley was rocked by the free speech movement, an effort by students to retain their right to distribute political material on campus. Many of the leaders of the free speech movement had worked for SNCC in the South the summer before and a number of Freedom Summer tactics were adopted at Berkeley. Students used mass civil disobedience and sit-ins to pressure campus officials in November and December. They were generally successful. But the next spring, after the campus had quieted, a new twist came. A nonstudent who hung around in New York beat circles drifted to Berkeley to (in his words) "make the scene." On 3 March he stood on Bancroft and Telegraph and held up a sign that just said "FUCK." When asked to clarify his meaning, he added an exclamation point. His arrest threw the campus into another controversy. Other "dirty speech" protests were held, with other students arrested for obscenity.

The counterculture of the 1960s can be traced back to the beats of the 1950s, earlier still to artistic modernism, and even before that to Rousseau's mid-eighteenth-century attack on politeness. But if there is a long subterranean history, a very visible counterculture began to surface in 1964. The first underground newspapers appeared; they were dominated by countercultural themes. By 1966 the counterculture was a mass media phenomenon. Perhaps its height of popularity were the years 1967 and 1968. And while no precise date marks its end, by the early 1970s it was fading fast at least in its most utopian projections.

From Rousseau through the 1960s, advocates of a counterculture valued authenticity over civility. The command to be polite (that is, to *be nice*) does not encourage personal expression. It suppresses impulsive behavior, relying on established social forms to guarantee comity. As Norbert Elias has put it, the civilizing process is about affect control. Counterculture advocates challenged these presumptions, arguing for the liberation of the self. In the name of personal freedom they attacked the restraints and compromises of civil society. In a phrase introduced to American life by sixties freaks, they were dedicated to "doing their own thing."

This translated into an extraordinarily colorful form of life. Shoulder-length hair on men, Victorian dresses on women, day-glo painted bodies, elaborate slang, and more open sexuality—it was all far removed from "straight" (that is, civil) society. Hippies looked different, acted different, were different. At its best, there was a glorious joy in the freedom of hippie life-styles. The "be-ins" of 1967 celebrated the love that would replace the stilted conformity of the established world. In the 1967 rock musical *Hair,* the music builds to a rousing crescendo to support this playful celebration of counterculture style:

> Let it fly in the breeze
> And get caught in the trees
> Give a home to the fleas
> In my hair
>
> A home for the fleas
> A hive for the bees
> A nest for the birds
> There ain't no words
> For the beauty and splendor
> The wonders of my
> Hair. . . .

It was not only long hair that signaled liberation. Language also had to be freed, as did sex. Hippies are "more tolerant than most people," one hippie told a New York journalist. "Like you can be hung up, say, on eating twat and never want to screw, or I might want to just go to bed with boys, or somebody can be hung up on astrology. But the hippies don't really care." The same was true of psychedelic dress, beads, and long hair: "Basically, it's just a question of freedom. It's your body—you can do with it what you want to."

Drugs too were often defended as a liberating experience. (I myself did so ingenuously in the late sixties.) "It's like seeing the world again through a child's eye," one user noted in 1967. Drugs were "a transcendental glory." "When I first turned on," the owner of a San Francisco head shop reported in 1968, "it pulled the rug out from under me. Suddenly I saw all the bullshit in the whole educational and social system. . . . The problem with our schools is that they are turning out robots to keep the social system going." So "turning on, tuning in, and dropping out means to conduct a revolution against the system."

Intellectuals supportive of the counterculture echoed these themes. For Charles Reich, in *The Greening of America,* the new way of life was profoundly liberating. Straight society, according to Reich, was repressive, committed to "role-playing," to following patterned forms. The new consciousness, on the other hand, began "the moment the individual frees himself from automatic acceptance of the imperatives of society." The psychologist R. D. Laing took it even further, arguing that it was the "normal" people who were the real crazies. In such an insane world, precisely those who knew enough to ignore the rules—schizophrenics—were the sane ones. That was also a theme of Ken Kesey's *One Flew over the Cuckoo's Nest* (1962). The view gained more than a little currency within the counterculture.

To those with no respect for the counterculture, the alternative decorum was gross. There was just too much dirt. Hippies did not have the discipline to hold a job. The sex was too loose. The drugs were destructive. Some critics completely missed the claims to liberation and denounced hippies as simply negative. When *U.S. News & World Report* asked a leading psychiatrist about the changes "beatniks or hippies" might bring to "American manners," he responded by contrasting the thoughtful questioners of the establishment with those "arrogant" kids who "make us more uncomfortable." "They may have long hair and be a little careless in their dress and hygiene," the psychiatrist added. "They may not wear their neckties the way we think they should." He thought them mentally unstable.

Yet while the distance from straight culture was deep, the counterculture might best be seen not so much an attack on politeness as an alternative politeness, one not based on the emotional self-restraint of traditional civility but on the expressive individualism of liberated human beings. It is no surprise that "love" was an important theme running throughout the counterculture. We were, according to *Hair*, at the dawning of the Age of Aquarius, where "peace will guide the planets and love will steer the stars." The vision was explicitly utopian:

Harmony and understanding
Sympathy and trust abounding
No more falsehoods or derisions
Golden living dreams of visions
Mystic crystal revelations
And the mind's true liberation

Even some of the behavior that most provoked the straight world was often connected with a new communal sensibility. One typical counterculture youth noted that "smoking grass makes people feel very warm and tender and loving and emotional. This is why, you know, they call it the herb of love." Liberating the self was connected with a new communal culture.

The counterculture, at least in its more utopian moment, did not survive the decade. Already by the end of 1967 hippies in San Francisco were announcing the "death of hippie." The anarchistic Diggers (often called the conscience of the counterculture) were by that time trying to alert newcomers to the ways that some long-haired men preyed on naive young girls who came unsuspecting to the city. The girls were fed drugs they did not understand as a prelude to sex. By 1968 Andy Warhol was noting that the mood had changed in New York, with more distrust and even violence in counterculture circles than during the year before. If the image of Woodstock, with hundreds of thousands of young people coming together and enjoying themselves for three days, signaled the best of the counterculture, that of Altamount, with Hell's Angels beating and killing a fan, conjured up the dark side.

The limits might be found in the vision itself. For communalism and authenticity were harder to combine than one might think. The very lack of roles and restraint, the absence of Elias's affect control, would work only if there was a respect for the group that was not always there. As one more cynical New York hippie put it in 1968: "See, hippie society is a lot more ruthless and a lot more deceptive than straight society. In straight society you have your established rules and regulations, you know; in hippie society anything goes. Some of them will live with you and consume everything you have."

The counterculture, at its most utopian, tried to invent a new civility. It attacked the social roles of straight society and the implied social order contained within it. But it held firm to the other dimension of civility—that of being nice. But in the end, it could not be yoked together as easily as one thought. To some degree, the roles involved in civil etiquette are connected with the avoidance of discord.

To say this, however, is not to condemn the counterculture tout court. It is rather to simply point out the problems in its most utopian dreams and to remind readers in the 1990s how real and prevalent those dreams were in the mid-1960s. For if the counterculture, chastened, fed into the relaxation of mainstream etiquette in the late sixties, it should not be confused with that more moderate, reformist goal. At its most heady, the counterculture thought of itself as a revolution in consciousness, something that could reshape the world. That dream was not realized.

THE POLITICAL LEFT

By 1965, as the counterculture was coming to national consciousness, there was another debate going on about the civil society. At least some radical activists had moved beyond the talking stage. Violent behavior became a considered option.

This happened first among black activists, later among whites. African American radicals like H. Rap Brown and Stokely Carmichael decisively split with the earlier civil rights movement. Carmichael's 1966 call to let the cities burn, the stream of urban riots after 1965, and the growing militancy in general frightened numerous Americans. To be sure, many whites missed the nuances of the shift. Groups like the Black Panthers conjured violence only as a defensive tactic. Still, the situation was complicated. An activist like Rap Brown loved the effect his talk of violence had on whites. And there was rhetoric that legitimated revolt. Franz Fanon's *Wretched of the Earth* explicitly called for violence, and certain African American radicals did promote it by 1967.

Some white student and antiwar activists were making their own transition. The move from dissent to resistance was accompanied by a shift in rhetoric. "We're now in the business of wholesale disruption and widespread resistance and dislocation of the American society," Jerry Rubin reported in 1967. To be sure, not all white radicals accepted this, but some did, and the thought of disruption scared Middle America, whose more conservative press responded with almost breathless reports about imminent revolution. The heightened rhetoric, on both sides, contributed to the sense that the center might not hold. A string of burned buildings on university campuses as well as a handful of bombings over the next few years contributed as well.

Real violence, against property or person, however, was actually rare. Far more important was the *talk* about violence. The escalation of rhetoric, the easy use of hard words made more centrists very nervous. It reflected, in their eyes, a lack of faith in civil politics.

For these radicals, the hard words were part of their sense that polite society had its priorities backward. There was something grotesquely misguided about a middle-class decorum that masked the profound inequalities of America. The true obscenities, they argued, were the Vietnam War and racial hatred. In fact, some thought, the very idea of obscenity had to be rethought. "The dirtiest word in the English language is not 'fuck' or 'shit' in the mouth of a tragic shaman," one activist wrote, "but the word 'NIGGER' from the sneering lips of a Bull Conner."

Exposing the "real" obscenities of America led to a wave of shock tactics. One of the most provocative was in the May 1967 *Realist*, a monthly partly of the Left, partly just absurdist. The article in question was supposed to be suppressed bits of William Manchester's *Death of a President*, which had been published two years before. In one section of the parody, "Jackie Kennedy" recounted an incident that took place on Air Force One after her husband's assassination. The author has the first lady say that she saw Lyndon B. Johnson "crouching over the corpse" while "breathing hard and moving his body rhythmically." She at first did not understand what was going on, but then "I realized—there is only one way to say this—he was literally fucking my husband in the throat. He reached a climax and dismounted. I froze. The next thing I remember, he was being sworn in as the new President."

The incident, of course, had never occurred. The *Realist*'s editor, Paul Krassner, made it up. It created an enormous stir. The paper was banned in some parts of Boston. Krassner's usual printer, a socialist himself, refused to print it. Subscribers cancelled. The Left-oriented journalist Robert Sheer worried that the magazine's real exposés would lose credibility. On the other hand, *Ramparts* editor Warren Hinckle called it a "brilliant dirty issue." One reader raised the question of whether it really was the most obscene thing imaginable: "I don't cancel my subscription to the *Chronicle* because I read every day of the horror, the obscenities, the crimes committed by LBJ. . . . That grisly image was *not* burned children in Vietnam, crying mothers, bombed villages or starving black kids in Oakland."

By the late sixties, then, countercultural politics might mesh with political radicalism. To be sure, the two movements never fit perfectly together. But there were connections. Even long hair could be a threatening statement laden with political overtones. One participant in the Columbia University uprising in 1968 welcomed the "bad vibrations" his long hair brought: "I say great. I want the cops to sneer and the old ladies swear and the businessmen worry. I want everyone to see me and say: 'There goes an enemy of the state,' because that's where I'm at, as we say in the Revolution game."

To the extent that the New Left was connected with more elaborate countercultural themes, it went the way of the counterculture. Even if most did not sell out in the way Jerry Rubin did (going to Wall Street in the 1970s), for thousands there was a scaling down of dress, decorum, and drugs in the ensuing years. This should not be confused with any sort of move to the Right, for despite what some popular retrospectives on the sixties have claimed, like the movie *The Big Chill*, there is good scholarly evidence that the political sympathies of radical activists have remained steady over the decades, whatever the length of their hair.

Nevertheless, as an organized political force the New Left was dead by the mid-1970s. But the New Left's strategic disruption of decorum did not completely fade away. If random bombings stopped, there are still echoes of the New Left's politics of incivility in the verbal assaults on fur wearers in the late 1980s. And more than one commentator has noted that the shock tactics of the late 1980s conservative student newspapers on American campuses aped the tone of the 1960s New Left. In a civil society that relies on the mass media to define public life, one of the best ways to bring attention to your point of view is by strategic acts of incivility.

INFORMALITY

The debate in the late sixties was clouded by the polarization of the times. Hippies and violent political radicals were tailor-made for the mass media. But despite the preoccupation with the more extravagant behavior, the nation's manners were changing in more subtle ways. There was a large move toward the informalization of American society.

Informalization is a term invented by sociologists to describe periodic efforts to relax formal etiquette. These periods of informality are then followed by a more conservative "etiquette-prone" reaction. While Americans in the sixties pressed toward more informal social relations, the phenomenon was by no means unique to that period. A significant relaxation of manners took place in Jacksonian America, tied to both egalitarian sentiment and the desire for authenticity. Still another important stage was the 1920s. And as Barbara Ehrenreich has pointed out, sexual mores were becoming less rigid inside mainstream society in the 1950s, a prelude for the next decade.

The counterculture of the mid-1960s was only picking up on debates already under way in mainstream America. Disputes about long hair surfaced not in 1966 with the counterculture but in 1963 when the Beatles first became known in the United States. The *New York Times* first reported on the issue in December 1964, four months after the Beatles began their first full-length tour in the United States. In those early years, the debate over long hair had a very different feel than it would beginning in 1966. The discussion was *not* about basic rottenness of a civilization. Rather, for the boys involved, it was about fun and girls. The look, as it evolved in the United States, was a surfer look. The "mop top," as it was called, was simply a bang swooped over the forehead. The sides were closely and neatly cropped. It was moderate hair by 1966 standards (and by 1994 standards).

Between 1963 and 1965, however, it was controversial. Adults who disliked the bangs claimed they blurred gender lines. Boys looked like girls, something both disquieting and disgusting. Nevertheless, the conservatives on this issue were like the "long hair" kids in not talking about the mop top as a frontal assault on civilization but in the more restricted terms of a threatening relaxation of order. It was only in 1966 that certain forms of male hair became associated with a wholesale attack on what was known as "the American way of life."

Something similar can be said about sexual mores. The urge to liberalize "official" sexual codes was certainly a prominent theme of the counterculture, but it was also a theme of Hugh Heffner's *Playboy*, first published in 1953. And a female variant, Helen Gurley Brown's *Sex and the Single Girl*, was a huge bestseller as early as 1962. By the mid-1960s there were a host of middle-class advocates for a more liberal sexuality, a trend culminating in the early 1970s in books like Alex Comfort's *The Joy of Sex*. The counterculture contributed, but it was neither the beginning nor the end of the change.

The same was true of obscenity. While counterculturalists by 1965 were fighting over "dirty words" at Berkeley, there was a corresponding effort in the mainstream to relax norms. Liberal judges had softened obscenity laws in the 1950s and 1960s. The pornography industry was growing throughout the sixties, with, to take one example, magazines catering to sadists making their appearance early in the decade. In 1965 authorities filed twice as many pornography complaints as in 1959. By the early 1970s, X-rated movie theaters were dotting every city and many towns across the nation. And in 1970 the President's Commission on Obscenity and Pornography "reported" that there was no empirical evidence that exposure to pornography played a significant role in crime, violence, rape, or antisocial behavior of any kind.

In countless ways you could see the mainstream's mores changing. In 1969, for the first time in history, a major dictionary of the English language included the words *fuck* and *cunt*. In August 1971 *Penthouse* magazine first contained pictures of female genitalia. *Playboy* followed five months later. The *New York Times* reported in the fall of 1967 that even doctors and stockbrokers, "traditional squares" the paper called them, were starting to let their hair grow longer. The miniskirt, which first appeared in the mid-1960s, was by no means only worn by girls and women hopelessly alienated from the culture. For its creator, the mini was explicitly tied to sexual liberation. "The old taboos are dead or dying," *Newsweek* reported in 1967. "A new and more permissive society is taking shape."

In the portrayal of violence, as well, mainstream culture was breaking civil taboos. *Night of the Living Dead* (1968) is considered to be a historic turning point in the history of horror films. Its graphic portrayals of splattered brains, dismemberment, cannibalism, and matricide set the stage for later films like *The Texas Chainsaw Massacre* and the *Halloween* series. In 1972 a new type of romance novel, sometimes known in the trade as "sweet savagery," introduced rape to the genre. The first of these novels, Kathleen Woodiwiss's eight-hundred-page *The Flame and the Flower,* sold two and a half million copies by 1978.

The changes touched all sorts of mainstream venues. To trace *Cosmopolitan* magazine between 1964 and 1970 is to chart one variation of the move. In 1964 it ran rather staid articles such as "Catholics and Birth Control" and "Young Americans Facing Life with Dignity and Purpose." By 1969, however, *Cosmo* was reporting on "The Ostentatious Orgasm" and "Pleasures of a Temporary Affair." A piece lauding "hippie capitalists" noted how "loose" and "free form" the new entrepreneur was, not tied to confining restraints of Wall Street. "Nobody, *but nobody,*" it observed, "calls the boss by anything except his first name." In 1972 *The Cosmo Girl's Guide to the New Etiquette* was published to provide help for the contemporary world. There was advice about language ("But unless you have been wearing blinders and earmuffs for the last ten years, there is not likely a four-letter expletive a nice girl has never heard or even used."), about "women's lib" ("Coexisting with our militant sisters takes intelligence and tact."), and about household help (Don't be like your mother in the 1950s. Being your maid's "friend" will "probably get you lots farther . . . than being her icky, finicky, stuck-up employer.")

Parallel changes might be found in other magazines with no commitment to the counterculture, as *Esquire,* with its growing respect for sideburns, or *Ebony,* with its increasing tolerance for moderate Afros. This widespread informalization at the center was often missed during the sixties. It lacked the flair of the counterculture or the drama of the Left.

By the early 1970s, however, the changes were becoming apparent. A spate of articles appeared with titles like "Buzz Off, Mrs. Post, It's Time for the New Etiquette" and "Good Manners for Liberated Persons." The old forms were out of date, one writer noted, but that just raised new questions: "The trouble is that the first principle of the way we live now is nonintervention, also known as letting people do their own thing." This *Saturday Review* article included advice about unmarried cohabitation, breast-feeding in public, dress ("Virtually no one tells his guests how to be clad anymore."), even about drugs ("It is the responsibility of the host to provide a roach clip."). Even Amy Vanderbilt tried to update her *Etiquette* to accommodate the changes, although that did not stop partisans of the new from vigorously noting how hopelessly outdated she continued to be.

For writers like Doris Grumbach and Lois Gould, a main point of attack was the older male/female etiquette. If there was one place where the new principle of "nonintervention" was set to the side, it was here. Calling grown women "girls," having men invariably take the lead in dancing, and presuming that men asked women out on dates were mentioned as suspect behavior. These authors introduced to mainstream audiences feminist arguments about the part that male "chivalry" played in female subordination. "If there is to be a new etiquette," Lois Gould wrote in the *New York Times Magazine,* "it ought to be based on honest mutual respect, and responsiveness to each other's real needs."

The two moves—toward informality and toward egalitarian male/female etiquette—indicate the complicated cross-currents of reform. For the informality was rooted in a critique of the "inauthenticity" of the old manners, while complaints about chivalry were connected with the ways that decorum upheld patterns of inequality. To oversimplify, the former was a part of the romantic critique and loosely associated with the same push of the counterculture. The latter was a democratic critique with more in common with the civil protests of black Americans during the decade.

LEGALIZING AN INCIVIL SOCIETY

This shift at the center of American culture did not take place without opposition. There were plaints for the older norms. Nor did the changes take place independent of the law. In fact, they were sanctioned and encouraged through new attitudes toward decorum promulgated by the federal courts, principally the U.S. Supreme Court. A number of decisions, most coming between 1966 and 1973, changed the relationship of the "civilizing process" to the rule of law. This was the legal version of informalization.

In a number of instances, the Court refused to use arguments of bad taste or decorum to uphold the law. In one celebrated case, a young man opposed to the Vietnam War had been arrested in the corridor of the Los Angeles County Courthouse for wearing a jacket with the words "Fuck the Draft" prominently inscribed on it. The Court overturned the conviction, noting that there was no sign of imminent violence at the courthouse and that while the phrase was crude and vulgar to many, the open debate the First Amendment guaranteed necessitated its protection. In a far-reaching departure from earlier decisions, the Court also raised doubts about the possibility of any evaluation of taste: "For, while the particular four-letter word being litigated here is perhaps more distasteful than others of its genre, it is nevertheless true that one man's vulgarity is another's lyric." Since government officials "cannot make principled decisions in this area," it was important to leave "matters of taste and style largely to the individual."

This was a far cry from *Chaplinsky v. New Hampshire* (1942), in which the Court simply asserted that some utterances were of "such slight social value" that the First Amendment did not protect them. In the Chaplinsky case, the defendant was convicted for calling someone a "damned racketeer" and a "damned Fascist." In the next few years, the Court would protect the use of "motherfucker" in public debate. In *Chaplinsky*, the Court also upheld a local ordinance that rather explicitly outlawed incivil behavior: "No person shall address any offensive, derisive, or annoying word to any other person who is lawfully in any street or other public place nor call him by any offensive or dismissive name." In the early 1970s the Court struck down similar ordinances as too broad.

The Supreme Court also addressed differing conceptions of the place of civility in relation to violence. In *Gooding v. Wilson* (1972), it took up an ordinance

that made any "opprobrious words or abusive language" a possible misde-
meanor. An appellate court had made the case for the older standard: "The
term 'breach of peace' is generic, and includes all violations of the public peace
or order, or decorum." The Supreme Court, however, rejected this defense of
civil society, which made it a crime to "merely speak words offensive to some
who hear them, and so sweeps too broadly."

What the Court was doing in these cases was to open up "civil society" to
incivil behavior. It was explicitly granting certain "offensive" behavior constitutional protection. In *Gooding,* a protester scuffling with police was arrested for
yelling "White son of a bitch, I'll kill you" and "You son of a bitch, I'll choke you
to death." In the next couple of years, a number of similar cases came to the
Court's attention. In one, a man was arrested at a school board meeting of 150
people (about 40 children) for calling teachers, the school board, and others
"motherfuckers." The Court overturned the conviction. In still another decision,
a state university student code mandating "generally accepted standards of conduct" and prohibiting "indecent conduct or speech" was struck down. Here,
too, decorum was the issue. A graduate student at the university had been expelled for publishing and distributing a paper with a cartoon of a policeman
raping the Statue of Liberty and an article entitled "Mother Fucker Acquitted."
(This was in reference to the acquittal of a member of a radical student group
that called itself "The Motherfuckers.") The Court declared the student code unconstitutional, arguing that a state university had no right to shut off the flow of
ideas merely "in the name of the conventions of decency," "no matter how offensive to good taste."

If the Court moved to open up public space to certain sorts of incivil behavior, there were limits. At no time did it accept the legitimacy of violence. The
Supreme Court held fast to the notion that the state had a monopoly on the legitimate use of force. What the Court was doing was rewriting the line between
behavior and violence, allowing far more space for aggressive words. Earlier
laws had defended civil demeanor precisely because "incivil" behavior was
thought to *lead* to discord. Now there was to be a toleration of more insulting
behavior although it still had to stop short of violence.

At the same time that this whole string of cases opened up room for more
"incivil" action in public, there was a parallel set of cases arguing that decorum
had to be maintained. These cases all had to do with the functioning of institutions. In courts, schools, even the workplace, the Court upheld the need for civil
decorum and left authorities broad discretion in setting standards.

One case, which had to do with a defendant whose "vile and abusive language" disrupted his criminal trial, prompted the Court to argue that "dignity,
order, and decorum" must be "the hallmarks of all court proceedings." The
"flagrant disregard of elementary standards of proper conduct . . . cannot be
tolerated."

In cases like this, the Court explicitly called attention to the decorum of the
protest. As it said in *Grayned v. Rockford* (1971), a case on picketing outside a
school: "The crucial question is whether the manner of expression is basically
incompatible with the normal activity of a particular place at a particular time."

When protest inside an institution was upheld, it was because it was not disruptive. No doubt the most important case of this kind was *Tinker v. Des Moines*, decided in 1969. A handful of students were suspended from a Des Moines high school in 1965 for wearing black arm bands to protest the escalation of the Vietnam War. Prior to this, the school board had voted to forbid the activity. The Court four years later vindicated the students, but precisely because of the civility of their action. The Court noted how the case did not relate "to regulation of the length of skirts or the type of clothing, to hair style or deportment." Nor did it concern "aggressive, disruptive action." There was no evidence "that any of the armbands 'disrupted' the school." The Court, however, added that activity that *did* disrupt a school was *not* protected by the First Amendment.

Debate over institutional decorum also extended to discussion of hair and clothing. In 1975 the Court took up the case of a policeman who had broken the department's dress code by wearing his hair modestly over the collar. While he argued that the code infringed upon his civil rights, the Court's majority disagreed, arguing that the department's need for "discipline, esprit de corps, and uniformity" was sufficient reason for a dress code. Only Justice William O. Douglas dissented, asserting that the policeman should have the right to wear his hair "according to his own taste."

The courts also debated the dress and hair codes of the public schools. Beginning in the late sixties, a number of lawsuits were introduced pitting the dress code of schools against the individual freedom of students and teachers. Although the Supreme Court was reticent to get involved in such cases, preferring to leave them to local authorities, it did say in 1971 that it had no objection to such codes. Lower courts around the country handled a number of these cases. They were split on whether a boy's hair length could be regulated or whether miniskirts and slacks could be forbidden for girls. Blue jeans were also a source of contention. And while the lower courts generally allowed teachers to grow beards, dress codes for employees were routinely upheld. Although these decisions were not uniform, they generally indicate some distance from the old decorum in favor of commitment to the new informality. At the same time, however, state courts almost universally upheld the right of a school board to set some sort of code. For example, even if a court allowed long hair, it often noted that cleanliness could be required. Some institutional authority was sanctioned.

All regimes wind up taking a stand on where decorum can be broken and where it has to be enforced. It is only where there is an abstract commitment to universal equal rights that decorum becomes legally problematic. But, to again repeat, there are different ways that such regimes can handle the issue. In the late 1960s there was a shift in American practice and law. The Supreme Court opened up all sorts of behavior in private life and in public. The Court would do nothing about people yelling "motherfucker" at school board meetings or in street protests. It declared unconstitutional broad ordinances that outlawed incivil behavior because it "tended" to lead to a breach of the peace. It does not seem inaccurate to suggest that the Court was giving certain leeway to an "incivil society." At the same time, however, the Court also carefully maintained the authority of institutions. The running of a school, a courtroom, or a workplace (for example, a police department) all demanded decorum. Here civil behavior, as defined by authorities, could be enforced by law.

Earlier thought had stressed the continuity between everyday life, public drama, and the avoidance of violence. To keep violence from erupting, the first two had to remain "polite." The new thinking cut that relationship. If one thinks about civil behavior as "affect control," the hiding of emotions, some of these new norms were not civil. The courts might then be interpreted as trying to impose a new level of tolerance by *demanding* that citizens respond to abusive language with restraint. But if one understands the courts as partaking in changes already under way in society at large, then its defense of "Fuck the Draft" or "motherfucker" meant something different. Such words were no longer expected to provoke a violent response, and the Supreme Court was only writing into law the higher state of emotional control in the populace at large.

It should be remembered that the courts only allowed incivil behavior in special settings—in "civil" society. At the same time that they were legalizing certain public incivilities in the name of democratic debate, they were also firmly reinforcing the authority of institutions to maintain order. In schools, courtrooms, and the workplace, some decorum could be imposed. Taken together, the informalization in civic forums and the reaffirmation of institutional authority indicated a strategic response by the Supreme Court to late sixties cultural and social pressures. The two streams of thought on decorum were complementary, defining how the state would give ground to informalizing forces and still shore up the authority of institutions.

The decisions of the Court bear resemblance to the image of social order suggested by Immanuel Kant in his essay, "What Is Enlightenment?" Kant had argued that enlightenment required public freedom so that discussion could take place. On the other hand, he claimed that in our "private" capacities, by which *he* meant basically positions in the civil service (including Protestant ministers, state bureaucrats, and university professors), there was a stronger need for institutional order. In such settings the vigorous use of reason "may often be very narrowly restricted." This is, of course, not to say that Kant would have endorsed the Supreme Court decisions of the late sixties, only that they can be seen as part of one tradition of liberal thought.

By the early 1970s this position had become liberal dogma. John Rawls, in his 1971 neo-Kantian treatise, *A Theory of Justice,* made distinctions very similar to those that contemporary courts were working out. In a just society, Rawls argued, the intolerant must be tolerated. Repression was justifiable only when someone's personal security was threatened or when "the institutions of liberty are in danger." Just as the courts were doing at the very same time, Rawls drew the relevant lines at the point of imminent violence and at the disruption of functioning institutions. Within this frame of reference, the felt need for robust civic discussion would trump any discomfort about the lack of civil etiquette or occasional expressions of irrational bigotry. As the liberal historian C. Vann

Woodward put it in 1975, "freedom of expression is a paramount value, more important than civility or rationality."

By 1990 this would be a controversial position within Left and liberal circles. In the late 1980s the notion of "offensiveness" reentered progressive political thought, at this point connected with arguments about the debilitating effect of rude insults and slurs on historically subjugated peoples. Speech codes adopted by a few campuses explicitly used "offensiveness" as a criterion to forbid some forms of expression. Some law professors indicated qualified respect for *Chaplinsky v. New Hampshire.* For them, it was no longer a matter of principle that the intolerant must be tolerated. The other side on this debate continued to argue that the concern for verbal niceties undermined free speech. In 1989 and 1991, cases reviewing campus codes outlawing offensive speech reached the federal courts. In both, the codes were declared unconstitutional. By the early 1990s, these debates not only divided progressives from conservatives but also split the Left-liberal community itself into those defending the "1970 position" and those adhering to arguments developed in the late 1980s. To some, at least, C. Vann Woodward's attitudes about free speech no longer sounded particularly progressive.

Institutional decorum coupled with a relatively unregulated civic forum is one historic way liberal politics has handled the issue of order and freedom. This was the path chosen by U.S. courts in the late 1960s, a legal version of the informalization going on in American society at large. While this perspective was no longer universally accepted on the left of the American spectrum by the early 1990s (perhaps *because* it was no longer universally accepted on the Left), it gained credence at the center and the right. And for the time being, at least, it has remained the law of the land.

THE COUNTERCULTURE: A PHOTO ESSAY

Many Americans formed opinions of the hippie counterculture by looking at photos like the ones in this visual essay. For the moment, imagine that you are a forty-year-old factory worker, trying to make some sense of the counterculture from these photographs. What can be learned from the pictures? What conclusions might one draw about countercultural attitudes toward gender? The body? The Vietnam war? Patriotism? Are the young people in these photographs engaged in acts of incivility? Do they look uncivil?

A San Francisco Hippie, Peddling a Local Newspaper, 1967.
National Archives.

358

Cornell University Freshmen, 1972.
National Archives.

A Rally Against the Vietnam War, Bryant Park, New York City, April 1970.
National Archives.

THE UNCIVIL WORLD
OF THE BLACK PANTHERS

By the late 1960s, the Black Panther Party for Self-Defense had become a touch-stone for those fearful of the politics of incivility. Founded in 1966 by Huey Newton and Bobby Seale, the Panthers were perhaps best known for the open bearing of weapons, for a program of free breakfasts for schoolchildren, and for a series of violent confrontations with local police departments, most initiated by the police with the intent of destroying an organization considered dangerous.

In 1970, the Committee on Internal Security of the House of Representatives opened hearings on Black Panther activities in Philadelphia, Detroit, Indianapolis, Omaha, and other cities. Of special concern to the committee was the Panthers' hostility toward the police, reflected in the Panthers' frequent use of the phrase "off the pig" and in cartoons appearing in the party's newspaper, The Black Panther. *Several of the cartoons, and a selection from the hearings, are reprinted here. If you were a member of the Committee on Internal Security, what would you have recommended? What does the episode reveal about the era?*

From *The Black Panther,* **November 16, 1968.**

The Black Panther cartoons appeared in the Black Panther Party newspaper, *The Black Panther.* They are reprinted in U.S., Congress, House, Committee on Internal Security, *Hearings before the Committee on Internal Security,* 91st Cong., 2nd sess., July 21–24, 1970, *Black Panther Party,* part 3: *Investigation of Activities in Detroit, Mich.; Philadelphia, Pa.; and Indianapolis, Ind.* (Washington, D.C.: GPO, 1970), Appendix, Committee Exhibit No. 1. The testimony is from U.S. Congress, House, Committee on Internal Security, *Hearings before the Committee on Internal Security,* 91st Cong., 2nd sess., October 6, 7, 8, 13, 14, 15, and November 17, 1970, *Black Panther Party,* part 4: *National Office Operation and Investigation of Activities in Des Moines, Iowa, and Omaha, Nebr.* (Washington, D.C.: GPO, 1971).

From *The Black Panther*, November 23, 1967.

TESTIMONY OF DONALD BERRY (JULY 21, 1970)

MR. [STEPHEN] ROMINES [ASSISTANT COUNSEL]. Will you state your full name for
    the record, please?

MR. BERRY. Donald Berry.

MR. ROMINES. Where do you reside, Mr. Berry?

MR. BERRY. Detroit, Mich.

MR. ROMINES. How long have you lived in Detroit?

MR. BERRY. All my life.

MR. ROMINES. How old are you?

MR. BERRY. Thirty-eight. . . .

MR. ROMINES. Where were you a member of the Black Panther Party?

MR. BERRY. In the city of Detroit, Mich.

MR. ROMINES. When did you join the party?

MR. BERRY. Around 1967, the year after it was formed. . . .

MR. ROMINES. Why did you join the Black Panther Party, Mr. Berry?

MR. BERRY. At the time I joined the Panthers, for the good the Panthers were doing. I had studied the Panthers before I joined and I seen a lot of good things they were doing for the black community. This I wanted to be a part of, as long as they were helping our people working in the community, helping the children, working with the people, this was good. I wanted to be a part of this.

MR. ROMINES. How long did you remain a member of the Panther Party?

MR. BERRY. For approximately 3 years. . . .

MR. ROMINES. Mr. Berry, I hand you what has been marked Committee Exhibit No. 1, which is a collection of cartoons which have appeared in various issues of the Black Panther Party newspaper on certain dates. The dates are indicated on each page of the exhibit with each cartoon. I ask you to look at that and see if you have observed those cartoons before.

MR. BERRY. Yes, I have.

MR. ROMINES. Where have you seen those cartoons before?

MR. BERRY. In the Black Panther paper.

MR. ROMINES. Would you have an opinion, Mr. Berry, as to the reason or the purpose that the Black Panther Party paper publishes these cartoons?

MR. BERRY. I think they are trying to say something to the people, in other words, this is what should be done or this is what we should do or this is what needs to be done. In other words, like saying one picture can be worth more than a thousand words. In other words, rather than sit down and tell you this they will show you a picture, even to a kid. Now, the average kid, he will look at this and say is this what I am supposed to do or should I be doing this? Then he sits down and looks at the picture and that gives him some kind of idea.

MR. ROMINES. How would you yourself describe and characterize these cartoons? What do they represent to you?

MR. BERRY. To me they represent a bunch of foolishness, that is all, and silly ideas.

MR. ROMINES. Would you have an opinion as to what they are intended to represent to the people?

MR. BERRY. To me they intend to represent the killing and sniping and killing of policemen. . . .

MR. ROMINES. We discussed a few moments ago the Panther concept of racism. As I look through Exhibit 1, I see a number of cartoons depicting either policemen or pigs, depending on how you want to use your terms. I notice that none of them is depicted as being black. There are black policemen, I presume?

MR. BERRY. Yes, there are; there are quite a few. You know I have thought about that, too. The Panthers say we are not racist, we don't believe in separation, but I have never yet seen a cartoon in a Panther paper with anything being done to a black policeman.

MR. ROMINES. What is the Black Panther attitude toward black policemen?

MR. BERRY. Now in Detroit they feel the same. They talk the same toward a black policeman as they do a white policeman because they have even put pictures of certain ones in the paper that were working as undercover agents that were found out they were policemen. They put their pictures in the paper saying this is a pig, watch out for him, and all that. They speak the same, but I never see any drawings of any black policemen. They feel the same toward them, a policeman is a policeman.

TESTIMONY OF FRANK BENSON JONES (OCTOBER 7, 1970)

MR. ROMINES. Will you please state your full name for the record?

MR. JONES. Frank Benson Jones.

MR. ROMINES. Where do you reside, Mr. Jones?

MR. JONES. 5050 Creeley Avenue, Richmond, California.

MR. ROMINES. Are you currently employed?

MR. JONES. Yes, I am.

MR. ROMINES. Mr. Jones, did you serve in the Armed Forces?

MR. JONES. Yes, I did.

MR. ROMINES. In which branch?

MR. JONES. The United States Air Force.

MR. ROMINES. When were you discharged?

MR. JONES. February 23, 1966.

MR. ROMINES. What is the date of your birth, please?

MR. JONES. August 21, 1938.

MR. ROMINES. Mr. Jones, are you now or have you ever been a member of the Black Panther Party?

MR. JONES. Yes, I have been but I am not now.

MR. ROMINES. When did you join the Black Panther Party?

MR. JONES. The date is a little difficult; I can't give you an exact date, sometime in May or June of 1968.

MR. ROMINES. Where did you join the party?

MR. JONES. In Oakland, California.

MR. ROMINES. Why did you join the party?

MR. JONES. I thought the Black Panther Party was doing something that needed to be done. They were opposing racism, and I felt that because racism was a problem in the United States that the party was serving the necessary need.

MR. ROMINES. What, Mr. Jones, in your opinion, is the purpose of the cartoons?

MR. JONES. I consider them sort of political satire. How often I have had to explain this before and I often use the analogy of, say, a political cartoon stating, "Stamp out litter bugs." You might see a giant shoe about to smash a bug, but that in no sense means that you are to kill the next guy you see throw paper on the streets, you know. This is the way the cartoons in the Black Panther paper are used. There has been some discussion about how this affects people, and I often say the way the cartoon effects a person is dependent upon their psychological bent.

MR. ROMINES. Let's back up and go at it first of all from the way they are intended. You say as a political satire?

MR. JONES. Yes.

MR. ROMINES. You use your analogy, but tell me exactly what you think they are trying to satirize.

MR. JONES. I think they are saying that policemen who don't conduct themselves as police officers and who engage in criminal activity in the black community could be removed from the black community.

MR. [JOHN] ASHBROOK [REPRESENTATIVE, OHIO]. Is that really the case? I have in front of me a cartoon which shows, as you pointed out, a police officer depicted as a pig, and I suppose what they refer to as one of the brothers stabbing him in the back with all kinds of blood oozing out. And it says underneath it, "The only good pig, is a dead pig." There isn't any real way you could construe that into being a satire or being a commentary. That is about as definite as one could be. "The only good pig, is a dead pig," and here it is in the so-called Black Panther Coloring Book. How could that be construed to be satire in the context of what you have just said, that it is all in the mind of a person? What possible connotation could there be in the mind of a beholder that would not be violence prone, murder prone or in a sense opening up a dialogue. That is what I gather from your statement, but it is not borne out by some phenomena.

MR. JONES. Is that from the Black Panther paper?

MR. ASHBROOK. It is from the Black Panther Coloring Book.

MR. JONES. Some of those cartoons may have been used in the paper. But to answer your question, you said that the caption states that the only good pig is a dead pig. Then you have to define what is meant by "pig." If a pig is intended to be or if you believe that a pig is a policeman who conducts himself improperly and in a criminal manner in a black community or in any community, then I would like for you to tell me how you could ever call this person, if he is alive, indeed a good policeman, you see.

MR. ASHBROOK. That is not what it says. It says the only good pig is a dead pig.

MR. JONES. That is right, because a pig would be the pig who was most criminal, you see what I mean? Either the pig who is going to come in and brutalize people——

MR. ASHBROOK. Up is down, fair is foul, in is out.

MR. JONES. You might say the only good polio germ is the dead polio germ.

MR. ASHBROOK. That is the point you are starting out with the connotation that he has to be bad.

MR. JONES. They don't say the only good policeman is a dead policeman; it says the only good pig is a dead pig. In other words you are using the phrase, the only good bad policeman is a dead bad policeman.

MR. ASHBROOK. In your Black Panther newspaper have you ever referred to a policeman as a policeman or to a good policeman? Isn't there almost an incessant use of the word "pig"? I read it fairly closely and I don't ever recall seeing the word policeman.

MR. JONES. I believe the word policeman has been used in the paper and I believe it was used while I was editor. But the majority of the time they will use the term "pig," yes.

MR. ASHBROOK. I found it particularly interesting because of your response, which I think is a reasonable response, that it is all in the mind of a person, it is what a person thinks, but I just don't see any connotation, to be quite honest with you, that would be read into this, particularly somebody stabbing the knife in the back and saying, "The only good pig is a dead pig." Maybe the average person goes through a semantical exercise that you are suggesting, but I just really don't see it, to be quite honest with you. I would have to respectfully disagree with that connotation.

MR. JONES. It really depends on your starting point. If you start with the assumption that the Black Panthers advocate killing policemen, then you would probably draw from that cartoon, you would think the cartoon implies the Black Panthers are advocating the killing of policemen.

MR. ASHBROOK. Usually if you have a knife in somebody's back, normally the average person would be advocating killing somebody.

MR. JONES. If you start with the assumption or the belief that the Black Panther Party is in favor of removing policemen from the community who do not conduct themselves properly, then you might see this is a cartoon depicting the removal of a policeman who does not conduct himself in a proper manner.

MR. ASHBROOK. We are not talking about remove, we are talking about killing somebody. This is about the most violent way you could remove somebody from the scene, good or bad.

MR. JONES. That, of course, is the cartoonist's prerogative, how he depicts the removal.

MR. ASHBROOK. I just wanted to make sure this was part of the record. It is a little bit like I was talking to what I would call a more liberal-minded minister the other day and I asked him about the Black Panther Coloring Book. And he said there is some deep-seated psychological meaning behind this and he said, "I think they are just trying to tell us something."

I said, "Yes, with a knife in your back and a gun in your nose." I suppose you could read anything into it at all.

MR. JONES. I can give you another example, possibly, of how cartoons have been used to depict this. During World War II it was not unusual to see a cartoon in the GI Joe comic books of GI Joe killing a Japanese soldier who might have been drawn to some outrageous proportions or have outrageously ethnic physical characteristics, and this was accepted because at the time the Japanese were considered to be enemies of the United States. So now if you think of this, if you saw that same cartoon now while there is peace existing among the Japanese people and the American people, you would not be influenced by this particular cartoonist's depiction.

Now if you start with the assumption that there must be something wrong to make people visualize the police this way, as an enemy, then you see what actually motivates a person to draw that type of picture and why it would be accepted by anyone. It would only be accepted by a person who believes that the police is indeed his enemy. You don't advocate killing the policeman, and I don't.

MR. ASHBROOK. I accept that. If you start from the idea that the police is the enemy, this is logical. I merely want to put in the record also a comment which was in the Black Panther magazine, a cartoon signed "Emory," as you know, and it says:

> So, here is where we began to create our revolutionary art—we draw pictures of our brothers with stoner guns with one bullet going through forty pigs taking out their intestines along the way—another brother comes along, rips off their technical equipment; brothers in tanks guarding the black house and the black community—also launching rockets on U.S. military bases—Minister of Justice H. Rap Brown burning America down; he knows she plans to never come around; Prime Minister of Colonized Afro-American Stokely Carmichael with hand-grenade in hand pointed at the Statue of Liberty; preaching we must have undying love for our people; LeRoi Jones asking, "Who will survive in America?" "Black people will survive in America"—taking what they want— Minister of Defense Huey P. Newton defending the black community—two pigs down two less to go.

And so on and so on. Again this opens up a constructive dialogue, probably. I would have to be frank, among those who miss the point. If you start from the theory that the policeman is an enemy, then what they refer to, I suppose, is revolutionary art and they make a lot of sense.

But I think the record ought to show that it is not exactly correct to say, and the only criticism I would have of your testimony is I don't think it is exactly correct to say you could look at a cartoon like this and conclude that it is only what is in the mind of the beholder. I don't think many reasonable people would have a difference of opinion. When you see a policeman being stabbed in the back and blood coming out, this is not something that opens up a constructive dialogue; this is something that is inciting to violence.

MR. JONES. This is because it is a popular usage. To keep the record straight that statement you read was a statement by Emory Douglas, not by the Black Panther Party or anybody that represents the Black Panther Party as spokesman.

MR. ASHBROOK. It was printed by the Black Panthers?

MR. JONES. Under the byline of Emory Douglas, so it is attributed to Emory, not to the Black Panther Party. Popular usage has actually altered the use of the term "pig." So when you see the cartoon there and you see a pig in a policeman's uniform, this does not necessarily connote to you a policeman who conducts himself improperly, it merely carries the connotation or indicates the inference of that being any policeman.

MR. ASHBROOK. That is correct, I would buy that.

MR. JONES. What you are doing in essence is applying a kind of ex post facto logic.

MR. ASHBROOK. Murdering somebody whether he is good or bad is not ex post facto.

MR. JONES. It depends on the status of the murder. For instance it is happening in Vietnam.

MR. ASHBROOK. Here is a man stabbing him in the back; there is no way you can make that something you are striking a blow for.

MR. JONES. If a Vietcong would turn and run, you would shoot him in the back.

MR. ASHBROOK. You will admit that Black Panthers virtually rule out the possibility that a policeman can be a good guy?

MR. JONES. No, I don't, because the Black Panther Party has circulated a petition in Oakland asking for community control of the police. They are merely saying the police must be responsive to the community they are serving. When they are not responsive and live outside that community and have an opportunity to conduct themselves in a violent manner, then we are saying that they must change this situation.

From *The Black Panther*, May 4, 1969.

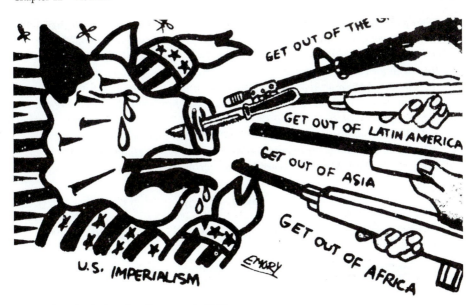

From *The Black Panther*, **January 4, 1969.**

VIETNAM

For more than two decades, the United States tried, and failed, to create a Vietnam suitable to its own vision of the postwar world. This failure became most apparent in the 1960s, when the fighting of the war divided Americans into bitter factions. Apologists for John Kennedy believed that he would have avoided full-scale involvement. But Kennedy had remarked that a withdrawal from Vietnam would mean collapse in Southeast Asia; and by 1963 he had sent 15,000 advisers to the country, more than fifteen times Dwight Eisenhower's commitment. Lyndon Johnson also believed in the domino theory and defined the Vietnam problem as simple communist aggression, and in 1964, he inaugurated systematic air attacks on North Vietnam. But neither the air war nor an additional half-million American troops were sufficient to bring anything resembling victory. Even before the January 1968 Tet offensive, when Viet Cong and North Vietnamese attacks on major South Vietnamese cities made clear that the American claim to be winning the war was a sham, many Americans had come to question the war in moral terms. Over 200,000 marched against the war in Washington, D.C., in 1967. When Richard Nixon in 1970 moved ground troops into Cambodia, students closed down many colleges and universities in protest. By 1973, as Nixon withdrew the last of the nation's ground troops, the Eisenhower consensus lay in ruins.

To illustrate the polarization that the Vietnam War produced, and to offer some sense of how reasonable people could find themselves at loggerheads over this conflict, we have assembled two disparate views on the war. The first, a

1965 address by President Lyndon Johnson, reveals how a socially engaged, activist president could see the war as a high priority and, indeed, allow the war to interfere with his domestic agenda. The second, a 1971 statement delivered to a Senate committee by John Kerry (a future senator), representing the Vietnam Veterans Against the War, condemned the conflict with as much passion, conviction, and eloquence as Johnson had brought to his defense of the war six years earlier.

How did Johnson defend the war in Vietnam? How would Kerry have responded to Johnson's arguments? According to Kerry's statement, what had happened in the intervening years to make the war seem so unpalatable?

Lyndon Johnson

PATTERN FOR PEACE IN SOUTHEAST ASIA (1965)

Last week seventeen nations sent their views to some two dozen countries having an interest in Southeast Asia. We are joining those seventeen countries and stating our American policy tonight, which we believe will contribute toward peace in this area of the world.

I have come here to review once again with my own people the views of the American government.

Tonight Americans and Asians are dying for a world where each people may choose its own path to change. This is the principle for which our ancestors fought in the valleys of Pennsylvania. It is a principle for which our sons fight tonight in the jungles of Vietnam.

Vietnam is far away from this quiet campus. We have no territory there, nor do we seek any. The war is dirty and brutal and difficult. And some 400 young men, born into an America that is bursting with opportunity and promise, have ended their lives on Vietnam's steaming soil.

Why must we take this painful road? Why must this nation hazard its ease, its interest, and its power for the sake of a people so far away?

We fight because we must fight if we are to live in a world where every country can shape its own destiny, and only in such a world will our own freedom be finally secure.

This kind of world will never be built by bombs or bullets. Yet the infirmities of man are such that force must often precede reason and the waste of war, the works of peace. We wish that this were not so. But we must deal with the world as it is, if it is ever to be as we wish.

The world as it is in Asia is not a serene or peaceful place.

The first reality is that North Vietnam has attacked the independent nation of South Vietnam. Its object is total conquest. Of course, some of the people of

Speech made at Johns Hopkins University, Baltimore, Maryland, April 17, 1965, Department of State *Bulletin,* April 26, 1965, pp. 606–610.

South Vietnam are participating in attack on their own government. But trained men and supplies, orders and arms, flow in a constant stream from north to south.

This support is the heartbeat of the war.

And it is a war of unparalleled brutality. Simple farmers are the targets of assassination and kidnapping. Women and children are strangled in the night because their men are loyal to their government. And helpless villages are ravaged by sneak attacks. Large-scale raids are conducted on towns, and terror strikes in the heart of cities.

The confused nature of this conflict cannot mask the fact that it is the new face of an old enemy.

Over this war—and all Asia—is another reality: the deepening shadow of Communist China. The rulers in Hanoi are urged on by Beijing. This is a regime that has destroyed freedom in Tibet, attacked India, and has been condemned by the United Nations for aggression in Korea. It is a nation that is helping the forces of violence in almost every continent. The contest in Vietnam is part of a wider pattern of aggressive purposes.

Why Are We in South Vietnam?

Why are these realities our concern? Why are we in South Vietnam?

We are there because we have a promise to keep. Since 1954 every American president has offered support to the people of South Vietnam. We have helped to build, and we have helped to defend. Thus, over many years, we have made a national pledge to help South Vietnam defend its independence.

And I intend to keep that promise.

To dishonor that pledge, to abandon this small and brave nation to its enemies, and to the terror that must follow, would be an unforgivable wrong.

We are also there to strengthen world order. Around the globe, from Berlin to Thailand, are people whose well-being rests in part on the belief that they can count on us if they are attacked. To leave Vietnam to its fate would shake the confidence of all these people in the value of an American commitment and in the value of America's word. The result would be increased unrest and instability, and even wider war.

We are also there because there are great stakes in the balance. Let no one think for a moment that retreat from Vietnam would bring an end to conflict. The battle would be renewed in one country and then another. The central lesson of our time is that the appetite of aggression is never satisfied. To withdraw from one battlefield means only to prepare for the next. We must say in Southeast Asia—as we did in Europe—in the words of the Bible: "Hitherto shalt thou come, but no further."

There are those who say that all our effort there will be futile—that China's power is such that it is bound to dominate all Southeast Asia. But there is no end to that argument until all the nations of Asia are swallowed up.

There are those who wonder why we have a responsibility there. Well, we have it there for the same reason that we have a responsibility for the defense of

Europe. World War II was fought in both Europe and Asia, and when it ended we found ourselves with continued responsibility for the defense of freedom.

Our objective is the independence of South Vietnam and its freedom from attack. We want nothing for ourselves—only that the people of South Vietnam be allowed to guide their own country in their own way. We will do everything necessary to reach that objective, and we will do only what is absolutely necessary.

In recent months attacks on South Vietnam were stepped up. Thus it became necessary for us to increase our response and to make attacks by air. This is not a change of purpose. It is a change in what we believe that purpose requires.

We do this in order to slow down aggression.

We do this to increase the confidence of the brave people of South Vietnam who have bravely borne this brutal battle for so many years with so many casualties.

And we do this to convince the leaders of North Vietnam—and all who seek to share their conquest—of a simple fact:

We will not be defeated.

We will not grow tired.

We will not withdraw, either openly or under the cloak of a meaningless agreement.

We know that air attacks alone will not accomplish all these purposes. But it is our best and prayerful judgment that they are a necessary part of the surest road to peace.

The Path of Peaceful Settlement

We hope that peace will come swiftly. But that is in the hands of others besides ourselves. And we must be prepared for a long continued conflict. It will require patience as well as bravery—the will to endure as well as the will to resist.

I wish it were possible to convince others with words of what we now find it necessary to say with guns and planes: armed hostility is futile—our resources are equal to any challenge—because we fight for values and we fight for principle, rather than territory or colonies, our patience and our determination are unending.

Once this is clear, then it should also be clear that the only path for reasonable men is the path of peaceful settlement. Such peace demands an independent South Vietnam—securely guaranteed and able to shape its own relationships to all others—free from outside interference—tied to no alliance—a military base for no other country.

These are the essentials of any final settlement.

We will never be second in the search for such a peaceful settlement in Vietnam.

There may be many ways to this kind of peace: in discussion or negotiation with the governments concerned; in large groups or in small ones; in the reaffirmation of old agreements or their strengthening with new ones.

We have stated this position over and over again fifty times and more to friend and foe alike. And we remain ready with this purpose for unconditional discussions.

And until that bright and necessary day of peace we will try to keep conflict from spreading. We have no desire to see thousands die in battle—Asians or Americans. We have no desire to devastate that which the people of North Vietnam have built with toil and sacrifice. We will use our power with restraint and with all the wisdom that we can command.

But we will use it.

A Cooperative Effort for Development

This war, like most wars, is filled with terrible irony. For what do the people of North Vietnam want? They want what their neighbors also desire—food for their hunger, health for their bodies, a chance to learn, progress for their country, and an end to the bondage of material misery. And they would find all these things far more readily in peaceful association with others than in the endless course of battle.

These countries of Southeast Asia are homes for millions of impoverished people. Each day these people rise at dawn and struggle through until the night to wrest existence from the soil. They are often wracked by diseases, plagued by hunger, and death comes at the early age of forty.

Stability and peace do not come easily in such a land. Neither independence nor human dignity will ever be won, though, by arms alone. It also requires the works of peace. The American people have helped generously in times past in these works, and now there must be a much more massive effort to improve the life of man in that conflict-torn corner of our world.

The first step is for the countries of Southeast Asia to associate themselves in a greatly expanded cooperative effort for development. We would hope that North Vietnam would take its place in the common effort just as soon as peaceful cooperation is possible.

The United Nations is already actively engaged in development in this area, and as far back as 1961 I conferred with our authorities in Vietnam in connection with their work there. And I would hope tonight that the secretary-general of the United Nations could use the prestige of his great office and his deep knowledge of Asia to initiate, as soon as possible, with the countries of that area, a plan for cooperation in increased development.

For our part I will ask the Congress to join in a billion-dollar American investment in this effort as soon as it is under way. And I would hope that all other industrialized countries, including the Soviet Union, will join in this effort to replace despair with hope and terror with progress.

The task is nothing less than to enrich the hopes and existence of more than a hundred million people. And there is much to be done.

The vast Mekong River can provide food and water and power on a scale to dwarf even our own TVA [Tennessee Valley Authority]. The wonders of modern medicine can be spread through villages where thousands die every year from lack of care. Schools can be established to train people in the skills needed to manage the process of development. And these objectives, and more, are within the reach of a cooperative and determined effort.

I also intend to expand and speed up a program to make available our farm surpluses to assist in feeding and clothing the needy in Asia. We should not allow people to go hungry and wear rags while our own warehouses overflow with an abundance of wheat and corn and rice and cotton.

So I will very shortly name a special team of outstanding, patriotic, and distinguished Americans to inaugurate our participation in these programs. This team will be headed by Mr. Eugene Black, the very able former president of the World Bank.

The Dream of Our Generation

This will be a disorderly planet for a long time. In Asia, and elsewhere, the forces of the modern world are shaking old ways and uprooting ancient civilizations. There will be turbulence and struggle and even violence. Great social change—as we see in our own country—does not always come without conflict.

We must also expect that nations will on occasion be in dispute with us. It may be because we are rich, or powerful, or because we have made some mistakes, or because they honestly fear our intentions. However, no nation need ever fear that we desire their land, or to impose our will, or to dictate their institutions.

But we will always oppose the effort of one nation to conquer another nation.

We will do this because our own security is at stake.

But there is more to it than that. For our generation has a dream. It is a very old dream. But we have the power, and now we have the opportunity to make that dream come true.

For centuries nations have struggled among each other. But we dream of a world where disputes are settled by law and reason. And we will try to make it so.

For most of history men have hated and killed one another in battle. But we dream of an end to war. And we will try to make it so.

For all existence most men have lived in poverty, threatened by hunger. But we dream of a world where all are fed and charged with hope. And we will help to make it so.

The ordinary men and women of North Vietnam and South Vietnam, of China and India, of Russia and America, are brave people. They are filled with the same proportions of hate and fear, of love and hope. Most of them want the same things for themselves and their families. Most of them do not want their sons to ever die in battle, or to see their homes, or the homes of others, destroyed.

Well, this can be their world yet. Man now has the knowledge—always before denied—to make this planet serve the real needs of the people who live on it.

I know this will not be easy. I know how difficult it is for reason to guide passion, and love to master hate. The complexities of this world do not bow easily to pure and consistent answers.

But the simple truths are there just the same. We just all try to follow them as best we can.

Power, Witness to Human Folly

We often say how impressive power is. But I do not find it impressive at all. The guns and the bombs, the rockets and the warships, are all symbols of human failure. They are necessary symbols. They protect what we cherish. But they are witness to human folly.

A dam built across a great river is impressive.

In the countryside where I was born, and where I live, I have seen the night illuminated, and the kitchen warmed, and the home heated, where once the cheerless night and the ceaseless cold held sway. And all this happened because electricity came to our area along the humming wires of the REA [Rural Electrification Administration]. Electrification of the countryside—yes, that, too, is impressive.

A rich harvest in a hungry land is impressive.

The sight of healthy children in a classroom is impressive.

These—not mighty arms—are the achievements that the American nation believes to be impressive. And if we are steadfast, the time may come when all other nations will also find it so.

Every night before I turn out the lights to sleep I ask myself this question: Have I done everything that I can do to unite this country? Have I done everything I can to help unite the world, to try to bring peace and hope to all the peoples of the world? Have I done enough?

Ask yourselves that question in your homes—and in this hall tonight. Have we, each of us, all done all we can do? Have we done enough?

We may well be living in the time foretold many years ago when it was said: "I call heaven and earth to record this day against you, that I have set before you life and death, blessing and cursing: therefore choose life, that both thou and thy seed may live."

This generation of the world must choose: destroy or build, kill or aid, hate or understand. We can do all these things on a scale that has never been dreamed of before.

Well, we will choose life. And so doing, we will prevail over the enemies within man, and over the natural enemies of all mankind.

John Kerry

VIETNAM VETERANS AGAINST THE WAR (1971)

Thank you very much, Senator Fulbright, Senator Javits, Senator Symington, Senator Pell. I would like to say for the record, and also for the men behind me who are also wearing the uniform and their medals, that my sitting here is really symbolic. I am not here as John Kerry. I am here as one member of the group of 1,000, which is a small representation of a very much larger group of

Statement by John Kerry, April 23, 1971, to the Senate Committee on Foreign Relations, *Congressional Record*, vol. 117, pp. 11738–11740.

veterans in this country, and were it possible for all of them to sit at this table they would be here and have the same kind of testimony.

I would simply like to speak in very general terms. I apologize if my statement is general because I received notification yesterday you would hear me and I am afraid that because of the court injunction I was up most of the night and haven't had a great deal of time to prepare for this hearing.

I would like to talk on behalf of all those veterans and say that several months ago in Detroit we had an investigation at which over 150 honorably discharged, and many very highly decorated, veterans testified to war crimes committed in Southeast Asia. These were not isolated incidents but crimes committed on a day to day basis with the full awareness of officers at all levels of command.

It is impossible to describe to you exactly what did happen in Detroit—the emotions in the room and the feelings of the men who were reliving their experiences in Vietnam. They relived the absolute horror of what this country, in a sense, made them do.

They told stories that at times they had personally raped, cut off ears, cut off heads, taped wires from portable telephones to human genitals and turned up the power, cut off limbs, blown up bodies, randomly shot at civilians, razed villages in fashion reminiscent of Genghis Khan, shot cattle and dogs for fun, poisoned food stocks, and generally ravaged the countryside of South Vietnam in addition to the normal ravage of war and the normal and very particular ravaging which is done by the applied bombing power of this country.

We call this investigation the Winter Soldier Investigation. The term Winter Soldier is a play on words of Thomas Paine's in 1776 when he spoke of the Sunshine Patriot and summer time soldiers who deserted at Valley Forge because the going was rough.

We who have come here to Washington have come here because we feel we have to be winter soldiers now. We could come back to this country, we could be quiet, we could hold our silence, we could not tell what went on in Vietnam, but we feel because of what threatens this country, not the reds, but the crimes which we are committing that threaten it, that we have to speak out.

I would like to talk to you a little bit about what the result is of the feelings these men carry with them after coming back from Vietnam. The country doesn't know it yet but it has created a monster, a monster in the form of millions of men who have been taught to deal and to trade in violence and who are given the chance to die for the biggest nothing in history; men who have returned with a sense of anger and a sense of betrayal which no one has yet grasped.

As a veteran and one who feels this anger I would like to talk about it. We are angry because we feel we have been used in the worst fashion by the administration of this country.

In 1970 at West Point Vice President Agnew said "some glamorize the criminal misfits of society while our best men die in Asian rice paddies to preserve the freedom which most of those misfits abuse," and this was used as a rallying point for our effort in Vietnam.

But for us, as boys in Asia whom the country was supposed to support, his statement is a terrible distortion from which we can only draw a very deep sense of revulsion, and hence the anger of some of the men who are here in Washington today. It is a distortion because we in no way consider ourselves the best men of this country; because those he calls misfits were standing up for us in a way that nobody else in this country dared to; because so many who have died would have returned to this country to join the misfits in their efforts to ask for an immediate withdrawal from South Vietnam; because so many of those best men have returned as quadruplegics and amputees—and they lie forgotten in Veterans Administration Hospitals in this country which fly the flag which so many have chosen as their own personal symbol—and we cannot consider ourselves America's best men when we are ashamed of and hated for what we were called on to do in Southeast Asia.

In our opinion, and from our experience, there is nothing in South Vietnam which could happen that realistically threatens the United States of America. And to attempt to justify the loss of one American life in Vietnam, Cambodia or Laos by linking such loss to the preservation of freedom, which those misfits supposedly abuse, is to us the height of criminal hypocrisy, and it is that kind of hypocrisy which we feel has torn this country apart.

We are probably much more angry than that, but I don't want to go into the foreign policy aspects because I am outclassed here. I know that all of you talk about every possible alternative to getting out of Vietnam. We understand that. We know you have considered the seriousness of the aspects to the utmost level and I am not going to try to dwell on that. But I want to relate to you the feeling that many of the men who have returned to this country express because we are probably angriest about all that we were told about Vietnam and about the mystical war against communism.

We found that not only was it a civil war, an effort by a people who had for years been seeking their liberation from any colonial influence whatsoever, but also we found that the Vietnamese whom we had enthusiastically molded after our own image were hard put to take up the fight against the threat we were supposedly saving them from.

We found most people didn't even know the difference between communism and democracy. They only wanted to work in rice paddies without helicopters strafing them and bombs with napalm burning their villages and tearing their country apart. They wanted everything to do with the war, particularly with this foreign presence of the United States of America, to leave them alone in peace, and they practiced the art of survival by siding with whichever military force was present at a particular time, be it Viet Cong, North Vietnamese or American.

We found also that all too often American men were dying in those rice paddies for want of support from their allies. We saw first hand how monies from American taxes were used for a corrupt dictatorial regime. We saw that many people in this country had a one-sided idea of who was kept free by our flag, and blacks provided the highest percentage of casualties. We saw Vietnam ravaged equally by American bombs and search and destroy missions, as well as by Viet Cong terrorism, and yet we listened while this country tried to blame all of the havoc on the Viet Cong.

We rationalized destroying villages in order to save them. We saw America lose her sense of morality as she accepted very cooly a My Lai and refused to give up the image of American soldiers who hand out chocolate bars and chewing gum.

We learned the meaning of free fire zones, shooting anything that moves, and we watched while America placed a cheapness on the lives of orientals.

We watched the United States falsification of body counts, in fact the glorification of body counts. We listened while month after month we were told the back of the enemy was about to break. We fought using weapons against "oriental human beings." We fought using weapons against those people which I do not believe this country would dream of using were we fighting in the European theater. We watched while men charged up hills because a general said that hill has to be taken, and after losing one platoon or two platoons they marched away to leave the hill for re-occupation by the North Vietnamese. We watched pride allow the most unimportant battles to be blown into extravaganzas, because we couldn't lose, and we couldn't retreat, and because it didn't matter how many American bodies were lost to prove that point, and so there were Hamburger Hills and Khe Sahns and Hill 81s and Fire Base 6s, and so many others.

Now we are told that the men who fought there must watch quietly while American lives are lost so that we can exercise the incredible arrogance of Vietnamizing the Vietnamese.

Each day to facilitate the process by which the United States washes her hands of Vietnam someone has to give up his life so that the United States doesn't have to admit something that the entire world already knows, so that we can't say that we have made a mistake. Someone has to die so that President Nixon won't be, and these are his words, "the first President to lose a war."

We are asking Americans to think about that because how do you ask a man to be the last man to die in Vietnam? How do you ask a man to be the last man to die for a mistake? But we are trying to do that, and we are doing it with thousands of rationalizations, and if you read carefully the President's last speech to the people of this country, you can see that he says, and says clearly, "but the issue, gentlemen, the issue, is communism, and the question is whether or not we will leave that country to the communists or whether or not we will try to give it hope to be a free people." But the point is they are not a free people now under us. They are not a free people, and we cannot fight communism all over the world. I think we should have learned that lesson by now.

But the problem of veterans goes beyond this personal problem, because you think about a poster in this country with a picture of Uncle Sam and the picture says "I want you." And a young man comes out of high school and says, "that is fine, I am going to serve my country," and he goes to Vietnam and he shoots and he kills and he does his job. Or maybe he doesn't kill. Maybe he just goes and he comes back, and when he gets back to this country he finds that he isn't really wanted, because the largest corps of unemployed in the country—it varies depending on who you get it from, the Veterans Administration says 15 percent and various other sources 22 percent—but the largest corps of unemployed in this country are veterans of this war, and of those veterans 33 percent of the unemployed are black. That means one out of every ten of the nation's unemployed is a veteran of Vietnam.

The hospitals across the country won't, or can't meet their demands. It is not a question of not trying; they haven't got the appropriations. A man recently died after he had a tracheotomy in California, not because of the operation but because there weren't enough personnel to clean the mucus out of his tube and he suffocated to death.

Another young man just died in a New York VA Hospital the other day. A friend of mine was lying in a bed two beds away and tried to help him but he couldn't. He rang a bell and there was nobody there to service that man and so he died of convulsions.

I understand 57 percent of all those entering the VA hospitals talk about suicide. Some 27 percent have tried, and they try because they come back to this country and they have to face what they did in Vietnam, and then they come back and find the indifference of a country that doesn't really care.

Suddenly we are faced with a very sickening situation in this country, because there is no moral indignation and, if there is, it comes from people who are almost exhausted by their past indignations, and I know that many of them are sitting in front of me. The country seems to have lain down and shrugged off something as serious as Laos, just as we calmly shrugged off the loss of 700,000 lives in Pakistan, the so-called greatest disaster of all times.

But we are here as veterans to say we think we are in the midst of the greatest disaster of all times now because they are still dying over there—not just Americans, but Vietnamese—and we are rationalizing leaving that country so that those people can go on killing each other for years to come.

Americans seem to have accepted the idea that the war is winding down, at least for Americans, and they have also allowed the bodies which were once used by a President for statistics to prove that we were winning that war, to be used as evidence against a man who followed orders and who interpreted those orders no differently than hundreds of other men in Vietnam.

We veterans can only look with amazement on the fact that this country has been unable to see there is absolutely no difference between ground troops and a helicopter crew, and yet people have accepted a differentiation fed them by the administration.

No ground troops are in Laos so it is all right to kill Laotians by remote control. But believe me the helicopter crews fill the same body bags and they wreak the same kind of damage on the Vietnamese and Laotian countryside as anybody else, and the President is talking about allowing that to go on for many years to come. One can only ask if we will really be satisfied only when the troops march into Hanoi.

We are asking here in Washington for some action; action from the Congress of the United States of America which has the power to raise and maintain armies, and which by the Constitution also has the power to declare war.

We have come here, not to the President, because we believe that this body can be responsive to the will of the people, and we believe that the will of the people says that we should get out of Vietnam now.

We are here in Washington also to say that the problem of this war is not just a question of war and diplomacy. It is part and parcel of everything that we are trying as human beings to communicate to people in this country—the question of racism, which is rampant in the military, and so many other questions such as the use of weapons; the hypocrisy in our taking umbrage in the Geneva Conventions and using that as justification for a continuation of this war when we are more guilty than any other body of violations of those Geneva Conventions; in the use of free fire zones, harassment interdiction fire, search and destroy missions, the bombings, the torture of prisoners, the killing of prisoners, all accepted policy by many units in South Vietnam. That is what we are trying to say. It is part and parcel of everything.

An American Indian friend of mine who lives in the Indian Nation of Alcatraz put it to me very succinctly. He told me how as a boy on an Indian reservation he had watched television and he used to cheer the cowboys when they came in and shot the Indians, and then suddenly one day he stopped in Vietnam and he said "my God, I am doing to these people the very same thing that was done to my people," and he stopped. And that is what we are trying to say, that we think this thing has to end.

We are also here to ask, and we are here to ask vehemently, where are the leaders of our country? Where is the leadership? We are here to ask where are McNamara, Rostow, Bundy, Gilpatric and so many others? Where are they now that we, the men whom they sent off to war, have returned? These are commanders who have deserted their troops, and there is no more serious crime in the law of war. The Army says they never leave their wounded. The Marines say they never leave even their dead. These men have left all the casualties and retreated behind a pious shield of public rectitude. They have left the real stuff of their reputations bleaching behind them in the sun in this country.

Finally, this administration has done us the ultimate dishonor. They have attempted to disown us and the sacrifices we made for this country. In their blindness and fear they have tried to deny that we are veterans or that we served in Nam. We do not need their testimony. Our own scars and stumps of limbs are witness enough for others and for ourselves.

We wish that a merciful God could wipe away our own memories of that service as easily as this administration has wiped away their memories of us. But all that they have done and all that they can do by this denial is to make more clear than ever our own determination to undertake one last mission—to search out and destroy the last vestige of this barbaric war, to pacify our own hearts, to conquer the hate and the fear that have driven this country these last ten years and more, so when 30 years from now our brothers go down the street without a leg, without an arm, or a face, and small boys ask why, we will be able to say "Vietnam" and not mean a desert, not a filthy obscene memory, but mean instead the place where America finally turned and where soldiers like us helped it in the turning.

Thank you.

the big picture

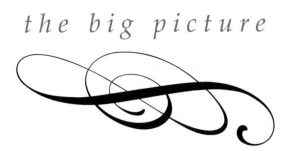

You're home for the holidays. Dad has a few beers and gets riled up. He rants and raves about the glorious and orderly 1950s, and he explains how the "sixties" came along and ruined everything with needless attacks on authority. You have just finished reading about both eras. How do you respond?

chapter thirteen

AMERICA UNDER SIEGE

Whether understood as an era of destructive social upheaval or of productive social reformism, the "sixties" had a number of hard and bitter endings. Politically, the sixties began to end in 1968, when many union and working-class voters, long the mainstay of the Democratic Party, helped elect Richard Nixon. The era definitively terminated in 1972, when Nixon thrashed the liberal Democratic candidate, George McGovern, whose nomination had been made possible by internal changes in the party (motivated by the reformist energies of the sixties) that had given blacks and women larger roles in the political process. Economically, the sixties may have ended in 1971, when the United States experienced its first international trade deficit since 1893. Or they may have ended on October 16, 1973, when the Arab-dominated Organization of Petroleum Exporting Companies (OPEC) responded to American intervention in the Arab-Israeli war by cutting off oil shipments to the United States, Japan, and Western Europe. By early 1974 the stock market was in free fall and problems of inflation and economic stagnation had surfaced that would last nearly another decade. Culturally, one might mark the end of the 1960s by the breakup of the Beatles in 1970, an event that brought to an end the band's effort to produce creative music in a framework of group cooperation—and ushered in an era focusing on self and family, typified by Paul McCartney's self-conscious anthem to his wife, "Lovely Linda" (1971), in which McCartney played all the parts himself.

For those who would like to see the "fall" of the 1970s as a product of the excesses of the 1960s, consider the event known as Watergate. Watergate had its origins in 1969, when the Nixon administration embarked on a campaign to isolate and discredit the peace movement. By 1971 the people charged with this responsibility had moved to the Committee for the Reelection of the President (CREEP), where they were working with former Attorney General John Mitchell on an illegal effort to gather information on political opponents. In June 1972, five CREEP operatives were apprehended at Democratic National Committee headquarters in Washington's Watergate apartment complex. Two years later, when the president's own tape recordings revealed that he had conspired to cover up the break-in, a humiliated Nixon resigned. His legacy (although it also owed something to Lyndon Johnson's lack of candor in handling the war in Vietnam) focused on a new and troublesome attitude toward politics: credibility. He didn't have any. Simply put, many Americans no longer believed what the politicians told them.

Given the depressed economic conditions of the decade, the crisis of confidence in politics, and the working-class-led backlash against the social reform energies of the sixties, it is not surprising that there was little progress made on "reform" fronts in the seventies. To be sure, powerful lobbies of the elderly were able to bring their constituents tangible gains: a new system that indexed social security to changes in the cost of living and a 1978 law that abolished mandatory retirement in most employment. Campaigns for gay rights and women's rights also remained vital through the 1970s. And environmental issues proved able to generate an ongoing consensus for continued government action. But on the critical issues that the sixties had courageously and optimistically raised to prominence—poverty, racism, the decaying inner cities—the consensus was washing away. What was left was a new and mistaken reliance on the mandatory busing of schoolchildren as the solution to all these ills. It was a solution that relied too much on the sacrifices of the white working class and on schools that were inadequate no matter who attended them. It was a solution bound to fail.

Above all it was an age of survival, of getting by until things got better, of coming to terms with limited opportunities. Hence the quintessential movie star of the day was John Travolta, whose characters were ordinary guys whose main task was to achieve a modicum of self-respect, and whose triumphs were limited ones—learning to ride a mechanical bull, or winning a dance contest—won in bars and discos. As for discos, there was no more consensus over the music than over anything else in the 1970s, and its origins in the gay and black communities in the early part of the decade did not endear it to the white working class. Yet disco was enormously popular because it spoke so clearly to the question of survival, with the darkened disco a haven of refuge from a difficult world and the pulsating, irrepressible beat a pacemaker for the walking (or dancing) wounded. In the words of the Bee Gees' 1977 hit, it all came down to "stayin' alive."

Jimmy Carter spoke this language, too, and for four years he ministered to the needs of the population like Mom with a bowl of chicken soup. He worked at labeling the nation's illness—a "malaise" in one speech, a "crisis of purpose" in another. And he patiently explained to Americans how they could survive the new regime of limits by conserving energy and living simpler lives. It was not bad advice at all, and for a time Americans responded enthusiastically to a president that at least seemed honest and credible. But Carter could not solve the riddle of "stagflation"—high rates of inflation and unemployment at the same time. Nor could he do anything much about the Iranian militants who in 1979 took fifty-two American hostages and held them for 444 days—for many Americans, the last in a long series of national humiliations. By 1980, Americans wanted more than survival, and they were willing to listen to anyone who promised to give them back the nation they had lost.

interpretive essay

Susan J. Douglas

GROWING UP FEMALE WITH THE MASS MEDIA

For many years, it was convenient to associate the start of the modern feminist movement with the publication in 1963 of Betty Friedan's best-seller The Feminine Mystique, *which claimed that women had been denied the careers they wanted and deserved because they were depicted only as mothers and homemakers in the women's magazines of the day. Friedan became the first president of the National Organization for Women, founded in 1966. More recently, scholars have emphasized the impact of World War II in producing a generation of women that would want their daughters to do more than have babies and raise children; the civil rights movement, which encouraged women to think of their own lives in terms of egalitarian principles; and the needs of business for a new pool of talented labor, drawing women into the labor force in ever-increasing numbers. Moreover, Friedan's book has come under fire for its neglect of the needs and values of working-class and minority women.*

The feminist movement that emerged in the 1960s was the third such movement of the nineteenth and twentieth centuries. The first culminated in the Seneca Falls [New York] Declaration of 1848, which listed the "repeated injuries on the part of man toward woman, having in direct object the establishment of an absolute tyranny over her." The second culminated in the Nineteenth Amendment to the Constitution (1920), granting suffrage to those women who did not already have it as a result of state action. The most recent movement appeared headed for a similar triumph—the ratification of the Equal Rights Amendment, which would have done little more than grant rights that most women already enjoyed—only to see the amendment defeated in 1982 by a hysterical right wing that conjured up images of men and women forced by the Constitution to use the same toilets.

In the following essay, Susan J. Douglas describes and analyzes media coverage of the feminist movement in the 1970s. How does Douglas characterize that coverage? How does she explain it? What impact did the media have?

On August 26, 1970, Howard K. Smith, the anchorman at ABC News, smirked slightly and read the following lead-in to one of the day's major stories: "Quote. Three things have been difficult to tame. The ocean, fools, and women. We may soon be able to tame the ocean, but fools and women will take a little longer. Unquote." In case viewers missed the gist of the quip, the text of the quotation was projected to the right of Smith on the screen. He continued. "The man who made that statement is Spiro Agnew. He is now touring Asia, wisely, because today all over this nation, the women's liberation movement is marking the fiftieth anniversary of women gaining the vote by demonstrations and strikes." This was the lead-in to ABC's coverage of the Women's Strike for Equality, the largest demonstration in American history up to that time for women's rights. Opening with such a dismissive little epigram from the official verbal hit man and all-around sleazeball—oh, pardon me, vice president—of the Nixon administration, Smith was able to frame ABC's coverage of the strike with considerable condescension while absolving himself and the network of responsibility for such an obviously neanderthal remark. After airing the reports of several correspondents from around the country, Smith ended the segment by quoting West Virginia Senator Jennings Randolph, who characterized the women's movement as "a small band of bra-less bubbleheads." The last thing the viewer saw was the phrase "bra-less bubbleheads" projected on the right portion of the screen. Kinda made you wanna join right up.

Over on CBS, also spurred by the strike, Eric Sevareid, the TV commentator I screamed at most in the early 1970s, dedicated his evening's commentary to the women's movement. He opened by noting that "no husband ever won an argument with a wife, and the secret of a happy marriage is for the man to repeat those three little words, 'I was wrong.'" Dismissing the movement as led by "aroused minorities . . . who are already well off by any comparative measurement," Sevareid asserted that "the plain truth is, most American men are startled by the idea that American women generally are oppressed, and they read with relief the Gallup poll that two-thirds of women don't think they're oppressed either." Reflecting again on the evolution of social movements, he observed, "Many movements grow by simple contagion, thousands discovering they are in pain, though they hadn't noticed it until they were told." After some further commentary about how difficult it was to think of women simply as people, he concluded by lecturing, "As for the organized movement itself, it remains to be seen whether it will unify and remain effective, or will fragment into quarreling, doctrinal groups like the far left student movement and the black movement. It now has the unavoidable opportunity to prove that the masculine notion that women can't get along with other women is another item from the ancient shelf of male mythology." The camera then switched to Walter Cronkite, who added with his usual finality, "And that's the way it is."

These are just two excerpts from the extensive coverage the women's liberation movement received in 1970, but they are typical of how the news media framed what was and continues to be, by almost any measure, one of the most consequential social movements of the twentieth century. Aside from the big yucks the gents shared over "bra-less bubbleheads" and the Agnew quotation, words such as *contagion* likened feminism to a social disease, and there was incessant emphasis on the divisions, real or imagined, within the movement. The news media's stereotypes about feminism—which flattened this complex, rich, multipronged, and often contradictory movement into a cardboard caricature— were of urgent concern to feminist organizers, since most women first learned about the movement through the media. "Rage would not be too strong a word to describe the emotion felt by large numbers of feminists about the media's coverage of the women's movement," noted the first chroniclers of the movement, Judith Hole and Ellen Levine, in 1971. And though rage was exactly the correct response, it should not have been the only response. For what is provocative here is that despite this coverage—perhaps even because of it—increasing numbers of women, and men, came to support varying versions of feminist ideology, and to change their aspirations and their lives accordingly. Membership in NOW, to pick only one example and the most mainstream of the feminist organizations, skyrocketed from 1,200 in 1967 to 48,000 in 1974, with 700 chapters in the United States and nine other countries. By 1972, the movement had an anthem—Helen Reddy's "I Am Woman"—which went gold, hit number one on the charts, and won Reddy a Grammy.

There is no doubt that the news media of the early 1970s played an absolutely central role in turning feminism into a dirty word, and stereotyping the feminist as a hairy-legged, karate-chopping commando with a chip on her shoulder the size of China, really bad clothes, and a complete inability to smile—let alone laugh. But at the same time, by treating the women's liberation movement as a big story, the news media also brought millions of converts to feminism, even if the version many women came to embrace was a shriveled compromise of what others had hoped was possible. And while some stories were shockingly derisive, others were sympathetic. Many reports were ambivalent and confused, taking feminism seriously one minute, mocking it the next. In this way, the news media exacerbated quite keenly the profound cultural schizophrenia about women's place in society that had been building since the 1940s and 1950s.

In 1970, the women's liberation movement burst onto the national agenda. It would not be an exaggeration to say, even with everything else going on then, that this was the story of the year. And in the capable hands of our nation's highly objective journalists, the women's liberation movement seemed to come out of nowhere—or, more frequently, from Pluto. The movement fit the criteria of newsworthiness perfectly. People were demonstrating in the streets, they were charging that America was *not* the democratic, egalitarian oasis its mythology said it was, they were saying and doing outrageous things, *and* they were women. The protesters clashed starkly with the women elsewhere on TV: young, perfectly groomed, always smiling, never complaining, demure, eager to please, eager to consume. Unlike Katy Winters, who urged us to be cool, calm, and collected in all those revolting Secret commercials, these women were angry; they yelled, argued, and accused; they raised their fists and shook them; and they mounted a full-scale attack against Madison Avenue and the prevailing media stereotypes of women. They violated the nation's most sacred conceits about love, marriage, the family, and femininity. They denounced illegal, back-alley abortions, a previously taboo subject, as a form of butchery that had to stop. They talked back to men, invaded their bars and clubs, and even challenged the very fabric of American language, coining terms such as *sexism* and *male chauvinism* while exposing the gender biases in the words *mankind*, *chairman*, and *chick*, to name just a few. They insisted that "the personal is political," that motherhood, marriage, sexual behavior, and dress codes all had to be considered symptoms of a broader political and social system that kept women down. *This* was news. After 1970, there was simply no going back.

Consider what happened in this one year. Women charged *Newsweek* magazine with sex discrimination in hiring and promotion, and their sisters over at the competition filed a similar suit with the New York State Division of Human Rights against Time Inc. In March alone, over one hundred feminists staged an eleven-hour sit-in at the *Ladies' Home Journal,* NBC and CBS each ran a multipart series on the women's movement on their nightly newscasts, *Time* printed a special report called "The War on 'Sexism'" (they still felt compelled to put the offending word in quotation marks), and *The New York Times Magazine* ran a major article by Susan Brownmiller titled "Sisterhood Is Powerful." The *Times* magazine also ran articles that year on the Equal Rights Amendment, on Betty Friedan, and on whether there were biologically determined sex differences between men and women. Kate Millett's *Sexual Politics* became the most talked about best-seller of the year, and Millett herself appeared on the cover of *Time.*

August was another landmark month. On the third, the U.S. Justice Department, prodded by outraged female workers, filed suit against the Libbey-Owens-Ford Company of Toledo, Ohio—the department's first suit against sex discrimination in the workplace. A week later, on August 10, the House of Representatives, prompted by the brilliant tactical work of Representative Martha Griffiths (D-Michigan), passed the ERA. Two weeks after that, on August 26, the Women's Strike for Equality took place in cities around the country. And the *Ladies' Home Journal* included in its August issue an eight-page supplement titled "The New Feminism," written by some of the women who had occupied the *Journal's* offices five months earlier. Stickers reading "This Ad Insults Women" appeared on billboards, subway posters, and the sides of buses. Bella Abzug was elected to Congress; Shirley Chisholm was reelected. Hawaii and New York State liberalized their abortion laws. Feminists began appearing on talk shows, Gloria Steinem or Germaine Greer debating the likes of Hugh Hefner or William F. Buckley, Jr. And *The Mary Tyler Moore Show* premiered in September, noteworthy because, despite its overly accommodating and compliant heroine who said "Oh geez, oh golly" too much (not to mention "Oh, Mr. Grant"), it actually featured a single woman on her own without a steady boyfriend and with a steady job.

The watershed year of 1970 actually began in November 1969, when *Time* became the first mass magazine to feature a major article on the movement. It was written by Ruth Brine, one of the few female contributing editors at the magazine, who was also (the publisher's note hastened to emphasize) a mother of three, as if this ensured her objectivity and immunized her against contamination from this latest ideological plague. Headlined "The New Feminists: Revolt Against 'Sexism' " and placed in the "Behavior" section of the magazine, the article oscillated wildly between dismissive ridicule and legitimation of certain feminist grievances. Thus it was typical of the schizoid coverage of feminism. Brine suggested that the movement was highly derivative, its activities and its charges of oppression "all borrowed, of course, from the fiery rhetoric of today's militant black and student movements." The implication, often repeated elsewhere, was that this was a copycat movement, a frivolous imitation, with no genuine basis in true oppression, true hardship.

Labeling feminists as, simply, "the angries," Brine observed, "Many of the new feminists are surprisingly violent in mood, and seem to be trying, in fact, to repel other women rather than attract them." It went without saying—and so, of course, it had to be said—that feminists "burn brassieres." The most prominent image of feminism, a seemingly required illustration for any article on the topic, and one brandished here, was a photograph of women learning karate, to signify the movement's deadly seriousness and its hostility toward men and femininity. This was a familiar, and deliberate, journalistic strategy. As the journalist Susan Brownmiller described it, male editors would insist, succinctly, "Get the bra burning and the karate up front." "Soon," Brine predicted, "we may expect legions of female firemen, airline pilots, sanitation men and front-line soldiers (although anthropologist Margaret Mead thinks that they would be too fierce)." Yet despite this alleged fierceness, the article emphasized that "women themselves do not, in truth, have a record of soaring achievement." The message was clear: women were, by nature, a bunch of incompetents who, if you gave them just a little power, would turn into megalomaniacs and become as lethal as Snow White's stepmother.

The story also suggested that women had to be brainwashed in order to become part of the movement. This, too, was a common theme, that feminists, like the pods in *Invasion of the Body Snatchers,* cannibalized perfectly happy women and turned them into inhuman aliens. Young women were especially "fertile ground for the seeds of discontent" that were sown in consciousness-raising groups. According to *Time,* these were "rap sessions" in which women "drum their second-class status into each other by testifying to various indignities." Radical feminists "soon attracted a number of women who otherwise had no radical leanings at all. The latest recruits include factory workers, high school girls, a number of discontented housewives, and even a coven [!] or two of grandmothers." The discourse of invasion recurred over and over again, resonating with the still powerful anti-Communist rhetoric of the cold war. Brine described the "radical wing of Women's Liberation" as consisting of "groups, or cells, which constantly split and multiply in a sort of mitosis." One could readily imagine a sci-fi horror film, "Invasion of the Mutant Feminist Bitches" against whom conventional male weaponry was helpless.

At the same time, and in less suggestive language, the article acknowledged that feminists "have also drawn attention to some real problems," such as the wage gap between men and women, the lack of decent day care, and the fact that two-thirds of the women who worked did so because they needed the money. In a small sidebar, highlighted in pink, *Time* listed a series of statistics documenting women's low salaries and their underrepresentation in business, the professions, and politics. Like virtually every other mainstream news organization, *Time* legitimated liberal feminism's charges about economic discrimination. For one thing, the statistics were irrefutable. But, also, the news media embraced the conceit that the United States was a society of equal opportunity, and where it wasn't it had to change, especially after prodding from a sanctimonious, and often hypocritical, press. "Equal pay for equal work" was a slogan quickly accepted by many journalists as a reasonable and moderate goal; it was a concrete, measurable reform, it built on the rhetoric of democracy, and it suggested that women *could* be integrated into male jobs without insisting that they *would*. "Equal pay for equal work" was also handy for journalists: they could affirm it to show they weren't sexists, then use that support to marginalize other, more sweeping feminist critiques as deviant and extreme.

Four months later, in March 1970, *Newsweek* featured its own "Special Report" story, "Women in Revolt." The cover illustration featured a silhouette of a naked woman, her arm raised and fist clenched, breaking through the circle and cross symbol for woman, cracking the circle in half. The article, "Women's Lib: The War on 'Sexism,'" was initially assigned to Lynn Young, an assistant editor at the magazine, who claimed that her male colleagues attacked it for not being objective enough. One editor asserted, "Only a man could portray 'the ludicrous soul of this story,'" and had a man rewrite her article. The piece was reportedly rewritten every week for two months before her editors decided not to run it. Then *Newsweek* hired Helen Dudar, the wife of one of its senior editors and a writer for the *New York Post*, to write the piece.

Dudar's article was surprisingly sympathetic, although she reinforced existing metaphors, like the one that cast feminism as a science project gone berserk. She wrote that "women's lib groups have multiplied like freaked-out amebas," and she found the feminists' hostility "gravely infectious." But she also provided one of the least sensationalized accounts of radical feminism and wrote about women's second-class status with passion. As a newcomer to feminism, she recorded her own reactions to her topic. "As I sat with many of the women I have discussed here, I was struck by how distorting the printed word can be. On paper, most of them have sounded cold, remote, surly, tough, and sometimes a bit daft. On encounter, they usually turned out to be friendly, helpful, and attractive. Meeting the more eccentric theoreticians, I found myself remembering that today's fanatics are sometimes tomorrow's prophets." At the end of the article she admitted that she had gotten a real education, that she'd had to question some very basic assumptions about her own position in life, and that the process was deeply unsettling. Nonetheless, "the ambivalence is gone; the distance is gone. What is left is a sense of pride and kinship with all those women who have been asking all the hard questions. I thank them and so, I think, will a lot of other women."

To balance this out, *Newsweek* featured a one-page insert titled, "Other Voices: How Social Scientists See Women's Lib." This piece was filled with the typically pompous comments of primarily male "experts" who endorsed equal pay for equal work, but cited a range of studies to show that, in a host of areas, feminists were simply ignorant, wrongheaded, and misguided women prone to hyperbole. (Marilyn Goldstein of *Newsday* revealed to a fellow journalist in 1970 that whenever her paper covered the movement, one of her editors instructed reporters to "get out there and find an authority who'll say this is all a crock of shit.") *Newsweek's* assortment of dispassionate blowholes asserted that men and women really were biologically different, that girls were by nature more nurturing and passive, boys more active and aggressive. Each expert was introduced as someone "famous," "eminent," "distinguished," and "the most knowledgeable" in his field about sex roles. Dr. Abram Kardiner of Columbia maintained, "From what I've seen of the liberationists, their most conspicuous feature is self-hatred. I see tremendous vituperativeness and lack of feeling." Dr. Mary Calderone, "distinguished for her work on sex education," denounced the movement "because the women in it are militant, unpleasant and unfeminine."

This same mixture, grudging acknowledgment of a few feminist critiques infused by a disdain for feminists themselves, characterized TV's equally schizophrenic coverage. The CBS network began its three-part evening news series on "the blossoming of the feminist movement" on March 3, choosing David Culhane to cover the story. The first installment focused on economic discrimination against women, pointing out that their median salary was $4,000 a year, about half that of men. Culhane noted that women were confined to "women's jobs," such as teacher, secretary, or nurse, and discouraged from entering the professions. He added that there were fewer women holding Ph.D.'s in 1970 than there were in 1940. Although women made up 51 percent of the population, they were an "oppressed majority," a position backed up by an interview with Betty Friedan. Then the story cut to a women's meeting in Northridge, California, in which moderate middle-class women, young and middle-aged, calmly discussed the dilemmas they faced. "Most women are going to have to work as head of households to support an entire household and taxed the same as a man," explained one woman, "and yet paid one-third as much for identical work. How do we make the public understand that this woman can't compete . . . she can't compete in the labor market enough to feed her children?" In this story we learned that women had a legitimate point about their second-class economic status.

But when women, especially young women, showed their anger, this was less acceptable. The story cut to Senate hearings on the safety of the birth control pill, which younger, more "militant" women had "disrupted" by standing up and yelling at committee members. "Women are not going to sit quietly any longer—you are murdering us for your profit and convenience," yelled one young woman. Added another, "I'd like to know why is it that scientists and drug companies are perfectly willing to use women as guinea pigs, but as soon as a woman gets pregnant in one of these experiments she's treated like a common criminal." When the chairman asked the young women to sit down, one shot back, *"No,* we aren't going to sit down—why don't you give us some solid answers to our questions?"

Whatever the intended effect of this footage, young women like me, watching this on TV, were yelling, "Right on!" because it was so thrilling to see women my age taking on these bloated, self-righteous senators who thought girls should be quiet, smile, and serve tea. The story moved on to other disorderly women demonstrating against sex-segregated bars, and as they angrily confronted a bar's owner, they equated having a "men only" bar with having "whites only" facilities. After one woman was attacked by a male patron of the bar, the women discussed their need to learn how to defend themselves physically. The last scene showed what reporters repeatedly referred to as "militant feminists" learning judo and karate. The final image of the story was of a woman hurling a man to the floor and pinning him there. No one could miss the point. "Militant feminists," meaning anyone more outspoken than Pat Nixon, favored brass knuckles and Molotov cocktails as the only way to achieve women's liberation.

The second installment opened with Walter Cronkite sitting in front of a picture of Sigmund Freud. Those of us already sick of being told that we suffered from "penis envy" and that our biology was our destiny, braced ourselves for the worst whenever we saw Freud invoked, and we were not to be disappointed here, as Cronkite intoned, "Sigmund Freud, an expert on women if there ever was one, said that despite his thirty years of research, he was unable to answer one great question: What does a woman want?" (Well, Walter, he might have found out if he'd actually *listened* to them.) Freud might be even more confused today, opined Cronkite, if he saw the current "militant demonstrations" staged by women. Culhane then opened his story with footage of the Miss America demonstration, a protest that was anything but "militant." While he cited Playboy Clubs as a special target of feminists, the camera zoomed in on the jiggling cleavage of a particularly well-endowed bunny, and Culhane described these watering holes as places "where men come to observe remarkable displays of female pulchritude," thereby embracing the objectification of women that feminists deplored and suggesting that it was, in fact, harmless. He hastened to add, however, that it wasn't just "sour grapes" that led feminists to protest the objectification of women's bodies. "They can and indeed have won beauty contests," he reported, as if it was newsworthy—and shocking—to think that a feminist would be anything but hideously ugly, then cut to an interview with Alice Denham, a former model and playmate of the month who had become a feminist.

Just when you wanted to punch Culhane in the snout, he changed tone, reporting quite movingly on Jean Temple, a college-educated divorced mother of four in her forties who was agitating for child-care centers because she was "unable to work and take care of her children at the same time." Speaking of her constant worry about her children while she was at work, and about how her family was always on the verge of poverty, Temple said simply, "My children now have to bring themselves up." Here Culhane demonstrated how male journalists got it about the oppression of economic discrimination and didn't get it at all about the bondage of sexual objectification. He closed the story by delineating the differences between liberal and radical feminism. The moderates wanted "equal job opportunities, equal pay with men for the same jobs, child-care centers, and more or less unrestricted abortion." The more militant feminist groups, however, "say even these goals are not enough." He promised that the next report would look at the "revolutionary views of these radical women," the word *radical* receiving especially heavy emphasis.

The final segment pulled out all the stops. Several radical feminists, including Ti-Grace Atkinson, Shulamith Firestone, and Anselma dell'Olio, were interviewed by a female reporter, Conchita Pierce. The sections of the interviews the network chose to air focused on these women's critiques of marriage and the family as institutions that can't help but oppress women. As Atkinson asserted, "If you had equality between men and women, you couldn't have marriage." "What would you substitute for marriage?" asked Pierce. "What would you substitute for cancer?" Atkinson replied. Firestone argued that "pregnancy is barbaric" and that women should not have to bear the burden of reproduction alone. Scientific research should be directed toward what Culhane paraphrased as "the so-called bottled baby. . . . That, of course, is one of the most radical visions of feminism."

Here we see how vexed the relationship was between radical feminism and the mainstream media. What radical feminists presented as revolutionary and utopian, the mainstream media saw as a bad acid trip. Some radical feminists refused to cooperate at all with anyone in the media, alienating women journalists who wanted to give their views a wider hearing. Yet radical feminists were right to be wary of media that delighted in the superficial and the shocking because this approach endorsed reformism rather than a complete break with the past. Ti-Grace Atkinson became a media darling because she gave great sound bites like "Marriage means rape" or "Love has to be destroyed." But the coverage she received used such disembodied quotations to make radical feminists seem like crazed freaks. Now it's true, most radical feminists were over the top in their condemnation of patriarchy, and their pronouncements were outside mainstream thought. But rarely did any reporter acknowledge the thoughtful analysis, or the painful realities for many women, that led to such conclusions.

Culhane concluded the series in a typical way, pitting women against women and acting as if male sexism was a completely insignificant barrier to change: "So far, the women's rights movement has had one fundamental problem; not so much to persuade men, but to convince the majority of American women that there is something basically wrong with their position in life." After some final footage of women singing a feminist version of the "Battle Hymn of the Republic," the camera cut to a smirking Walter Cronkite, eyebrows raised in amusement, as he softly chuckled, "And that's the way it is."

Two weeks after the CBS series ended, NBC weighed in with its own, which turned out to be one of the most sympathetic pieces done on the movement. This point of view was due in no small part to the firmness and persuasiveness of NBC's female reporters—Liz Trotta, Norma Quarles, and Aline

Saarinen—who covered the story. In Saarinen's first report, a rapid-sequence montage of Barbie dolls, fashion models, women in print ads, and footage from a Virginia Slims commercial drove home how women are victimized by "degrading stereotypes." And Saarinen was one of the few to highlight feminists' emphasis on personal choice, by reporting their insistence that "domesticity and motherhood should be one option among many options." In just a few minutes, Saarinen had acknowledged the legitimacy of the major points underlying the 1968 Miss America protest and broadcast them to millions.

Liz Trotta followed up this report with a review of society's sexist attitudes toward girls. "Discrimination begins early in a girl's life," noted Trotta, as she interviewed expectant fathers in a hospital waiting room, all of whom hoped they would be getting boys. Over footage of children playing, she pointed out that the girl "learns that her place is in the home. The boy learns his place is not in the home." Trotta then went to Austin, Minnesota, and asserted that "by the time she's in high school, a girl has been brainwashed." She then aired a classroom debate among high school students over women's rights, in which the boys claimed that girls only go to college to find a husband and that girls are inferior and simply want an easy life. As one young man summed it up, "Like, my mother, she went to college, you know, she got some dietary deal, and she doesn't know anything." (I wonder what kind of a reception he got from his know-nothing mom that night.) Trotta let these retrograde comments speak for themselves. She concluded, "There are young girls here who are bright, enthusiastic, and full of hopes, but, like most women, they'll go out in the world knowing their place, and that place is secondary to men." This was powerful and persuasive stuff.

Norma Quarles covered economic discrimination against women, offering such statistics as "only 1 percent of the 31 million working women earn $10,000 or more." Some "exceptional" women can make it, but they will "be fighting man's prejudice all the way." In an especially savvy and effective ploy, Quarles edited together, on the audio track, a series of quotations by men about how women can't concentrate like men, aren't levelheaded, can't be aggressive at work, and are basically domestic. These she played over footage of women working with computers, in banks, in heavy industry, and in offices, images that directly contradicted the men's dismissive comments and dramatized the ignorance and stupidity of sexism.

In the final report, Saarinen conveyed the richness and diversity of feminism, describing movement members as ranging from "reformers to revolutionaries." She showed women in demonstrations getting arrested and being dragged to police vans. Cutting to footage of a demonstration by the Women's International Terrorist Conspiracy from Hell (WITCH), Saarinen described the "flashier, more original" WITCH as "uniquely satirical and witty in a movement that, like all crusades, is rather humorless." This was one of the few moments when a journalist laughed with, not at, radical feminists and understood what they were poking fun at, and why. Saarinen concluded, "There's a group for every taste, from militant man-haters and lesbians to happily mated." While acknowledging that there were disagreements among these groups, she emphasized that "the strength of the movement lies in what the groups hold in common," their determined fight against discrimination. She closed with a powerful plea from suffragist Alice Paul, then in her eighties, who asked, "Mr. President, how long must women wait for liberty?" Viewers of the NBC series saw an extremely convincing and sympathetic account of the pressing need for women's liberation, an account that would soon be pooh-poohed elsewhere.

The biggest story of the year, and the one that received the most coverage, was the Women's Strike for Equality on August 26, to commemorate the fiftieth anniversary of the ratification of the Nineteenth Amendment. Women were urged to drop their stenographer's pads, their laundry baskets, and their compliant, nurturing demeanor, to strike for a day in protest of sexism in the United States. Organizers of the strike agreed on the following demands, which you can read with a wistful sigh, since none of them has been achieved: equal opportunity for women in employment and education, twenty-four-hour childcare centers, and abortion on demand. To drive home the role played by the media in reinforcing women's oppression, organizers also urged women to boycott four products whose advertising was offensive and degrading to women: *Cosmopolitan* magazine, Silva Thins cigarettes, Ivory Liquid, and Pristeen, the infamous "feminine hygiene" spray. The strike was probably the most important public action of the movement, and given the number of women who participated, and the even larger number who were converted to feminism, it was a huge success.

Newsweek described the movement as a "shaky coalition of disparate groups" and asserted that "there is plenty of reason to doubt that [it] will ever be able to unite women as a mass force. Certainly it has not done so yet." What Aline Saarinen of NBC had characterized as a strength—the fact that the movement sustained a wide spectrum of groups with different ideological positions—was cast by *Newsweek* as an insurmountable weakness. *Time* opened its story with the world-weary, oh-what-we-boys-must-endure quip, "These are the times that try men's souls, and they are likely to get much worse before they get better." Women had better button their lips and keep their anger to themselves, *Time* warned, quoting no less an authority than Margaret Mead: "'Women's Liberation has to be terribly conscious about the danger of provoking men to kill women. You have quite literally driven them mad.'" Noting that the movement "has not produced much humor," the article cited *Sexual Politics* as the new bible for feminists and described Kate Millett as "the Mao Tse-Tung of women's liberation," "a brilliant misfit in a man's world" who lived in a dashiki and work pants and didn't wash her hair enough. Reading *Sexual Politics*, warned Millett's doctoral-thesis adviser, "is like sitting with your testicles in a nutcracker."

Commentary on television before the strike mingled amused condescension with outright contempt, and no network was more notorious than ABC and its virulently sexist anchormen Harry Reasoner, Howard K. Smith, and Frank Reynolds. On August 11, in his commentary, Reynolds observed that now there were "lady" jockeys, "lady" generals, and a female president of the U.N. General Assembly, and that "even the House of Representatives has finally decided that women are entitled to the same rights as men." The first major implication of the ERA Reynolds chose to highlight was that women might be required to pay alimony, which, he noted sarcastically, "would restore the ancient and honorable profession of gigolo to its rightful glory." The second implication of the ERA was that women would be subject to the draft, which would decidedly end "America's role of world policeman." He explained why with a chuckle. "Female draftees would presumably retain at least some of their civilian prerogatives, so it would be obviously impossible to fly a regiment halfway around the world at a moment's notice when at least one-half the regiment could simply never be ready on time. It is not that there is anything inherently unequal about women in such matters, it is just that they are, well, different." Oh, Frankie, such a wit.

On August 25, Reynolds's colleague Howard K. Smith weighed in with his thoughts on women's liberation. "Like the majority of Americans," Smith said, he was "weary of the abrasive type of group protest." While sympathetic to "Indians and Negroes," who had been "genuinely mistreated," Smith confessed to a "modified *un*sympathy with women's liberation." He found "a few of their demands," such as equal pay, equal access to "some jobs," and child-care centers, to be "good." He suggested women were already more than equal, since they constituted 53 percent of the population and "they get the most money, inherited from worn-out husbands." He derided what he saw as a demand for "sameness," which he denounced as "abhorrent." Then, in a bizarre non sequitur, Smith observed that European cities traditionally have had more charm than those in America. "But when American women adopted the miniskirt, displaying much more woman, it was the biggest advance in urban beautification since Central Park was created in Manhattan." Winding down from such lyrical heights, Smith said, "To me, women's lib has that in common with the midi, which is now threatening us—that it is a kind of defeminization." Praising the differences between men and women, Smith concluded, "Vive la différence!" This, I remind you, passed for journalistic analysis in 1970.

When August 26 arrived, there were marches and rallies in most major cities, and in New York the day's events culminated in a march down Fifth Avenue, followed by speeches and a rally behind the New York Public Library. The police had cordoned off one lane for the parade, but the barricades got pushed aside as somewhere between 20,000 and 50,000 marchers filled all the lanes of Fifth Avenue. Although few women actually went on strike during the day, thousands participated in lunchtime and after-work demonstrations.

Not every female reporter was as sympathetic as the women at NBC. Linda Charlton reported for *The New York Times*, "In New York, as elsewhere in the country, the impact of the day of demonstrations beyond those already involved or interested in the women's liberation movement appeared to be minimal." I hasten to emphasize that there were no featured interviews—zero—with any of the thousands of women who participated in the march, and whose lives may indeed have been changed by the experience. A small sidebar piece next to the article was headlined "Leading Feminist Puts Hairdo Before Strike." Girls will be girls, of course, and it was eminently newsworthy that Betty

Friedan was no exception: she was twenty minutes late for her first scheduled appearance because of a "last minute emergency appointment with her hairdresser." A larger story on the same page, by Grace Lichtenstein, was titled "For Most Women, 'Strike' Day Was Just a Topic of Conversation." The story began, "For the vast majority of women, yesterday was a day simply to go about one's business—whether that meant going to a job, attending a Broadway matinee, having one's hair done or washing the baby's diapers." A female employee of Doyle, Dane and Bernbach was described as spending the day in "the most liberated way possible. She took off to play golf." A spokesman for the Equitable Life Assurance Society told Lichtenstein, "The movement is regarded with some ridicule here." A typist for the company added, "I'm against the whole equality thing. . . . I'm afraid of being drafted." Lichtenstein also interviewed suburban women. As one folded diapers, she said, "Women's liberation? Never thought much about it, really." But those who *had* thought about it apparently eluded the reportorial staff of the nation's newspaper of record.

One of my favorite pieces on the strike was another story in *The Times* titled "Traditional Groups Prefer to Ignore Women's Lib." The Daughters of the American Revolution, the Women's Christian Temperance Union, and the Junior League, which were described as "traditional groups" that had "for decades championed women's rights," were cast as "facing a challenge from a movement that many consider bizarre, alien, and totally unacceptable." The traditionalists, according to the article, considered women of the movement "ridiculous exhibitionists, a 'band of wild lesbians,'" or "communists." Mrs. Saul Schary, incoming president of the National Council of Women, asserted, "There's no discrimination against women like they say there is . . . women themselves are just self-limiting. It's in their nature and they shouldn't blame it on society or men." After describing the women in the movement as self-seeking exhibitionists, she added, "And so many of them are just so unattractive. . . . I wonder if they're completely well."

This was a consistent media device: to have "refined" women denounce "grotesque" women. In its leading editorial on August 27, *The Times* echoed Mrs. Schary's remarks, condemning the demonstrations as "publicity seeking exhibitionism" and "attention getting antics." The newsmagazines were no better. *Time* snickered that the Fifth Avenue march provided "some of the best sidewalk ogling in years" but seemed disappointed that there were no "charred bras." *Newsweek* emphasized that "lib supporters came up short" in getting women out in the streets, except for "small detachments" who formed "unstructured battalions" of presumably warlike, fearsome commandos ready to nuke sexist men and housewives to kingdom come.

On television, the three networks used varying approaches in their coverage. But they had one thing in common: they *all* showcased the Jennings Randolph "bra-less bubblehead quip," giving this bonehead more coverage than any woman involved in the strike. On NBC, the advances of the Saarinen-Quarles-Trotta series were forgotten, as not-so-subtle editing strategies delivered a new message: that the movement was filled with preposterous exaggerations and thus was naturally off-putting to more sensible gals. In the network's footage on strike activities in Washington, DC, viewers saw and heard a black woman in a park singing, "And before I'll be a slave, I'll be buried in my grave. . . . Yes, goodbye slavery, hello freedom." As the woman sang these powerful lyrics about the oppression of slavery, the camera cut to white women in dresses and pearls lounging lazily on the lawn and languorously eating ice cream in the sun while they listened. The striking juxtaposition of the song's lyrics and the images of extremely comfortable women enjoying a leisurely pic-nic put the lie to claims that women were "oppressed" in any way like other groups had been. In its report on Los Angeles, NBC showed marchers chanting repeatedly, "Sisterhood is powerful, join us now," as they punched the air with clenched fists. On the words "join us now," the camera zoomed in on two wait-resses watching the march who scurried back to safety behind the doors of the restaurant. Again, in pictures alone, without any commentary, NBC conveyed the gap between feminists and "real" women. In his commentary at the end of the program, Frank McGee derided the "nonsense being mouthed today by some of the more extreme members of the current women's liberation move-ment" and scolded them for trying to make wives and mothers feel inferior. But it was usually McGee and other male commentators, not feminists, who pushed this equation between being a housewife and being inferior.

The coverage on CBS was, not surprisingly, in line with that network's ear-lier news reports. Right after an ad for Playtex bras, Walter Cronkite introduced the protest by calling its participants a "militant minority of women's libera-tionists." Of the four stories about the strike from around the country, three were by male reporters, and they discounted the strike and thus the movement as ridiculous, inconsequential, and having little bearing on most women's lives. Bob Schakne in New York opened his story over footage of a small group of women carrying placards with this introduction: "It turned out there weren't a lot of would-be liberated women willing to stop their work for the day in New York. Early demonstrations tended to be small, and the onlookers were by no means always sympathetic." When the film cut to the march on Fifth Avenue, which Schakne severely underrepresented by saying it drew "several thousand people," viewers nonetheless saw an enormous crowd of marchers jamming the street, arm in arm, some with raised fists, some with signs. Schakne noted that "the tone of the protest stayed moderate and orderly. The radical feminists of the movement attempted no confrontation," as if viewers should have ex-pected women in fatigues, firing bazookas.

Bill Kurtis, reporting from Los Angeles that "several hundred" women's lib-erationists "shared the spotlight with an opposing group," focused on the con-frontation between the two groups. As men holding signs reading "Viva la Différence" heckled the feminists, the women turned on them, chanting, "Go do the dishes! Go do the dishes!" Then several women grabbed the signs from the men, tore them in pieces, and threw them back in the men's faces. The strike was thus cast as nothing more elevated than a playground spat. The story then cut to Richard Threlkeld in San Francisco, who announced, "Women's liberation day went largely unnoticed in San Francisco's middle-class neighborhoods, where housewives were too busy just being housewives to pay it all much mind." He interviewed a woman in a supermarket parking lot, who said, "I think it's ridiculous," which evoked a loud and approving chuckle from Threlkeld. She continued, "I think it's stupid. I don't think women should just stay home all the time, but I don't think they belong out either." (Say what?) Another woman, carrying her shopping bags out of the store, said she was a happy housewife and a happy mother, and a third woman echoed this sentiment.

This juxtaposition—in which women with complaints were shown only in highly charged, dramatic, public demonstrations, yelling loudly and tussling with men, while women without complaints were in more tranquil, everyday settings—made women shoppers opposed to the movement appear more thoughtful, rational, and persuasive than their feminist counterparts. The visual positioning of them, in places such as supermarket parking lots, suggested these women were much more connected to the fabric of daily life. The juxtaposition also suggested that women had only two choices of how to be and where to be: compliant, calm, and sexually rewarded in private; or aggressive, strident, and sexually mocked in public. The network's pattern of framing the story, especially Threlkeld's segment, suggested that most women were quite contented with their lot, were well treated financially and emotionally, and simply could not comprehend a series of complaints that seemed exaggerated and irrelevant to their lives.

After a commercial break, Eric Sevareid offered his commentary on the day's events. He dismissed the notion that women were oppressed, cast women's liberation as a minority movement, and echoed the feminism-as-disease metaphor by suggesting that it spread by "contagion" as women's libbers indoctrinated previously happy women. Yet Sevareid endorsed "three practical aims with which a great many men also agree: equal opportunities in employment and education, abortion on demand, and child-care centers. Nor does this end the list of realistic inequities." So even in the midst of his pompous dismissal of female oppression, Sevareid put his seal of approval on three revolutionary feminist goals. How could viewers not feel torn about feminism when commentators like this kept trying to have it both ways? . . .

One of the most striking, though hardly surprising, aspects of the media coverage of the women's movement is the way that news organizations repeatedly—almost desperately, one is tempted to note—ignored, erased, and dismissed male opposition to women's liberation. Male commentators and reporters, positioning themselves as the wise, dispassionate onlookers, used their alleged endorsement of equal pay for equal work, or their appreciation of women's thighs, to demonstrate that *they* weren't male chauvinist pigs and to suggest that their other attacks on feminism stemmed not from sexism but from simple common sense. Male observers of the movement weren't hostile; they were "amused." Opposition to the women's movement, reporters insisted, came from women, not men, and they included plenty of interviews with unsympathetic women to prove their point. Rarely, however, were there interviews with male attorneys, college professors, doctors, or corporate executives, let alone with shop foremen, union stewards, or construction workers, about why they had so few women co-workers and how they would regard the entrance of women into their ranks. Men were simply not put on the spot, nor were their attitudes flushed out.

Instead, women with no economic or political power were used as stand-ins for men who opposed feminism. Through this tactic, male journalists could ask why men should support changes even most women didn't want, and they could smirk over one of their favorite events, the catfight, while smiling knowingly and maintaining that women *were* different from men, and weren't the differences cute and delightful. Thus was misogyny naturalized, transformed into a kind of world-weary tolerance of what everyone understood to be women's inherent foibles.

Even if most women *did* want a liberation movement, its success was doomed, according to news accounts, because women were constitutionally incapable of cooperating with one another. Certainly there were real divisions within what was broadly termed the women's movement. Yet by playing up such divisions, the news media reinforced the stereotype that women were completely incompetent as politicians, tacticians, and organizers and had proved, once again, that they didn't deserve to be active anywhere but in the kitchen, the bedroom, and the nursery.

Possibly the most important legacy of such media coverage was its carving up of the women's movement into legitimate feminism and illegitimate feminism. Mainstream journalists, most of whom were men, endorsed a narrow, white, upper-middle-class slice of liberal feminism and cast the rest off as irresponsible, misguided, and deviant. Nearly every story and editorial about the women's movement acknowledged that women really did suffer from economic discrimination and approved of "equal pay for equal work." Many also endorsed child-care centers and the legalization of abortion. They supported, in other words, going through the courts and legislatures for redress and establishing one or two new institutions to help working mothers. Feminism, in this view, should only redraw the workplace, and this only slightly. Other regions of society, like a man's home, his marriage, his family, should be cordoned off from feminist surveyors. Yet for young women like me, these issues were exactly the locus of the movement: we got it that the personal was indeed political. While inequities in employment were carefully documented, neither the print media nor television devoted news time to inequities in marriage, divorce, and child rearing. Critiques of marriage and the family were much too explosive, and hit too close to home, for male journalists to be comfortable analyzing them. But since such criticisms were, in 1970, articulated primarily by radical feminists, they were easy to dismiss as loony and bizarre. This reinforced the media's insistence that the personal was *still* the personal and should never be politicized. The overall message was that women had no business trying to imagine wholesale social change; that was man's work.

Perhaps the biggest difficulty for feminists was that the most basic and pernicious forms of female oppression did not lend themselves to visual documentation. Women's real grievances—the burdens, frustrations, and inequities in their lives—occurred behind closed doors. Unlike the civil rights movement, there were no protesters being hosed down or attacked by dogs. There was no war footage, or photographs of napalm burning people's skin. There were just these women, most of whom looked OK on the outside but who were, on the inside, being torn apart. Feminists had to make the private public, the invisible visible, and the personal political. This was an extremely difficult assignment, especially with a media increasingly hooked on dramatic, violent pictures.

Time and again the media emphasized that members of the women's liberation movement were completely out of touch with, hostile to, and rejected by most American women, when, in fact, many women's attitudes toward feminism were much more complicated and were constantly moving toward support. And the movement was much broader-based than the images revealed. No black feminists, with the exception of Shirley Chisholm, appeared in these news stories, even though Florynce Kennedy, Frances Beal, and Eleanor Holmes Norton, to name just a few, were already active in the movement.

The news media's ambivalent representation of feminism was simultaneously empowering and crippling, for it legitimated middle-class, liberal feminism and applauded legalistic reform at the same time that it dramatized the severe psychological and emotional costs to women who challenged patriarchal versions of female sexuality and who publicly violated the boundary between the public (male) and private (female) spheres. The word *militant* was tossed around all too loosely to marginalize any woman who wanted more than a few legislative reforms and served to demonize female behavior that refused to remain friendly, accommodating, compliant, docile, and obsequious. Women, in other words, might get pay raises and child-care centers if they just asked nicely and kept smiling at men. Karate images, which overflowed with anxieties about female anger, male castration, and the possible dissolution of amicable heterosexual relations, marked "militant feminism" as a potentially deadly trend. And the repeated use of *militant* as an adjective imparted to many feminists attitudes from female separatism to a love of violence that they did not, in fact, embrace.

But let's consider what else we did see and hear, and why such coverage may have been empowering to some women viewers. The media did enable us to hear speakers on television attack the sexual objectification of women and the impossible beauty standards imposed by advertisers. They provided a platform for women furious over their inability to control their own bodies and their reproductive lives. They showed us women challenging men in the streets, chanting to them to "go do the dishes." I remember being initially intrigued and repelled by what I saw. At the age of twenty, I had just discovered how much fun boys could really be, and now this? At first I bought into the media dismissal that comfy young women like me couldn't possibly be oppressed. And the reduction of sophisticated feminist critiques into "man-hating" made me wary. But, like millions, I stayed tuned; I read *The Female Eunuch* and *The Golden Notebook*; and I woke up. The messages from feminists I saw and heard in the news resonated with my own experiences, while the representation of women in ads and TV shows undermined my aspirations and ambitions. So when Harry Reasoner trashed the women's movement from his privileged podium on ABC, it made me even more angry, more committed to feminism, and more determined than ever to hurl a series of expletives—or whatever else was handy—at the next paunchy, middle-aged man I met (and I met too many of them) who treated me as if I couldn't possibly be serious about having a career of my own.

While the coverage repudiated feminists as ugly, humorless, disorderly man-haters in desperate need of some Nair, it also endorsed selected feminist principles, particularly those premised on equality of opportunity. It showed that while women who got together in the public sphere were subject to male derision, they could also change society. And at the same time that radical feminists and their often shocking pronouncements were marginalized, portions of their vision were folded into the mainstream, thus reconfiguring what constituted the middle ground.

The news coverage pinioned women between the same messages we had grown up with, only now the stakes were higher. On the one hand, by endorsing a few liberal reforms like equal pay, the media reinforced the message that women had every right to expect to be treated as equal citizens, with the same rights, responsibilities, and opportunities as men. On the other hand, by mocking and dismissing the way feminist activists looked and behaved, and by marginalizing many of their critiques of society, the media also endorsed the notion that in some cases female subordination and sexual objectification were not only fine but desirable. In one moment, the media exhorted women to be equal and active; in the next, they urged them to be subordinate and passive. Sound familiar? We had been hearing it all our lives.

What was different now was that many women, especially young women, were aware of these contradictions and pointed to them in their demonstrations, newsletters, and speeches, holding them up as untenable. Understanding that the internal conflicts we faced weren't our own lonely struggle but resulted from being raised female in America was, in the language of the times, mind-blowing, and, as such, a colossal relief. Finally, the demonstrators and the female reporters said, out loud, on television, that women were in an absolutely impossible situation because they couldn't ever live up to the mutually exclusive traits society demanded. Women like me started to seek some kind of satisfactory resolution to these contradictions, not in ourselves but in society. We had become conscious not only of our inequality but also of how our identities had been fragmented. The warring pieces, we saw, were virtually impossible to hold together without constant posing, dissembling, and the abandonment of our own needs and desires.

There were other blind spots in the media coverage that worked to women's advantage. The media failed to convey the exhilaration of participating in the women's movement. Yes, there were divisions, battles, and internecine strife. But there was also a compelling utopian vision, a great unity of purpose, and a respect for diversity. Once a woman experienced the sheer joy of uniting with her sisters to effect personal and societal change, only to see on television and in the press an image of grimness and humorlessness, it was hard to trust the media again. The antidote to this was the consciousness-raising group, which spread rapidly throughout the country, forming an alternative, behind-the-spotlight communications center for women to discuss what the news ignored or belittled. These underground networks were quite consciously independent of and often at odds with the dominant media. Here, working through their ambivalent positions, women came to appreciate how they had been socialized—especially by the media—to be all things to all people. Now, when we went back and forth between the girl talk of our groups and the mostly boy talk of the news, we understood more clearly why much of what we had grown up with on TV, and what we still saw, made us uncomfortable, insecure, and furious. We learned—and loved—the power of rejecting media pronouncements and of giving guys like Howard K. Smith a big Bronx cheer. We also learned that feminism itself, unlike the one-dimensional caricature we saw in the media, was many things to different women. It was becoming apparent that there were as many ways to adopt a feminist perspective as there were ways to be a woman. Most important, we realized that it was within our power to accept or resist the new stereotypes, picking up some shards, kicking away others. Feminism, like womanhood itself, became a pastiche.

While the media helped spread the word about feminism, producing converts and enemies, they had one particularly pernicious, lasting effect. By demonizing prominent feminists like Kate Millett, the media effectively gutted one of feminism's most basic challenges to gender roles: that women should be taken seriously and treated with respect regardless of whether they were conventionally "attractive." The media countermanded this heresy, not only in the news but through entertainment shows in the 1970s that offered up Charlie's Angels and the Bionic Woman as the new exemplars of the liberated woman. The media representation of feminism reinforced the division between the acceptable and the deviant, between the refined and the grotesque, between deserving ladies and disorderly dogs. This false dichotomy helped to reaffirm, more than ever, the importance of female attractiveness to female success, and the utter folly of taking to the streets. Even as the media attention accelerated the spread of the women's movement throughout the country, it stunted the movement's most liberatory potential, a handicap that cripples all of us, women and men alike, to this day.

NEW-STYLE FEMINISM

Modern feminism emerged in the early 1960s, with John Kennedy's Commission on the Status of Women, the Equal Pay Act of 1963, and the publication that year of Betty Friedan's The Feminine Mystique. *During the 1960s, feminists emphasized their exclusion from the mainstream—from politics, from the professions, from Princeton and Yale, from ordinary good jobs. Through the National Organization for Women (NOW) and other organizations, they demanded equality in the workplace and assailed the idea, captured in the phrase "the feminine mystique," that women could live full, rich lives in purely domestic roles. By the 1970s, vocal critics of this position had emerged. Some believed that there could be no equality that did not involve significant changes in the family and domestic relations. Others rejected the assumption, implicit in the earlier view, that women should strive to be like men. This new-style feminism emphasized that feminists should understand, value, and utilize their qualities as women.*

Our Bodies, Ourselves (1971) was part of this new brand of feminism. What kinds of information did the book contain? Why did the women who wrote the book think it was necessary? What connection is there between its publication and the Roe v. Wade *decision, handed down by the Supreme Court in 1973, which made invalid all laws prohibiting abortion during the first three months of pregnancy?*

OUR BODIES, OURSELVES

The Boston Women's Health Book Collective

Preface

A Good Story

The history of this book, *Our Bodies, Ourselves,* is lengthy and satisfying.

It began at a small discussion group on "women and their bodies" that was part of a women's conference held in Boston in the spring of 1969. These were the early days of the women's movement, one of the first gatherings of women meeting specifically to talk with other women. For many of us it was the very first time we got together with other women to talk and think about our lives and what we could do about them. Before the conference was over some of us decided to keep on meeting as a group to continue the discussion, and so we did.

In the beginning we called the group "the doctor's group." We had all experienced similar feelings of frustration and anger toward specific doctors and the medical maze in general, and initially we wanted to do something about those doctors who were condescending, paternalistic, judgmental, and noninformative. As we talked and shared our experiences with one another, we realized just how much we had to learn about our bodies. So we decided on a summer project—to research those topics that we felt were particularly pertinent to learning about our bodies, to discuss in the group what we had learned, then to write papers individually or in small groups of two or three, and finally to present the results in the fall as a course for women on women and their bodies.

As we developed the course we realized more and more that we were really capable of collecting, understanding, and evaluating medical information. Together we evaluated our reading of books and journals, our talks with doctors and friends who were medical students. We found we could discuss, question, and argue with each other in a new spirit of cooperation rather than competition. We were equally struck by how important it was for us to be able to open up with one another and share our feelings about our bodies. The process of talking was as crucial as the facts themselves. Over time the facts and feelings melted together in ways that touched us very deeply, and that is reflected in the changing titles of the course and then the book—from *Women and Their Bodies* to *Women and Our Bodies* to, finally, *Our Bodies, Ourselves.*

When we gave the course we met in any available free space we could get—in day schools, in nursery schools, in churches, in our homes. We expected the course to stimulate the same kind of talking and sharing that we who had prepared the course had experienced. We had something to say, but we had a lot to learn as well; we did not want a traditional teacher-student relationship. At the end of ten to twelve sessions—which roughly covered the material in the current book—we found that many women felt both eager and competent to get together in small groups and share what they had learned with other women. We saw it as a never-ending process always involving more and more women. . . .

You may want to know who we are. We are white, our ages range from twenty-four to forty, most of us are from middle-class backgrounds and have had at least some college education, and some of us have professional degrees. Some of us are married, some of us are separated, and some of us are single. Some of us have children of our own, some of us like spending time with children, and others of us are not sure we want to be with children. In short, we are both a very ordinary and a very special group, as women are everywhere. We are white middle-class women, and as such can describe only what life has been for us. But we do realize that poor women and nonwhite women have suffered far more from the kinds of misinformation and mistreatment that we are describing in this book. In some ways, learning about our womenhood from the inside out has allowed us to cross over the socially created barriers of race, color, income, and class, and to feel a sense of identity with all women in the experience of being female.

We are twelve individuals and we are a group. (The group has been ongoing for three years, and some of us have been together since the beginning. Others came in at later points. Our current collective has been together for one year.) We know each other well—our weaknesses as well as our strengths. We have learned through good times and bad how to work together (and how not to as well). We recognize our similarities and differences and are learning to respect each person for her uniqueness. We love each other.

Many, many other women have worked with us on the book. A group of gay women got together specifically to do the chapter on lesbianism. Other papers were done still differently. For instance, along with some friends the mother of one woman in the group volunteered to work on menopause with some of us who have not gone through that experience ourselves. Other women contributed thoughts, feelings, and comments as they passed through town or passed through our kitchens or workrooms. There are still other voices from letters, phone conversations, a variety of discussions, etc., that are included in the chapters as excerpts of personal experiences. Many women have spoken for themselves in this book, though we in the collective do not agree with all that has been written. Some of us are even uncomfortable with part of the material. We have included it anyway, because we give more weight to accepting that we differ than to our uneasiness. We have been asked why this is exclusively a book about women, why we have restricted our course to women. Our answer is that we are women and, as women, do not consider ourselves experts on men (as men through the centuries have presumed to be experts on us). We are not implying that we think most twentieth-century men are much less alienated from their bodies than women are. But we know it is up to men to explore that for themselves, to come together and share their sense of themselves as we have done. We would like to read a book about men and their bodies.

We are offering a book that can be used in many different ways—individually, in a group, for a course. Our book contains real material about our bodies and ourselves that isn't available elsewhere, and we have tried to present it in a new way—an honest, humane, and powerful way of thinking about ourselves and our lives. We want to share the knowledge and power that comes with this way of thinking, and we want to share the feelings we have for each other—supportive and loving feelings that show we can indeed help one another grow.

From the very beginning of working together, first on the course that led to this book and then on the book itself, we have felt exhilarated and energized by our new knowledge. Finding out about our bodies and our bodies' needs, starting to take control over that area of our life, has released for us an energy that has overflowed into our work, our friendships, our relationships with men and women, for some of us our marriages and our parenthood. In trying to figure out why this has had such a life-changing effect on us, we have come up with several important ways in which this kind of body education has been liberating for us and may be a starting point for the liberation of many other women.

First, we learned what we learned equally from professional sources—textbooks, medical journals, doctors, nurses—and from our own experiences. The facts were important, and we did careful research to get the information we had not had in the past. As we brought the facts to one another we learned a good deal, but in sharing our personal experiences relating to those facts we learned still more. Once we had learned what the "experts" had to tell us, we found that we still had a lot to teach and to learn from one another. For instance, many of us had "learned" about the menstrual cycle in science or biology classes—we had perhaps even memorized the names of the menstrual hormones and what they did. But most of us did not remember much of what we had learned. This time when we read in a text that the onset of menstruation is a normal and universal occurrence in young girls from ages ten to eighteen, we started to talk about our first menstrual periods. We found that, for many of us, beginning to menstruate had not felt normal at all, but scary, embarrassing, mysterious. We realized that what we had been told about menstruation and what we had not been told, even the tone of voice it had been told in—all had had an effect on our feelings about being female. . . .

Learning about our bodies in this way really turned us on. This is an exciting kind of learning, where information and feelings are allowed to interact. It has made the difference between rote memorization and relevant learning, between fragmented pieces of a puzzle and the integrated picture, between abstractions and real knowledge. We discovered that you don't learn very much when you are just a passive recipient of information. We found that each individual's response to information is valid and useful, and that by sharing our responses we can develop a base on which to be critical of what the experts tell us. Whatever we need to learn now, in whatever area of our life, we know more how to go about it.

A second important result of this kind of learning has been that we are better prepared to evaluate the institutions that are supposed to meet our health needs—the hospitals, clinics, doctors, medical schools, nursing schools, public health departments, Medicaid bureaucracies, and so on. For some of us it was the first time we had looked critically, and with strength, at the existing institutions serving us. The experience of learning just how little control we had over our lives and bodies, the coming together out of isolation to learn from each other in order to define what we needed, and the experience of supporting one another in demanding the changes that grew out of our developing critique—all were crucial and formative political experiences for us. We have felt our potential power as a force for political and social change.

The learning we have done while working on *Our Bodies, Ourselves* has been such a good basis for growth in other areas of life for still another reason. For women throughout the centuries, ignorance about our bodies has had one major consequence—pregnancy. Until very recently pregnancies were all but inevitable, biology *was* our destiny—that is, because our bodies are designed to get pregnant and give birth and lactate, that is what all or most of us did. The courageous and dedicated work of people like Margaret Sanger started in the early twentieth century to spread and make available birth control methods that women could use, thereby freeing us from the traditional lifetime of pregnancies. But the societal expectation that a woman above all else will have babies does not die easily. When we first started talking to each other about this we found that that old expectation had nudged most of us into a fairly rigid role of wife-and-motherhood from the moment we were born female. Even in 1969 when we first started the work that led to this book, we found that many of us were still getting pregnant when we didn't want to. It was not until we researched carefully and learned more about our reproductive systems, about birth-control methods and abortion, about laws governing birth control and abortion, not until we put all this information together with what it meant to us to be female, did we begin to feel that we could truly set out to control whether and when we would have babies.

This knowledge has freed us to a certain extent from the constant, energy-draining anxiety about becoming pregnant. It has made our pregnancies better, because they no longer happen to us; we actively choose them and enthusiastically participate in them. It has made our parenthood better, because it is our choice rather than our destiny. This knowledge has freed us from playing the role of mother if it is not a role that fits us. It has given us a sense of a larger life space to work in, an invigorating and challenging sense of time and room to discover the energies and talents that are in us, to do the work we want to do. And one of the things we most want to do is to help make this freedom of choice, this life space, available to every woman. That is why people in the women's movement have been so active in fighting against the inhumane legal restrictions, the imperfections of available contraceptives, the poor sex education, the highly priced and poorly administered health care that keeps too many women from having this crucial control over their bodies.

There is a fourth reason why knowledge about our bodies has generated so much new energy. For us, body education is core education. Our bodies are the physical bases from which we move out into the world; ignorance, uncertainty —even, at worst, shame—about our physical selves create in us an alienation from ourselves that keeps us from being the whole people that we could be. Picture a woman trying to do work and to enter into equal and satisfying relationships with other people—when she feels physically weak because she has never tried to be strong; when she drains her energy trying to change her face, her figure, her hair, her smells, to match some ideal norm set by magazines, movies, and TV; when she feels confused and ashamed of the menstrual blood that every month appears from some dark place in her body; when her internal body processes are a mystery to her and surface only to cause her trouble (an unplanned pregnancy, or cervical cancer); when she does not understand nor enjoy sex and concentrates her sexual drives into aimless romantic fantasies, perverting and misusing a potential energy because she has been brought up to deny it. Learning to understand, accept, and be responsible for our physical selves, we are freed of some of these pre-occupations and can start to use our untapped energies. Our image of ourselves is on a firmer base, we can be better friends and better lovers, better *people*, more self-confident, more autonomous, stronger, and more whole.

Our Changing Sense of Self

Changing Our Internalized Sexist Values

When we started talking to each other we came to realize how deeply ingrained was our sense of being less valuable than men.

> In my home I always had a sense that my father and brother were more important than my mother and myself. My mother and I shopped, talked to each other, and had friends over—this was considered silly. My father was considered more important—he did the real work of the world.

Rediscovering Activity

Talking to each other, we realized that many of us shared a common perception of men—that they all seemed to be able to turn themselves on and to do things for themselves. We tended to feel passive and helpless and to expect and need men to do things for us. We were trained to give our power over to men. We had reduced ourselves to objects. We remained children, helpless and giving other people power to define us and objectify us.

As we talked together we realized that one of our central fantasies was our wish to find a man who could turn us on, to do for us what we could not do for ourselves, to make us feel alive and affirm our existence. It was as if we were made of clay and man would mold us, shape us, and bring us to life. This was the material of our childhood dreams: "Someday my prince will come." We were always disappointed when men did not accomplish this impossible task for us. And we began to see our passive helpless ways of handing power over to others as crippling to us. What became clear to us was that we had to change our expectations for ourselves. There was no factual reason why we could not assert and affirm our own existence and do and act for ourselves.

There were many factors that affected our capacity to act. For one, the ideal woman does less and less as her class status rises. Most of us, being middle class, were brought up not to do very much. Also, the kind of activity that is built into the traditional female role is different in quality from masculine activity. Masculine activity (repairing a window, building a house) tends to be sporadic, concrete, and have a finished product. Feminine activity (comforting a crying child, preparing a meal, washing laundry) tends to be repetitive, less tangible, and have no final durable product. Here again our sense of inferiority came into play. We had come to think of our activity as doing nothing—although essential for maintaining life—and of male activity as superior. We began to value our activity in a new way. We and what we did were as valuable as men and what they did.

On the other hand, we tried to incorporate within us the capacity to do more "male" product-oriented activity. . . .

We have also come to enjoy physical activity as well as mental and emotional activity. Again, the realm of physical strength is traditionally male. Once again we realized that we were active in our own ways, but we did not value them. As we looked at the details of our lives—the shopping and the cleaning—we realized that we used up a lot of physical energy every day but that we had taken it for granted and thought of it as nothing. We did avoid heavy, strenuous activity. . . .

We are learning to do new things—mountain climbing, canoeing, karate, auto mechanics.

Rediscovering Our Separateness

. . . During this period of building up our own sense of ourselves we tried to find out what we were like on our own, what we could do on our own. We discovered resources we never thought we had. Either because we had been dependent on men to do certain things for us or because we had been so used to thinking of ourselves as helpless and dependent, we had never tried.

It is hard. We are forever fighting a constant, inner struggle to give up and become weak, dependent, and helpless again. . . .

As we have come to feel separate we try to change old relationships and/or try to enter new relationships in new ways. We now also feel positive about our needs to be dependent and connect with others. We have come to value long-term commitments, which we find increasingly rare in such a changing society, just as we value our new separateness.

VISUALIZING FEMINISM

The following photographs illustrate the enormous changes that occurred in feminism between 1945 and 1975. The first photograph, of a display celebrating the 100th anniversary of the Women's Rights Convention at Seneca Falls, New York, reflects the ambivalence of women's position at midcentury. The second, of a 1971 rally in Washington, D.C., reveals no ambivalence at all. Look at the photographs carefully. What can be learned from each of them?

National Archives, Women's Bureau.

Photo by Dennis Brack from Black Star.

FILM AND CULTURE

In an era of VCRs, movie rentals, and cable television, students increasingly carry with them substantial knowledge of the history of film—enough, we hope, to have some fun with the lists that follow. Do the films on the 1970s list reflect some of the seventies themes discussed in this chapter, such as survival, narcissism, environmentalism, and the retreat from social reformism? What other themes might one suggest? The original Superman *was a product of the 1930s. How do you explain the reemergence of the character in the 1970s? Can you see any difference between the films of the 1960s and those of the 1970s?*

TOP TEN MONEYMAKING FILMS FROM THE SEVENTIES

1. *Star Wars* (1977)
2. *Jaws* (1975)
3. *Grease* (1978)
4. *The Exorcist* (1973)
5. *The Godfather* (1972)
6. *Superman* (1978)
7. *The Sting* (1973)
8. *Close Encounters of the Third Kind* (1977)
9. *Saturday Night Fever* (1977)
10. *National Lampoon's Animal House* (1978)

Runners-Up

1. *Smokey and the Bandit* (1977)
2. *One Flew Over the Cuckoo's Nest* (1975)
3. *American Graffiti* (1973)
4. *Rocky* (1976)
5. *Jaws II* (1978)
6. *Love Story* (1970)
7. *Towering Inferno* (1975)
8. *Every Which Way But Loose* (1978)
9. *Heaven Can Wait* (1978)
10. *Airport* (1970)

Cobbett S. Steinberg, *Film Facts* (New York: Facts on File, 1980), pp. 13–14.

TOP TEN MONEYMAKING FILMS FROM
THE SIXTIES

1. *The Sound of Music* (1965)
2. *The Graduate* (1968)
3. *Doctor Zhivago* (1965)
4. *Butch Cassidy* (1969)
5. *Mary Poppins* (1964)
6. *Thunderball* (1965)
7. *Funny Girl* (1968)
8. *Cleopatra* (1963)
9. *Guess Who's Coming to Dinner* (1968)
10. *The Jungle Book* (1967)

Runners-Up

1. *2001: A Space Odyssey* (1968)
2. *Goldfinger* (1964)
3. *Bonnie and Clyde* (1967)
4. *The Love Bug* (1969)
5. *It's a Mad, Mad, Mad, Mad World* (1963)
6. *Midnight Cowboy* (1969)
7. *The Dirty Dozen* (1967)
8. *The Valley of the Dolls* (1967)
9. *The Odd Couple* (1968)
10. *West Side Story* (1961)

John Travolta in His Famous Disco-Dancing Pose in *Saturday Night Fever* (1977).
Travolta's characters were working-class young men operating within the economic
and social constraints of the 1970s.
Corbis Images.

the big picture

This chapter is mostly about the modern women's movement. Where did it come from? What strategies or approaches did it pursue? What were the movement's greatest enemies? How might John Travolta's film *Saturday Night Fever* be used to analyze the women's movement?

chapter fourteen

CULTURE WARS

When he took office as president in 1981, Ronald Reagan had many constituencies. As the oldest man ever to assume the presidency, he was the candidate of the elderly. His promises to restore American "strength" and "pride" brought him the support of millions of working-class and middle-class Americans who could not understand or accept the defeat in Vietnam, humiliation at the hands of the Arab nations, or the nation's weakness in the international marketplace. Reagan appealed to the business community and to growing numbers of other Americans who believed that welfare, the welfare state, liberalism, big government, unions, or high taxes were responsible for the nation's ills. And he had the support of fundamentalist Christians, who interpreted the nation's troubles as a fall from grace and sought a remedy in the restoration of traditional values and practices: an end to abortion, prayer in the public schools, sexual abstinence before marriage, old-fashioned gender roles, censorship of the pornographic or salacious.

For twelve years Reagan and his successor, George Bush, held this curious coalition together. They did it partly with bravado and posturing, partly with American lives. Reagan did his best to revive a foundering Cold War and to restore the Soviet Union as the "evil empire" that Americans loved to hate. He even imagined a technology, familiarly known as "Star Wars," that would miraculously protect Americans from missile attacks. Americans responded by shelling out billions for Star Wars and celebrating the October 1983 invasion of the tiny

Caribbean island of Grenada, with its Marxist government, as a sign of a reemerging America that once again had control of its destiny. Almost a decade later, when the Cold War had ended, Bush found a new, and even worthy, enemy: Iraq's Saddam Hussein, who had invaded oil-rich Kuwait. Once again, the American public responded, greeting "Operation Desert Storm" with a frenzy of patriotism and, rather pointedly, offering returning troops (136 Americans were killed) the lavish homecomings that Vietnam veterans had been denied.

On the domestic front, Reagan and Bush appeared to have made some progress, especially in reconstructing the nation's faltering economy. The catastrophic inflation rates of the Carter years had been dramatically reduced. Unemployment, which had reached a post–World War II peak of 10 percent in the second year of Reagan's first term, had been reduced as well. The Reagan administration had found a remedy for "stagflation."

Yet problems remained. In the midst of the prosperity of the mid-1980s, unemployment stayed at a level more than twice that considered reasonable a generation earlier. Major industries, including machine tools, clothing, steel, and automobiles, remained at the mercy of foreign competition. The United States was losing its heavy industry and, increasingly, its light industry, too. Most of the new jobs—and there were millions of them—were in nonunion service industries that paid low wages and did not offer their employees health insurance or pension plans. More Americans were working, but poor, too—and frightened about the future. When Bush proved ineffectual at dealing with recession in 1992, the voters replaced him with Arkansas Governor Bill Clinton.

Facing the economic uncertainties that were part of the ordinary round of life, Americans turned mean, aggressive, and deadly. Violent crimes—assaults, murders, and rapes—became commonplace events in major cities, and the ghettos of some cities, where drug traffic was heavy, became zones of terror, where people were afraid to leave their homes. Despite Bush's call for a "kinder, gentler" nation, all manner of real and fictitious Americans—talk show hosts, comedians, rock stars, cartoon characters—seemed to revel in insults, abuse, and hate-mongering. The victims were predictable: blacks, women, Asians, Arabs, welfare recipients, Jews, homosexuals, and (for rap artists like N.W.A.) the police. It was—and is—an ugly age.

As the twenty-first century approached, the search for ways of understanding the nation's difficult recent history increasingly took the form of forays into the realm of culture. One set of conservative critics attacked the emerging "multicultural" focus of the high schools and universities, calling for a return to a traditional curriculum that emphasized the nation's European roots. Book-banning made a comeback when fundamentalist, "pro-family" groups went to court to prove that some school districts were using public-school textbooks to teach the "religion" of secular humanism. Under Reagan and Bush—but not Clinton—the National Endowment for the Arts withdrew its support from projects—usually ones with some erotic content—that did not have "the widest audience."

One of the more interesting cultural battles of the 1980s was waged by Tipper Gore, the wife of Albert Gore, Jr., the Tennessee senator who would become Clinton's vice president. Working through a variety of family groups, including her own Parents' Music Resource Center, Gore focused her criticism on heavy metal rock music, a genre she claimed was characterized by harmful images of sadism, brutality, and eroticism. After congressional hearings in 1985, the record industry agreed to a voluntary system of warning labels. Later in the decade and into the 1990s, cultural censors turned their guns on the misogynist lyrics of rap group 2 Live Crew and the violent lyrics of what had become known as "gangsta" rap. And the beat goes on.

Americans have always had a prudish streak, and perhaps the culture wars of the 1980s and 1990s were just another outbreak of the nation's obsession with morality. More likely they are the other face of the American postindustrial economy. One face—whether under Reagan, Bush, or Clinton seems to make no difference—looks outward toward a new, post-American world in which the United States is just another player in the international marketplace. The other face looks inward, contemplating the damage already wrought by these changes and anticipating problems to come. It is this face—the face of a pervasive anxiety about the future—that seeks some modicum of control in the "culture wars."

interpretive essay

James Davison Hunter

CULTURE WARS

In this thoughtful analysis of recent controversies over art, music, television, and other aspects of culture, James Davison Hunter offers us a picture of two cultural camps, one conservative and "orthodox," the other liberal and "progressivist." Because each camp has its own idea of what is vital and important, they appear in this story almost as shadowboxers, struggling furiously against their opponents yet somehow never landing a blow.

While reading Hunter's essay, look for evidence that would indicate the author's sympathies. Is Hunter consistently evenhanded, or does his account lean toward the orthodox or progressivist camp? Consider, too, the meaning of Hunter's overall analysis for American history in the late twentieth century. That is, what kind of society does Hunter describe? Is it healthy or sick? Furthermore, if the culture wars are, indeed, "the struggle to define America" (the words of the subtitle of Hunter's book), which definitions of Americans have been offered in this debate? Perhaps more significant, which definitions have been left out? In the end, can anything significant be accomplished through wars over culture?

One does not need to endure a thousand bleary-eyed evenings with Dan Rather or Tom Brokaw to understand how important a role the media of mass communications play in our lives. Television, radio, magazines, newspapers, news magazines, the popular press, as well as music, film, theater, visual arts, popular literature, do much more than passively reflect the social and political reality of our times. Like the institutions of public education . . . , these institutions actively define reality, shape the times, give meaning to the history we witness and experience as ordinary citizens. This outcome is unavoidable in many ways. In the very act of *selecting* the stories to cover, the books to publish and review, the film and music to air, and the art to exhibit, these institutions effectively define which topics are important and which issues are relevant—worthy of public consideration. Moreover, in the *substance* of the stories covered, books published and reviewed, art exhibited, and so on, the mass media act as a filter through which our perceptions of the world around us take shape. Thus, by virtue of the decisions made by those who control the mass media—seemingly innocuous decisions made day to day and year to year—those who work within these institutions cumulatively wield enormous power. In a good many situations, this power is exercised unwittingly, rooted in the best intentions to perform a task well, objectively, fairly. Increasingly, however, the effects of this power have become understood and deliberately manipulated. Is it not inevitable that the media and the arts would become a field of conflict in the contemporary culture war?

There are at least two matters to consider here. First, the contest to define reality, so central to the larger culture war, inevitably becomes a struggle to control the "instrumentality" of reality definition. This means that the battle over this symbolic territory has practically taken shape as a struggle to influence or even dominate the businesses and industries of public information, art, and entertainment—from the major television and radio networks to the National Endowment for the Arts; from the Hollywood film industry to the music recording industry, and so on. But there is more. At a more subtle and symbolic level, the tensions in this field of conflict point to a struggle over the meaning of "speech" or the meaning of "expression" that the First Amendment is supposed to protect. Underlying the conflict over this symbolic territory, in other words, are the questions "What constitutes art in our communities?" "Whose definition of entertainment and aesthetic appreciation do we accept?" "What version of the news is fair?" And so on.

TAKING ON THE ESTABLISHMENT

We begin by considering a brief vignette of an event that occurred at a pro-life march in Washington, D.C. The day was filled with speeches from politicians, religious leaders, pro-life leaders, and other luminaries. Several hundred thousand people listened attentively, cheered, chanted, prayed, and sang songs. Such are the rituals of modern political rallies. At one point during the rally, however, a number of pro-life advocates spontaneously turned toward a television news crew filming the event from atop a nearby platform and began to chant in unison, "Tell the truth!" "Tell the truth!" What began as a rumble within a few moments had caught on within the crowd. Soon, tens of thousands of people were chanting "Tell the truth!" "Tell the truth!" "Tell the truth!" Of all the aspects of the rally covered in the newscast that evening or in the newspapers the following day, this brief and curious event was not among them.

The story highlights the conviction held by virtually everyone on the orthodox and conservative side of the new cultural divide that the media and arts establishment is unfairly prejudiced against the values they hold dear. They do not tell the truth, the voices of orthodoxy maintain, and what is worse, they do not even present opposing sides of the issues evenhandedly. . . .

Exaggerated [though] they may be, the general perceptions are not totally born out of illusion. Studies of the attitudes of media and entertainment elites, as well as of television news programming and newspaper coverage of various social issues and political events, have shown a fairly strong and consistent bias toward a liberal and progressivist point of view. The field over which these particular battles are waged, then, is uneven—and the contenders recognize it as such. One contender takes a position of defending territory already won; the other strives to reclaim it. There are three major ways in which traditionalists have sought to reclaim this symbolic (and institutional) territory.

One way has been in a direct assault against the media and arts establishment. Acquiring a large-circulation newspaper or a network was something that had been "a dream of conservatives for years," according to Howard Phillips of the Conservative Caucus. Early in 1985, such an assault was made. After years of frustration with what it called "the liberal bias" of CBS, a group called Fairness in Media (FIM) spearheaded a move to buy out the television network. . . . Ultimately, of course, the bid to take over the network failed, but those who supported the idea were not put off. "It may take a while to accomplish [this goal]," one editorialized, "but it's a goal well worth waiting—and striving—for."

The persistent effort of the orthodox alliance to hold the media establishment accountable for the content it presents is another strategy. Numerous national and local organizations are committed to this task, covering a wide range of media. Morality in Media, for example, is an interfaith organization founded in 1962 by three clergymen in order to stop traffic in pornography and to challenge "indecency in media" and to work "for a media based on love, truth and good taste." Accuracy in Media has, since 1969, sought to combat liberal bias by exposing cases where the media have not covered stories "fairly and accurately." The Parents' Music Resource Center, established in 1985, is concerned to raise the awareness of parents about the content of modern rock music, especially heavy metal music. Its specific focus is, according to one of its founders, "not the occasional sexy rock lyric . . . [but] the celebration of the most gruesome violence, coupled with explicit messages that sadomasochism is the essence of sex." One of the most visible of all media watchdog groups is the American Family Association and the affiliated CLeaR-TV, or Christian Leaders for Responsible Television. Founded by the Reverend Donald Wildmon, the American Family Association membership claims ordinary believers and religious leaders from all Christian faiths, Protestant, Catholic, and Orthodox, and together they propose to combat the "excessive, gratuitous sex, violence, profanity, [and] the negative stereotyping of Christians."

These organizations are joined by many others both national and local, including town and city councils around the country that share a similar concern about the content of public information and entertainment. They are effective because they are grass roots in orientation (or at least they pose as being locally connected to the grass roots), and they make use of proven techniques

of popular political mobilization: letter writing, boycott, countermedia exposure, and the like.

As much a support structure for the various orthodox and conservative
subcultures as a weapon in the culture war, communities within the orthodox
alliance have created an entire network of alternative electronic media. These
alternative media challenge the media and arts establishment a third way, then,
through competition, offering programming that defines a fundamentally different and competing reality and vision of America. . . .

. . . Vigorous challenges have been made by the Evangelical-dominated television and radio industry. Within the Evangelical subculture alone there were
over 1300 religious radio stations, over 200 religious television stations, and 3 religious television networks broadcasting in the United States by the early 1990s.
The Catholic place in this industry is relatively small by comparison, but it does
make an important contribution. The programming goes far beyond televised
religious services or radio broadcasts of sacred music to include religious talk
shows, soap operas, drama, Bible studies, and news commentary. In addition to
these enterprises is a billion-dollar book industry (made up, within the
Evangelical orbit alone, of over eighty publishing houses and over 6000 independent religious bookstores) that publish and market books on, for example,
how to be a better Christian, how to raise children, how to cope with a mid-life
crisis, not to mention a sizable literature on what is wrong about America and
what you can do about it. And a multimillion-dollar music industry extends far
beyond the latest rendition of "Blessed Assurance" by George Beverly Shea to
Hasidic and Christian rock and roll, folk, heavy metal (groups called Vengeance,
Petra, or Shout singing such releases as "In Your Face"), and even rap music.

THE POLITICS OF FREE SPEECH

What makes these battles over the media and arts especially interesting is that
they reveal a conflict that is several layers deeper. The first layer of conflict concerns the nature and meaning of art and music, as well as the nature and meaning of information. Inevitably this conflict leads to the more philosophical and
legal disputes over the nature of "speech" and "expression" protected by the
First Amendment. There is no end to the number of "headline cases" in which
these sorts of issues are worked out. The fact is that each dispute contains
within it all the underlying philosophical and legal tensions as well.
Collectively, they make the matter a crisis over which actors on both sides of the
cultural divide urgently press for resolution.

To demonstrate how this conflict is played out at these different levels, it is
necessary to get down to specific cases. . . .

The Avant-Garde and Its Discontents

It begins with the quest for novelty. This impulse is undeniably a driving force
in the arts, entertainment, and news media. The quest is based on the premise

that the new will somehow be better than the old, a premise that fits well with America's utilitarian demand for improvement. The expectation that the media and arts will continue to innovate keeps an audience coming back for more. Cultural tensions, of course, inhere within the quest and on occasion they erupt into full-blown controversy.

Art

Out of a budget of more than $150 million a year, the National Endowment for the Arts funds literally hundreds upon hundreds of projects in theater, ballet, music, photography, film, painting, and sculpture. In the late 1980s, however, it became widely publicized that the National Endowment for the Arts had indirectly funded two controversial photographic exhibits. One project, by Andres Serrano, included, among others, a photograph of a crucifix in a jar of Serrano's urine, entitled *Piss Christ;* the other project, by Robert Mapplethorpe, included, among many others, a photograph that turned an image of the Virgin Mary into a tie rack as well as a number of homoerotic photos (such as one showing Mapplethorpe with a bullwhip implanted in his anus and another showing a man urinating in another man's mouth). All of this was well publicized. Avant-garde? To say the least! But Serrano and Mapplethorpe are, their defenders maintained, "important American artists." One critic called the photograph *Piss Christ* "a darkly beautiful photographic image." Likewise, the director of the Institute of Contemporary Art in Boston concluded of Mapplethorpe's exhibit, "Mapplethorpe's work is art, and art belongs in an art museum."

For those in the various orthodox communities, the controversial aspects of the Serrano and Mapplethorpe exhibits were not art at all but obscenity. "This so-called piece of art is a deplorable, despicable display of vulgarity," said one critic. "Morally reprehensible trash," said another. Of Serrano himself, a third stated, "He is not an artist, he is a jerk. Let him be a jerk on his own time and with his own resources." The American Family Association responded with full-page advertisements in newspapers asking, "Is this how you want your tax dollars spent?"

These voices had a sympathetic hearing in the halls of government as well. In response to the National Endowment for the Arts funding of these projects and the likelihood that it would fund still other such projects in the future, Senator Jesse Helms introduced legislation that would forbid the endowment from supporting art that is "obscene or indecent." The National Endowment for the Arts agreed to make grants available only to those who pledge not to do anything of this nature. The endowment, a Helms ally argued in support of this proposal, should not showcase "artists whose forte is ridiculing the values . . . of Americans who are paying for it." Conservative columnist Doug Bandow argued similarly. "There's no justification for taxing lower-income Americans to support glitzy art shows and theater productions frequented primarily by the wealthy." Still others cited Thomas Jefferson's dictum that it is "sinful and tyrannical" to compel a person to contribute money for the propagation of opinions with which he or she disagrees.

Music

Rap is just one more innovation in youth-oriented music that began decades before with rock and roll. Serious questions were raised about the form and content of this innovation, however, with the 1989 release of *As Nasty As They Wanna Be* by the Miami-based rap group 2 Live Crew. On just one album, there were over 200 uses of the word *fuck,* over 100 uses of explicit terms for male and female genitalia, over 80 descriptions of oral sex, and the word *bitch* was used over 150 times. And what about the work of groups like Mötley Crüe, which invokes images of satanism, and the rap group the Beastie Boys, who mime masturbation on stage, or N.W.A., who sing about war against the police (in "Fuck tha Police"), or Ozzy Osbourne, who sings of the "suicide solution"? Was this really music?

The arts establishment responded with a resounding "yes." Its endorsements were positive and sympathetic. Notwithstanding the violence and irreverence, one essay in the *Washington Post* described rap in particular as "a vibrant manifestation of the black oral tradition. . . . You cannot fully understand this profane style of rapping if you disregard the larger folklore of the streets." A review of 2 Live Crew and rap in general in the *New York Times* claimed that this form of musical expression "reveals the tensions of the communities it speaks to. But with its humor, intelligence and fast-talking grace, it may also represent a way to transcend those tensions." Even at its grossest, one critic wrote in *Time,* this entire genre of music represents "a vital expression of the resentments felt by a lot of people."

Needless to say, the opinions within the orthodox communities were less enthusiastic. One American Family Association member called the work of the rap poets of 2 Live Crew as well as other exemplars of popular music, such as the heavy metal of Mötley Crüe, Twisted Sister, and the like, "mind pollution and body pollution." An attorney involved in the controversy commented, "This stuff is so toxic and so dangerous to anybody, that it shouldn't be allowed to be sold to anybody or by anybody." Because this album was being sold to children, he continued, the group's leader, Luther Campbell, was nothing less than "a psychological child molester." Judges in Florida agreed with the sentiment, finding the lyrics to *As Nasty As They Wanna Be* to violate local obscenity laws. Police arrested Campbell for performing the music in a nightclub after the decree, as well as record store owners who continued to sell the album. In response, Campbell promised two things: a legal appeal and a new album—"this one dirtier than the last."

Television

Every year during the ratings sweep, the major networks display their raciest and most innovative programming. In years past, television shows like "Miami Vice," "Dream Street," "Knots Landing," "thirty-something," "A Man Called Hawk," "The Cosby Show," among many others have made strong showings within the national television audience. These, in turn, become strong draws for corporations wanting to advertise their products. Critics admit that the amount of sexual intimacy outside marriage, violence, and profanity portrayed on some of these shows is very high, yet they also have been quick to point out that many of these shows are technically innovative and treat many issues such as homosexuality, child abuse and incest, and the ambiguities of ethical behavior in law enforcement, marriage, student culture, and the like, with great sensitivity.

Sensitivity is the last thing these television shows display, in the view of many with orthodox commitments. To the contrary, "television," claimed a letter from the American Family Association, "is undermining the Judeo-Christian values you hold dear and work hard to teach your children." For this reason, leaders from CLeaR-TV visited with executives from the three major networks in order to express their concerns. According to Reverend Wildmon, "They used the same words that I used, but we certainly didn't mean the same thing by them." From this point on, the leaders decided to approach the advertisers rather than the networks. "Advertisers don't give you a cold shoulder. They want to be your friend." In line with this strategy, the American Family Association and CLeaR-TV began to approach advertisers. Sponsors who did not respond positively to their concerns very often faced the threat of a boycott. PepsiCo, for example, pulled a commercial featuring pop star, nude model, and actress Madonna and their promotion of her world tour; General Mills, Ralston Purina, and Domino's Pizza pulled advertising from "Saturday Night Live"; Mazda and Noxell were also influenced in this way; and of the 400 sponsors of prime-time television in the 1989 rating sweeps, CLeaR-TV focused on the Mennon Company and the Clorox Corporation, pledging to boycott their products for a year for their sponsorship of programs containing sex, violence, and profanity. . . .

Decoding Art and Avant-Garde

The preceding examples are but a few well-publicized illustrations of cultural warfare in various media and forms of public expression. The point of reviewing them was to demonstrate, across media, certain patterns of cultural conflict. Despite the variations of situation and media, one can trace a common and consistent thread of sentiment on each side of the new cultural divide.

On the progressivist side, there is a tendency to value novelty and the avant-garde for their own sake. This in itself is not controversial. What is controversial is *how* avant-garde is defined. Progressives implicitly define the "avant-garde" not so much as the presentation of classic social themes in new artistic forms, but rather as the symbolic presentation of behavior and ideas that test the limits of social acceptability. More often than not this means the embrace of what the prevailing social consensus would have called "perverse" or "irreverent," what Carol Iannone calls "the insistent and progressive artistic exploration of the forbidden frontiers of human experience." Lucy Lippard acknowledges as much in her review of the Serrano corpus in *Art in America:* "His work shows," she contends, "that the conventional notion of good taste with which we are raised and educated is based on an illusion of social order that is no longer possible (nor desirable) to believe in. We now look at art in the context of incoherence and disorder—a far more difficult task than following the prevailing rules." A similar theme can be found in each of the other cases reviewed. In rap music and in television programming, the boundaries of social consensus around human relationships are tested through excessive sex and violence. . . . In each case, an earlier consensus of what is "perverse" and what is "irreverent" is challenged, and as it is challenged, it inevitably disintegrates.

The issue is sharpened when considering the special case of art. Here too the underlying controversy is over how art is to be defined. In general, progressivists tend to start with the assumption that there is no objective method of determining what is art and what is obscene. Historical experience demonstrates time and again that even if a consensus declares that a work has no enduring artistic value, the consensus may change; the work could, over time, come to be viewed as art. For this reason one must recognize and at all times respect and defend the autonomy of the artist and of artistic effort. Artists should not be bound by legal constraints or inhibited by social conventions, for artistic genius may yet emerge, if it is not already evident. Indeed, modern criticism does regard art "as a 'sacred wood,' a separate universe, a self-contained sovereignty" and the artist, in writer Vladimir Nabokov's words, as responsible to no one but himself. One artist expressed this theme when he said, "It is extremely important that art be unjustifiable."

Out of this general perspective comes the implicit understanding that a work is art if "experts" are willing to call it art and if it symbolically expresses an individual's personal quest to understand and interpret one's experience in the world. Both themes were evident in the expert testimony given at the 1990 obscenity trial of the Contemporary Arts Center in Cincinnati where the question "What is art?" was posed directly in view of the Mapplethorpe retrospective. Jacquelynn Baas, director of the University Art Museum at the University of California at Berkeley, responded to the question of why one should consider Robert Mapplethorpe's work as art by declaring: "In the first place, they're great photographs. Secondly, in this work he dealt with issues that our society, modern society is grappling with . . . what it means to be a sexual being, and also race, that was an important part of the show." . . .

For the orthodox and their conservative allies, expert opinion is not a reliable measure of artistic achievement and the artist's intentions are completely irrelevant to determining whether a work is art. Rather, artistic achievement is measured by the extent to which it reflects the sublime. Critic Hilton Kramer endorses this view in speaking of federal funding for art that reflects "the highest achievements of our civilization." George F. Will similarly favors the view that art, at least art worthy of support, is recognized in its capacity to "elevate the public mind by bringing it into contact with beauty and even ameliorate social pathologies." Art worthy of government funding, therefore, should be justifiable on the grounds that it serves this high public purpose. Congressman Henry Hyde, in reflecting about his role in the public policy process, argues that "art detached from the quest for truth and goodness is simply self-expression and ultimately self-absorption." . . .

In sum, for the orthodox and their conservative allies artistic creativity is concerned to reflect a higher reality. For their opponents, art is concerned with the creation of reality itself. Art for the progressivist is, then, a statement of being. To express oneself is to declare one's existence. Hilton Kramer may be correct that the professional art world maintains a sentimental attachment to the idea that art is at its best when it is most extreme and disruptive, but he is probably wrong if he believes this to be its chief or only aim. More fundamentally, if only implicitly, the contemporary arts project is a statement about the meaning of life, namely that life is a process of self-creation. As this enterprise takes public form, however, contemporary art and the avant-garde come to represent nothing less than the besmearing of the highest ideals of the orthodox moral vision.

When all is said and done, however, the events taking place in each of the contexts mentioned earlier—the action and reaction of progressivists and cultural conservatives—represent only the first state in the development of a deeper debate about the limits of public expression in American society.

CENSORSHIP

Progressivist Accusations

The immediate reaction of the progressivists is that those who complain about art do so because they "do not know enough about art," or simply "do not care about art." All the protest demonstrates, as the *Washington Post* put it, "the danger of a cultural outsider passing judgement on something he doesn't understand." Such comments may sound elitist (and undoubtedly are), but their significance goes beyond implying that those who do not share progressive aesthetic taste are simple philistines. The real significance of such sentiments is that they reaffirm the basic characteristic of the contemporary culture war, namely the nigh complete disjunction of moral understanding between the orthodox and progressivist communities—in this case, on what constitutes art. The progressivist communities and the arts establishment display a certain arrogance in believing that their definitions of "serious artistic merit" should be accepted by all, and this leads them to categorize various cultural conservatives as "Know-Nothings," "yahoos," "neanderthals," "literary death squads," "fascists," and "cultural terrorists."

The response of progressivists to this situation, however, quickly evolves beyond this. In a way, what we hear after this initial response is less an argument than a symbolic call to arms, a "Banzai!" that reveals a spontaneous, unified, and passionate indignation every bit as deep as that expressed by the orthodox in reaction to tarnishing of their ideals. Irrespective of the circumstances or media, the orthodox protest evokes among progressives the cry of "censorship."

Nowhere has this alarm sounded more loudly than in the case of the protest against network television. People for the American Way, Americans for Constitutional Freedom, *Playboy*, and many others have viewed the boycotting of corporate advertisers of television programming as acts of "economic terrorism" that are tantamount to censorship. "What is more intrusive than the attempt by fundamentalist censors to dictate what we can watch in the privacy of our own homes?" asked the founder of Fundamentalists Anonymous. Donald Wildmon, whom *Playboy* called the "Tupelo Ayatollah," is nothing short of "dangerous." Said the executive director of Americans for Constitutional Freedom, "We intend to do everything to prevent him from setting himself up as a censor who can re-make America in his own image."

Similar accusations are leveled in every other situation where the orthodox protest the content of public media. The music industry viewed the efforts of the Parents' Music Resource Center to have albums labeled "contains explicit lyrics" as an act of censorship. Frank Zappa called it a conspiracy to extort. . . . And, fi-nally, efforts to prohibit flag burning have been called political censorship.

Implicit within this accusation, of course, is the legal judgment that the con-stitutionally guaranteed right to freedom of speech is either threatened or ac-tually violated by conservative protest. For this reason, the Bill of Rights is al-most always invoked by progressives or by artists themselves. When, for example, Nikki Sixx of Mötley Crüe was told in an interview that there were those who objected to the band stating on stage that their "only regret is that [they] couldn't eat all the pussy [they] saw here tonight, he responded, 'I say fuck 'em. It's freedom of speech; First Amendment!' " Thomas Jefferson himself might not have put it quite that way or even necessarily agreed with the appli-cation, but without fail, the legacy of Jefferson directly informs the content of the progressivist reply. Luther Campbell of 2 Live Crew echoed this sentiment when he said, "We give America what they want. Isn't there such a thing as free enterprise here? Isn't there such a thing as freedom of speech?" The record store owner in Florida arrested for selling *As Nasty As They Wanna Be* put the matter in a slightly larger context. "We tell the Lithuanians, you know, fight for free-dom. . . . And yet, we're trying to censor our own country. . . . We don't need nobody to censor us and they're violating our civil rights and our freedom of speech. And next—what else will it be next?" . . .

The pounding repetition of this accusation is in accord with the general po-sition taken by the People for the American Way, who believe that this brand of censorship is not only on the increase, it "has become more organized and more effective" with haunting implications. The very language employed by cultural conservatives when they insist it is time to "clean up our culture" or to "stop subsidizing decadence" is, as several writers contend, "chillingly reminiscent of Nazi cultural metaphors." Robert Brustein, writing in the *New Republic,* goes so far as to dismiss the distinction between censorship and the effort to influ-ence the distribution of taxpayers' money (as in the effort to defund "offensive art" at the National Endowment for the Arts), insisting that defunding art is a form of censorship. He concludes that "only government—in a time when other funding has grown increasingly restrictive and programmatic—can guarantee free and innovative art. And that means acknowledging that, yes, every artist has a First Amendment right to subsidy."

The progressivist response to this backlash has gone beyond rhetoric into direct political action as well. Full-page newspaper ads criticizing the censorious impulse have appeared. Individual artists, the ACLU [American Civil Liberties Union], Playboy Enterprises, *Penthouse,* the American Booksellers Association, and many other individuals and organizations have initiated litigation against a number of organizations, such as Concerned Women for America and the American Family Association. . . .

To the accusation of censorship, the reply of cultural conservatives is "nonsense!" *Christianity Today* editorialized that the media and arts establishment

> use freedom of speech as a means to flout standards of common public decency. We must not throw in the towel. Christians must unite in mounting a counteroffensive through our families, churches, schools, and other institutions. The legal issues surrounding public standards may be complex, but the moral imperatives are not. We must not abandon the ring of public debate to those who would use freedom of speech as an excuse to be as morally offensive as they "wanna" be.

Implicit here and in much of the orthodox and conservative rhetoric is the view that communities have the right to decide for themselves what standards will be used to discriminate between art and obscenity. If, through the democratic process, standards are agreed upon, why should communities not be entitled to uphold them through official means?

Donald Wildmon also rejects the idea that he and his compatriots are somehow violating the First Amendment protections of free speech, but he takes a slightly different tack. He insists that artists do have the right to express themselves as they please but that he too has a right to speak out against them. This posture is expressed paradigmatically in his rationale for acting against Pepsi for its plans to fund the Madonna tour.

> Here is a pop singer who makes a video that's sacrilegious to the core. Here's a pop star that made a low-budget porn film. Here's a pop star who goes around in her concerts with sex oozing out, wearing a cross. Now Pepsi is saying to all the young people of the new generation, "Here is the person we want you to emulate and imitate." They can do that. They've got every right to give Madonna $10 million dollars, put it on television every night if they want to. All I'm saying is "Don't ask me to buy Pepsi if you do it." . . .

Tipper Gore of the Parents' Music Resource Center called the cry of censorship "a smoke screen," a dodge for taking corporate responsibility for their product. In asking for labels on record albums, her group claimed, they were asking for more information, not less. The group's approach, then, "was the direct opposite of censorship." Morality in Media takes the argument one step further in maintaining that "freedom of expression is not the exclusive right of producers, publishers, authors or a handful of media executives. Freedom of expression belongs . . . to the entire community. . . . [it is only a] vocal, unremitting, organized community expression [that] will bring about a media based on love, truth and good taste." . . .

Some complain that progressivists and a liberal educational establishment censor, through exclusion, material on traditional religion in the public school textbooks. . . . The same kind of de facto censoring occurs, it is maintained, when major magazines and newspapers, through editorial edict, refuse to review books written and published by conservative Catholics or Evangelical Protestants, or deny them the recognition they deserve by not including these works on their best-seller lists. The Evangelical writer Francis Schaeffer, for example, sold over 3 million copies of his books in the United States, and yet his books were never reviewed in the *New York Times Book Review* or *Time* and never counted on any best-seller list. The same was true of Hal Lindsey's *Late Great Planet Earth,* a book that was the top nonfiction seller in America in the 1970s— for the entire decade. The book was not reviewed by the literary establishment nor did it appear on weekly best-seller lists until it was later published by a secular publishing house. For publishing elites to ignore this literature, for whatever reasons—even if they do not believe such works constitute "serious literature or scholarship"—is, they say, to "censor." . . .

Decoding Free Speech

Back and forth the arguments go. After a time, the details of this conflict become tediously predictable. One side claims that a work is "art"; the other claims it is not. One claims that a work has enduring aesthetic or literary appeal; the other claims it appeals only to the eccentric interests of a deviant subculture. At least on the face of it, one is tempted to agree with Justice John Marshall Harlan, who concluded that "one man's vulgarity is another's lyric." Such relativism may not be desirable but it seems to be the necessary outcome of the present cultural conflict. In this light, it is entirely predictable that each side would claim that the other side is not committed to free speech but to a systematic imposition of its values and perspectives on everyone else. Alas, one person's act of "censorship" has become another's "commitment to community standards."

Thus, in the contemporary culture war, regard for rights to the freedom of speech has become a matter of "whose ox is being gored" at the moment. The fact is, both sides make a big mistake when they confuse *censuring* (the legitimate mobilization of moral opprobrium) with *censoring* (the use of the state and other legal or official means to restrict speech). Censuring, say through economic boycott or letter-writing campaigns, is itself a form of political speech protected by the First Amendment and employed legally all the time whether in boycotts against South Africa, Nestle's, or California lettuce growers, or against the purveyors of sexually explicit or theologically controversial art. But the finer points of distinction are lost on many of the activists in this debate. Even when the protest is merely the expression of disapproval, what each side invariably hears are the footsteps of an approaching cadre of censors. In most cases, however, neither side presents a genuine threat to the rights of the other to free expression. The cry of censorship from both sides of the cultural divide, then, becomes an ideological weapon to silence legitimate dissent.

This being said, it must also be stated that real censorship *is* taking place and the voices of both cultural conservatism and progressivism perpetuate it in their own ways. Censorship, again, is the use of the state or other official means to restrict speech. In every case it is justified by the claim that "community standards" have been violated. The use of the police to arrest the members of 2 Live Crew in Florida and the use of law to shut down the Contemporary Arts Center in Cincinnati because they violated community standards of obscenity are, then, textbook cases of such censorship. Censorship is also perpetuated on the other side of the cultural divide. It is seen in the efforts of student groups and universities to prohibit, in the name of community standards, defamatory remarks and expressions against minorities, gays, and women. (Would progressives throw their support or legal weight behind a similar code that prohibited say, unpatriotic, irreligious, or sexually explicit "expressions" on the community campus?) Censorship is also seen, to give another example, in the suspension of Andy Rooney from his job at CBS in 1990 for making remarks against gays. On both sides of the cultural divide, the concept of "community standards" is invoked as an ideological weapon to silence unpopular voices. Understanding how the standards of one moral community can be so diametrically opposed to the standards of the other takes us back to the root of the cultural war itself.

ART, EXPRESSION, AND THE SACRED

A critic quoted earlier warned of the danger of a cultural outsider passing judgment on something he does not understand. The reality of the culture war is that the cultural conservative and the progressivist are each outsiders to the other's cultural milieu. Accordingly, each regularly and often viciously passes judgment on the other. That judgment is not at all bad in itself. Such is the back and forth of democratic discourse. The danger is not in passing judgment but in the failure to understand why the other is so insulted by that judgment. *That* is the measure of their mutual outsiderness.

The orthodox, for example, demonstrate such a position when they view certain artistic work in isolation from the larger aesthetic project of an artist and label it obscene, pornographic, and prurient. Who are these people, progressivists ask, to label the life work of Serrano and Mapplethorpe as vulgarity? That they cannot see the "enduring artistic achievement" of an artist's oeuvre is a gauge of their alienation from "high art" discourse. The same kind of obtuseness is found among progressivists. Consider the controversy surrounding *The Last Temptation of Christ*. A *Washington Post* editorial stated with no equivocation that audiences would not find the film blasphemous. Another reviewer, from *Newsweek*, said, "One can think of hundreds of trashy, thrill-happy movies devout Christians could get upset about. Instead, they have taken to the airwaves to denounce *the one movie that could conceivably open a viewer's heart to the teachings of Jesus.*" Still another reviewer, from Newhouse Newspapers, called the film, "The most realistic biblical film ever made." Who are these people, orthodox Christians ask, to proclaim universally that *The Last Temptation of Christ* was not blasphemous? For millions of Americans it certainly was, and it was a measure of progressives' outsiderness that they could not acknowledge it to be.

This kind of mutual misunderstanding reveals once more that the conflict over the media and the arts is not just a dispute among institutions and not just a disagreement over "speech" protected by the First Amendment. Ultimately the battle over this symbolic territory reveals a conflict over world views—over what standards our communities and our nation will live by; over what we consider to be "of enduring value" in our communities; over what we consider a fair representation of our times, and so on. As a bystander at the Contemporary Arts Center in Cincinnati observed during the controversy over the Mapplethorpe exhibit, "This isn't just an obscenity prosecution. This is a trial of a good part of American culture."

But even more, these battles again lay bare the tensions that exist between two fundamentally different conceptions of the sacred. For those of orthodox religious commitments, the sacred is obvious enough. It is an unchanging and everlasting God who ordained through Scripture, the church, or Torah, a manner of life and of social relationship that cannot be broached without incurring the displeasure of God. On the other side of the cultural divide, the sacred is a little more difficult to discern. Perhaps Tom Wolfe had it right when he observed that art itself was the religion of the educated classes. Maybe this is why Broadway producer Joseph Papp said as he observed the police coming into the Cincinnati Contemporary Arts Center to close the Mapplethorpe exhibit, "It's like an invasion. It's like they're coming into a church or coming into a synagogue, or coming into any place of worship. It's a violation." Such an insight makes sense if we see art as a symbol of conscience. To place any restrictions on the arts, therefore, is to place restrictions on the conscience itself; it is to place fetters on the symbol of being. Such an insight also makes sense if we see art as a symbol of immortality—of that which will outlive us all. To place restrictions on art is to place restrictions on the (secular) hope of eternity. Perhaps this is why the procedural guarantee of freedom of expression has also acquired a sacred quality in progressivist circles.

The idea that the battle over the arts is related to the tensions between two different conceptions of the sacred is not far-fetched. How else can one explain the passion and intensity on both sides of the cultural divide were it not that each side, by its very being and expression, profanes what the other holds most sublime? If this is true, we are again reminded of the reasons that the larger culture war will not subside any time soon.

RAP WARS

*Rap music emerged in the South Bronx ghetto in the late 1960s and was first
recorded in 1979. During the mid-1980s, rap entered the mainstream, and by
1988, white ten-year-olds in the suburbs were plugged into "wholesome"
black rappers like Young MC or white rappers like Vanilla Ice. At the same
time, however, a new generation of confrontational hard-core rappers—among
them Public Enemy, N.W.A., and 2 Live Crew—had begun to record forms of
rap music that many thought were simply unacceptable. In 1990, 2 Live
Crew's album* As Nasty As They Wanna Be *was ruled obscene by a U.S.
District Court in Florida, and the band was arrested and tried on obscenity
charges for its performance at an adults-only concert in Hollywood, Florida.*

*Concerned about the content and tone of rap music, Tipper Gore (see the
introduction to this chapter) offered her thoughts in a January 1990 editorial
in the* Washington Post; *the piece was written before the controversy over 2
Live Crew erupted. Henry Louis Gates, Jr., professor of English at Duke
University and an authority on African-American culture, joined the fray six
months later, when 2 Live Crew was at the center of things, with a brief column for the* New York Times.

*Is Gates's defense of 2 Live Crew convincing? Do his arguments address
Tipper Gore's concerns?*

Tipper Gore

HATE, RAPE AND RAP

Words like bitch and nigger are dangerous. Racial
and sexual epithets, whether screamed across a
street or camouflaged by the rhythms of a song,
turn people into objects less than human—easier to degrade, easier to violate,
easier to destroy. These words and epithets are becoming an accepted part of

Washington Post, January 8, 1990.

our lexicon. What's disturbing is that they are being endorsed by some of the very people they diminish, and our children are being sold a social dictionary that says racism, sexism, and antisemitism are okay.

As someone who strongly supports the First Amendment, I respect the freedom of every individual to label another as he likes. But speaking out against racism isn't endorsing censorship. No one should silently tolerate racism or sexism or antisemitism, or condone those who turn discrimination into a multimillion-dollar business justified because it's "real."

A few weeks ago television viewers saw a confrontation of depressing proportions on the Oprah Winfrey show. It was one I witnessed firsthand; I was there in the middle of it. Viewers heard some black American women say they didn't mind being called "bitches" and they weren't offended by the popular rap music artist Ice-T when he sang about "Evil E" who "f——ed the bitch with a flashlight/pulled it out, left the batteries in/so he could get a charge when he begins." There is more, and worse.

Ice-T, who was also on the show, said the song came from the heart and reflected his experiences. He said he doesn't mind other groups using the word nigger in their lyrics. That's how he described himself, he said.

Some in the audience questioned why we couldn't see the humor in such a song.

Will our kids get the joke? Do we want them describing themselves or each other as "niggers?" Do we want our daughters to think of themselves as "bitches" to be abused? Do we want our sons to measure success in gold guns hanging from thick neck chains? The women in the audience may understand the slang; Ice-T can try to justify it. But can our children?

One woman in the audience challenged Ice-T. She told him his song about the flashlight was about as funny as a song about lynching black men.

The difference is that sexism and violence against women are accepted as almost an institutionalized part of our entertainment. Racism is not—or at least, it hasn't been until recently. The fact is, neither racism, sexism nor antisemitism should be accepted.

Yet they are, and in some instances that acceptance has reached startling proportions. The racism expressed in the song "One In A Million" by Guns N' Roses, sparked nationwide discussion and disgust. But, an earlier album that featured a rape victim in the artwork and lyrics violently degrading to women created barely a whisper of protest. More than 9 million copies were sold, and it was played across the radio band. This is only one example where hundreds exist.

Rabbi Abraham Cooper of the Simon Wiesenthal Center, who also appeared on the Oprah Show, voiced his concerns about the antisemitic statements made by Professor Griff, a nonsinging member of the rap group Public Enemy; statements that gain added weight from the group's celebrity. "Jews are wicked," Professor Griff said in an interview with the *Washington Times*. . . . "[Responsible for] a majority of wickedness that goes on across the globe."

The Simon Wisenthal Center placed a full-page ad in *Daily Variety* calling for self-restraint from the music industry, a move that prompted hundreds of calls to the center. Yet Rabbi Cooper's concerns barely elicited a response from Oprah Winfrey's audience.

Alvin Poussaint, a Harvard psychiatrist who is black, believes that the widespread acceptance of such degrading and denigrating images may reflect low self-esteem among black men in today's society. There are few positive black male role models for young children, and such messages from existing role models are damaging. Ice-T defends his reality: "I grew up in the streets— I'm no Bryant Gumbel." He accuses his critics of fearing that reality and says the fear comes from an ignorance of the triumph of the street ethic.

A valid point, perhaps. But it is not the messenger that is so frightening, it is the perpetuation—almost glorification—of the cruel and violent reality of his "streets."

A young black mother in the front row rose to defend Ice-T. Her son, she said, was an A student who listened to Ice-T. In her opinion, as long as Ice-T made a profit, it didn't matter what he sang.

Cultural economics were a poor excuse for the south's continuation of slavery. Ice-T's financial success cannot excuse the vileness of his message. What does it mean when performers such as Ice-T, Axl Rose of Guns N' Roses and others can enrich themselves with racist and misogynist diatribes and defend it because it sells? Hitler's antisemitism sold in Nazi Germany. That didn't make it right.

In America, a woman is raped once every six minutes. A majority of children surveyed by a Rhode Island Rape Crisis Center thought rape was acceptable. In New York City, rape arrests of thirteen-year-old boys have increased 200 percent in the past two years. Children eighteen and younger now are responsible for 70 percent of the hate crime committed in the United States. No one is saying this happens solely because of rap or rock music, but certainly kids are influenced by the glorification of violence.

Children must be taught to hate. They are not born with ideas of bigotry— they learn from what they see in the world around them. If their reality consists of a street ethic that promotes and glorifies violence against women or discrimination against minorities—not only in everyday life, but in their entertainment— then ideas of bigotry and violence will flourish.

We must raise our voices in protest and put pressure on those who not only reflect this hatred but also package, polish, promote, and market it; those who would make words like nigger acceptable. Let's place a higher value on our children than on our profits and embark on a remedial civil rights course for children who are being taught to hate and a remedial nonviolence course for children who are being taught to destroy. Let's send the message loud and clear through our homes, our streets and our schools, as well as our art and our culture.

Henry Louis Gates, Jr.

2 LIVE CREW, DECODED

Durham, N.C.

The rap group 2 Live Crew and their controversial hit recording *As Nasty As They Wanna Be* may well earn a signal place in the history of First Amendment rights. But just as important is how these lyrics will be interpreted and by whom.

For centuries, African-Americans have been forced to develop coded ways of communicating to protect them from danger. Allegories and double meanings, words redefined to mean their opposites (*bad* meaning *good,* for instance), even neologisms *(bodacious)* have enabled blacks to share messages only the initiated understood.

Many blacks were amused by the transcripts of Marion Barry's sting operation, which reveals that he used the traditional black expression about one's *nose being opened.* This referred to a love affair and not, as Mr. Barry's prosecutors have suggested, to the inhalation of drugs. Understanding this phrase could very well spell the difference (for the Mayor) between prison and freedom.

2 Live Crew is engaged in heavy-handed parody, turning the stereotypes of black and white American culture on their heads. These young artists are acting out, to lively dance music, a parodic exaggeration of the age-old stereotypes of the oversexed black female and male. Their exuberant use of hyperbole (phantasmagoric sexual organs, for example) undermines—for anyone fluent in black cultural codes—a too literal-minded hearing of the lyrics.

This is the street tradition called *signifying* or *playing the dozens,* which has generally been risqué, and where the best signifier or "rapper" is the one who invents the most extravagant images, the biggest "lies," as the culture says. (H. "Rap" Brown earned his nickname in just this way.) In the face of racist stereotypes about black sexuality, you can do one of two things: you can disavow them or explode them with exaggeration.

2 Live Crew, like many "hip-hop" groups, is engaged in sexual carnivalesque. Parody reigns supreme, from a take-off of standard blues to a spoof of the black power movement; their off-color nursery rhymes are part of a venerable western tradition. The group even satirizes the culture of commerce when it appropriates popular advertising slogans ("Tastes great!" "Less filling!") and puts them in a bawdy context.

2 Live Crew must be interpreted within the context of black culture generally and of signifying specifically. Their novelty, and that of other adventuresome rap groups, is that their defiant rejection of euphemism now voices for the mainstream what before existed largely in the "race record" market—where the records of Redd Foxx and Rudy Ray Moore once were forced to reside.

Rock songs have always been about sex but have used elaborate subterfuges to convey that fact. 2 Live Crew uses Anglo-Saxon words and is self-

New York Times, June 19, 1990. Copyright © 1990 by the New York Times Company. Reprinted by permission.

conscious about it: a parody of a white voice in one song refers to "private personal parts," as a coy counterpart to the group's bluntness.

Much more troubling than its so-called obscenity is the group's overt sexism. Their sexism is so flagrant, however, that it almost cancels itself out in a hyperbolic war between the sexes. In this it recalls the intersexual jousting in Zora Neale Hurston's novels. Still, many of us look toward the emergence of more female rappers to redress sexual stereotypes. And we must not allow ourselves to sentimentalize street culture: the appreciation of verbal virtuosity does not lessen one's obligation to critique bigotry in all its pernicious forms.

Is 2 Live Crew more "obscene" than, say, the comic Andrew Dice Clay? Clearly, this rap group is seen as more threatening than others that are just as sexually explicit. Can this be completely unrelated to the specter of the young black male as a figure of sexual and social disruption, the very stereotypes 2 Live Crew seems determined to undermine?

This question—and the very large question of obscenity and the First Amendment—cannot even be addressed until those who would answer them become literate in the vernacular traditions of African-Americans. To do less is to censor through the equivalent of intellectual prior restraint—and censorship is to art what lynching is to justice.

Legacies: The Monument Controversy

A decade after the last American soldiers left Vietnam in 1973, Americans quarreled again over Vietnam; they re-fought the conflict—this time in the realm of culture. Hollywood led the way, looking back at the war in a series of important films, including Platoon *(1986),* Full Metal Jacket *(1987),* Hamburger Hill *(1987),* Born on the Fourth of July *(1989), and several featuring Sylvester Stallone as the alienated veteran, John Rambo, especially* First Blood *(1982) and* Rambo: First Blood, Part II *(1985). Most of these films were as much about masculinity, and about how men were dealing with the consequences of de-industrialization, as they were about anything that happened in Southeast Asia.*

Differences over the meaning of Vietnam inevitably affected the shape of a monument to commemorate the Vietnam War dead. The two most prominent proposals were for a sunken wall, inscribed with the names of the dead, and a statue of combat soldiers. The upshot was a memorial incorporating both designs; the statue is positioned a short distance from the wall. What was at stake in the monument controversy? What, in your opinion, is the message or theme of each design, and how might each represent a distinct understanding of the war?

The Wall Portion of the Vietnam Memorial. The design by Yale University architecture student Maya Ying Lin was the winning entry in an open competition. *National Park Service.*

The Statue Portion of the Vietnam Memorial, Sculpted by Frederick Hart. *National Park Service.*

BACK TO THE FUTURE

"Future Adaptation of Man." In a cartoon drawn in 1982, Tom Toles presented this rather pessimistic view of humanity's future. Which of Toles's anxieties have been confirmed by recent history? Which no longer seem as significant? If Toles were drawing the strip in 2000, how might it be different?

Reprinted with permission of Tom Toles and the Buffalo and Erie County Historical Society.

the big picture

What was being contested in the "culture wars" of the 1980s and 1990s? What were the basic values that underpinned the different arguments? Was conflict over "culture" new? Or had it been present in earlier periods, too?

chapter fifteen

CLOSING THE CENTURY:
MORE OF THE SAME

*I*n many ways, the last decade of the century resembled the one before it. Culture remained a battlefield, as New York City's Republican Mayor Rudolph Giuliani demonstrated in the fall of 1999, when he withheld city funds from The Brooklyn Museum of Art because of an exhibit that included a painting of a black Madonna featuring a clump of elephant dung and cutouts from pornographic magazines. "As the mayor of the city of New York," Giuliani asked on *Meet the Press*, "am I going to approve the hard-earned dollars of the people of this city supporting this? I have to say no. And for standing up for that principle, I'm being attacked by the First Amendment hysterics."

Liberalism of the New Deal/Great Society kind remained an endangered species. The liberal panaceas of the 1970s—affirmative action and mandatory busing to achieve integrated public schools—were increasingly seen as wrong or harmful. Although Bill Clinton talked the liberal talk on issues as diverse and important as race relations, the environment, literacy, and health care, his two-term presidency produced remarkably few liberal triumphs. A major administration effort to revamp the nation's medical care delivery system to provide something close to universal coverage—a goal of public policy liberals since the 1910s—found little support among Americans too selfish to care about the basic needs of others or wary of anything that smacked of bureaucracy and big government. The most important piece of domestic legislation passed in the Clinton years—the Personal Responsibility and Work Opportunity Act (1996)—had been on the conservative agenda for decades. The law did what Clinton had promised to do in the 1992 campaign, "to end welfare as we know it." It ended the federal government's role in AFDC (Aid to Families with Dependent Children, the heart of the welfare system since 1935) and required the states to develop their own programs under restrictive federal guidelines that limited recipients to two years of continuous benefits, and five years over a lifetime. The law was based on several ideas and assumptions held by Republicans and Democrats: that the welfare system was somehow responsible for the nation's ills, and especially for conditions in the inner cities; that welfare mothers were black, lazy, and promiscuous; that work outside the home would punish welfare mothers and make them more moral; and that welfare encouraged women to remain outside of marriage. Whatever the assumptions, the result was that poor, single women were forced to work outside the home or to rely on charity.

The economy absorbed much of Clinton's attention, and here, too, the administration held the political center. The president was an ardent supporter of the North American Free Trade Agreement (1994), which incorporated Mexico into a free-trade zone with the United States and Canada, embraced the Republican goal of a balanced budget, and, in his second term, made economic cooperation in Asia a high priority, even at the expense of human-rights considerations in China. Driven by expanding international markets, a revolution in computer technology that dramatically increased the productivity of American workers, a decline in inefficient Cold War military spending, and judicious monetary policy under the direction of Federal Reserve chief Alan Greenspan, the economy responded with year after year of strong growth and low inflation. With the unemployment rate at about 4 percent by century's end, employers in many industries were scrambling to find the labor they needed.

Prosperity, jobs, new technologies, abundant consumer goods, the free enterprise system humming along—Americans should have been pleased, proud, and satisfied. But the moment was more complex than that, and more unsettling. Though real enough, the prosperity of the 1990s was appallingly uneven. While a small percentage of Americans made huge profits in a raging bull market on Wall Street, millions of others just survived, holding down low-wage jobs in service industries and in a declining manufacturing sector buffeted by foreign competition and damaged by free trade. Hispanics, African Americans, women who headed households, inner-city youth, the 10 percent of the U.S. population that was foreign-born—all these groups had substantial rates of poverty in a decade described by one magazine as "a golden age in American history."

No less disturbing was what had happened to politics. For most of the century, Americans had used the political system to help the unfortunate, to deal with social problems, or to remedy injustice. In the progressive era, reformers used politics to protect children from the hazards of the workplace. In the Great Depression, New Dealers used politics to aid the unemployed, to build housing for the poor, and to provide retirement security for the elderly. In the 1960s, the Great Society used the political sphere to fight a "War on Poverty" and to insure that the poor and the old had adequate medical care. By the end of the 1990s, little remained of this sense of political efficacy. Instead, Americans had transferred their allegiance from politics to economics, from the body politic to the business corporation, from confidence that government could solve major social problems to a reliance on solutions that focused on the smallest unit of social organization: the family.

It was a long process, one that began in the late 1960s; and as it occurred, politics became what it is today: "undignified, disreputable, vaguely ridiculous, and thoroughly outmoded," in the words of twenty-five-year-old social critic Jedediah Purdy. A politics of issues becomes a politics of personality, the province of scandal, a setting for pointless talk—that is, the politics of Bill Clinton. Hence we should not be surprised that Clinton had sexual relations with a White House intern; that he lied to cover up the affair; that he was impeached and nearly removed from office; or that Americans became addicted to following the story in all its lurid detail. The Clinton-Lewinsky scandal is the quintessence of modern politics.

To be sure, the decade has witnessed efforts to forge a new politics that speaks more directly than the existing free-market consensus to the needs and values of ordinary Americans. Interestingly, most of these efforts invoked criticism of the emerging economic system. Public cynicism about politics sparked enthusiasm for the 1992 third-party candidacy of businessman Ross Perot, who announced that NAFTA would produce a "giant sucking sound" as American jobs went to Mexico. He received 19 percent of the vote. In the 1996 campaign, growing opposition to the economics of free trade fueled Pat Buchanan's challenge within the Republican Party. And 1999 brought perhaps the most significant oppositional movement of the decade—a massive demonstration in Seattle, Washington, protesting the policies of the World Trade Organization (WTO). A giant black puppet, cast as a combination of the WTO and death, carried a sign reading "FREE TRADE . . . Free to exploit people & nature." In communities across the country, residents unwilling to accept the social costs of increased efficiency defeated proposals for WalMarts and other "big box" stores. More ominous were the Branch Davidians, the militias, the Patriots, Timothy McVeigh, some millenialists, and other groups whose disaffection with politics was so complete that they could see the federal government only as an evil conspiracy against individual freedom. Although most Americans wanted nothing to do with such fringe groups, they did watch *The X-Files* and films such as *JFK* (1991), which presented and validated the idea that the government could not be trusted. More commonly, they simply refused to vote.

In his charming book, *For Common Things* (1999), Purdy argues that the most widespread response to the decline of politics has not been violence or protest or images of conspiracy, but rather a stance of ironic detachment. The ironist remains aloof, distanced from a politics that has proven untrustworthy. "The point of irony," writes Purdy, "is a quiet refusal to believe in the depth of relationships, the sincerity of motivation, or the truth of speech—especially earnest speech." In the 1990s, he continues, the exemplar of this ironic sensibility was a television personality named . . . well, think about it, and read on.

interpretive essay

Stephanie Coontz

THE AMERICAN FAMILY: IN SEARCH OF THE GOOD OLD DAYS

In the increasingly conservative era between the election of Richard Nixon in 1968 and the triumph of the Republican right wing in the congressional elections in 1994, three issues focused the new conservatism and stimulated national debate: abortion, the growth of "welfare," and the "decline" of the family. Evidence of family decline seemed incontrovertible. Between 1966 and 1976, the divorce rate doubled. By 1980, almost a quarter of the American population was living alone, and less than 10 percent of all families conformed to the pattern that once had seemed standard: a working husband, a homemaking wife, and two children. Most social critics believed that family deterioration was a particular problem in the black community, where many families were headed by women. Hollywood explored family decline in a series of films, including Kramer vs. Kramer *(1979) and* Ordinary People *(1980), most of which found women and feminism at the root of the problem.*

Something had gone terribly wrong, or so it seemed. Inevitably, Americans looked back, searching the past for the "good old days" when the family was whole and strong, convinced that somewhere in that past was the key to rebuilding the family. In the following essay, family historian Stephanie Coontz takes us on this historical journey, tracing the history of the American family over the course of two centuries. What does she find? When did anxieties about the family emerge? Did the family have its "golden age"? How can knowledge of the history of the family help Americans understand—and perhaps remake—today's families?

The American family is under siege. To listen to the rhetoric of recent months, we have all fallen down on the job. We're selfish; too preoccupied with our own gratification to raise our children properly. We are ungrateful; we want a handout, not a hand.

If only we'd buckle down, stay on the straight and narrow, keep our feet on the ground, our shoulder to the wheel, our eye on the ball, our nose to the grindstone. Then everything would be all right, just as it was in the family-friendly '50s, when we could settle down in front of the television after an honest day's work and see our lives reflected in shows like *Ozzie and Harriet* and *Father Knows Best*.

But American families have been under siege more often than not during the past 300 years. Moreover, they have always been diverse, both in structure and ethnicity. No family type has been able to protect its members from the roller-coaster rides of economic setbacks or social change. Changes that improved the lives and fortunes of one family type or individual often resulted in losses for another.

A man employed in the auto industry, for example, would have been better off financially in the 1950s than now, but his retired parents would be better off today. If he had a strong taste for power, he might prefer Colonial times, when a man was the undisputed monarch of the household and any disobedience by wife, child, or servant was punishable by whipping. But woe betide that man if he wasn't born to property. In those days, men without estates could be told what to wear, where to live, and whom to associate with.

His wife, on the other hand, might have been happier in the 1850s, when she might have afforded two or three servants. We can be pretty sure, though, that the black or Irish servants of that day would not have found the times so agreeable. And today's children, even those scarred by divorce, might well want to stay put rather than live in the late 19th century, when nearly half of them died before they reached their late teens.

A HISTORY OF TRADEOFFS

These kinds of tradeoffs have characterized American family life from the beginning. Several distinctly different types of families already coexisted in Colonial times: On the East Coast, the Iroquois lived in longhouses with large extended families. Small families were more common among the nomadic Indian groups, where marital separation, though frequent, caused no social stigma or loss of access to group resources. African-American slaves, whose nuclear families had been torn apart, built extended family networks through ritual coparenting, the adoption of orphans, and complex naming patterns designed to preserve links among families across space and time.

White Colonial families were also diverse: High death rates meant that a majority spent some time in a stepfamily. Even in intact families, membership ebbed and flowed; many children left their parents' home well before puberty to work as servants or apprentices to other households. Colonial family values didn't sentimentalize childhood. Mothers were far less involved in caring for their children than modern working women, typically delegating the task to servants or older siblings. Children living away from home usually wrote to their fathers, sometimes adding a postscript asking him to "give my regards to my mother, your wife."

A REVOLUTION OF SORTS

Patriarchal authority started to collapse at the beginning of the Revolutionary War: The rate of premarital conception soared and children began to marry out of birth order. Small family farms and shops flourished and, as in Colonial days, a wife's work was valued as highly as her husband's. The revolutionary ferment also produced the first stirrings of feminism and civil rights. A popular 1773 Massachusetts almanac declared: "Then equal Laws let custom find, and neither Sex oppress: More Freedom give to Womankind or to Mankind give less." New Jersey women had the right to vote after the Revolution. In several states slaves won their freedom when they sued, citing the Declaration of Independence.

But commercial progress undermined these movements. The spread of international trade networks and the invention of the cotton gin in 1793 increased slavery's profits. Ironically, when revolutionary commitment to basic human equality went head-to-head with economic dependence on slavery, the result was an increase in racism: Apologists now justified slavery on the grounds that blacks were *less* than human. This attitude spilled over to free blacks, who gradually lost both their foothold in the artisan trades and the legal rights they'd enjoyed in early Colonial times. The subsequent deterioration in their status worked to the advantage of Irish immigrants, previously considered nonwhite and an immoral underclass.

Feminist ideals also faded as industrialization and wage labor took work away from the small family farms and businesses, excluding middle-class wives from their former economic partnerships. For the first time, men became known as breadwinners. By the post-Civil War era of 1870–90, the participation of married women in the labor force was at an all-time low; social commentators labeled those wives who took part in political or economic life sexual degenerates or "semi-hermaphrodites."

WOMEN LOSE; CHILDREN LOSE MORE

As women left the workforce children entered it by the thousands, often laboring in abysmal conditions up to ten hours a day. In the North, they worked in factories or tenement workshops. As late as 1900, 120,000 children worked in Pennsylvania's mines and factories. In the South, states passed "apprentice" laws binding black children out as unpaid laborers, often under the pretext that their parents neglected them. Plantation owners (whose wives and daughters encased themselves in corsets and grew their fingernails long) accused their former female slaves of "loaferism" when they resisted field labor in order to stay closer to home with their children.

So for every 19th-century middle-class family that was able to nurture its women and children comfortably inside the family circle, there was an Irish or German girl scrubbing floors, a Welsh boy mining coal, a black girl doing laundry, a black mother and child picking cotton, and a Jewish or Italian daughter making dresses, cigars, or artificial flowers in a sweatshop.

Meanwhile, self-styled "child-saver" charity workers, whose definition of an unfit parent had more to do with religion, ethnicity, or poverty than behavior, removed other children from their families. They sent these "orphans" to live with Western farmers who needed extra hands—or merely dumped them in a farm town with a dollar and an earnest lecture about escaping the evils of city life.

THE OUTER FAMILY CIRCLE

Even in the comfortable middle-class households of the late 19th century, norms and values were far different from those we ascribe to "traditional" families. Many households took in boarders, lodgers, or unmarried relatives. The nuclear family wasn't the primary focus of emotional life. The Victorian insistence on separate spheres for men and women made male-female relations extremely stilted, so women commonly turned to other women for their most intimate relationships. A woman's diary would rhapsodize for pages about a female friend, explaining how they carved their initials on a tree, and then remark, "Accepted the marriage proposal of Mr. R. last night" without further comment. Romantic friendships were also common among young middle-class men, who often recorded that they missed sleeping with a college roommate and laying an arm across his bosom. No one considered such relationships a sign of homosexuality; indeed, the term wasn't even invented until the late 19th century.

Not that 19th-century Americans were asexual: By midcentury New York City had one prostitute for every 64 men; the mayor of Savannah estimated his city had one for every 39. Perhaps prostitution's spread was inevitable at a time when the middle class referred to the "white meat" and "dark meat" of chicken to spare ladies the embarrassment of hearing the terms "breast" or "thigh."

THE ADVENT OF THE COUPLE

The early 20th century brought more changes. Now the emotional focus shifted to the husband and wife. World War I combined with a resurgence of feminism to hasten the collapse of Victorian values, but we can't underestimate the role the emergence of a mass consumer market played: Advertisers quickly found that romance and sexual titillation worked wonders for the bottom line.

Marriage experts and the clergy, concerned that longer lifespans would put a strain on marriages, denounced same-sex friendships as competitors to love; people were expected to direct all their emotional, altruistic and sensual impulses into marriage. While this brought new intimacy and sexual satisfaction to married life, it also introduced two trends that disturbed observers. One was an increased dissatisfaction with what used to be considered adequate relationships. Great expectations, social historian Elaine Tyler May points out in her book of the same name, could generate great disappointments. It's no surprise that the U.S. has had both the highest consumption of romance novels and the highest divorce rates in the world since the early part of the 20th century.

The second consequence of this new cult of married bliss was the emergence of an independent and increasingly sexualized youth culture. In the late 19th century, middle-class courtship revolved around the institution of "calling." A boy was invited to call by the girl or her parents. It was as inappropriate then for a boy to hint he'd like to be asked over as it was in the 1950s for a girl to hint she'd like to be asked out. By the mid-1920s, calling had been almost totally replaced by dating, which took young people away from parental control but made a girl far more dependent on the boy's initiative. Parents especially worried about the moral dangers the automobile posed—and with reason: A middle-class boy was increasingly likely to have his first sexual encounter with a girlfriend rather than a prostitute.

The early part of the century brought a different set of changes to America's working class. In the 1920s, for the first time, a majority of children were born to male-breadwinner, female-homemaker families. Child labor laws and the spread of mass education allowed more parents to keep their children out of the workforce. Numerous immigrant families, however, continued to pull their offspring out of school so they could help support the family, often arousing intense generational conflicts. African-American families kept their children in school longer than other families in those groups, but their wives were much more likely to work outside the home.

THERE GOES THE FAMILY

In all sectors of society, these changes created a sense of foreboding. *Is Marriage on the Skids?* asked one magazine article of the times; *What Is the Family Still Good For?* fretted another. Popular commentators harkened back to the "good old days," bemoaning the sexual revolution, the fragility of nuclear-family ties, the cult of youthful romance, and the threat of the "emancipated woman."

The stock market crash, the Great Depression, and the advent of World War II moved such fears to the back burner. During the '30s and '40s, family trends fluctuated from one extreme to another. Depression hardship—contrary to its television portrayal on *The Waltons*—usually failed to make family and community life stronger. Divorce rates fell, but desertion and domestic violence rose sharply; economic stress often translated into punitive parenting that left children with emotional scars still apparent to social researchers decades later. Murder rates in the '30s were as high as in the 1980s; rates of marriages and births plummeted.

WWII started a marriage boom, but by 1946 the number of divorces was double that in 1941. This time the social commentators blamed working women, interfering in-laws and, above all, inadequate mothers. In 1946, psychiatrist Edward Strecker published *Their Mothers' Sons: The Psychiatrist Examines an American Problem*, which argued that women who were old-fashioned "moms" instead of modern "mothers" were emasculating American boys.

Moms, he said disapprovingly, were immature and unstable and sought emotional recompense for the disappointments of their own lives. They took care of aging parents and tried to exert too much control over their children. Mothers, on the other hand, put their parents in nursing homes and derived all their satisfaction from the nuclear family while cheerfully urging independence on their children. Without motherhood, said the experts, a woman's life meant nothing. Too much mothering, though, would destroy her own marriage and her son's life. These new values put women in an emotional double-bind, and it's hardly surprising that tranquilizers, which came on the scene in the '50s, were marketed and prescribed almost exclusively to housewives.

THE '50S: PARADISE LOST?

Such were the economic and cultural ups and downs that created the 1950s. If that single decade had actually represented the "tradition" it would be reasonable to argue that the family has indeed collapsed. By the mid 1950s, the age of marriage and parenthood had dropped dramatically, divorce rates bottomed out and the birthrate, one sociologist has recently noted, "approached that of India." The proportion of children in Ozzie-and-Harriet type families reached an all-time high of 60 percent.

Today, in contrast, a majority of mothers, including those with preschool children, work outside the home. Fifty percent of children live with both biological parents, almost one quarter live with single parents and more than 21 percent are in stepfamilies. Three quarters of today's 18–24-year-olds have never been married, while almost 50 percent of all first marriages—and 60 percent of remarriages—will end in divorce. Married couples wait longer to bear children and have fewer of them. For the first time there are more married couples without children than with them. Less than one quarter of contemporary marriages are supported by one wage earner.

Taking the 1950s as the traditional norm, however, overstates both the novelty of modern family life and the continuity of tradition. The 1950s was the most atypical decade in the entire history of American marriage and family life. In some ways, today's families are closer to older patterns than were '50s families. The median age at first marriage today is about the same as it was at the beginning of the century, while the proportion of never-married people is actually lower. The number of women who are coproviders and the proportion of children living in stepfamilies are both closer to that of Colonial days than the 1950s. Even the ethnic diversity among modern families is closer to the patterns of the early part of this century than to the demographics of the 1950s. And the time a modern working mother devotes to childcare is higher than in Colonial or Revolutionary days.

The 1950s family, in other words, was not at all traditional; nor was it always idyllic. Though many people found satisfactions in family life during that period, we now know the experiences of many groups and individuals were denied. Problems such as alcoholism, battering, and incest were swept under the rug. So was discrimination against ethnic groups, political dissidents, women, elders, gays, lesbians, religious minorities and the handicapped. Rates of divorce and unwed motherhood were low, but that did not prevent 30 percent of American children from living in poverty, a higher figure than at present.

IT'S ALL RELATIVE

Why then, do many people remember the 1950s as so much easier than today? One reason is that after the hardships of the Depression and WWII, things *were* improving on many fronts. Though poverty rates were higher than today, they were falling. Economic inequality was also decreasing. The teenage birthrate was almost twice as high in 1957 as today, but most young men could afford to marry. Violence against African-Americans was appallingly widespread, yet many blacks got jobs in the expanding manufacturing industries and for the first time found an alternative to Southern agriculture's peonage.

What we forget when politicians tell us we should revive the 1950s family is that the social stability of that period was due less to its distinctive family forms than to its unique socioeconomic and political climate. High rates of unionization, heavy corporate investment in manufacturing, and generous government assistance in the form of public-works projects, veterans' benefits, student loans and housing subsidies gave young families a tremendous jump start, created predictable paths out of poverty, and led to unprecedented increases in real wages. By the time the "traditional male breadwinner" reached age 30, in both the 1950s and '60s, he could pay the principal and interest on a median-priced home on only 15–18 percent of his income. Social Security promised a much-needed safety net for the elderly, formerly the poorest segment of the population. These economic carrots combined with the sticks of McCarthyism and segregation to keep social dissent on the back burner.

THE NEW TRENDS

Because the '60s were a time of social protest, many people forget that families still made economic gains throughout the decade. Older workers and homeowners continued to build security for their retirement years. The postwar boom and government subsidies cut child poverty in half from 1949 to 1959. It was halved again, to its lowest levels ever, from 1959 to 1969. The high point of health and nutrition for poor children came in 1970, a period that coincided with the peak years of the Great Society, not the high point of the '50s family.

Since 1973, however, a new phase has emerged. Some things have continued to improve: High school graduation rates are at an all-time high; minority test scores rose steadily from 1970 to 1990; poverty rates among the elderly have continued to fall while life expectancy has risen.

Other trends show mixed results: The easy availability of divorce has freed individuals from oppressive or even abusive marriages, but many divorces have caused emotional and economic suffering for both children and adults. Women have found new satisfaction at work, and there's considerable evidence that children can benefit from having a working mother, but the failure of businesses—and some husbands—to adjust to working mothers' needs has caused much family stress and discord.

In still other areas, the news is quite bleak. Children have now replaced seniors as the poorest segment of the population; the depth and concentration of child poverty has increased over the past 20 years so it's now at 1965 levels. Many of the gains ethnic groups made in the 1960s and '70s have been eroded.

History suggests that most of these setbacks originate in social and economic forces rather than in the collapse of some largely mythical traditional family. Perhaps the most powerful of these sources is the breakdown of America's implicit postwar wage bargain with the working class, where corporations ensured labor stability by increasing employment, rewarding increased productivity with higher wages, and investing in jobs and community infrastructure. At the same time, the federal government subsidized home ownership and higher education.

Since 1973, however, real wages have fallen for most families. It increasingly requires the work of two earners to achieve the modest upward mobility one could provide in the 1950s and '60s. Unemployment rates have risen steadily as corporations have abandoned the communities that grew up around them, seeking cheap labor overseas or in nonunionized sectors of the South. Involuntary part-time work has soared. As *Time* magazine noted in 1993, the predictable job ladders of the '50s and '60s have been sawed off: "Companies are portable, workers are throwaway." A different article in the same issue found, "Long-term commitments . . . are anathema to the modern corporation."

During the 1980s the gap between the rich and middle-class widened in 46 states, and each year since 1986 has set a new postwar record for the gap between rich and poor. In 1980 a CEO earned 30 to 40 times as much as the average worker; by 1994 he earned 187 times as much. Meanwhile, the real wages of a young male high school graduate are lower today than those earned by his 1963 counterpart.

These economic changes are not driven by the rise in divorce and unwed motherhood. Decaying wage and job structures—not changing family structures—have caused the overwhelming bulk of income redistribution. And contrary to what has been called a new bipartisan consensus, marriage is not the solution to poverty. According to sociologist Donald J. Hernandez, Ph.D., formerly with the U.S. Census Bureau, even if every child in America were reunited with both biological parents, two thirds of those who are poor today would still be poor.

OUR UNCERTAIN FUTURE

History's lessons are both positive and negative. We can take comfort from the fact that American families have always been in flux and that a wide variety of family forms and values have worked well for different groups at different times. There's no reason to assume that recent changes are entirely destructive. Families have always been vulnerable to rapid economic change and have always needed economic and emotional support from beyond their own small boundaries. Our challenge is to grapple with the sweeping transformations we're currently undergoing. History demonstrates it's not as simple as returning to one or another family form from the past. Though there are many precedents for successfully reorganizing family life, there are no clear answers to the issues facing us as we enter the 21st century.

sources

Dan Quayle

"MURPHY HAS A BABY . . . QUAYLE HAS A COW"

"Murphy has a Baby . . . Quayle has a Cow"—that was the headline in the Philadelphia Daily News *the day after Vice President Dan Quayle, in a May 19, 1992, address to the Commonwealth Club of California, criticized prime-time television character Murphy Brown for having a baby out of wedlock. The story line for the last episode of the season had Murphy getting pregnant accidentally by her former husband, then deciding to have the baby on her own, rather than marry or have an abortion. The speech caused an uproar. Some took it as an attack on single mothers, noting that President Bush's divorced daughter was raising two children by herself. Others emphasized that by rejecting abortion, Murphy Brown was acting like a good, right-to-life Republican. For still others, the speech revived the debate over the impact of television on social norms and values. And many thought Quayle's effort to link Murphy Brown's conduct with the recent riots in Los Angeles was especially ill-considered. Of course, the vice president also had his defenders. What is your view? Why would the political right wing be especially attracted to arguments about "family values"?*

. . . When I have been asked during these last weeks who caused the riots and the killing in L.A., my answer has been direct and simple: Who is to blame for the riots? The rioters are to blame. Who is to blame for the killings? The killers are to blame. Yes, I can understand how people were shocked and outraged by the verdict in the Rodney King trial. But there is simply no excuse for the mayhem that followed. To apologize or in any way to excuse what happened is wrong. It is a betrayal of all those people equally outraged and equally disadvantaged who did not loot and did not riot—and who were in many cases victims of the rioters. No matter how much you may disagree with the verdict, the riots were wrong. And if we as a society don't condemn what is wrong, how can we teach our children what is right?

Historical Documents of 1992 (Washington, D.C.: Congressional Quarterly), pp. 446–51.

Dan Quayle.
Library of Congress.

But after condemning the riots, we do need to try to understand the underlying situation.

In a nutshell: I believe the lawless social anarchy which we saw is directly related to the breakdown of family structure, personal responsibility and social order in too many areas of our society. For the poor the situation is compounded by a welfare ethos that impedes individual efforts to move ahead in society, and hampers their ability to take advantage of the opportunities America offers.

If we don't succeed in addressing these fundamental problems, and in restoring basic values, any attempt to fix what's broken will fail. But one reason I believe we won't fail is that we have come so far in the last 25 years.

There is no question that this country has had a terrible problem with race and racism. The evil of slavery has left a long legacy. But we have faced racism squarely, and we have made progress in the past quarter century. The landmark civil rights bills of the 1960s removed legal barriers to allow full participation by blacks in the economic, social and political life of the nation. By any measure the America of 1992 is more egalitarian, more integrated, and offers more opportunities to black Americans—and all other minority group members—than the America of 1964. There is more to be done. But I think that all of us can be proud of our progress.

And let's be specific about one aspect of this progress: This country now has a black middle class that barely existed a quarter century ago. Since 1967 the median income of black two parent families has risen by 60 percent in real terms. The number of black college graduates has skyrocketed. Black men and women have achieved real political power—black mayors head 48 of our largest cities, including Los Angeles. These are achievements.

But as we all know, there is another side to that bright landscape. During this period of progress, we have also developed a culture of poverty—some call it an underclass—that is far more violent and harder to escape than it was a generation ago.

The poor you always have with you, Scripture tells us. And in America we have always had poor people. But in this dynamic, prosperous nation, poverty has traditionally been a stage through which people pass on their way to joining the great middle class. And if one generation didn't get very far up the ladder—their ambitious, better-educated children would.

But the underclass seems to be a new phenomenon. It is a group whose members are dependent on welfare for very long stretches, and whose men are often drawn into lives of crime. There is far too little upward mobility, because the underclass is disconnected from the rules of American society. And these problems have, unfortunately, been particularly acute for Black Americans. . . .

It would be overly simplistic to blame this social breakdown on the programs of the Great Society alone. It would be absolutely wrong to blame it on the growth and success most Americans enjoyed during the 1980s. Rather, we are in large measure reaping the whirlwind of decades of changes in social mores.

I was born in 1947, so I'm considered one of those "Baby Boomers" we keep reading about. But let's look at one unfortunate legacy of the "Boomer" generation. When we were young, it was fashionable to declare war against traditional values. Indulgence and self-gratification seemed to have no consequences. Many of our generation glamorized casual sex and drug use, evaded responsibility and trashed authority. Today the "Boomers" are middle-aged and middle class. The responsibility of having families has helped many recover traditional values. And, of course, the great majority of those in the middle class survived the turbulent legacy of the 60's and 70's. But many of the poor, with less to fall back on, did not.

The intergenerational poverty that troubles us so much today is predominantly a poverty of values. Our inner cities are filled with children having children; with people who have not been able to take advantage of educational opportunities; with people who are dependent on drugs or the narcotic of welfare. To be sure, many people in the ghettos struggle very hard against these tides—and sometimes win. But too many feel they have no hope and nothing to lose. This poverty is, again, fundamentally a poverty of values.

Unless we change the basic rules of society in our inner cities, we cannot expect anything else to change. We will simply get more of what we saw three weeks ago. New thinking, new ideas, new strategies are needed. . . .

And for those concerned about children growing up in poverty, we should know this: marriage is probably the best anti-poverty program of all. Among families headed by married couples today, there is a poverty rate of 5.7 percent. But 33.4 percent of families headed by a single mother are in poverty today. . . .

Answers to our problems won't be easy.

We can start by dismantling a welfare system that encourages dependency and subsidizes broken families. We can attach conditions—such as school attendance, or work—to welfare. We can limit the time a recipient gets benefits. We can stop penalizing marriage for welfare mothers. We can enforce child support payments.

Ultimately, however, marriage is a moral issue that requires cultural consensus, and the use of social sanctions. Bearing babies irresponsibly is, simply, wrong. Failing to support children one has fathered is wrong. We must be unequivocal about this.

It doesn't help matters when prime time TV has Murphy Brown—a character who supposedly epitomizes today's intelligent, highly paid, professional woman—mocking the importance of fathers, by bearing a child alone, and calling it just another "lifestyle choice."

I know it is not fashionable to talk about moral values, but we need to do it. Even though our cultural leaders in Hollywood, network TV, the national newspapers routinely jeer at them, I think that most of us in this room know that some things are good, and other things are wrong. Now it's time to make the discussion public.

It's time to talk again about family, hard work, integrity and personal responsibility. We cannot be embarrassed out of our belief that two parents, married to each other, are better in most cases for children than one. That honest work is better than hand-outs—or crime. That we are our brothers' keepers. That it's worth making an effort, even when the rewards aren't immediate.

So I think the time has come to renew our public commitment to our Judeo-Christian values—in our churches and synagogues, our civic organizations and our schools. We are, as our children recite each morning, "one nation under God." That's a useful framework for acknowledging a duty and an authority higher than our own pleasures and personal ambitions.

If we lived more thoroughly by these values, we would live in a better society. For the poor, renewing these values will give people the strength to help themselves by acquiring the tools to achieve self-sufficiency, a good education, job training, and property. Then they will move from permanent dependence to dignified independence. . . .

Though our hearts have been pained by the events in Los Angeles, we should take this tragedy as an opportunity for self-examination and progress. So let the national debate roar on. I, for one, will join it. The president will lead it. The American people will participate in it. And as a result, we will become an even stronger nation.

THE IRONIC SENSIBILITY

Jerry, Elaine, and Kramer, in *Seinfeld.*
PhotoFest.

For five years in the mid-1990s, Seinfeld was television's most popular program. It starred comedian Jerry Seinfeld, who played some version of himself, and a small cast of narcissistic characters who, like Seinfeld, seemed always to be obsessed about the trivial details of life. The comment most often made was that it was a show about "nothing." For Jedediah Purdy (see p. 443) Seinfeld's character represents the ironic sensibility of the late twentieth century. What does that mean? Are there other programs that feature the ironic stance? Would you consider Jay Leno or David Letterman ironic?

the big picture

Are you convinced that the American family is a troubled institution? If so, what causes of those troubles can you identify, and how would you go about strengthening the family? If not, why is there so much talk about the decline of the family?